Legal Rules, Moral Norms and Democratic Principles

Dia-Logos

Schriften zu Philosophie und Sozialwissenschaften
Studies in Philosophy and Social Sciences

Herausgegeben von/Edited by
Tadeusz Buksiński and Piotr W. Juchacz

Bd./vol. 15

PETER LANG
EDITION

Bartosz Wojciechowski
Piotr W. Juchacz
Karolina M. Cern
(eds.)

Legal Rules, Moral Norms and Democratic Principles

PETER LANG
EDITION

Bibliographic Information published by the Deutsche Nationalbibliothek
The Deutsche Nationalbibliothek lists this publication in the Deutsche Nationalbibliografie; detailed bibliographic data is available in the internet at http://dnb.d-nb.de.

This book has been prepared within the framework
of the research project: NN 110 237839
financed by the Polish Ministry of Science.

ISSN 1619-005X
ISBN 978-3-631-64008-1

Peter Lang Edition is an imprint of Peter Lang GmbH

www.peterlang.de

Contents

Appendix

Preface

We live in a world of rapid global change; nonetheless, we try to manage the seemingly universal development in a consistent manner. Any fruitful description of such a world in change must take into account many differing factors. Among these, we can distinguish a specific world-wide tendency towards the democratisation of our lives in the social, individual and political dimensions. As some point out, there are just a few political orders that do not claim to be founded on democratic principles.

However, this peculiar global trend does give rise to doubts as well as problems, of which the most profound seems to concern the question whether the "democratic turn" is a real or just a virtual one. Democracy generally means governance by the people – but who are the people? What kind of governance by the people can be claimed as democratic – all of the various types that exist or only a single, chosen one?

What – if any – is the normative issue of such a governance? Democracy, after all, is not a simple descriptive model of governance; it is deeply rooted in our preferences and hence normative patterns of conduct, which are not yet to be understood as the norm but rather as founding principles. Democracy is a thoroughly normative model. It is always as constructed and uttered in the picture of life at the same time.

Does this mean that democracy, as a normative project, can fit only a part of our world and not the other part, that which maintains beliefs in different gods, philosophies or systems of values? Or maybe democratic principles are to be understood from a secular-rational value perspective (post-Weberian values) as formal frames that give people the real possibility to fill the created form with their convictions of the preferred norms that should be obeyed in the name of equality and freedom. But does not the concept of democracy presume a special civil engagement and a strong civil participation? Further, does it not entail self-expression built on a strong feeling of a self-direction? All of these issues can be viewed as post-traditional values that are not yet dominant throughout the world. For this reason, the following question must be raised: What, if any, is the legal issue of the democratic political order? Are the normative, institutional normative and institutional orders - following Sir Neil MacCormick - three different cases or do they cross themselves somewhere or do they even comprise the same issue, which keeps dividing itself into different orders?

In a pluralistic world, should morally impartial legal rules exist for the great as well as the humble, if not providing the only support for peace? But then, altering Ronald Dworkin's question, we can ask how is democracy possible here - if it is at all? To answer this question is the aim of the authors of this book.

Part I

Moral and Legal Discourse in a Constitutional Democratic State

Karolina M. Cern & Bartosz Wojciechowski
Adam Mickiewicz University & University of Łódź, Poland

Postmetaphysical Approach to Moral Autonomy and the Justification of the Thesis of the Necessary Relations between the Legal and Moral Discourse

Abstract: The following paper discusses the significance as well as the role of legal discourse in relation to morality from the point of view of the discourse theory. Reflections of three "fathers-founders" of the theory of discourse (Jürgen Habermas, Karl-Otto Apel and Robert Alexy) are presented in the strict relations to their roots, namely, to Kantian practical philosophy and above all to the categorical imperative. The basic task of the paper is to highlight the importance of the issue in question for current debates in field of practical philosophy.

Keywords: discourse, autonomy, categorical imperative, laws of law-making

Introduction

The arena of the twentieth-century philosophy was full of turbulent events, turnabouts and changes in the paradigms, which often remained under the unmistakable influence of the nineteenth-century thought. One could even say that it inferred the radical implications from the considerations of its ancestors, drawing from this its exceptional power of influence from the perspective of its achievements to date.

A special role in the past century was granted to the category of *facticity*. The latter constitutes a peculiar modification of the concept of *sensibility*, which casted an important role in the philosophy of Immanuel Kant. It concerned, generally speaking, the relations of time and space and, together with the concept of reason, it constituted the source of cognition, and practical action. By indicating the basis for the possibility of referring reason to that what is phenomenal (what appears in time and space as forms of our intuition pre-conditioning any experience), Kant made the Copernican revolution which involves, inter alia, indicating the ground for the connections between thinking based on rational and empirical categories.

However, it was only Martin Heidegger who modified the concept of sensibility (going in-depth in understanding concepts of time and space as intuitions (*Anschauungen*)), so that until now it plays a vital role in various areas of philosophical considerations, including social ones. What Heidegger did was giving a broader meaning to the concept of sensibility, by means of using William Dilthey's researches to prove methodological specificity of the human sciences (*Geisteswissenschaften*) by applying a fundamental category for the latter, namely the category of *understanding* (in Dilthey it was still of a distinct psychological provenance) in opposition to the category of explanation that characterizes the methodology of the natural sciences. Facticity, indeed, began to stand not just simply for the appearance of something at some time and in some space, but also to indicate randomness, contingency - in the sense of the medieval connotation: non-necessity of certain phenomena (including human existence, the formation of such and not other social or political institutions, etc.). This implies an inevitable perspectivity of understanding, because one cannot go towards the general (and somewhat necessary), exceeding the specific embedding of understanding in what is 'already always' there and what was formed in a certain way. Facticity has become a constitutive attribute of human existence in the world and of undertaking an interpretation from a specific historical - cultural and social perspective.

Heidegger's reflections were used in a significant way by Hans-Georg Gadamer who, on the one hand, gave specific dynamics to the category of facticity and, on the other hand, for this purpose he used the potential of Heidegger's category of understanding, by emphasizing the importance of language for the possibility of understanding the world and our lives in it. Gadamer's well-known sentence from *Truth and Method*: "Being that can be understood is language" ("*Sein, das verstanden verden kann, ist Sprache*"[1]) clearly shows that the twentieth-century philosophy realizes that the only way to reach the world and to question it is language itself. In other words, it is impossible to query about the relations between thinking and the world without perceiving them by means of the language.

The results of Gadamer's researches converge at this point in some way with the considerations of those philosophers who derive from other philosophical traditions, for example, Ludwig Wittgenstein and John Langshaw Austin. The former, already in the early stage of his work, clearly expressed the opinion that "the limits of language mean the limits of my world."[2] On the other hand, Austin in his book *How to Do Things with Words*, in which he presented his theory of locutionary, illocutionary and then perlocutionary acts, showed that the language we use is the actual way of influencing the world and other people.[3] According to Austin, by means of speech acts we can actually operate in the world.

The above changes that have taken place in philosophy - and it must be emphasized that these are not only unique, but also they are not the only ones which were relevant to the current state of philosophical thought - resulted in a theory according to which, when misquoting Arthur Schopenhauer that the world is our representation, the world is the result of our cooperative interpretation of the situation in which we find ourselves together as interpreters. Therefore, the thesis of communicative nature of law has been fully accepted in the methodology of contemporary jurisprudence. The law constitutes the subject of a cultural nature, and therefore it can be said that it is both a product of communication activities, as well as the subject of

---

[1] Hans-Georg Gadamer, *Wahrheit und Methode. Grundzüge einer philosophischen Hermeneutik*, in: idem, *Gesammelte Werke 1, Hermeneutik I*, Tübingen: J.C.B. Mohr (Paul Siebeck), 1990, p. 478.

[2] Ludwig Wittgenstein, *Tractatus logico-philosophicus*, transl. C.K. Ogden, Routledge 2005, thesis 5.60.

[3] Locution is a specific phonic chain containing information about a certain state of things, i.e. propositional content. When such a phonic chain is expressed with a specific intention (even if for the purpose of making some observations), then we are dealing with illocution (so-called illocutionary force of expression). Moreover, if the statement triggers off some effect in the recipient, involving the change of his mental state, then such action is called perlocution.

discourse, which is, in addition, embedded in certain socio-cultural references. This follows from the belief that the speech (or rather the discourse) constitutes a common and essential communications medium of all people, and therefore a great part of human interaction takes place in it and with it. What characterises human interactions, in turn, is that they are both an expression of our understanding (interpretation) of the world, as well as the way of constituting it. Thus, a philosophical – legal reflection is one of the moments of reconstructing our socio-cultural self-understanding and yet it always co-constitutes the latter.

The point here is that the world is the result of our communicative cooperation oriented at the agreement on the validity claims which are related to the answers to the following questions: what in this world really is; how one should conduct; what does everyone experience? Nevertheless, the central question in the theory of discourse is how it is possible (if it is at all possible) to reach an agreement (defined as a consensus, that is an active rather than passive consent or approval), on threefold issues that are significant for us? And accordingly, how should one proceed on the basis of this commonly and cooperatively developed consensus? Another emerging question concerns the issue of how to coexist and cooperate with one another, in order to maintain this consensually reached agreement, and thus to ensure the peaceful coexistence of human beings.

In other words, the theory of discourse is focused on the issue of the possibility of resolving various conflicts without violence. Validity claims, in particular those normative ones, which say how to proceed, consensually taking into account the interests of all their addressees "*mediate a mutual dependence* of language and the social world that does not exist for the relation of language to the objective world."[4] The latter is the case because for the judgments of truth their relation to the corresponding states of affairs is fundamental, while for the claims to validity of a legislative nature what is important in the first place is not so much whether they actually impose a commitment on us, but whether they are regarded by all affected (namely their addressees) as valid and binding, so that they all recognize the commit-

---

[4] Jürgen Habermas, *Moral Consciousness and Communicative Action,* transl. Christian Lenhardt, Shierry Weber Nicholsen, Cambridge, Mass.: The MIT Press, 1999, p. 61.

ment to the activities identified by these very norms. The moment of the normative commitment is obviously not included in the sphere of states of affairs. A search for its source, or determining its binding force is at the heart of the theory of discourse, whose main representatives are Jürgen Habermas, Karl-Otto Apel and Robert Alexy.

1. The structure of the issue of discourse theory and its Kantian foundations

It can be stated in the initial and general approach that the central question in the theory of discourse is the issue of peaceful settlement of various conflicts, and more precisely, of settling them by means of rational argumentation, in which what matters most is the force of applied arguments rather than the argument of force (not so much physical, but social, political or even cultural - symbolic one). Since the essence of this theory is the problem of justifying the rules of rational use of the arguments, Alexy points out that in contrast to other philosophical and theoretical proposals, "the theory of rational discourse is a normative theory of discourse."[5] Resolving the problem of justifying the rules of discourse allows to go on to the next question which, referring to Habermas, can be formulated as a question of how and due to what the actual coercion, which we are subject to (whether morally or legally) is (or rather may be) legitimated?

The above formulation of the basic problem for the theory of discourse refers directly to the practical philosophy of Kant, that constitutes a vital source for this theory, despite being already equipped with the twentieth century philosophical and theoretical tools. Due to the fact that all of the three abovementioned thinkers assume or have assumed transcendental perspective as a starting point of the discourse theory, on the basis of which they formulated the transcendental justification for this theory (which is in each case, undoubtedly, different on account of the additional assumptions adopted by each of

[5] Robert Alexy, *A Theory of Legal Argumentation. The Theory of Rational Discourse as Theory of Legal Justification*, transl. Ruth Adler, Neil MacCormick, Oxford: Clarendon Press, 1989, p. 180.

its contributors), so a detailed analysis of the theory of discourse will start from indicating its Kantian foundations.

In *Groundwork of the Metaphysic of Morals*, Kant points to the need for a *final* validation of moral philosophy.[6] Due to his division of rational cognition, i.e. one that provides certainty of cognitive performance, the subject of moral philosophy able to cause the above legitimacy, and therefore "pure," meaning free from empiricism, are the principles and ideas of pure *will*, i.e. such on account of which man should act necessarily, as long as s/he is to be recognised as a moral subject. In Kant's philosophy, this cognition is a priori cognition of some object (principles, rules and ideas of the pure human will), namely it has the nature of material a priori cognition, so it is a metaphysical understanding. Kant's twentieth-century heirs who brood upon the justification of the principles or rules of action that would result in consensual resolution of problems or disputable issues, use the tools that have been gained already after the so-called linguistic turn (Heidegger, Wittgenstein, Austin) which proved that all the queries about the world actually relate to acts of speech and language. Therefore, they do not go in for metaphysics - like Kant did - but rather for transcendental philosophy that is of formal nature since it concerns the conditions enabling the universally valid (obliging) rights (moral or legal) that would only allow to generate universally valid normative content. And because these conditions of possibility are inherently contained - according to the creators of the theory of discourse - in the linguistic rules and speech acts, so they go in for transcendental pragmatics, or at least by forming the foundations of the theory of discourse, they start with the arguments indicated on its basis.

Therefore, one of the tasks of the theory of discourse is transcendental-pragmatic justification of discourse principles (and not, as in Kant: principles and ideas of the pure human will), which is to demonstrate that the validity of certain principles is an enabling condition[7] of forming interpersonal communication. Abandoning speech

---

[6] Immanuel Kant, *Grundlegung zur Metaphysik der Sitten*, in: *Werke in sechs Bänden*, Band 3, Könemann 1995, *Vorrede*, [387–392], pp. 173–179.

[7] This method is of transcendental character because one examines *the conditions of the possibility* of establishing communication. However, this issue is not unambiguous in the course of the development of the discourse theory, since Habermas, who was

acts is thus impossible without negating such modes of action that must be considered typically human. Even a methodical attitude of a sceptic is not possible without establishing communication on the basis of these particular rules. This follows from the belief that the validity of certain rules is indispensable in order to undertake specific speech acts. Abandoning these speech acts, on the other hand, would imply giving up such forms of behaviour that are perceived as typically human.[8]

Because in Kant's philosophy theoretical cognition and motivation to act are in some way rooted both in the rational dimension (general, universal structures of thinking) as well as in the dimension if sensibility (specific relations - determined by time and space - which constitute the form of appearance of the phenomena; however time and space - as forms of intuitions - reveals the original phenomena in the very sense of the term), so all the moral principles of human action somehow have always two aspects: objective and subjective. Objective aspect, has therefore the nature of a general and universal form, namely the form of practical law. On the other hand, the subjective aspect takes the form of the principle of moral action, called the maxim of action that has the character of *representing* (*Vorstellung*) the said moral law in such way that whilst being *represented* (namely, in a particular way referred to time and space within which a moral problem comes to voice), the moral law may - in a given situation in life -

---

initially talking about this very transcendental - pragmatic argument at some point (in *Was ist Universalpragmatik*) departs from referring to the method as transcendental one in favour of identifying it simply as universal one. He undertakes the latter primarily for two reasons. Firstly, in his opinion, it is difficult to distinguish a purely logical element from an empirical one in the analysis used by him, notably that he uses the analysis of informal logic, expressing the standpoint that pure deduction cannot provide any substantive input on pragmatics. Secondly, the theory of discourse does not deal with the conditions enabling experience, but with the conditions of communication capabilities or, ultimately, with the conditions under which arguments are generated, thus referring to the method as transcendental one is not fully legitimate according to Habermas (see R. Alexy, *A Theory of Legal Argumentation*, op. cit., p. 185). However, in *Between Facts and Norms*, he definitely dissociates himself from the transcendental research perspective.

8 Jürgen Habermas, *Vorstudien und Ergänzungen zur Theorie des kommunikativen Handelns*, Frankfurt am Main: Suhrkamp Verlag, 1984, p. 353 ff.

here and now motivate us, people of flesh and blood, to a certain type of action.[9] It may - yet it does not have to - motivate us to act in a particular situation, since we can be also motivated by something else (e.g., by some interest which is currently crucial for us, pleasure that is within our reach or anything that here and now affects us - sensible beings). In other words, as human beings we always can but never have to act morally. If this action was not just a possibility, that is, if acting morally was necessary, we could not speak of freedom and we would deal with determinism. What is thus *necessary* is a *form* of the motive of our action, as long as the action itself is to be moral, namely *conformity of a maxim of an act with* moral law, i.e. a *universal and general form of moral law*.[10]

Due to the fact that we can listen to our own reason, but we do not need to, that reason must somehow necessitate our wills.

> The representation of an objective principle, so far as it necessitates the will, is called a commandment (of reason); and a formula expressing such is called **an imperative**.[11]

This categorical imperative is the only one, because one can meaningfully talk only about one ultimately justified moral law, and the latter has the nature of a synthetic-practical proposition *a priori*,[12] namely such proposition which combines two comparatively semantic-independent elements: *a priori* element with (in the case of moral philosophy) empirical one. An *a priori* element (i.e. formulated prior to any empirical experience) is a *necessary form* of representing moral law (the maxim of action, that is our actual motive of conduct), which is of a general nature and hence of a universal validity. The *synthetic* element, therefore, is the *maxim* of our conduct itself, namely the *representation* (*Vorstellung*) of *moral law* (due to the form) which is in this way already defined as to its content. After all, what can really motivate a person to act is not a "blank" form of the law, but "determined with regard to its meaning" law in its general formulation.

---

[9] I. Kant, *Grundlegung...*, op. cit., p. 205 [412/413].

[10] Ibidem, p. 215 [420/421].

[11] Ibidem, p. 205 [413].

[12] Ibidem, p. 214 [420].

What is of fundamental importance for understanding the intention of discourse theory is Kant's answer to the question of how we can *represent* this moral law. According to Kant, the pure practical power of judgement (*Urteilskraft*) operates differently than the theoretical power of judgement and it is not sensing (does not rely to phenomenal appearance) - in some equivalent of transcendental schematism of imagination (*Einbildungskraft*)[13] - the categories (that is: pure concepts) of freedom that allowed representation of the moral law due to which they would at last gain the objective validity (and were not merely "empty abstractions"). This is so because, as the philosopher from Königsberg believed, on the one hand, the categories of freedom "immediately (*sogleich*) are cognitions"[14] whilst, on the other hand, in order to represent the moral law as a maxim, in our particular problem situation, we have to formulate the principle of action, and then "subject it to a test" - whether in terms of form it meets the requirement of generality and universality, and therefore whether it can be determined (in terms of its form) as "the *Type* of moral law" (*Typus des Sittengesetzes*).[15]

What is essential here is that these categories of freedom are immediately of objective meaning.[16] However, we understand how they relate to this reality of human motives, solely by "departing from" the specific situation, the type of which we seek to recognize, so that an appropriate motive of action in a given situation could be recognized by us - on account of its form - as a model of typical moral law, so that this motive of conduct could be regarded as a model one (typically binding) for a given *type* of situation. Thanks to this, the will of every man is "individually" of legislative nature, on account of which one can say that he is acting on the basis of a principle of autonomy of will, while the rank of the law which everyone individually and independently imposes on oneself is - with regard to its form - universal.

[13] Immanuel Kant, *Kritik der praktischen Vernuft*, in *Werke in sechs Bänden*, Band 3, Könemann 1995, p. 361 [68/69].

[14] Ibidem, p. 357 [66].

[15] Ibidem, p. 362 [69].

[16] Yet, as they relate to determination of the human will (action), and not to the objects of the sensibility.

From the perspective of autonomy of will – understood in the above way – Kant holds that every reasonable being must be "in all his actions addressed to him as well as to other reasonable beings always *also as an end* considered, *not as a mere means* to be used by any will whatsoever."[17] This entails that the will of every reasonable being should have the possibility to function autonomously, that is, it should have the possibility to act morally recognised. Consequently, Kant puts forward a postulate, which can be understood as an ideal shining upon our actual actions. It is a postulate of "the realm of ends," namely of "the systematic connection of different reasonable beings through common laws [*gemeinschaftliche Gesetze*]"[18] in such a way that even though everyone independently made laws, which s/he would be subject to, however, these laws – based on the actual implementation of the principle of autonomy – would have universal validity and, as a result, they would be the same for everyone on the account of a universal form. What follows from this is a universal principle of law:

> Every action is *right*, the maxim of which makes that the freedom of everybody's arbitrary will can coexist with the freedom of all other's according to a universal law.[19]

The above reconstructed form and content of the categorical imperative is essential for the theory of discourse on the grounds that it demonstrates both the need to link together the universal form of practical reflection with some specific content, which is to be included in this form, as well as the impossibility of a legitimate indication (enumeration) of the norms of action set out on account of their content, which would not matter (not take into account) all the specific circumstances of life, namely such norms which would in solely discretionary manner plan necessary modes of conduct. This is the very issue that the theory of discourse undertakes, looking for a legitimate, universal form of discourse, which would in the actual processes of reaching an agreement generate a consensus between all affected,

---

[17] I. Kant, *Grundlegung…*, op. cit., p. 224 [428].

[18] Ibidem, p. 231 [433].

[19] Immanuel Kant, *Die Metaphysik der Sitten*, in *Werke in sechs Bänden*, Band 3, Könemann 1995, p. 277 [230].

rather than impose a solution incomprehensible for a given person, even "under the guise" of expert and far-sighted judgement. Other words round, it is a power of judgement that is at stake in the discourse theory – whether be it internal human faculty or external mode of being already co-existed in the world.

It is precisely because of this "dual nature" of categorical imperative that morality becomes the issue of "how one answers the question concerning the possibility of a rationally resolving practical questions in general."[20] It refers to the fact that the categorical imperative can be understood as an explanation of how it is possible to formulate impartial moral judgment, namely on the basis of *best available reasons*, deciding between competing norms of action.[21] According to Habermas, in this way, perhaps paradoxically, Kant caused a turn toward postmetaphysical approach to moral autonomy.

Why is this turn perceived as a postmetaphysical? Because from the point at which Kant redefines morality in such way that on its ground we ask about most legitimate moral claim (moral norm), the general moral question ceases to have Aristotelian form: "what is good *for me / for us*?" and it takes the form of "what should *one* do?"[22] Thus, it is no longer happiness interpreted through the prism of *eudaimonia*, but justice and autonomy become *par excellence* moral issues. The question of what is good is placed in purely subjective and private perspective. There is a split between what is good and what is right. Practical reason no longer functions in the context of lifeworlds, but it becomes a pure reason, free from the contextual determination.

This turn implies redefinition of the term "*good* for me / for us", too. It designates no longer the type of situation, that is the particular situation captured in the universal form, that would indicate a typical kind of obligation, but instead it articulates an *authentic* life which in the contrary is not to be classified neither standardised.[23] Thus the question concerning 'the good' becomes a question about authentic

---

[20] Jürgen Habermas, *Justification and Application. Remarks on Discourse Ethics*, transl. C.P. Cronin, Cambridge, MA: The MIT Press, 2001, p. 117.

[21] Ibidem, p. 118.

[22] Ibidem.

[23] The concept of 'authenticity' and authentic life or form of life is most often referred to certain groups comprehended as communities and to their characteristic life forms (broadly understood cultural background).

forms of life to which the lancet of rational justification has no application anymore.

Now it appears that as connecting moral discourse with the legal one is fully manifested in the questions about (possible) just and fair law, namely such which does not favour any of the possible concepts of the "good life," questioning the legal argumentation becomes specific activity of the practical reason focused on processes of legitimation (best justified) fair norms.

Therefore, an arising question whether one can find universal normative claims, independent of the contexts of lifeworlds in which, after all, the totality of life is embedded, becomes the crucial question in the theory of discourse. The structure of the answer to this question is determined by a dual nature of the categorical imperative: what is sought is a universal form able to generate consensus by means of real discourse. It is such a form, which will provide appropriate reasons to talk about valid normative regulation of social reality. Since this form must, due to its nature, essentially have the form of universality that guarantees the generality of normative resolutions undertaken within it, it shall be therefore of utterly moral character. It results from the fact that - as Hegel noted[24] - it has been assumed already since Kant that the definitional element of morality is to formulate normative claims with a *universal* form and a *general* scope of validity.

Based on the perspective outlined above, it can be stated that the Kantian foundations of justifying moral law lay the grounds for the theory of discourse. Each of its representatives is focused on slightly different "parts of the structure". Karl-Otto Apel undertakes the issue of a definitive justification of the moral law. The goal which he is guided by is to respond the idea of the realm of ends that - due to the theoretical tools by means of which he operates - he considers "metaphysical prefiguration of *a priori* ideal community of communication", which again must be regarded as "a regulative idea of human com-

[24] More precisely, Hegel writes about the major change that has taken place in our culture with the advent of Socrates who first raised decency, due to reflection, to the moral level; yet it is Kant who places this universal form of reflection in the centre of his considerations.

munication."[25] With reference to this idea, Apel develops the ethics of responsibility, particularly in the global dimension - the so-called universal macro ethics of co-responsibility. This dimension contrasts with the ethics that functions in the dimensions from small social groups, up to the national level, referred to by him as micro ethics.[26]

Conversely, Robert Alexy, who is of the view that legal discourse constitutes a special case of practical discourse (so-called *Sonderfallthese*), seeks to identify the normative (in the moral sense) core of legal discourse.[27] What forms the core of his argument is the thesis that even a nonpositivist conception of law must be based on at least rudimentary nonrelativistic ethics.[28] For this purpose, the law must be morally falsificable whereas the rules and principles of discourse ethics remain the criteria for assessing whether a legal norm is morally correct.[29]

Jürgen Habermas, on the other hand, addresses the issue of mutual balance between moral autonomy and popular sovereignty ex-

---

[25] Karl-Otto Apel, *Diskurs und Verantwortung. Das Problem des Übergangs zur postkonventionellen Moral*, Frankfurt am Main: Suhrkamp Verlag, 1997.

[26] Karl-Otto Apel, „Diskursethik als Ethik der Mit-Verantwortung vor den Sachzwängen der Politik, des Rechts und der Marktwirtschaft," in: K.-O. Apel, Holger Burckhart (eds.), *Prinzip Mitverantwortung. Grundlage für Ethik und Pädagogik*, Würzburg: Königshausen & Neumann, 2001, pp. 69–96.

[27] Critical and representative analysis of this thesis in Polish literature has been presented by Andrzej Grabowski in the article „Dyskurs prawniczy jako przypadek szczególny ogólnego dyskursu praktycznego" [Legal Discourse as a Special Case of General Practical Discourse], in: Jerzy Stelmach (ed.), *Studia z filozofii prawa* [Studies in Philosophy of Law], vol. 2, Kraków: Wydawnictwo UJ, 2003, pp. 45–64. He rightly points out that *Sonderfallthese* may not be reliable if it is presented descriptively or empirically because of its inadequacy. This is the case because it does not correspond to all parts of the legal discourse undertaken within the judicial application of law (e.g. in a criminal trial, which by its very nature is of illiberal nature and it has a distorted principle of equality between the parties), as well as to the description of dogmatic-legal discourse. This leads to the conclusion that what should be taken into account is the possibility of normative-analytical methodological status of the "thesis on a particular case."

[28] Robert Alexy, *Begriff und Geltung des Rechts*, Freiburg–München: Verlag Alber, 1992, p. 93.

[29] However, as Alexy highlights, "Every violation of human rights is unjust, but not every injustice is a violation of human right" (Robert Alexy, "Law, Morality, and the Existence of Human Rights," *Ratio Juris* 2012, March, vol. 25, no. 1, pp. 2–14, here at: p. 9), which implies that not every injustice immediately falisficates the law.

pressed through the medium of positive law. His aim is in a way to indicate "the third way" of justifying laws, that is, instead of grounding the notion of the popular sovereignty on the notion of moral autonomy (like Kant did), or conversely, making the notion of sovereignty the basis for the notion of moral autonomy (like Rousseau), it should be demonstrated that these two concepts can mutually overlap so that none of them has an advantage over the other (so-called 'co-originality thesis').

2. Transcendental-pragmatic / universal-pragmatic justification of discourse ethics

2.1. Principium of universalization

As Habermas says, the form of the categorical imperative consists of a triple abstraction which determines this test for the maxim as to whether it falls under the model of typical moral law or not: (a) the abstraction from (*a posteriori*) motives of action, namely those related to the considered situation; (b) "abstraction from the particular situation"; (c) "abstraction from existing institutions and forms of life"[30] (of the one who asks about how s/he should act in a given situation). What is specifically meant here are the following operations: (a) abstraction and individualization as the distinction between autonomy and heteronomy; (b) reflection as understanding and applying reflective norms or principles; (c) generalization.[31] Other words round, this precise operations are needed in order to formulate best reasons in favour of one of competing norms.

Because of this abstraction it can be considered, inter alia, that Kant expects to indicate the best *reasons* in favour of resolving certain *moral* dilemma. This is the essence of post-metaphysical turn, which is undertaken in his practical philosophy. The request to indicate the best reasons implies that these arguments will provide - in an *analogous* manner to the facts - a kind of justification for the formulation

[30] J. Habermas, *Justification and Application…*, op. cit., p. 118.

[31] Jürgen Habermas, "Moral development and Ego Identity," in: *Communication and the Evolution of Society*, transl. Th. McCarthy, Boston: Beacon Press, 1979, pp. 83–87.

and selection of certain norm of action. So the norm of action itself will correspond to an *analogue* of truth-based qualification of descriptive propositions[32] - a judgment whether it is well justified or not. In other words, based on the theory of discourse (in the case of each of its creators) normative judgments are given cognitivistic (*cognitive*) character, which clearly protects them against any relativization. The latter is crucial because this theory, taking Kantian ideas, points to justifiability of some specific (normative) claims of a universalist character.

The thesis of justifiability of normative claims is in the theory of discourse closely related to another thesis, namely that the reasoned argument is the one which 'deserves recognition by all concerned,'[33] and therefore to whom it is addressed. This conviction - shared jointly by Apel, Habermas, or Alexy - stems from the possibility of the claim to universal validity of the norm at issue. The universal validity implies the widespread application. As a result, the objectivity of the categories of freedom is replaced by "a priori of 'facticity' of real community of communication, namely the socio-cultural form of life"[34], through *a priori* assumption that somehow we are all immersed in certain historically shaped lifeworlds that found massive contexts of understandability of our existence. In a sense, this is based on the assumption of the need to take into account Gadamer's pre-judgments. Indeed, Gadamer claims that

> ... who wants to understand a text, always undertakes a projection (*ein Entwerfen*). He throws a sense of a whole, once the very first sense shows oneself in a text. Such a one shows oneself but only, whereas man reads the text with specific expectations for a certain sense. Understanding of what is contained there consists in developing such a pre-project that is of course constantly revised by what turns out with further penetration into the sense.[35]

---

[32] Jürgen Habermas, *The Inclusion of the Other. Studies in Political Theory*, ed. by Ciaran Cronin, Pablo De Greiff, Polity Press, 2002, p. 98; idem, *Moral Consciousness and Communicative Action*, op. cit., p. 56, p. 68.

[33] Jürgen Habermas, "Discourse Ethics," in: idem, *Moral Consciousness and Communicative Action*, op. cit., p. 65.

[34] K.-O. Apel, *Diskurs und Verantwortung*, op. cit., p. 19.

[35] H.-G. Gadamer, *Wahrheit und Methode*, op. cit., p. 271.

Understanding is, therefore, inextricably linked with the process of socialization and enculturation.

In the Kantian philosophy, the test verifying whether a given maxim could be considered as a model type of the moral law is undertaken by making three kinds of abstractions on the proposed maxim determining in moral terms an action of a subject in the particular situation, namely situation embedded in terms of the sensibility (particular temporal and spatial relations). In view of the circumstances that a particular situation - defined in terms of time and space - means the actual life situation of potential addressees of the tested norm, Kant's test of universalization is modified in the discourse theory in favour of the *actual (real) discourse* between all interested in (and affected by) the settlement of disputed issue, which appeared in those lifeworlds.

It can be, therefore, said that Kantian practical power of judgment is transformed into democratically hold public discourse whose aim is, without doubt, the indication of the best legitimate reasons in favour of a particular norm-candidate, which will to the greatest extent meet the requirements laid down by the very principle of universality. The focus lies here on non-monological (as was the case even in Kant) and intersubjective justification of norm- candidate because the place of transcendental (universal) structure of the subject is already taken by transcendental structures of pragmatically defined inter-subjectivity. This is certainly such intersubjectivity which in particularly determined conditions must be heard, and then agree to adjust its real vital interests. It is how Apel himself puts it:

> The most important point of transformation is as follows: The place (as required by Kant from an individual) of the fitness of maxim of action to [become] the law is taken by regulative idea - accepted by all individuals as binding, but in a real discourse implemented, where possible, approximatively - of reachability of consensus by all affected as to any valid norms. It is this universal reachability of consensus that - according to the discourse ethics - constitutes the basis for introducing sense [*Sinnimplementierung*] and concretization of Kant's determination of the fitness to be law at the level of intersubjectivity - in a way postmetaphysical, yet pragmatically and transcendentally justifi-

able, deciphering of 'the realm of ends' as a regulative idea of human communication.[36]

In view of the above, Habermas formulates two principles corresponding to two moments in Kant's categorical imperative: to *a priori* moment, which points to a necessary form of what is to lay claim to being the moral law, and to the synthetic moment, namely the maxim whose conformity with the form of the moral law is necessary, but reachable by deriving from what is essential in particular, actual situation. These are respectively: the formal principium of universalization (U) and discourse principle (D). The principle of universalization is as follows:

> *All* affected (*Betroffenen*) can accept the consequences and the side effects its *general* observance can be anticipated to have for the satisfaction of *everyone's* interests (and these consequences are preferred to those of known alternative possibilities for regulation).[37]

On the other hand, the principle of discourse ethics (D) - already assuming the justifiability of the principle (U) - takes the following form:

> Only those norms can claim to be valid that meet (or could meet) with the approval of all affected in their capacity as participants in a practical discourse.[38]

Only such determined rule of discourse, according to Habermas, guarantees the impartiality of justification of normative decisions, which is one of the necessary conditions for rational agreement reaching, the one, that on the other hand, has its possibility embodied or presumed, in his opinion, in this principium of universalization. Other words speaking, principium of universalization stands for recognition of this form of a norm-candidate that meets Kantian demand

---

[36] K.-O. Apel, "Etyka dyskursu jako etyka odpowiedzialności - postmetafizyczna transformacja etyki Kanta" [Discourse ethics as ethics of responsibility - the postmetaphysical transformation of Kantian ethics], *Principia* 1992, t. V, p. 19.

[37] J. Habermas, "Discourse Ethics," op. cit., p. 65.

[38] Ibidem, p. 66.

of its conformity with the moral law, and the starting point of individual moral test performance via triple abstraction - namely, moral problem embodiment in the specific situation - is replaced by the communicative community of individuals emerging from their life worlds towards impartial formulations of norms which they all would become addresses of.

Hence, the basic theoretical as well as practical premise for discourse is a "primordial situation" in the sense of "a situation of argumentation" that allows every individual to realize that they are members of the real community of communication. This is reflected in adopting the principle of action which - in Apel's approach - takes the form of formally defined principle of universalization:

> Act only according to the maxim (norm) which allows you, on the basis of the actual agreement with all affected (*Betroffenen*), or their representatives or - as a substitute - on the basis of equivalent thought experiment, to assume that the outcomes and side effects that result from their widespread application to satisfy the interests of each probably interested in individual, may be without coercion accepted in some real discourse by all affected (concerned).[39]

This leads to the further conclusion that the norm is binding only when its results could be accepted without coercion by any party in any possible discourse.

Apel finally formulates a maxim - corresponding to the greatest extent with Kant's categorical imperative - which reads as follows: "(Always) act as if you were a member of the ideal community of communication."[40] In other words, each participant in the discourse must realize that s/he is a member of a real community of communication, or even of counterfactually assumed ideal community of communication. The assumption of an ideal transcendental communi-

---

[39] K.-O. Apel, *Diskurs und Verantwortung*, op. cit., p. 123.

[40] Karl-Otto Apel, "Diskursethik vor der Problematik von Recht und Politik: Können die Rationalitätsdifferenzen zwischen Moralität, Recht und Politik selbst noch durch die Diskursethik normativ-rational gerechtfertigt werden?," in: K.-O. Apel and Matthias Kettner (eds.), *Zur Anwendung der Diskursethik in Politik, Recht und Wissenschaft*, Frankfurt am Main: Suhrkamp Verlag, 1992, p. 123.

ty of communication is significant because within the latter is constituted a precondition for interpersonal communication. Consequently, we realize that we are actually the members of a real community of communication. Indeed, "the institution of linguistic communication" is not removable and it is realised in any language, in every community. Naturally, as for the ideal community of communication, which the principle of universalization of discourse ethics counterfactually concerns, in fact, there are only some efforts made in order to realize it.[41]

According to Habermas, the validity of the above rules in terms of assuming them as valid, is a constitutive force for undertaking all acts of speech. In other words, if we, making speech acts, have made no assumptions about the universal validity of these rules, then we would not rationally and, in a consequence, effectively communicate with others. Consequently, we counterfactually commonly make such assumptions in our everyday actions. Communication in fact means, as Apel holds with Habermas, that

> ... the one who argues, *implicitly* recognizes all the possible claims of all participants in the community of communication, which can be justified by rational arguments ... and he also undertakes to justify all his claims vis-à-vis others by delivering arguments.[42]

2.2. The ideal conditions of communication generated by the rules of discourse

Nonetheless, there appears a serious problem, namely these counterfactually adopted rules (always accepted by each participant of a linguistic game) have a perfect character which actually is not always, or even it is never fully implemented. What is therefore the sense of constructing perfect rules and - consequently - indicating the ideal conditions of discourse? According to Alexy, it is even crucial. The required ideal rules along with the ideal conditions for communica-

---

[41] Ibidem, p. 36 ff.

[42] Karl-Otto Apel, *Transformation der Philosophie*, Band 2: *Das Apriori der Kommunikationsgemeinschaft*, Frankfurt am Main: Suhrkamp Verlag, 1973, p. 424.

tion generated by the former, may in fact serve a critical function vis-à-vis the actual conditions or vis-à-vis the agreement on the normative claims reached in them.[43] Secondly, it should be noted that the approximation of an ideal situation, founded on ideal rules is yet possible.[44] Habermas himself puts it as follows, clearly explaining why this seemingly "weak point" of discourse theory is in fact a decisive issue:

> The ideal moment of unconditionality is deeply ingrained in the factual processes of communication, because validity claims are Janus-faced: as claims they overshoot every context; at the same time, they must be both raised and accepted here and now, if they are to support an agreement effective for coordination – for this there is no "null context." The universalistic meaning of the claimed validity exceeds all contexts, but only the local, binding act of acceptance enables validity claims to bear the burden of social integration for a context-bound everyday practice.[45]

In view of the above, Alexy takes up the task of explaining these rules which would extract to the full the ideal conditions of discourse that have the potential critical function to realistically undertaken discussions, so that they could lead to bringing up such norms (with already identified content) which could be reasonably said that they deserve universal recognition by all those whom they concern. Since the theory of discourse, let us recall, is of normative character, therefore the said explication has the character of justifying the universalization principium in the sense that it is implied by these rules of general practical discourse. Alexy treats these rules of discourse as a contribution to formulating a "code of practical reason" which "would be a synopsis and an explicit formulation of all the rules and forms of rational practical argumentation."[46] In other words, the rules of general practical discourse provide a necessary foundation of *rational* practical argumentation.

---

[43] R. Alexy, *A Theory of Legal Argumentation*, op. cit., p. 122.

[44] Ibidem, p. 123.

[45] J. Habermas, *Between Facts and Norms. Contributions to a Discourse Theory of Law and Democracy*, transl. W. Rehg, Cambridge, Mass.: The MIT Press, 1999, pp. 20–21.

[46] R. Alexy, *A Theory of Legal Argumentation*, op. cit., p. 188.

The rules of general practical discourse can be divided into:

1) basic rules that apply to:
   (1.1) logical rules (both in classic and deontic terms) also applying to normative statements,
   (1.2) sincerity of expression, which is constitutive for all communication,
   (1.3) a consistent method of using terms by one speaker,
   (1.4) common (in the meaning of commonly and consistently determined) use of terms by various speakers;[47]
2) rules of rationality, namely '*the general justification rule,*'[48] and – correlated with the latter – three rules which express:
   (2.1) universalistic dimension of discourse - everyone can enter it,
   (2.2) equality of the position of each participant in the discourse for the argumentative openness of discourse,
   (2.3) freedom of discourse from any coercion;[49]
3) 'rules for allocating the burden of argument' which, as Alexy succinctly puts it, are to protect the discourse both against 'driving it into a corner' by 'childish and mechanical repetition of the question "why?"'[50] as well as against polilogically saying anything, because everyone can speak in any case freely.

Alexy then goes on to define the forms of arguments,[51] justification rules[52] and rules of transitivity.[53] When analysing justification rules, he considers three formulations of universalization principium: Hare's, Habermas', and Baier's. He tries to show that none of these approaches is fully satisfactory from the perspective of the rules indicated by him, and yet all of them, according to Alexy, constitute the terms of rational discourse. In reference to Habermas, he says that his version of universalization principium 'is the direct result of the structure of discourse as determined by the rationality rules ((2.1)–(2.3))."[54]

[47] Ibidem, pp. 188–191.
[48] Ibidem, p. 192.
[49] Ibidem, pp. 193–195.
[50] Ibidem, p. 195–197.
[51] Ibidem, pp. 197–202.
[52] Ibidem, pp. 202–205.
[53] Ibidem, p. 206.
[54] Ibidem, p. 203.

Finally he concludes that all three formulations of universalization principium should be complemented by two additional rules, which say that "(5.2.1.) the moral rules underlying the moral views of a speaker must be able to withstand critical testing in terms of their historical genesis"[55] and the rule stating that the above critical restriction of moral rules in fact contains a reference to empirical knowledge.[56]

Habermas tries to refute Alexy's interpretation. In his view, the rules from (1) to (3), as indicated by the philosopher from Kiel, can be interpreted through the angle of Aristotle's theory of rhetorical art as, respectively:

1) The rules based on the logical (i.e., determining the form) level of argumentation that guarantees that the reasoning is consistently conducted; in other words it is about the logical-semantic rules of language which, however, have no ethical content.[57]

2) The rules based on dialectical level indicating the application of procedures during argumentation[58] due to which the presentation of arguments on the issues which are disputable for the discussants is so structured that this order allows them to further "test the arguments." It is here, according to Habermas, where

> ... are located the pragmatic presuppositions of a special form of interaction, namely everything necessary for a search for truth organized in the form of a competition. Examples include recognition of the accountability and truthfulness of all participants in the search. At this level also situate general rules of jurisdiction and relevance that regulate themes for discussion, contributions to the argument, etc.[59]

It is here, Habermas argues, that there appear *ethically* essential components of discourse rules, such as mutual recognition of the participants in the discourse. And since this discourse has the nature of competition (between the arguments made by its participants), therefore, according to Habermas, it is thoroughly postmetaphysical be-

[55] Ibidem, p. 204.

[56] Ibidem, p. 205.

[57] J. Habermas, "Discourse Ethics," op. cit., p. 87.

[58] Ibidem.

[59] Ibidem.

cause it assumes a critical attitude rather than, as it was the other day, protects "a dogmatic core of convictions" from the criticism.[60]

3) Rules based on rhetorical level, defining the process and the course of the argumentation.[61]

They must demonstrate the ability to generate such structures of statements that will withstand the various pressures, violence and inequalities, that is, those that "present itself as a form of communication that adequately approximates ideal conditions"[62] so that any competent speaker must assume as adequately fulfilled an overall symmetry of the terms of discourse. According to Habermas, what is also important here is to demonstrate that the rules which Alexy refers to, are not merely conventions (such as playing chess), but actually they are necessary conditions of discourse. This means that they must be regarded as 'merely the *form* in which we present the implicity adopted and intuitively known pragmatic presuppositions of a special type of speech, presuppositions that are adopted implicitly and known intuitively.'[63]

Habermas states from this point of view that the assumptions necessary to infer his version of universalization principium (U) have just been accepted. It is a moral principium being at the same time the 'rule of argumentation' that also constitutes a 'part of the logic of practical discourse.'[64] It is supplemented by 'the principle of discourse ethics (D), which stipulates the basic idea of a moral theory but does not form part of a logic of argumentation.'[65] In this way, according to Habermas, the rule of discourse was justified.

2.3. The final justification of discourse rules

The above justification of the rules of discourse is, however, not satisfactory for all representatives of discourse theory. According to

[60] Ibidem, p. 88.
[61] Ibidem, p. 88 ff.
[62] Ibidem, p. 88.
[63] Ibidem, p. 91.
[64] Ibidem, p. 93.
[65] Ibidem.

Apel, what is necessary is a *final* justification of the rules that constitute communication.[66] In his view, human nature shows that the negation of this idea, and thus negating the process of argumentation, would lead to schizophrenia and self-destruction.[67]

According to the author of *Diskurs und Verantwortung*, it is therefore necessary to complete the Kantian project, as it were "putting a dot over the 'i'", which, in fact, Kant failed to put. As Apel reproaches Kant - the philosopher from Königsberg announced in *The Groundwork of the Metaphysic of Morals* the final justification of the moral law. Meanwhile, in the *Critique of Practical Reason* he abandoned this project, settling for the observation that

> ... freedom is certainly *ratio essendi* of moral law, but moral law is *ratio cognoscendi* of freedom. So if the moral law was not sooner in our reason clearly thought, then we would never deem ourselves justified to adopt something like freedom.[68]

How can we, nonetheless, know this moral law?

> The moral law is also given as if it were a fact of pure reason, which we are *a priori* aware of and which is apodeictically certain, even when assuming that in experience one could not find any example of its strict compliance.[69]

This very observation does not satisfy Apel. He is therefore looking for answers why Kant failed to provide this ultimate justification of moral law and, consistently, what would be able to satisfy this request on the grounds of modern philosophy.

He notes that Kant assumed the perspective of universal, yet still subjective structures of the subject, and meanwhile "the moral law – as opposed to the law of nature – clearly obtains its meaning in *regu-*

---

[66] K.-O. Apel, *Transformation der Philosophie*, Band 2: *Das Apriori der Kommunikationsgemeinschaft*, op. cit., p. 222: "In einer modernen Transzendentalphilosophie geht es m.E. primär um die Reflexion auf den Sinn ... des Argumentierens überhaupt. Dies allerdings ist für den, der argumentiert ... offenbar das *Letzte, Nichthintergehbare*."

[67] Ibidem, p. 414.

[68] I. Kant, *Kritik der praktischen Vernuft*, op. cit., p. 274 [4]; footnote.

[69] Ibidem, p. 333 [47].

lating intersubjective relations of actors."[70] Nevertheless, intersubjective dimension is still closed for him, namely, on the basis of his philosophy it can reach the so-called other, that is another person, exclusively on the basis of reason, i.e. on the grounds of the abovementioned universal, general structures. From the perspective of perception we can always talk only about the objects of perception, which never give us the appropriate tools to distinguish among these "objects of perception" those which are human beings, from those that are not human beings. It was Edmund Husserl who learned about this when his struggle with the constitution of the other in his brilliant *Cartesian Meditations* ended in a failure. It was only Heidegger who – by deconstructing the category of subjectivity (i.e. these general and universal structures that were to appropriately describe us as people) in favour of the open-structures of understanding – restored philosophy from this peculiar impasse involving "impossibility of one human to reach another."[71] Category of understanding is what allows us to already assume the coexistence of the other and the philosophical research simply focuses in this perspective on modes of honest and original reaching this other – another human being (*Dasein*).

In this regard, the category of understanding oriented philosophical researches at the above-mentioned categories of language. The final justification of moral rules is thus to demonstrate that they are 'always already' contained in the very rules of communication. It is, therefore, about the transformation of the basic premise of Kant's philosophy: "I think" into "I argue."[72] The latter always presupposes the recognition of our membership in two communities at the same time: the real, socially and historically defined community of communication, according to previously specified "*a priori* of facticity" and in "ideal, counterfactually anticipated" community which constitutes a regulative idea, as it sets "ideal and universally valid condi-

[70] K.-O. Apel, *Etyka dyskursu jako etyka odpowiedzialności* [Ethics…], op. cit., p. 9.

[71] On this issue see: Karolina M. Cern, *Koncepcja czasu wczesnego Heideggera* [The Conception of the Time by the Early Heidegger], Poznań: Wydawnictwo Naukowe Instytutu Filozofii UAM, 2007.

[72] K.-O. Apel, *Etyka dyskursu jako etyka odpowiedzialności* [Ethics…] op. cit., p. 11.

tions and presuppositions of communication"[73] which in the latter, actual community would *always* enable real communication.

In view of the above, Apel concludes as follows:

> In reading ... Kantian formula (opinion) about the obvious 'fact of reason' as the expression of a priori accomplished fact, one can say that the obvious fact of reason means precisely that we - as those who argue - together with the communicative reason [meant] as rationality of discourse have at the same time recognized the legitimacy of the moral law.[74]

Reflection on the rules of discourse at the same time reveals their two-stage character. On the one hand, Apel points to the formal and procedural final justification of universal rules of discourse, whereas on the other hand, to the justification of consensually and communicatively reached norms of content that are always related to a specific socially and historically determined community of communication. It should be at the same time clearly stressed that the norms of this second degree are still distinguishable from the material norms (and thus relating to particular situations) indicated by practical discourses,[75] because the issue here is about their justification (due to the implementation of the general norms, norms of first-level). In other words, the norms of the second-degree relate to the normative approximation (and in that sense to justification) of universal norms to certain socially and culturally determined life worlds.

3. Application of discourse ethics

Apel's two-stage discourse ethics is therefore composed of two respective parts. The aim of the first one, called A, is to transcendentally and pragmatically (in formal and procedural way) justify the ability of generating universal principles of discourse.[76] The second part - B

---

[73] Ibidem, p. 14.

[74] Ibidem, p. 15.

[75] K.-O. Apel, *Diskurs und Verantwortung*, op. cit., p. 122.

[76] "Part A includes a justification of an ideal procedural principle of solving all moral and normative problems in the sense of discursive (i.e., purely argumentative

is to *justify the reference* of consensually and communicatively reached norms that make claims to universal validity to historically determined socio-cultural contexts. Thus the heritage of the philosophy of "Heidegger, Gadamer, Peirce, Mead and Wittgenstein,"[77] making the transformation of the concept of sensibility into the concept of facticity, is being linked to the transformation of Kant's "fact of reason", that is the awareness of the moral law, to the form of "a normative-teleological measure at the reconstruction of human social and cultural history"[78] so that, as a result, this measure serves as a benchmark of "the discourse ethics as a post-Weberian, historically determined ethics of responsibility."[79] Discourse ethics is thus the basis and starting point to develop the ethics of responsibility, the guiding idea of which is to understand the historical situation of a given socio-cultural community and, accordingly, to postulate or to generate normative claims of universal validity.

From a "negative" perspective, the sense of this operation consists in "non-violation" of actual, historically shaped life worlds with abstract normative postulates. The aim of this operation is not to call for norms which are infeasible at a particular socio-historical moment, namely norms which might even be incomprehensible for their actual recipients. From a "positive" perspective it is "to combine the readiness to consensual-discursive resolution of the conflicts of interests, according to the assessment of the situation, with the willingness to a strategic action."[80] Infringing a moral norm in the name of the requirements of responsibility imposes a duty to set a

> ... commitment to cooperate with a long-term, approximative elimination of the difference between historically conditioned situation of real com-

and non-strategic, but free from authority) creation of a consensus". K.-O. Apel, „Diskursethik vor der Problematik von Recht und Politik," op. cit., p. 60 ff.

77 K.-O. Apel, *Etyka dyskursu jako etyka odpowiedzialności* [Ethics…], op. cit., p. 21.

78 Ibidem, p. 21.

79 Ibidem, p. 25.

80 K.-O. Apel, "Zasada samoufundowania swoich podstaw w hermeneutycznej rekonstrukcji historii" [The Principle of Self-Foundation of One's Own Basis in Hermeneutical Reconstruction of History], in: Tadeusz Buksiński (ed.), *Rozumność i racjonalność* [Reason and Rationality], Poznań: Wydawnictwo Naukowe IF UAM, 1997, p. 35.

munity of communication and counterfactually anticipated ideal situation in which conditions of discourse would be fulfilled. It is the principle of a duty of continuous involvement of moral progress.[81]

The above does not give us the possibility of evading liability by escapism or parasitism. Thus, democratic, constitutional rule of law should continuously mobilize its citizens to efficiently realize social and political conditions that allow for discursive co-responsibility for collective action at national and international level.[82] What is more, Apel believes that every individual should, already when reading the morning newspapers, think about how he or she may, according to their abilities, participate in the organization of collective responsibility.[83] This is because it involves the participation of all individuals in virtually momentous discourses taking place at the level of the various institutions starting, as Apel states, from the level of legislation through furnishing the kindergarten.

Habermas, like Apel, aware of the breakthroughs made in the philosophical arena of the twentieth century, uses in a specific way a method of understanding sociology of Weberian provenance, Mead's analysis and hermeneutic philosophy, so that by means of the theory of discourse he could 'reconstruct th[e] normative self-understanding in a way that resists both scientistic reductions and aesthetic assimilations.'[84] In other words, he undertakes the reconstruction of the processes which derive 'legitimacy out of legality,'[85] namely the processes of mutual overlapping between moral autonomy and popular sovereignty.[86] He carries out the analysis of historical changes in consciousness which in post-modern times breaks with conventionality in favour of a rational factor, although only slightly motivating to action. The above is complemented by the researches of historic transitions of liberal and republican models of statehood. In such a perspective, he concludes that the transformation of the public sphere

[81] Ibidem, p. 36.

[82] K.-O. Apel, *Diskurs und Verantwortung*, op. cit., pp. 205–206.

[83] Ibidem, p. 206.

[84] J. Habermas, *Between Facts and Norms*, op. cit. p. 11.

[85] Ibidem, p. 83.

[86] Ibidem, p. 107 ff.

can increase the area of freedom - both individual and collective one - so long as they are based on the principle of democracy. It is fundamentally important here that the principle of democracy, which Habermas refers to, constitutes the result of "the interpenetration of the discourse principle and the legal form. - And Habermas - understand[s] this interpenetration as a *logical genesis of rights*."[87]

The principle of discourse, used by Habermas to demonstrate how legitimation of law is possible, that is such law which is approved by all its addresses (and law-givers at the same time), is slightly modified as compared with his prior deliberations. What does this modification consist in? The German philosopher himself writes that in application to the sources of establishing a fully democratic society, namely the one in which moral autonomy of individuals will go hand in hand with popular sovereignty, the principle of discourse "is initially indifferent *vis-à-vis* morality and law. The discourse principle is intended to assume the shape of a principle of democracy only by way of legal institutionalization."[88] This means that the transformation of the discourse principle is at least twofold. At the starting point, it is not a complement of a principium of universalization (U), but it is treated as a "sufficient tool". This is why Habermas says that the principle of discourse "is indifferent to morality." Secondly, discourse principle applied in this way (theoretically) is institutionalized in law - creating a legal *medium* of balancing the autonomy of individuals and the sovereignty of the people, referred to as the principle of democracy. This in turn means that the discourse principle is "indifferent" to the law, because the principle of discourse ensuring discursive realization of political autonomy of citizens is only the crux of the legal system, that is the basis for making that law. What is involved here is that only institutionalized mutual balance between the moral and political autonomy, namely institutionalized principle of discourse - (i.e. embedded in the medium of law), referred to now as the principle of democracy - constitutes the genesis of the laws that could only determine what belongs to the realm of morality, and what belongs to the realm governed by positive law. Habermas thus says that

[87] Ibidem, p. 121.

[88] Ibidem.

codification of law and, at the same time, developing and clarifying the principle of democracy that legitimises this codification, will always co-constitute.

Eventually he comes to the conclusion that the procedural character of reconstruction of law expresses itself in the fact that only the principle of discourse limits and also provides the basis for generating other - new - laws, that is, positive laws, but the latter is not done by pre-positive laws (natural or moral). The principle of discourse therefore requires, in particular, the establishment of laws that govern the membership to a particular association of the common law, and thus protect the membership in that community. Moreover, what is particularly significant, Habermas argues that

> ... classic liberal rights – to personal dignity; to life, liberty, and bodily integrity; to freedom of movement, freedom in the choice of one's vocation, property, the inviolability of one's home, and so on - are interpretations of, and ways of working out, what we might call a "general right to individual liberties," however these may be specified.[89]

In other words, the legitimate law does not require anything other than the mobilization of communicative power of citizens who will every time specify and permeate the outlined kernel of rights, according to the socio-historical circumstances. However, on must keep in mind that the phrase "communicative power" evokes the concept of discourse and its rational rules. For Habermas "perfectly fair acceptability"[90] to be settled in an intersubjective social interaction demands a certain kind of "correctness." The author of *Theory of Communicative Action* undoubtedly emphasizes that moral cognition is naturally different in nature than empirical cognition, and as such should be considered in light of appreciating the recognition of some norm of some action.[91] Both in Habermas and Alexy, ideal conditions of communi-

---

[89] Ibidem, pp. 125–126.

[90] J. Habermas, „Richtigkeit versus Wahrheit. Zum Sinn der Sollgeltung moralischer Urteile und Normen," in: idem, *Wahrheit und Rechtfertigung. Philosophische Aufsätze*, Frankfurt am Main: Suhrkamp Verlag, 2004, p. 284.

[91] Comp. R. Alexy, „The Nature of Legal Philosophy," *Ratio Juris* 2004, June, vol. 17, no. 2, pp. 156–167, here p. 157: "Action, on the other hand, presupposes a conception about what ought to be done or is good."

cation and, as a result, universal, discursively and theoretically justified human rights will speak for the significance of norms or actions.

Therefore, in Alexy, the claim to correctness (*Richtigkeit*) justifies the need to combine legal and moral discourse. The claim to correctness might thus refer either to the formal level or procedural one, as well as to legally regulated substance or matter.[92] This second possibility is particularly important here, especially when it is linked to the formal correctness - then it constitutes the kernel of discussions and disputes between legal positivism and non-positivism[93] and it concerns the possible loss of legal validity. According to the philosopher from Kiel, "the judge who chooses a morally mistaken interpretation in a case, in which the positive law allows as well for a morally correct interpretation, would not be making a legally perfect decision."[94]

Meanwhile, the relations between morality and law are twofold: they may be of a classifying character (morality is the criterion for recognizing a given norm as valid) or qualifying one (morality is the criterion for identifying the defective legal regulations).[95] According to Alexy, who tries to justify the non-positivist concept of law,[96] using Radbruch formula, it can be meaningfully stated that moral defects of law do not always deny its validity, although in extreme situations where the law is grossly unfair - the latter may be the case because the law has a dual nature: it has a physical dimension - referring it to the dimension of social impact and authoritative regulation - as well as the ideal one, defined by the correctness, including the moral correctness which serves a critical function in respect to this first dimension.[97] More specifically, the content of the concept of law consists of the two abovementioned dimensions.

On account of that, the judge in the above example makes a mistaken interpretation, whereas the question here is about the qualify-

---

[92] Robert Alexy, *On the Concept and the Nature of Law*, Lecture in Honour of Leon Petrażycki, Warszawa: Foundation „Ius et Lex," 2006, p. 45.

[93] Ibidem, p. 23 ff.

[94] Ibidem, p. 48.

[95] Ibidem, p. 39.

[96] Robert Alexy, *W obronie niepozytywistycznej koncepcji prawa* [Defending Nonpositivist Conception of Law], „Państwo i Prawo" 1993, no. 11–12, p. 34.

[97] R. Alexy, *On the Concept and the Nature of Law*, op. cit., pp. 38–40.

ing relation of law from the perspective of its ideal dimension - the moral correctness. This alone demonstrates the necessary connection of law with morality,[98] but for now in respect of mere qualification of legal regulations. According to Alexy, in order to go to the classification of these regulations, we need the so-called additional reasons, which have a *normative* character and which may take the form of human rights or fundamental rights.[99] This is also a manifestation of another aspect of discourse theory. Alexy takes it further in his fundamental work *A Theory of Constitutional Rights*,[100] and distinctly presents it in *Begriff und Geltung des Rechts.*

Conclusions

The common goal for all the discussed representatives of the theory of discourse is to present a critical social theory, the essence of which is to ensure communicative rationality and its potential in self-reflection and self-control. Critical dimension of discourse theory is expressed mainly in the pursuit of extending the consensus based on a free and undistorted communication between participants in the discourse and in a demonstration - by means of slightly different arguments - of the necessary links between the legal and moral discourse. In other words, the criticism becomes the object of study of the conceptual and practical procedures enabling the formation of a rational consensus. As a result, the critical theory of the representatives of discourse theory, formulates a program to overcome the situation of reification and basing social life on ethical foundation by means of self-reflection concerning the process of reifying social relations.

The crux of the presented problematics is however this, that as connecting moral discourse with the legal one is fully manifested in the questions about (possible) just and fair law, namely such which does not favour any of the possible concepts of the 'good life,' ques-

---

[98] Ibidem, p. 48.

[99] Ibidem, p. 49.

[100] Robert Alexy, *A Theory of Constitutional Rights*, transl. J. Rivers, New York: Oxford University Press, 2002.

tioning the legal argumentation becomes specific activity of the practical reason focused on processes of legitimation (best justified) norms.[101] Undertaking a reflection over processes of legitimation is a critical attempt, for 'reflection necessarily has a critical dimension'[102] which, moreover, in case of practical philosophy including legal philosophy, is of normative burden, as normative considerations aim at 'distinguish[ing] what is correct from what is incorrect.'[103] The critical function of the theory of practical discourse in general is focused on one hand on differentiating moral issues from ethical issue and on the other hand the pivotal role plays the principium of democracy within the legal order.

Since the practical power of judgement had been exteriorised and manifested within structures of public spheres, the connection between the moral and legal discourse transformed into questioning legitimation processes on the account of the requirement of correctness. Paradoxically, in the heart of the possibility of meeting this requirement, one may find out the communicative power, precisely, the *conjunction* of universal form reflexivity *and* individual as well as cooperative action-taking on the basis of this reflexivity. As wisely points out Habermas there is: 'the evidence that democratic institutions of freedom disintegrate without the initiatives of a population *accustomed* to freedom.'[104] Therefore, in the very heart of practical philosophical investigations since thousands of years has remained *The Conjunction* of reflection and action.

---

[101] And it must be explicitly put, that Habermas and Alexy agree on this point: compare *Between Facts and Norms*, op. cit. (especially Chapters III and IV) and "Law, Morality, and the Existence of Human Rights," *Ratio Juris* 2012, March, vol. 25, no. 1, pp. 2–14, especially pp. 9–10.

[102] R. Alexy, *The Nature of Legal Philosophy*, op. cit., p. 157.

[103] Ibidem, p. 158.

[104] J. Habermas, *Between Facts and Norms*, op. cit., p. 130.

Marco Antonio Oliveira de Azevedo
Unisinos, University of Sinos Valley, Brazil

Commands and Claims

Abstract: Notwithstanding the widely accepted view that rights establish normative constraints on authority's powers, *command* is still a core notion in modern philosophical jurisprudence. Nevertheless, if Herbert Hart is correct in his analysis on the deficiencies of the traditional command theories, a command is binding only if there is a right of being obeyed implying authority. My main objective in this paper is to make explicit the semantical and normative relations between rights and commands. In the first part, after some remarks on Hobbes' semantics, I will note that, although commands are performative utterances paradigmatically addressed to "inferiors," claims, on the contrary, are utterances addressed also to "superiors." In the second part, assuming Wesley Newcomb Hohfeld's distinctions between claims, privileges, powers and immunities, I will discuss Joseph Raz's theory that authorities have a right of being obeyed. Looking for a more coherent theory, and taking a little bit of distance from Raz's definitions, I will present some refinements in the semantics of authority. My main point is that a command is valid only if it presupposes a right of being obeyed, a right that would be a claim-right in Hohfeld's sense; but since all claims are correlated to duties, this entails that the duty of being obeyed cannot be created by any acts of the authority which holds the claim. Anyway, since claims purport to present reasons for action, a command can only constitute a reason for action for persons who have a duty of obeying other persons with claims of being obeyed. In that case, commanding involves making an appeal not to fear, but to respect for authority.

Key-words: commands, claims, authority, right to obedience, Raz, Hart

Introduction

To say that "law is command" could strike someone as something very old and odd. Nonetheless, the conception that *law is command* was a commonplace in the philosophy of law at least until the middle of the 20th century. And in spite of Hans Kelsen's modifications[1] and even Herbert Hart's powerful objections to the command tradition, notably in *The concept of law*,[2] "commands" continue in the core of the conceptual domain of recent contemporary philosophical jurisprudence.[3]

However, law is not command. If Herbert Hart is correct, a command is legally binding only if there is a right of being obeyed implying legal authority. This presupposes that *law* or at least legal authority is prior to acts of making *commands*, and that the conceptually primary function of lawmaking is to establish legal authority, which includes the establishment of legal bounds for the exercise of all kinds of political authority. As I will explain, the authority to command is a kind of "right."

---

[1] Hans Kelsen, *Pure theory of Law*, The Lawbook Exchange, 2009; translated from the second revised and enlarged edition of the *Reine Rechtslehre* [1934]; and Hans Kelsen, *General theory of Law and State*, Harvard University Press, 1945.

[2] Herbert L.A. Hart, *The concept of law* [1961], Oxford University Press, 1997.

[3] Even though this story has no definite beginning, Gerald Postema remarks that the view of Law as a command has become a remarkable jurisprudential commonplace as from the 17th century. See: Gerald Postema, "Law as command: the modern of command in modern jurisprudence," *Noûs* 35. Supplement: Philosophical Issues 11, Social, Political and Legal Philosophy, 2001, pp. 470–501. Hobbes is probably its greatest leader in the seventies; further "command" has become the backbone of John Austin's positivist's theory of Law, and before him, albeit some non negligible and peculiar differences, of Jeremy Bentham's. The command law theorists saw acts of commanding in the origin of all kinds of political societies. Contrariwise, some modern natural law theorists, like John Locke, saw rights and all other legal bounds as not derived from any enforced commands of a powerful over others. Locke saw all rights (including the right to command) as derived from reason. But even Locke saw the laws of nature as declarations of the will of God (See: John Locke, "The second treatise on government," in: idem, *Political writings*, Hackett Publishing Company, 2003, pp. 261–369, Chapter XI, § 135: "Thus the law of nature stands as an eternal rule to all men, legislators as well as others. The rules that they make for other men's actions, must, as well as their own and other men's actions, be conformable to the law of nature, i.e. to the will of God, of which that is a declaration, and the fundamental law of nature being the preservation of mankind, no human sanction can be good, or valid against it"); reason, then, in its "practical sense," is seen by all modern natural lawyers as a dictate of a great superior will, hence as a command of a great sovereign (that is, God). Therefore, even for the modern natural law theorists, rights are viewed as ultimately derived from commands.

One of Hart's views is that law cannot be reduced to any group or set of "general commands" made by sovereigns. A recent interpretation of Hart's view has it that law is a *conventional* practice.[4] But it turns out that, for those "rule theorists" (or "conventionalists"), the central concept is no longer "command," but "authority." The problem comes to be why persons, agents or citizens have reasons to follow commands or orders issued by authorities. Even if they agree that authorities have "rights to command," there is the problem of explaining why this constitutes a reason for complying. Hence, even if we depart from the reductive notion that laws are commands, we still have a problem of understanding the place of commands within legal practices. This boils down to the problem of explaining legal authority.

At first sight, the connection between "command" and "authority" seems intuitive and obvious. "To command," says Hart, "is characteristically to exercise authority over man."[5] But, as we know, that thesis departs radically from the command conception as found in Austin. For according to this view, *to command* is something authorities are lawfully licensed to do. Hence it presupposes "authorization" rather than "authority." Anyway, we must pay attention to the use of those words. A superficial reader could conclude through this that the Law itself as well as persons can have authority, since, being "authoritative," Law not only *has* but it *is* also a kind of "authority" over men. Nevertheless, "Law's authority" is one thing; "official authority," another. Officials are authorities, but here we are talking about actual persons; Law in turn is not a person, it is a system of rules. One official can be indentified as "one authority;" but it does not make sense to say about the Law that it is "one authority" (besides others). It is very plausible, hence, that here we are dealing with two different senses of the term "authority" (and a very important difference that

[4] See: Jules Coleman, "The conventionality thesis," *Noûs* 35, Supplement: Philosophical Issues 11, Social, Political and Legal Philosophy, 2001, pp. 354–387; idem, *The practice of principle: In defence of a pragmatist approach to Legal Theory*, Oxford University Press, 2003; Scott Shapiro, "Judicial can't," *Noûs* 35, Supplement: Philosophical Issues 11, Social, Political and Legal Philosophy, 2001, pp. 530–557; and Frederick Schauer, *Playing by the rules: A philosophical examination of rule-based decision-making in Law and in life*, Oxford University Press, 1993.

[5] H.L.A. Hart, *The concept of law*, op. cit., p. 20.

was usually underestimated by almost all authors). If we conflate them, we would go back to the view of command theories that supposes there must be an ultimate sovereign, a supreme one, whose will is binding over all persons capable of being submitted to him, and it would represent a return to a voluntaristic conception of law bindingness, and not to a "rule conception" such as Hart's.

Hart tried to depart entirely from those voluntaristic assumptions. Law is not a mere habit of obedience to some supreme authority; neither presupposes any psychological bond between an authority's will and its targets (or their desires). But a command is an act; and being an act it presupposes *intention*.[6] Law, on the other hand, is not "an act." Law is intentional, but not in the same sense that acts are intentional (even if it is true that Law actually confers "intentionality" to actions). The reason here is that acts are *events*; but Law is not an event; it is rather a *state*.[7] Someone could still claim that Law is not

[6] Elizabeth Anscombe said that "a command is essentially a sign (or symbol), whereas an intention can exist without a symbol; hence we speak of commands, not of expression of commanding; but of the *expression of* intention," G.E.M. Anscombe, *Intention* [1957], Harvard University Press, 2000, p. 5. Taking commands as signs, Anscombe takes verbalized commands as locutions, that is, as "locutionary acts" in John Langshaw Austin's sense. See: John L. Austin, *How to do things with words* [1955], second edition, Harvard University Press, 1975. But a command is certainly also, in one sense, an expression of *commanding*; for verbalized commands comprise not only locutionary acts, but also distinct illocutionary acts, the illocutionary acts of commanding. Consequently, the command-locution is the expression of a "conventional intention" (John Searle, *Speech Acts: An essay in the Philosophy of Language*, Cambridge University Press, 1970), that is, the intention of commanding. Probably the intention Anscombe had in mind is not the illocutionary intention, but the perlocutionary one.

[7] Certainly an act of creating a law can be (actually, it must be) intentional, and an agent (that is, a citizen) can of course behave moved by that same intention. A group of legislators can approve a law with the intention (a perlocutionary intention, if we please) of promoting general happiness, and a citizen can also behave following that law with the same (perlocutionary) intention of promoting general happiness (that is, with the sincere expectation of adding his action to the general sum of happiness). We can, for example, imagine a situation where both legislators and citizens (or most of them) are honest (almost candid) utilitarians. But that would be a mere contingent situation. For the citizen's behavior must not be an expression of the same intentions that moved the legislators' acts. My suspicion is that Law becomes, after its promulgation (and if it turns to be effective), a *state*. Citizens' behavior must reaffirm or reimburse the state, independently anyway of their conformity with the prior intentions of

a state; Law, he could say, is a *social practice*.[8] But even if Law is a social practice, it does not follow that Law comprises a set of regular events, that is, that Law can be reduced to a set of events. Probably it cannot. Habits of obedience to general orders can actually be described by statements of frequency of compliance: if we have a high prevalence of compliance within the target group (formally registered by a high frequency of events, represented by a positive occurrence of a pair composed by the order and an individual of the group), we have a strong evidence in favor of the belief that there is an actual habit of obedience within this population.

But our problem is not this kind of "external compliance;" our problem is to understand what we mean by a *reason for* compliance. See Hart's remarks in *The concept of law* on the problem of succession of Rex I by Rex II. Here the problem is not a matter of habitual obedience. Rex I is a monarch in a kingdom whose vassals simply have a mere habit of obedience, a very personal relationship between each subject and Rex. Hart then supposes that after Rex's death, his son, Rex II immediately starts to issue general orders to the people. The problem is that, at this time, there is not any established habit of obedience to Rex II yet. Hence, we wouldn't have any explanation for the immediate compliance of the subjects in this case if we continue supposing that compliance is only a matter of mere habit. Hart sustains that it would be very different if, beyond the mere habit of obedience to Rex I, we suppose also the existence of a practice of obedience of some rule, such as the rule that conferred to the heir of Rex a right to rule as his lawful successor:

> If there is to be this right and this presupposition at the moment of succession there must, during the reign of the earlier legislator, have been somewhere in the society a general social practice more complex than

the acts that set up the normative state. On the difference between events and states (and other metaphysical entities), see: Michael Loux (ed.), *The possible and the actual: Readings in the metaphysics of modality*, Ithaca: Cornell University Press, 1979; idem, *Metaphysics: A contemporary introduction*, 3rd edition, Routledge, 2006; Helen Steward, *The ontology of mind: Event, processes and states*, Oxford: Oxford University Press, 2006.

[8] Practices plausibly cannot be reduced to mere states; they comprise also processes and events. Unfortunately we still do not have a clear metaphysical description of these kinds of "social entities."

> any that can be described in terms of habit of obedience; there must have been the acceptance of the rule under which the new legislator is entitled to succeed.[9]

Hence the conclusion that "the acceptance (and so the existence) of such a rule will be manifested during Rex I's lifetime" at least, says Hart, "in part by obedience to him, but" necessarily "also by acknowledgements that obedience is something to which he has a right by virtue of his qualifications under the general rule."[10] And "the statement that a new legislator has a right to legislate presupposes the existence, in the social group, of the rule under which he has this right."[11]

Hart understands that Law's authority is a special case of the phenomenon of following rules by the individual, or of the phenomenon of putting oneself under the "authority" of a social rule. But we must not be distracted here by the conclusion that saying that a rule is *actually* binding is the same as saying that it is taken as "authoritative." It would be circular to say that someone has a right to command *because* he is an authority, for that would be the same as saying that an *authority* has a right to command *because* he or she is an *authority*. Rather being in the position of an authority means holding some relevant cluster of rights. The "right to command" is hence nothing but one of those *rights*. And this means that "to exercise authority over men" cannot be simply reduced to "to command" them, since this would take us back to the command tradition, which reduced the right to authority to some collection of singular psychological and persuasive constraints.

It is of utmost importance to clarify the proper relation between commands and authority. And one important distinction here is that when we say that authorities have a "right to obedience," we are actually saying something more complex than a simple relation. Actually, we have a *complex* relation. And the "right to command" is only a part of that complex.

---

[9] H.L.A. Hart, *The concept of law*, op. cit., p. 55.

[10] Ibidem, p. 58.

[11] Ibidem, p. 59.

One of my aims in this work is to state that a "right to command" is a composite right in a broad sense, composed by the union of at least three kinds of "Hohfeldian units": some privileges, one distinct claim and some powers.[12] Probably some classes of authorities have

---

12 Wesley Newcomb Hohfeld's theory of rights is not uncontroversial (Wesley Newcomb Hohfeld, *Fundamental legal conceptions as applied in judicial reasonings* [1913, 1917], ed. by Walter Wheeler Cook with a foreword by Arthur L. Corbin, Union, New Jersey: The Lawbook Exchange, 2000), but it is unquestionably seminal and canonical. Hohfeld thought there were eight "fundamental legal relations," divided in a scheme of "opposites" and "correlatives" (ibidem, pp. 36, 65). It has appeared originally in the first of his two famous articles published in *The Yale Law Review* (Wesley Newcomb Hohfeld, "Some fundamental legal conceptions as applied in judicial reasoning," *The Yale Law Journal* 1913, vol. 23 (16), pp. 16–59; idem, "Fundamental legal conceptions as applied in judicial reasoning," *The Yale Law Journal* 1917, vol. 26, pp. 710–End.). In his presentations, Hohfeld avoided to use the term "right" to express what he understood as different kinds of legal entities: "[T]he term 'rights' tends to be used indiscriminately to cover what in a given case may be a privilege, a power, or an immunity, rather than a right in the strictest sense" (p. 36). Later, he amends that "if, as seems desirable, we should seek a synonym for the word 'right' in this limited and proper meaning, perhaps the word 'claim' would prove the best" (W.N. Hohfeld, *Fundamental legal conceptions as applied in judicial reasonings*, op. cit., p. 38). In a note, Hohfeld cites a legal decision, where it is written that "A right has been well defined to be a well-founded claim, and a well-founded claim means nothing more nor less than a claim recognized or secured by law" (ibidem, p. 38, note 32a). Hohfeld's view can plausibly be interpreted as the view that 'right' in a "primary sense" is a *claim-right*; only in a "secondary sense" it can be viewed on the same side of privileges, powers and immunities as "rights" (hence, in a "broad" or in a "generic," but not in a "specific" sense). See also Arthur Corbin's Foreword (ibidem, p. vii). My own philosophical interpretation is that rights are, in a metaphysically primary sense, (valid) *claims*. This is what I called *a claim conception of rights*. That view is plausibly semantically different from what I called *an entitlement view of rights* (for a more detailed explanation and argumentation, see: Marco A.O. de Azevedo, "Rights as entitlements and rights as claims," *Veritas* 2010, vol. 55, no. 1, pp. 164–182, available at: <http://revistaseletronicas.pucrs.br/ojs/index.php/veritas/article/view/7327>). Many people tried to develop Hohfeld scheme in a more formal way. Hohfeld, nevertheless, thought that, since the fundamental legal relations, the four pairs of "jural opposites" (right/no-right; privilege/duty; power/disability; and immunity/liability) and the four pairs of "jural correlatives" (right/duty; privilege/no-right; power/liability; and immunity/disability), are *sui generis*, the attempts of presenting them in a "formal definition are always unsatisfactory, if not altogether useless" (W.N. Hohfeld, *Fundamental legal conceptions as applied in judicial reasonings*, op. cit., p. 36). The difficulty in presenting a formal definition in clearly manifested in the version presented, for example, by Stig Kanger

also some special immunities. A very peculiar (and essential) trace of the so-called "right to obedience" is that it comprises a somewhat unique right-claim, the "claim to obedience"; nevertheless, authorities' rights include also a power over some people and their subordinates, besides a privilege of making commands.[13] An important point here is that since claims cannot be directly derived from or reduced to commands, the right-claim to obedience is not in any way created or derived from commands of the persons who have that claim, that is, the authorities which have also the independent privilege for making those commands.

(see: *Collected papers of Stig Kanger with essays on his life and work*, vol. I, ed. by Ghita Holmström-Hintikka, Sten Lindström and Rysiek Sliwinski, Kluwer Academic Publishers, 2001, pp. 104–106). It is not my aim here to analyze those alternative attempts (although it is plainly visible that the view presented by Kanger, notably on the concepts of legal power and legal immunity, departs equivocally from the soundly Hohfeld's views); neither here is the proper place for a more detailed defense of Hohfeld's semantics. Hence, I simply will invite the reader to accept the assumption of Hohfeld semantics (of course, if the reader does think that Hohfeldian semantics is not a good description of the actual meaningful use of the word 'right', then he coherently will think that my argument is not sound). For a good discussion on Hohfeldian concepts and some interesting relations with the Will and Interest Theory of Rights, see: Matthew H Kramer, N.E Simmonds and Hillel Steiner, *A debate over rights*, Oxford University Press, 1988. For a good introduction of Hohfeldian semantics, see: William Edmundson, *An introduction to rights*, Cambridge University Press, 2004. For a recent elaboration of Hohfeld's framework, see: Leif Wenar, "The nature of rights," *Philosophy & Public Affairs* 2005, vol. 33, no. 3, pp. 223–252. For a moral theory based on Hohfeld's semantics, see Judith Jarvis Thomson seminal book *The realm of rights* (Oxford University Press, 1990).

[13] The privilege of making commands counts as a mean-consequence of having a claim of being obeyed. If John has a valid claim against Peter of being obeyed, that is, if John can validly claim Peter's obedience of him, since commands can be counted as signs of someone's intention, then a command can be viewed as a mean for the claim's fulfillment; hence, having a claim of being obeyed implies having also a privilege of commanding. Could someone have a claim of being obeyed without having also a Hohfeldian privilege of commanding? If it would be true, then the claim of being obeyed would not imply a privilege or a permission to command. Note, nevertheless, that the privilege of commanding does not imply having a claim of being obeyed. Orders can be done without those claims. Someone who receives an order of another that does not have any claim of being obeyed by him has, of course, a privilege of disobeying. Those "commanders" cannot be entitled as legal authorities.

Another of my aims is to support the view that, since commands are utterances paradigmatically addressed to "inferiors," claims are utterances or statements addressed the other way round: claims are usually seen as utterances addressed to equals, but their strength is vividly showed when addressed just to "superiors."

That is the first part of this paper. In the second part, I will begin with the Hohfeldian (and canonical) distinction between claims, privileges and powers (besides immunities) as the core components of a right in a "broad sense." Then I will discuss Joseph Raz's well-known theory that authorities have a right of being obeyed.[14] Departing from Raz, I will propose some refinements (and some further considerations). Actually, since Raz has some complaints against Hohfeldian semantics (his theory of rights is what he himself has called a version of the "Bentham's beneficiary theory"[15]), I think that my differences with him derives from my adherence to the correlativity view between claims and duties, in a full agreement with a Hohfeldian analysis of rights relations. My main disagreement with Raz is that, since a right-claim to obedience implies a duty to comply, a right-claim to commanding is ever presupposed in case of authorities' legal recognition. Well, since all claims are duty-correlated (and in this I follow Hohfeld), the authority with the claim-right to obedience cannot create himself the subject's duty of obedience by means of his own act of commanding, for the subject's duty simply *is* (in other words) the authority's claim to obedience.[16] Raz, nevertheless, sees rights as grounds for holding others to be duty bound (for the sake of the protection of certain interests of the right-holder).[17] But a duty to loyalty is a citizen's duty imposed by authorities for the benefit of the citizens.[18] This creates the very problem of grounding

[14] Joseph Raz, *The morality of freedom*, Oxford University Press, 1988.

[15] Ibidem, p. 166, n. 2.

[16] It is arguably that the duty of obedience cannot be created by any commands of any authority. Even a sovereign, then, could create it at all. If I am correct, then authorities' right of being obeyed is a kind of "natural right" (in a Hartian sense), not of course in a Hobbesian or even in a Lockean sense (since by those natural lawyers there are not any authorities in the "natural state").

[17] Ibidem, p. 44.

[18] Ibidem.

claims and rights in the activity of commanding. Raz thinks that commanding is a kind of act that can create duties, in a sense similar to promises, that are alike acts that create and modify privileges and duties (in this case, of the promiser himself). But the duty to obey cannot be created by the commander, for the duty must be antecedent to the act of commanding. What the command can create is only a *particular* duty, the duty of *doing what the command instructs*. But if the duty to obey is prior to the duty of performing the action designated by the authority, then we must accept a Hohfeldian consequence, that is, that the authority has a claim of being obeyed as part of some cluster of Hohfeldian rights, including his power of creating a particular duty on the subservient and the privilege of commanding him. If I am correct, what authorities do when commanding is to afford directives to action that a subordinate must accomplish because he or she has a duty to obey. This explains why we can be unlawfully commanded, for if the commander would not be an authority, the addressee would not be bound to obey. But, first, let me try to distinguish these two different performative utterances, claiming and commanding, by means of some reflections on Hobbes' view.

*

The "superior-inferior" dichotomy is ubiquitous in the writings of the great authors of the command tradition. To them, the social relation understood by the name "law" is one binding those inferiors (vassals or citizens) to one or more superiors (and those, in this case, to an ultimate superior, the being endowed with sovereign or *supreme* power). We see then Thomas Hobbes trying to make fine distinctions between some different kinds of utterances, stating that only commanding can bind its addressee to the utterer's will. But Hobbes's distinction is faulty, since it blurs another important distinction (also neglected by almost all command theorists), the distinction between a *claim* and a *command*.

Hobbes realizes that imperatival speech is not always a device for issuing commands or orders. The locutions "Do this!" can be used also in paradigmatic cases of *counseling*. But counsels obviously do not bind their subjects to act. According to Hobbes and all the other command theorists, only commands create obligations. This is the way Hobbes has presented his distinction between these two different forms of speech in the *Leviathan*:

> COMMAND is, where a man saith, *do this,* or *do not this,* without expecting other reason than the will of him that says it. From this it followeth manifestly, that he that commandeth, pretendeth thereby his own benefit: for the reason of his command is his own will only, and the proper object of every man's will, is some good to himself.
>
> COUNSEL, is where a man saith, *do,* or *do not this,* and deduceth his reasons from the benefit that arriveth by it to him to whom he saith it. And from this it is evident, that he that giveth counsel, pretendeth only, whatsoever he intendeth, the good of him, to whom he giveth it.[19]

Hobbes immediately infers that "between counsel and command, one great difference is, that command is directed to a man's own benefit; and counsel to the benefit of another man." Nevertheless, the man Hobbes has supposed as benefited by a command is always the man who makes the command. Then he remarks another difference, "that a man may be obliged to do what he is commanded; as when he hath covenanted to obey: but he cannot be obliged to do as he is counselled, because the hurt of not following it, is his own." Nonetheless, if he was actually obliged to follow the counsel, "then is the counsel turned into the nature of a command."

But one of the manifest faults of Hobbes' distinction is that it is not true that orders or commands always look for benefiting the person who makes the command.[20] Even if the reason for following a command is that it was willed by a recognized superior, it does not follow that the superior necessarily has willed something for the sake

[19] Thomas Hobbes, *The Leviathan* [1651]. The English Works of Thomas Hobbes of Malmesbury, Collected and Edited by Sir William Molesworth, London: Bohn, 1839–1845), 11 vols (accessed from: <http://oll.libertyfund.org/title/585>), vol. 3, Chapter XXV: Of counsel, available at: <http://oll.libertyfund.org/title/585/89868/2025901> [on 2011-12-10].

[20] It is possible that this fault is a minor one in Hobbes description. My aim here is simply to note that the distinction between commanding and claiming is a missing point in his theory and probably in all other writings of the great authors of the Command Tradition.

of his own good. In other words, in the case of valid or lawful commands, it is true that the commanded must do something, or that he or she is bound to do something, even if he or she does not want or desire to do it. But it is not true that the action ordered is necessarily intended by the commander in order to satisfy his own benefit or interest. A superior can certainly make commands aiming at benefiting someone else (including, in some situations, the commanded himself). Even Hobbes concluded himself that:

> No man is bound by the words themselves, either to kill himself, or any other man; and consequently, that the obligation a man may sometimes have, upon the command of the sovereign to execute any dangerous, or dishonourable office, dependeth not on the words of our submission; ***but on the intention***, which is to be understood by the end thereof. When therefore our refusal to obey, frustrates the end for which the sovereignty was ordained; then there is no liberty to refuse: otherwise there is.[21]

Hence, commands serve, in general, to an end (that is, peace); commands are in a sense "words," but the obligation to follow a command depends on the commander's intention, which by itself serves to a general end. It seems that if the command's intention does not serve the appropriate end, it does not obligate. However, since for Hobbes the command's intention serves an *end*, it follows that a Sovereign and his officials not only *can*, but *should* make commands intentionally for the sake of some good (distant or proximate to the final end). That good must be, in the case of an official in charge, not his own good, but the good of someone other.[22]

Possibly Hobbes' interpretation of the submission to commands as submission not only to a sovereign will but also to his ultimate de-

---

[21] Th. Hobbes, *The Leviathan*, op. cit., available at: <http://oll.libertyfund.org/title/585/89860/2025820> [on 2011-12-10].

[22] It does not mean, of course, that a commander must make orders or acts in the interests of their subjects, that is, their commanded. A military commander "should put the defense of his country above the" immediate "interests of his soldiers. He may therefore order them to act against their own interests" (J. Raz, *The morality of freedom*, op. cit., p. 48). Nevertheless, if the command has some goals, ends or intentions, they are not done for the benefit of the commander. The view I am arguing for, by the way, is the same view claimed by Socrates against Thrasymachus in Plato's Republic.

sires (that is, to Sovereign benefit) is only well fitted to Hobbes's view of laws as imperatives made by, or ultimately originated from, God. But let us see now Hobbes' examples of commands in contrast to his examples of counsels or advices:

> Examples of the difference between command and counsel, we may take from the forms of speech that express them in Holy Scripture. *Have no other Gods but me; make to thyself no graven image; take not God's name in vain; sanctify the Sabbath; honour thy parents; kill not; steal not, &c.* are commands; because the reason for which we are to obey them, is drawn from the will of God our king, whom we are obliged to obey. But these words, *Sell all thou hast; give it to the poor; and follow me,* are counsel; because the reason for which we are to do so, is drawn from our own benefit; which is this, that we shall have *treasure in Heaven.* These words, *Go into the village over against you, and you shall find an ass tied, and her colt; loose her, and bring her to me,* are a command: for the reason of their fact is drawn from the will of their Master: but these words, *Repent and be baptized in the name of Jesus,* are counsel; because the reason why we should so do, tendeth not to any benefit of God Almighty, who shall still be king in what manner soever we rebel; but of ourselves, who have no other means of avoiding the punishment hanging over us for our sins.[23]

Observe that Hobbes said that the reason we have for obeying a God's command is *His* will *and* that we are obliged to obey him (we should note here that those are different normative situations, even for Hobbes - see more bellow). But here what is important is highlighting Hobbes's distinction between counsels and orders. See these two examples of commands: 'Do not kill him' and 'Go there and bring that gun to me'. We can understand those two "imperatives" as examples of "commands" (and, observe, of particular commands[24]). But why we must take that the first as, like the second, a directive for doing something for the benefit of the person who made the command?

---

[23] Th. Hobbes, *The Leviathan*, op. cit., available at: <http://oll.libertyfund.org/title/585/89868/2025909> [at 2011-12-10].

[24] We should understand "general commands" in two different kinds: as truly "general" commands (like orders directed to a group of people), and as "general" only by analogy, for these are "rules" rather than "commands." This is one of the most important modifications of the command tradition after Hart's criticisms.

Here we need to notice that even if the will of the commander is or can be the only reason for a subject submitting himself to a command (probably a kind of "sufficient" practical reason for Hobbes[25]) it doesn't follow that the command is or was made for the benefit of the commander. These are separate matters, and it should be noted here that the first does not imply the second, for it is plainly possible that a command can be willed for the sake of the interest or benefit of another person. Consider different utterances of the locution 'Do not kill me!'. We know (at least since Austin) that this locution can express different illocutionary acts: a person can be making a supplication (humbly), but he can also be making a threat ('If you kill me, you shall be cursed for eternity'). But 'Do not kill me!' can be also used to convey a claim. And a claim is very different from an advice (for example, of some undesirable consequences of the fulfillment of the act of killing). It is also not a mere request. It is a demand, a requirement, an exigency made over (or against) someone else.

Hence, besides counsels (and exhortations), we also have claims as utterances that differ in meaning (or in "illocutionary force") from commands. The expression of a claim conveys a right of the claimant to the person addressed. But expressions of claims are different from mere requests or mere solicitations. For the person addressed in a solicitation (if it is a *mere* solicitation) has (at least in "normal" situations) the liberty or, saying it more properly, the privilege of not complying with the request even if the request is entirely in order. Nonetheless, this is not a normal situation in the case of claims. The person to whom the claim is addressed does not have the privilege of not complying with the claim, not at least if the claim is entirely in order; he *must* have a reason for not complying and that reason cannot be that he simply does not want to do what was claimed. (Compare a person making a *mere* solicitation to someone and a person making a claim. For example, compare the difference between John simply asking Peter for a visit and John *claiming* it - we should suppose, in the se-

[25] In the context of practical reasonings, 'sufficient' cannot have the same logical meaning it has in deductions, that is, in the course of monotonic arguments (or reasonings). What we mean by 'sufficient' here is roughly the same as others called a *pro tanto* reason for action (Roger Crisp, *Reasons and the good*, Oxford University Press, 2008, pp. 56–61).

cond case, that Peter probably has promised to visit John. Compare also John asking Peter for his window seat in an airplane and John *claiming* that the seat belongs to him. Imagine now that Peter does not comply in either case. We all agree that, in the claim-situation, refusing to comply by simply saying that one does not want to do it is unacceptable.)

Here we have seen that the reason (the *pro tanto* reason) for the compliance of the person (to whom the performative claim is addressed) is drawn from the claimant's will (for, certainly, it could not be drawn from the other party, that is, the duty bound one). Hence, a salient difference between commands and claims is that claims are *always* made for the sake of the claimant; in the legal sphere, claims are made for the sake of the person legally or morally warranted as its proper right-holder. That is what license us saying that claim-rights are ever at the rights-holder interests' service;[26] commands (*pace* Hobbes) on the contrary can be made in a third party interest.[27] In some situations, this third party eventually or occasionally can actually have a claim over some authority for the promotion of some of his or her interests. This is especially the case of governmental authorities. A person can have a duty to obey an authority, which must have some rights (actually some privileges, powers and claims - see below) of commanding him justly because they are means for the execution of his duties correlated to (some) rights of a third party. Claims, then, are related to the ultimate interests and the good of their claim-holders; but official commands, that is, commands made by authorities, at least paradigmatically, are not made for the good of those rul-

---

[26] But let me be here a little apart from the controversy between the "will-theory" and the "interest-theory" of rights. On this controversy, see M.H. Kramer, N.E. Simmonds and H. Steiner, *A debate over rights*, op. cit. My bet is that we can make a compromise between both theories.

[27] Of course, claims can be made by a surrogate, but always, and obviously, in account of the proper right-holder. Could commands be made "by representation"? I do not think that it is appropriate to say that, but probably in some sense, yes, for someone can be instituted by some superior with the privilege of commanding by delegation. I do not think, anyway, that it invalidates my proposed contrast between the fact that commands can be made for the sake of the interests of a different person from the commander, and the fact that claims are always performed on account of the claim-bearer's interests.

ing persons, for the power ascribed to authorities are usually (politically) justified for the sake of promoting the end of someone else (being it an individual or a collectivity). We can also say here that commands' *telos* serve the promotion of someone else's interest.[28]

Hobbes and most of the command thinkers do not distinguish claims from orders or commands. But, as we have seen above, claiming is not commanding. A command is an authoritative directive made from someone endowed with authority over others; yet a claim is not an order or an instruction of some authority, but a demand for something thought as rightful or due. The difference is, of course, very subtle, but it is important to make it salient, and we can understand it better by pointing out some plain intuitive differences. For example, it would be very odd to describe an authority as "claiming" something to one of his subordinates by uttering an imperative sentence. A sergeant does not claim the fulfillment of something to soldiers under his command *when* he utters some order to them. *In* the act of ordering the sergeant is not actually claiming: that is, it is not a claim what he "does with words." Hence, the language of command is used in situations that are not fitted for claims. And the reason is that the illocutionary act of commanding is very different from the illocutionary act of claiming, even if those speech acts could be made by means of the same locutions.

But when we say that the sergeant does not *directly claim* the fulfilling of some act against his soldiers, since what he does is simply *commanding them* (to do something), this does not imply that the sergeant cannot *have* any claim-right against his subordinates.[29] The

[28] Possibly claim-rights are *always* related to the ultimate interests and the good of their claim-holders. David Copp suggested in a personal comment that if officials have a claim-right to obedience, then just as their commands might not be for their good so their claim-right might not always "relate" to their good. He is right; and Hobbes was obviously right in saying that commands can be made for the sake of the interests of the commander. My point however is only to put in contrast the fact that nowadays claims are *paradigmatically* made for the sake of the good of the claimant, but legal commands not. Perhaps the right to command is a special type of right whose legal and political existence is instrumentally tied to the promotion or protection of other's citizens' rights.

[29] It would be instructing here to remark an important distinction between *making* a claim and *having* a claim. This distinction was first made by Joel Feinberg, first in *The*

point is that superiors, if they are actually superiors in the legal sense (that is, *authorities*), must *have* actually some rights over their subordinates, rights some of them they exercise when commanding them. We must have in mind however that, as a matter of fact, the "right" the sergeant directly exercises is a privilege to command and, occasionally, some powers over the commanded, having the claim of being obeyed by him as presupposed. In effect, acts of commands are in a sense performances or actualizations of rights, that is, privileges and, occasionally, powers. We can understand of course rightful acts of commanding as acts backed by claims (that is, by the claim of being obeyed); but *to command* certainly is not the performance of a claim. Claims and commands are not the same performative utterances. Commanding is the act of making an authoritative directive for action to someone else; however, when claiming we are not directing persons or individuals submitted to our authority. Even persons not submitted to someone's authority can be liable to his claims.[30]

---

nature and value of rights (Joel Feinberg, "The nature and value of rights," *Journal of Value Inquiry* 1970, vol. 4, pp. 243–257) and after in his *Social philosophy*, where he said: "I would like to suggest that *having a claim consists in being in a position to claim in the performative sense*, that is, *to make claim to*" (Joel Feinberg, *Social philosophy*, Prentice Hall, 1973, p. 65). It can be concluded from that, that when we perform a claim, we do an action; and actions are particular occurrences, that is, they are *events*. But when we say that we *have* a claim we are not referring to any action (past-made, or actually-made). We are making a reference to a *fact*, possibly a legal fact (that we suppose legally occurs or "is the case"). If the legal state of having some claim actually exists, then it is true that *we have this claim* (and, in this case, the claim is a *fact*, that is, a *social* fact). It is not possible here to present a full argumentation for this metaphysical approach to rights. I'm satisfied here in presenting the contrast between *to have a claim* and *to make a claim* saying that "to have a claim" means being in the position of claiming of someone else that something occurs. Well, if I am in the (legal) position of claiming, then I *have* a claim. In another guise, claiming (as an action) is the actualization of my claim (the state). In spite of that, commands (the actions of commanding), are not actualizations of claims, yet they presuppose claims (that is, claims are legal positions that warrant acts of commanding – as we will see next).

30 My reference to persons and individuals as the possible liable subjects of commands and my reference to persons as the only liable subjects of our claims have a metaphysical intention. Only persons can be the target of claims – we call them the duty-bearers. But commands can obviously be directed to individuals that cannot bear duties. We can utter commands to animals, toddlers and human infants. But animals and human babies are not properly subject to our *authority* (at least, not in any strict

*

Let us assume that claims are rights and that superiors can have some claims over their subordinates. However, we would make this

sense). Infants can also be commanded; but we cannot say that infants are yet individuals to whom we have *plain* authority, in the strict *Razian* sense that we have against them a right to obedience. Nonetheless, for the command theorists, it seemed to be true that commanding them implies having authority. Hobbes, for example, saw the relation between parents and children as a relation of "dominion" (See: Th. Hobbes, *Leviathan*, op. cit., Chapter XX, & 565). But note that parental commands are not a consequence of any right of being obeyed; they are actually derived from children's claim of being cared. If we still continue to talk about parental's authority over their children, we must pay attention to some vagueness or even to different meanings of the word 'authority'. See for example the supposed authority a physician has over his patient. The word 'authority' is originated from the latin word *auctoritas*. But in Rome, *auctoritas* was linked to persons with general prestige. An *auctor* can improve the act and not only the juridical situation of someone. In this sense, a physician is or has "authority" over his patients and the laymen (of course, in matter of medicine). Nevertheless, physicians do not have any right of being obeyed by his patients (at least today, following a more modern conception of medical ethics). Anyway, it is true that in the past people used to think that physicians had not only expertise authority, but that they actually had a kind of political authority. In the past, medical prescriptions were seen as literal commands. But now, a medical "order" does not involve any kind of imposed duty on the patient. All privileges a physician has today are actually privileges of making prescriptions, not of making commands, for today we assume that patients have rights of not being forced of following medical prescriptions; they have a claim to consent. The expertise authority of physicians does not involve any kind of political or legal authority over the patients. Consequently, what we have here is a conceptual division between authority in a broad and ancient sense (as implying expertise authority) and political authority (as implying as I am claiming a right of being obeyed). This division can be tracked historically; as we know, such historical changes have political origins. This reveals also that the privilege to command is the basic or universal right-component in the composite authority's "rights." Powers and privileges are the most basic component of the concept of political authority, even if at present we only accept someone as an authority because we accept him as bearer of a valid claim of being obeyed. By the way: thanks for Stephen Skinner for personally reminding me that, at least in some historical legal systems, could have been an unprecedented command in its legal origins. It is plausible that some legal systems can have its origins in some "foundational act." This view was advanced by Professor João Carlos Brum Torres, in "Actes Fondateurs dans le domaine politique," *Les Cahiers de Fontenay* 1992, vol. 67/68, pp. 0–47).

clearer saying that the right to command is only a right in some special sense. Usually the right to command is only a *privilege* to command, and it sounds very odd to talk about "claims to command," since what can be claimed by the authority, as a claim-holder, is *obedience*. Moreover, claims can also be pronounced against superiors in force or in authority, but it would be nonsensical making a command to a superior. Even a soldier has and can pronounce claims against his superiors. A soldier, for example, can have a claim-right that the sergeant does not command him to do something against the military laws. Even if it this claim-right is not often insisted on (or claimed by its holder), it does not prove that the claim-right does not exist. Some claim-rights are paradigmatically claimed against superiors. It is actually very plausible that many of our human rights comprise negative or positive claim-rights against governmental authorities. In this sense, *claiming*, in the performative sense, is paradigmatically an action made by someone "inferior" against a "superior" (in strength or power, in a social or a legal position).

The crucial point is that superiors are never *directly* exercising (or performing) any claim *when* commanding: no claim is exercised in its performative sense in the course of acts of commanding, not at least in the same sense that commands can be directly exercised. Now we can see why it is important to say that "to have authority" is not *simply* having a right of being obeyed; because having authority is having a "right" in a broad sense, that is, a cluster formed by privileges, powers and claims. The Hohfeldian right that an authority exercises directly when commanding is his privilege to command; when commanding, his right-claim of being obeyed is presupposed.

Here is my chief complaint against Raz. Superiors actually have rights over their subordinates. But only one of those is a claim-right. If a superior has some claim-right over his subordinates, that claim-right is actually the claim of being obeyed by them. In our military example, the person who has that claim is the sergeant; but the person who fulfils the claim-content is not the sergeant, but the soldier. When I claim something of you (suppose that I'm demanding from you a loaned book of my property; or suppose in change that I'm saying: "Do not step on my feet!"), if it is true that I actually have the right that I claim, the person who executes, performs or fulfils the content of my claim is you, not me (I'm using "fulfilling" here in the sense of doing what makes himself discharged from some duty).[31] It is true that the soldier *must* fulfill the command, but he does not fulfill that demand in the same sense of your fulfilling my claim. For we can say two different things concerning the soldier: first, that when he fulfils an order from his sergeant he is following or complying with the sergeant's command; second, that since the sergeant has a claim of being obeyed, the soldier is fulfilling his duty, that is, he is fulfilling sergeant's claim of being obeyed. If I have a claim against you (but if I do not have any authority over you), you can be fulfilling your duty if it is true that whatever claim I have is actually satisfied. But it is also true that you are not fulfilling any command of mine. That applies even to the case of my demanding against you not stepping on my feet, for in this case I'm not an authority over you. "Obedience" in this case is simply a word out of place. When you return the book you have borrowed from me, you are not necessarily fulfilling any command of mine. This is true even if I actually have expressed my claim or demanded your compliance by saying to you: "Give me back my book!" The same applies in the case of my complaint against you for not stepping on my feet. If you are not actually stepping on them, you are not obviously following a command or fulfilling any order: you are simply fulfilling your duty. In conclusion: not all of our duties are connected to commands, neither is fulfilling a duty necessarily the fulfilling of a command. Commands then are only a part of the universe of normativity.

Nonetheless, the fact that superiors have authority over their subordinates does not imply that superiors cannot have claims against their inferiors. Actually, there can be cases in which the addressee of an order is without any duty of obedience. That is plainly true in the case of irregular and unlawful commands. Consider, for example, the commands made by robbers, bullies and tyrants. Hence, a robber can make a command to a person without having any claim to being

[31] See Thomson's phrase for the duty correlated to some claim: '*X* is under a duty toward *Y*, namely the duty that *Y* discharges if and only if not-*p*' as correlated to the claim '*X* has a claim against *Y* that *p*' (J.J. Thomson, *The realm of rights*, op. cit., pp. 41, 43).

obeyed. The difference is that while the robber has no right to the obedience of his victims, the official does have a right to the obedience of those within his subordination. But an official (even the most superior of them, the "sovereigns") can also make commands without having any right of being obeyed. These are cases that we usually call cases of abuse of authority. (Would a "command" made by someone who lacks any right to be obeyed not be strictly speaking a *command* at all? This could be stipulated, of course.)

Thus a command is valid only if the commander has a right of being obeyed. Consider Raz's assertion that the typical exercise of authority is done in the making of some kind of instructions, and that the appeal to compliance makes sense precisely for its invocation of the "duty to obey." It seems remarkable that Raz makes this claim but does not accept the Hohfeldian correlativity thesis between claims and duties. Actually, Raz coherently says that a "right" to command implies a *duty* to obey, since, in his definition, rights are "grounds for holding others to be duty bound to protect or promote certain interests of the right-holder."[32] He argued persuasively that the authority's invocation of a right to rule implies a correlated obligation to obey and that it is a known fact that authorities "claim such a right."[33] Authorities are *de facto* authorities just because they succeed in establishing and maintaining that ruling condition: "They have legitimate authority only if and to the extent that their claim is justified and that they are owed a duty of obedience" (idem). But the "right to command" is, for Raz, the right of *imposing* duties on others (that is, on the persons subordinated to the authority). But it would be more proper to say that when an authority "imposes" some duty on other he is rather exercising another Hohfeldian right, or rather another "incident"[34] within the scope of "rights in a broad sense," the kind of right Hohfeld has called "power" (which implies that the persons submitted to it have a correlated "liability").

But the duty to obey is not correlated to a legal power. The duty to obey is a normative state correlated to a *claim or a claim-right,* that is,

[32] J. Raz, *The morality of freedom,* op. cit., p. 44.

[33] Ibidem, p. 26.

[34] L. Wenar, "The nature of rights," op. cit.

the claim to obedience. And, besides these powers and claim-rights (a power to modify the broad rights of the persons submitted to authorities, and the claim of authorities of being obeyed by their "inferiors"), authorities also have some privileges. Those privileges include the privilege to command, but in some case authorities have other privileges, different from the privilege to command. For example, a police officer has privileges of using force for attaining some finality, such as public security, and it is not necessary that the persons affected by the officer's actions should have a duty of obedience, for what they logically must have is only the absence of a claim against the police officer that he does not use force. Hence, the right to authority is a complex right that includes at least three different kinds of "Hohfeldian incidents"[35]: some powers, some privileges and some claims (it is plausible that some authorities also have some immunities, but I suspect that not all of them have this - then, to have immunities is not something essential for the status of authority).

The ambiguity we can observe within Raz's theory between "to claim," in the sense of "to claim a right," and "to claim," in the more direct sense of "to *have* a right," is a consequence of his refusal of the Hohfeldian view that claims are correlated to duties - which makes, in my words, Raz's conception of rights an *entitlement view* in contrast to the more appropriated Hohfeld's *claim view*.[36] We should also remark (repeating what we have seen above) that commanding is not a performative act that directly invokes the duty to obey, for commanding is not an act of claiming obedience, at least not *directly*. That is, a commander does not directly make a *claim* for obedience when he utters a command. We wouldn't say that commands are acts directed from a superior to an inferior if, in addressing a command, the commander would be directly *claiming* the obedience of the subordinated person. It is especially obvious in the case of hierarchical organizations. It would be something preposterous to a military superior to describe himself as making claims to his inferiors when ordering them.

---

[35] The expression "hohfeld incidents" was introduced by Leif Wenar ("The nature of rights," op. cit.).

[36] M.A.O. de Azevedo, "Rights as entitlements and rights as claims," op. cit.

However, I agree with Raz's thesis that the fact of being in a position of command implies legal or moral authority and that all valid or justified authorities *can* claim obedience (what implies a duty of the commanded to obey). This is important to the claim that respecting authorities is a rational form of behavior.

However, here we should clarify the place of reasons in the activity of commanding. In one side, the superior can have reasons for making a command, but those reasons are not (or needn't be) the same reason or reasons for doing the ordered action by the inferior. Actually, the inferior must do the action, first, simply because it was commanded (that is, because it is an order). Hart and Raz have pointed out that a command represents a reason for action only if it is valid, that is, if it is done by a valid authority. Hart said that the difference between the robber case and the military order is that the robber, when commanding his victim (the bank clerk), is certainly not *giving him an order*; but the military-sounding phrase suggests "some right or authority to give orders."[37] Hart proposes then a difference between an "order backed by threats" and orders in a proper sense (the only case where the words 'obedience' and 'obey' make sense, since they include the claim for "compliance with such orders").

Following Hart, Raz has concluded that the authority's commands presuppose rights of obedience. But commands are not intuitively proper candidates of being "reasons for action." And, as we have seen, the authority's reason for commanding is not necessarily the same as the person commanded's reason for compliance. Additionally, some commands that are followed are not followed because they represent reasons for action to those who are commanded. Animals and infants can obey commands. Dogs, for example, can be trained to follow commands; and some people may follow commands only by habit; and certainly there are individuals, animals and people, who follow orders only by fear.

Following a command because of the recognition of a right of commanding is something only possible for persons.[38] But we should

[37] H.L.A. Hart, *The concept of law*, op. cit., p. 19.

[38] For a good definition, we can pick out the entities that have "second order desires." That's Harry Frankfurt's definition of persons, a definition also accepted by

not be distracted here by the controversial issue of what kind of entity is a "person." We can adopt here metaphysical neutrality concerning some conceptions of persons (even Raz's conception). We can simply adopt the view that persons are capable of acting for reasons. For the point is that agents (being what they are) can have different reasons to follow a command. One of reason might be that it is sensible to follow some command (for example, if the command is backed by an effective and reliable threat). Another might be that it is a reasonable demand (because the commander has a right to be obeyed). But an agent (a rational agent) can react to a command with compliance simply (or mainly) because he recognizes authority. How? Well, because he recognizes also the existence of a claim to obedience. He can, albeit incidentally, be a virtuous citizen who likes to view himself as a person who is committed to the law not from fear or from habit, but from respectfulness. Hence a duty to obey can be a reason to follow a command for at least some rational beings, that is, the kind of "rational being" who recognizes the practicality of claims (here I suppose we could say that the person is directly deriving an *ought* from the recognition of a *duty*, taken by him as a premise in the course of his practical reasoning).

Actually, a commander can claim obedience in the case of non-compliance. Hence, the commander can become a claimant if the relation of commander-commanded has become broken. But if the relation is not actually broken, the *claim* normally functions only as a presupposition (warranting the state of authority). This explains why we cannot say that a superior, when commanding, is making some claim against his subordinates; even if it is true that he has a claim of being obeyed, *when performing a command*, the commander is not actually making or performing this claim. *In* saying 'Stop!', an authority is actually making a command to someone, not a claim, even if it is true that he has a claim over him of being obeyed; the claim of being obeyed functions in this case only as the normative background of his authority relation.

Raz (*The morality of freedom*, op. cit., p. 294). See from Harry Frankfurt, "Alternate possibilities and moral responsibility," *The Journal of Philosophy* 1969, vol. 66, no. 23, pp. 829-839 and idem, "Freedom of the Will and the concept of a person," *The Journal of Philosophy* 1971, vol. 68, no. 1, pp. 5-20.

Valid claims are preeminent reasons for action; the same obviously applies to duties. When uttered, claims are directed to our reflective capacities. Acting intentionally for the sake of discharging a duty is always a rational activity. Assuming that duties are correlated to valid claims (even with the proviso that this is a quality of at least some kind of duties), to respect a claim is also, and correlatively, a rational activity. In order for a claim-right to be met, we must depend on the rational capacities of the correlated duty-bearers, those against whom the rights are held.[39]

But commands do not depend on the reflective capacities of their addressees for being complied with (animals besides people in general can also be the addressees of commands).[40] In this wide sense, commands are directed to what we should call simply our faculty of "following orders,"[41] since orders can be followed only by mere habit (that is, by an unreflective custom) and can be effective by any other means beyond their moral or legal authoritativeness (the unique character that depends on they're being reflectively apprehended). But since (legal) claims are preeminent reasons for action (and in some situations, even "sufficient" ones), a command can constitute a reason for action if it is true that the commanded has a duty to obey and the commander a right of being obeyed (that is, if the command is valid, because it is done by a valid authority). Here a command can be apprehended as a reason for action. This is connected with Raz understanding of the pre-emptive character of commands, that is, the fact that an order can displace other reasons contrary to the action commanded if the order was emitted by an authority (in the course of

---

39 There are of course duties that are accomplished by its duty-bearers "accidentally." It is notably true in the case of claims for the occurrence not of actions, but of "states-of-affairs." You can be discharged from your duty of restoring me the book you get borrowed in case I accidentally encounter the book at some place, or if another person delivers it to me.

40 Hart's imaginary Rex I ruling situation serves as a proof of this possibility.

41 See: Stanley Milgram, *Obedience to authority*, Harper Perenial, 1983. See also Harman's discussion on the implications of assuming Milgram's statements and other findings of experimental & observational psychology (Gilbert Harman, "Skepticism about character traits," *Journal of Ethics* 2009, vol. 13, pp. 235–242).

its official prerogatives).[42] It is precisely in that case that to command involves making an appeal not to fear, but to respect authority.

*

A concluding remark. The model of command appeared as an attractive model for the definition of Law, but the model is misleading. The view that Law can be composed by "commands without a commander"[43] can only be accepted at most as a metaphor. But even as a metaphor it turns to be equivocal, for we cannot have any command without commanders. In order to have authority over men, authorities must be lawfully authorized. We necessarily need to recur to law for the explanation of the rightfulness character of some command. To say that a person is entitled to authority is to say that this person has some specified legal powers, claims to obedience and privileges to command in order to be a *rightful* commander. If the authority's claim to be obeyed is valid, then the claim-holder (the person with authority) *has* this claim against someone else, and this other person *has* a correlative duty to comply. Law cannot be equated to commands, for the normativity of Law does not consist in some kind of "command-normativity" (for there is none). That is, there is not any kind of immanent normativity of which commands are endowed; commands' normativity is grounded on rights. Nonetheless, rights constitute a substantial part of Law's normativity, since primary and secondary rules are substantially related to the normativity of rights and their Hohfeldian constituents: powers and immunities, duties and *claims*.

Acknowledgements

This work was presented at the 9th IRSL - International Roundtable for the Semiotics of Law (Poznan, 2010). The author's participation was sponsored and supported by CAPES (Coordination for the

---

42 J. Raz, *The morality of freedom*, op. cit., pp. 38–62.

43 G. Postema, "Law as command: the modern of command in modern jurisprudence," op. cit., p. 495.

Improvement of Higher Level Education Personnel - Brazil) and Unisinos. Thanks to the comments and questions made by the meeting participants. Thanks to Stephen Skinner whose comments made me rethink some passages and arguments. Roger Crisp, Mark Timmons and Ricardo Rabenschlag also read an early draft and have made some very subtle criticisms on my intended distinction between commanding and claiming. Recently, this paper was friendly read by David Copp, who, with a Tibetan patience, made me several criticisms, besides important suggestions of textual changes and conceptual distinctions. I'm very indebted to him, but I'm not sure if I successively complied with his fine and gentle "commands."

Maciej Pichlak
University of Wrocław, Poland

The Autonomy from Morality as a Moral Claim: On Some Paradoxes of Legal Positivism

Abstract: The paper examines the legal positivist approach to the problem of the autonomy of law from morality. The idea of autonomy has to be seen as a pivotal component of the modern European legal culture; thus the theoretical expression of this idea is of practical significance as well. In the text I offer a description of the idea of autonomy within legal positivist tradition which equates this idea with so called identification thesis. Furthermore, I take under scrutiny the most common positivist justification of the idea discussed. Such justification is based upon functional argument; the best known positivist argument from "practical difference," offered by Scott Shapiro, or from law's "claim to authority," formulated by Joseph Raz, are the instances of functional justification. I claim that this mode of justification of the law's autonomy which is inevitably moral/political in nature drives to serious paradoxes which make legal positivism implausible, despite its theoretical and practical importance. At the end, I offer a brief outline of an alternative perspective which enables us to accept and respect that paradoxical nature of the idea of law's autonomy.

Key words: autonomy of law, legal positivim, law's claim to authority, practical authority, law and morality, function of law, legal functionalism, identification thesis, practical difference thesis

Introduction

One of the basic features of legal positivism, as well as one of its crucial claims, is a thesis on the autonomy of law from morality and politics.[1] Of course, the autonomy of law is an ambigous concept. Some of this ambiguity is inevitable, as legal positivism is a heterogenous

[1] I owe thanks to Ula Baj-Środa for helping me with making my Polish-English more English-English. Of course, for all mistakes I alone am responsible.

tradition; still, it is possible to give a more precise characterization of this concept. I will attempt to do so in the second section of this paper. As we shall see, autonomy of law may be understood as a matter of legal reasoning, which should be free from moral or political deliberations. Such an autonomy is best captured with the so-called identification thesis.

If the autonomy of law were the internal problem of legal positivism, one would not need to take interest in disputes about its meaning, and would treat it as an argument on positivism's own turf. Thus, we must remember that the significance of this question is much greater. As I show in the first section of this paper, the autonomy of law is one of the pivotal ideas of modern European legal culture, and establishes a route towards a practical understanding of the law. As Kaarlo Tuori says, for a typical European lawyer "the law is an autonomous, rational, consistent and coherent system of norms."[2]

Autonomy of legal reasoning may be justified in different ways. The most common and influential justification in contemporary positivism is the functional argument, which I examine in the third section. This argument may be treated in an analytical, descriptive or normative way; in sections four and five I shall try to explain why one should choose the latter. It seems that most contemporary positivist thinkers, who share an analytical attitude, try to "hide normative origins" of ther own tradition, "as an unpleasant family secret."[3] These roots are clear for so-called ethical positivism. Nevertheless, in both these varieties of positivist tradition, autonomy of law is an ethical or political claim.

This last statement, however, drives towards an obvious paradox: the autonomy from politics and ethics is justified on these very political and ethical grounds. But is that possible? Is there any way to solve this paradox regarding the autonomy of law? Positivist theory does not seem to give us an answer here, and that is why it cannot be plausible. We must reflect on the important problem of autonomy from a different perspective. At the end of the paper (section six), I will try to give an outline of such a perspective, which may solve the problem of

[2] Kaarlo Tuori, *Critical Legal Positivism,* Aldershot: Ashgate, 2002, p. 7.

[3] Gerald J. Postema, *Bentham and the Common Law Tradition,* Oxford: Clarendon Press, 1986, p. 330.

the paradoxical nature of the autonomy of law. In actuality, the word "solve" is not the proper one for this context. This is a common mistake of many theories of legal practice: attempting to solve the problem of autonomy. Rather, the perspective I offer explains how the idea of autonomy of law is possible despite all of its paradoxicality, and why we should respect the nature of such an idea.

I understand that my reconstruction of positivist theories is rather crude at some moments. Furthermore, I ignore some relevant differences in argumentation between various authors. This simplification is necessary not only because of lack of the room for a more detailed examination of various theoretical standpoints, but it also allows us to capture the most basic features and intuitions of positivist tradition – which is the main goal of this paper.

1. Why is the problem of autonomy important?

While discussing autonomy of law, the basic doubt may be the following: why should anyone bother with such a vague concept? Isn't it a matter of the internal dispute among positivist legal philosophers, trying to decide who is more positivist than the others? And isn't it a naive illusion, as law can never really be autonomous? In both cases, I claim that it is not. Autonomy of law has a broader role than only establishing the percentage amount of positivism in the positivist theory, and a picture of modern law as an autonomous system is far from being illusionary. It is widespread in our legal practices and among European lawyers, even if they do not always see it clearly. The idea of autonomy is present every time a court makes a distinction between arguments as legal or non-legal, as well as in many other, similar situations. Using quasi-Kantian language, the idea of autonomy is a condition of possibility of such activities.

As I stated when quoting Tuori in the introduction, the typical practical attitude to the law in our legal culture is to treat it as an "autonomous, rational, consistent and coherent system." This practical attitude to the law is rarely made explicit or even conscious; it is rather a kind of *habitus* or *world-picture*, to use the terms from Bourdieu and Wittgenstein. Thus, we may say that "spontaneus positivism" is typical for a European lawyer. On the other hand, positivism as a specific legal theory "can be understood as the reflexive level of this spontaneus positivism: positivistic theory has given an explicit and systematic expression to the self-understanding of the typical lawyer."[4]

To say that is not to deny the reverse impact of positivism, as legitimating and forming some types of legal practice. It is simply to claim that legal practice in the modern European legal culture is mostly positivistic in its character. The "double hermeneutics" of positivism as a theory of social practice establishes a circular relation, where a theory interprets a practice and in the same instance modifies it.[5]

Before going further with the positivist theory, we must first look inside this spontaneus *world-picture* that lawyers share. At first glance, we may think about it as a set of convictions that shape and order our activity; we would be wrong, though. While using this term, coined by Wittgenstein, we are not discussing some knowledge as a set of propositions that are primary to the practice and may be expressed independently of this practice. It is rather a "pre-knowledge" that we know only in and through the practice. *World-picture* is nothing else than some specific *form of life* (*Lebensform*), i.e. form of practice. Wittgenstein claims that it is similar to the rules of a game that we can learn purely practically, without explicit formulation.[6]

Therefore *world-picture* does not come before the practice it concerns; it is present *in the practice*. It is a set of practices that we perform almost automatically and unconsciously. According to the reality of law, they decide the basic features of a legal practice, but their role is even more significant. Recently Artur Kozak has shown how these practices create the ontology of law and enables its identity.[7] That is

---

[4] K. Tuori, *Critical Legal Positivism*, op. cit., p. 7.

[5] See Anthony Giddens, *The Constitution of Society: Outline of the Theory of Structuration*, Berkeley: University of California Press, 1984; Peter L. Berger, Thomas Luckmann, *The Social Construction of Reality. A Treatise in the Sociology of Knowledge*, New York: Anchor Books, 1967.

[6] Ludwig Wittgenstein, *On Certainty*, ed. by Gertrude E.M. Anscombe and Georg H. von Wright, transl. by Denis Paul and G.E.M. Anscombe, Oxford: Basil Blackwell, 1969, para. 95.

[7] Artur Kozak, *Myślenie analityczne w nauce prawa i praktyce prawniczej* [Analytical Thinking in Legal Science and Legal Practice], ed. by Maciej Pichlak, Wrocław: Wydawnictwo Uniwersytetu Wrocławskiego, 2010.

why a quasi-Kantian (or Fichtean, in fact) language is also legitimate in this context: practices that make up a form of life create their own object, and they are thus the transcendental conditions of the possibility of more complex practices. The act of treating a law as an autonomous system, as taken by lawyers, creates law as a symbolic reality of a special kind, which as a consequence is binding for those very lawyers.

2. The concept of autonomy

The idea of autonomy of law, which is embedded in legal practice, is still quite vague. When giving a theoretical expression to that idea, one has to formulate it more precisely. Probably the most complete articulation is given by Gerald Postema in his essay *Law's Autonomy and Public Practical Reason.*[8] Autonomy is understood here as a problem of 'the relation between legal considerations and moral considerations as they figure in the practical reasoning of officials and citizens.'[9] Postema describes with scrutiny what he calls the Autonomy Thesis, which according to him includes three basic components: the limited domain thesis, the sources thesis and the pre-emption thesis. These are not his original concepts, however. The first was formulated by Frederick Schauer, while the sources thesis along with the pre-emption thesis come from the writing of Joseph Raz. They are well known in contemporary debates and there is no need to give a full description of them here. Further in his essay, Postema gives us a very instructive examination of the mutual relations between these theses and the puzzles they bring about. Still the problem is, are they really necessary components of the idea of autonomy of law? I don't think so. Each of them might be seen as an important feature of legal culture, but each deals with slightly different issues and they do not necessarily have to go together. This is valid especially for the pre-emption thesis, whose relations to the other two are merely functional. Thus, we are left with the limited domain thesis and the sources

[8] Gerald J. Postema, "Law's Autonomy and Public Practical Reason," in: Robert P. George (ed.), *The Autonomy of Law. Essays on Legal Positivism*, Oxford: Clarendon Press, 1996.

[9] Ibidem, p. 82.

thesis, but even these two do not have equal weight for the autonomy thesis. Joseph Raz, one of the most important philosophers for Postema's own considerations, sees this in a similar way when he suggests that Postema has made a mistake by selecting ideas "from a variety of authors so that the combined picture is in fact no one's view, and all those cited as adhering to it would disagree with it."[10]

That is why it would likely be better to understand the idea of autonomy in a slightly more simplistic way, as limited only to the sources thesis - and in fact, to the special interpretation of the latter which stresses its epistemic sense. This interpretation might be called the identification thesis, and claims that "a determination of what law is does not depend on moral criteria or argument."[11] It should be noted that the identification thesis is not an exclusive idea of what is called exclusive positivism, nor of Raz who has given the formulation of sources thesis. Hart seems to share a similar view while considering the need for a recognition rule, despite his later affiliation to the inclusivist camp.[12] The idea of moral-free identification of law is also familiar for Bentham and even for Hobbes.[13] More recently, J. Coleman has shown the possibility of harmonizing the identification thesis with inclusive positivism.[14]

Even if we keep the autonomy thesis on such a general level, equating it with the identification thesis, some important remarks can be made. Firstly, the autonomy of law is a matter of legal reasoning: it

---

[10] Joseph Raz, "Postema on Law's Autonomy and Public Practical Reasons: A Critical Comment," *Legal Theory* 1998, vol. 4, p. 1.

[11] David Dyzenhaus, "Positivism's Stagnant Research Programme," *Oxford Journal of Legal Studies* 2000, vol. 20, no. 4, p. 706; this epistemic interpretation of sources thesis is crucial for Raz as well - see e.g. Joseph Raz, "Authority, Law and Morality," in: idem, *Ethics in the Public Domain: Essays in the Morality of Law and Politics,* Oxford: Clarendon Press, 1994, p. 195. In this interpretation of the idea of autonomy, limited domain thesis and pre-emptive thesis are still of major importance, not as a part of it, but rather as a second-order justification for the idea.

[12] Herbert L.A. Hart, *The Concept of Law,* 2nd ed., Oxford: Oxford University Press, 1994.

[13] G.J. Postema, *Bentham and the Common Law Tradition,* op. cit.; D. Dyzenhaus, "Positivism's Stagnant Research Programme," op. cit.

[14] Jules L. Coleman, *The Practice of Principle. In Defence of a Pragmatist Approach to Legal Theory,* Oxford: Oxford University Press, 2001.

is an autonomy of legal reasons from other arguments in practical reasoning. This point is pivotal not only for Dyzenhaus or Postema, who were quoted above, but also for Raz,[15] Schauer[16] and others.

Secondly, autonomy does not mean total separation, nor exclusiveness. To say that the law is autonomous obviously does not imply that there is no room for moral reasons within legal reasoning. The autonomy is built in a twofold activity of (juridicial) practical reason: in the first step the distinction between legal and non-legal (moral in this case) arguments is drawn, where the arguments of the latter kind are located outside the area of legal reasoning. In the next step, considering the default of the self-sufficiency of "purely legal" argumentation, moral arguments are brought back to legal reasoning. But the secondary nature of this step makes the return to legal reasoning in some sense "weaker" than prior foreclosure; the role and place of moral reasons is previously determined and limited.[17]

Thirdly, although it is a relation between law and morality that is under scrutiny here, it is clear that the problem of autonomy also concerns other kinds of practical reasons. First and foremost, political (what critical theories of law have shown persuasively) or economic reasons (Law and Economics) are to be mentioned here. Therefore, the problem of autonomy is a question of relation between legal reason and other dimensions (moral, political, economic) of practical reason.

As M. Kramer suggests, the identification thesis may be read in three different ways, depending on how one understands the ambigous term "does not depend": as *need not*, as *cannot*, or as *should not*. The first is assumed to be characteristic for 'soft' (inclusive) positivism, the second for "hard" (exclusive) positivism and the third for a normative (prescriptive) version of positivist theory.[18] We may

[15] See Joseph Raz, "On the Autonomy of Legal Reasoning," in: idem, *Ethics in the Public Domain*, op. cit.

[16] See Frederick Shauer, "The Limited Domain of the Law," *Virginia Law Review* 2004, no. 9.

[17] This is the view of Hart and Raz when writing about judicial discretion. See e.g. J. Raz, "On the Autonomy of Legal Reasoning," op. cit., pp. 314–319.

[18] Matthew H. Kramer, "Dogmas and Distortions: Legal Positivism Defended. A Reply to David Dyzenhaus," *Oxford Journal of Legal Studies* 2001, vol. 21, no. 4.

leave aside inclusive positivism, as it is generally irrelevant for current considerations; inclusive positivism is not interested in any particular legal culture so we may suppose it would be useless to examine special features of our own culture. For inclusivists, autonomy of law is a mere possibility, while for us it is a fact. Thus we have to choose between exclusive or normative interpretations, where the identification of law *cannot* or *should not* depend on moral reasons. In the next section I will try to explain why the only proper interpretation is the second, prescriptive one.

3. Autonomy, authority and the function of law

To say that "a determination of what law is *cannot* depend on moral criteria or argument" is to try to defend the autonomy thesis from an analytical standpoint. Two versions of such a defence are the best known and most influential in relevant literature: argument from practical difference, offered by Scott Shapiro, and argument from practical authority, formulated by J. Raz. The first argument, to give it possibly the most general expression, claims that existence of law must make a relevant difference in practical reasoning within particular social practice.[19] Taken this way, the argument is important but uncontroversial. It also captures the second argument as a specific variation of itself.[20] Still, Shapiro gives more detailed characteristics of the argument. Unfortunately, by doing this, he makes a number of seriously false assumptions that makes the entire argument dubious.[21]

[19] Law should make this difference at the 'social' level of practical reasoning; It's not clear, however, wether the difference in reasoning of particular agent is also necessary or not.

[20] See J.L. Coleman, *The Practice of Principle*, op. cit., p. xviii; Andrei Marmor, "Exclusive Legal Positivism," in: Jules Coleman and Scott Shapiro (eds.), *The Oxford Handbook of Jurisprudence & Philosophy of Law*, Oxford: Oxford University Press, 2004, p. 109. In fact, Raz takes this view by himself – "Authority, Law and Morality," op. cit., p. 204.

[21] There is no space to justify this judgment so I'll try to name some of these fallacies at least: In my opinion, Shapiro (a) takes the wrong, naturalistic conception of a social rule; (b) confuses epistemic problems of recognition of rules with purely psychological question of their motivational impact; (c) confuses the sociological level of

For this reason, I shall not examine it closer and will instead focus on the second argument, of law's claim to practical authority.

According to Raz, one of the basic conceptual features of law is its claim to legitimate practical authority.[22] It is important to remember that it is *a claim* only - not all actual legal systems are in fact legitimate. Nevertheless, if a particular system is legitimate or not, to claim the latter it must be capable of possessing an authority. Thus, if the claim to authority is part of the nature of law, then whatever else the law is it must be capable of possesing authority.[23] Here, Raz differentiates between moral and non-moral prerequisites of authority. While the first might be the subject of controversy, the second is usually taken for granted. If that were not the case, it would be odd to say that law claims authority. Thus, while moral attributes are conditions of law's actual legitimacy which is contingent, attributes of a non-moral nature are conditions of the very law's capacity to posses authority, which is conceptual. They are necessary, definitional features of law.

But what are these necessary conditions of law's capacity to posses practical authority? Raz expresses, among others, two such attributes: the mediating and exclusionary role of authoritative reasons. The very nature of practical authority is to mediate between subjects and genuine reasons for action that apply to them. The task of authority is to take into account all relevant reasons that apply to the subjects in specific circumstances, and to offer them a directive as a solution. However, this mediation means a displacement of genuine rea-

---

a theoretical reflection (the problem of social existence of a rule) with psychological considerations on perspective of particular agent; (d) from statements about legal system as a whole draws conclusions on particular rules, what is not plausibly justified; (e) finally, confuses legal rule which is formulated *in abstracto* with direct command formulated *in concreto*. See Scott Shapiro, "The Difference That Rules Make," in: Brian Bix (ed.), *Analyzing Law: New Essays in Legal Theory*, Oxford: Clarendon Press, 1998.

[22] J. Raz, "Authority, Law and Morality," op. cit. See also i.a. Kenneth E. Himma, "Law's Claim of Legitimate Authority," in: Jules Coleman (ed.), *Hart's Postscript. Essays on the Postscript to* The Concept of Law, Oxford: Oxford University Press, 2001; Kenneth E. Himma, "Inclusive Legal Positivism," in: *The Oxford Handbook of Jurisprudence & Philosophy of Law*, op. cit., pp. 147–157.

[23] J. Raz, "Authority, Law and Morality," op. cit., p. 199.

sons as well: an agent who has accepted authority is no longer expected to act according to genuine relevant reasons, but according to authorities' directives, which have now become the exclusive sound reasons for action (pre-emption thesis).

This is the mediating nature of authority that also justifies the autonomy of law, interpreted in accordance with the identification thesis. For authorities' directives to play their mediating role, they must be peremptory and exclusionary (pre-emptive), but they must also be identified without any recourse to the reasons they are supposed to displace. So, if law will mediate and replace moral and political reasons for some action, it cannot be identified using these very reasons.

If we accept the Razian concept of practical authority, we have no choice but to accept an analytically necessary autonomy of law as its consequence. Its theoretical depth, sophistication and internal coherence are truly persuasive. Still, the real question is, why should it be necessary for law to claim such an authority? Is there really no other option? In fact, there are authors who attempt to argue with Raz, showing alternatives to his mediating conception of authority.[24] It seems that even if law necessarily claims to be authoritative, it might be such in different ways.

Taking this into account, one may ask why Raz chooses the mediating conception as essential for understanding law. The answer goes towards what is seen as the fundamental, natural function of law. Raz gives different characteristics of that function at different stages of his writing. In his early book, *The Authority of Law,* he writes about "providing publicly ascertainable ways of guiding behaviour and regulating aspects of social life."[25] *Ethics in the Public Domain* no long-

---

[24] K.E. Himma, "Law's Claim of Legitimate Authority," op. cit., pp. 298–309; J. Coleman, *The Practice of Principle,* op. cit., p. 133; Heidi Hurd, "Challenging Authority," *The Yale Law Journal* 1991, vol. 100, no. 6. Hurt's considerations in particular seem to be indebted to more general philosophical conceptions of authority, like those offered by J. Bentham or H.-G. Gadamer.

[25] Joseph Raz, *The Authority of Law. Essays on Law and Morality,* Oxford: Oxford University Press, 1979, p. 51. In the same book we may find the chapter called *The Functions of Law* in which Raz describes this problem in a much more complex way. Still, all types of law's functions within classification he offers, or at least so-called "direct functions," seem to be variations on the general function quoted above.

er stresses such a function; instead, we find a much more complex view, according to which "the law - in its core - is the product of the activities of human institutions," thus, "it reflects the multiplicity of aims and beliefs held by various people ... It's natural to find reflected in the law conflicting values, goals and aims."[26] Nevertheless, all of these goals that law may serve are somehow subordinated to the law's main task of mediating between subjects and reasons for action.[27] Hence, it is justified to assume the existence of law's natural, ultimate function, namely the mediating one or, even more, the task 'to foster expectations' of participants of social practices.[28] Now, it is important to see that this task is not contradictory to the law's function stated in *The Authority of Law*. On the contrary, the latter justifies the former. In all his considerations, Raz is indebted to the suppositions of law's natural function.

Again, analogically to the idea of autonomous identification of law, this belief in essential function of law is not limited to Raz alone. It is broadly spread among writers belonging to the positivist community. Of course, there are some differences between them in the manner in which they describe this function: as "providing guides to human conduct" (Hart), "settlement of moral controversies" and "reducing the moral cost of disagreement" (Alexander and Sherwin), "coordination" (MacCormick, Postema) etc. All of these descriptions are still closely related to each other, and all of them are varieties of the "making a practical difference" function in its general interpretation explained above. Finally, what should not be underestimated is that such a supposition is not a peripheral statement but rather a crucial point of the whole theoretical characterization of law. We have noticed this with reference to Raz's theory, but it is true for most thinkers - even if not all of them see it with similar clarity.[29]

---

[26] J. Raz, "On the Autonomy of Legal Reasoning," op. cit., pp. 314–315.

[27] Further in the paper, I will show how one may plausibly explain this *prima facie* contradiction.

[28] J. Raz, "On the Autonomy of Legal Reasoning," op. cit., p. 321.

[29] In fact, Stephen Perry claims that Hart didn't notice the weight of that problem for his own theory - see Stephen R. Perry, "Interpretation and Methodology in Legal Theory," in: Andrei Marmor (ed.), *Law and Interpretation. Essays in Legal Philosophy*, Oxford: Clarendon Press, 1995, p. 121.

4. Two points of view on the point of law

The question is, how should we understand such references to the function of law? Hart probably treated them, much like the whole of his own theoretical project, as purely descriptive and morally neutral. But despite the fact that some authors still share the Hartian point of view,[30] most relevant thinkers (eg. Raz or MacCormick) take a more sophisticated perspective.

To find an answer we have to draw a distinction between practical and theoretical attitude to the point, or the function, of law.[31] The former one may describe as the perspective of participant, while the latter may be called the perspective of observer. The first is typical for someone who takes a part in a particular practice. It is a part of this practice in the sense of shaping the way people act and interpret their own actions. The second is typical for a scholar who builds a theoretical explanation of the practice. But this theoretical construct is not, or at least does not have to be, a part of the practice it describes. In some situations, it may be adapted by participants of this practice and then transformed, but there is no such conceptual need.

These two attitudes towards the point of law should not be confused with Hart's internal and external point of view. The reason for that is not only an ambiguity of the concept of an internal point of view in his theory. Even if we assumed that the meaning of the "critical-reflective attitude" was clear for us and it was equal to some kind of affirmative acceptance of the law, it still wouldn't tell us a great deal about the point or function of such a law. Furthermore, according to Hartian theory there is only one internal point of view, generally shared within society. This is the condition *sine qua non* of normativity of law.[32] Contrary to that, there may be a plenty of different

---

[30] See e.g. Larry Alexander, Emily Sherwin, *Demistifying Legal Reasoning*, Cambridge: Cambridge University Press, 2008.

[31] For clarity of considerations, I treat terms "function of law" and "point of law" as synonyms. Further in the text I will offer an interpretation of these which might be a basis to draw a distinction between them. Nevertheless, I don't face that problem directly.

[32] Even if we accept MacCormick's point that there are various kinds of internal points of view, they are still quite general and their number is limited. Furthermore,

beliefs about the point of law among participants of the same practice. As Raz writes, "It's natural to find reflected in the law conflicting values, goals and aims."[33]

If there is a difference between the concept of internal point of view and of participant's perspective on the point of law, there is an even greater one between the observer's perspective and the Hartian external point of view. On the one hand, the external point of view is typical not only for the external observer of some practice but also for its participant, and is sometimes described as a presupposition of the internal one. Thus, it could be understood as part of the practice; it is an outcome of practical, not theoretical, reasoning, to use Stephen Perry's words.[34] On the other hand, the theoretical observer's point on law's function is usually much more complex than the Hartian external point of view, as it contains fully interpretative statements (and often even some of moral kind, as we shall see).

With the distinction between practical and theoretical perspective in mind, we may ask, what the nature is of positivists' claims about the essential function of law. It should be clear that these are claims made from a theoretical point of view. Perry has shown this illuminatingly according to Hart's theory.[35] For Hart the function of law (which is, let us repeat, "providing guides to human conduct") seems to justify the conceptual characteristics of law in terms of secondary rules (first of all, the rule of recognition);[36] and this function is certainly an explanation of the need for an internal point of view as Hart describes it. But he "does not assume that judges and other persons who adopt the internal point of view within law have any views at all on the moral value of law as an institution."[37] Thus, that claim is in no case the report of participants' beliefs about the point or aim that law serves, beliefs that are constantly threatened with the possibility of changes. It's a purely theoretical statement that is seen as universally

---

we are still able to indicate one of them as fundamental. See Neil MacCormick, *Legal Reasoning and Legal Theory*, Oxford: Clarendon Press, 1978, pp. 275–292.

[33] J. Raz, "On the Autonomy of Legal Reasoning," op. cit., p. 315.

[34] S.R. Perry, "Interpretation and Methodology in Legal Theory," op. cit., p. 109.

[35] Ibidem, pp. 102–121.

[36] H.L.A. Hart, *The Concept of Law*, op. cit., pp. 91–93.

[37] S.R. Perry, "Interpretation and Methodology in Legal Theory," op. cit., p. 118.

valid. Otherwise the description of law as a bond of primary and secondary rules, or a claim on the need of internal point of view, could not be treated as analytically true.

The same remarks can be made with respect to Raz, whose project we have examined above. He explicitly names what Hart has suppressed: the difference between participants' "conflicting values, goals and aims," and the theoretical function of law which is one and fixed. Only the latter may serve as an explanation of law's conceptual claim to authority.

The preceding considerations drive towards the conclusion that the function of law in positivism is a theoretical concept. So far, so good. We must now take a further examination of the character of this concept and of positivist claim on law's function. Could these really be descriptive and morally neutral? Is there any natural or necessary function of law? I used to think that giving a positive answer to these questions implied taking positions of sociological functionalism.[38] Today I have to admit that there are more theoretical perspectives that make such an answer possible. Except for functionalism and its relative, organicism, one may indicate some variety of natural law theory ("the *true* law is only the law that serves some specific goals or values") or historic determinism, like that of a rather crude variant of marxist philosophy ("the function of law is to promote the interests of the dominant class"). Still, with all of these theoretical perspectives the same problem emerges: how is the existence of a function of law that is independent from views and consciousness of participants possible? And in what sense does it actually exist? Just notice that within such perspective the "real" essential function of law is not equal to some social effects that law may cause. It is quite clear that, because of some structural features of society, actions of social agents may cause some effects that were unintended by these agents;[39] the

[38] Maciej Pichlak, "Autonomia argumentacji prawniczej: między refleksją etyczną a analitycznym prawoznawstwem" [The Autonomy of Legal Argumentation: Between Ethical Reflection and Analytical Jurisprudence], in: Przemysław Kaczmarek (ed.), *Z zagadnień teorii i filozofii prawa. Lokalny a uniwersalny charakter interpretacji prawniczej* [Issues of Legal Theory and Philosophy of Law. Local and Universal Character of Legal Interpretation], Wrocław: Wydawnictwo Uniwersytetu Wrocławskiego 2009, pp. 247–250.

[39] See A. Giddens, *The Constitution of Society*, op. cit.

same is true with actions in the legal sphere. But to speak about the function of law is not the same as speaking about these effects, nor is it to say that such a function is simply a plausible theoretical explanation of the practice. The function is much more than that, it is a part of a practice that causes real effects within this practice. It is "natural" in the sense that it exists similarly to essential features of natural objects. But this is the fallacy of hypostatization: the reification of abstract concepts as if they were a part of real practices. This fallacy is common for all theoretical perspectives mentioned above.

If someone wants to avoid the fallacy of hypostatizing the concept of the function of law, the alternative is to treat it as a purely theoretical one. But if we then ask why someone should choose one function as essential for law rather than another one, we find no other criteria than a moral one. The law should be described by this particular function, because this is what the law should look like - that is how the argument, roughly speaking, goes. The function is equal to the moral point or value of the institution of law in which the theoretician believes. If such a theoretician draws any further conclusions from the point of law he adheres to, these further statements are of a necessarily moral nature as well.[40]

5. Law and morality: the paradox comes out

With all of this in mind, let us return to the problem of the autonomy of law. We have already seen how the thesis on law's epistemic autonomy (the identification thesis) is anchored in specific assumptions on the function of law. But when Raz, for instance, claims that

[40] This seems to be clear for representatives of so-called ethical or normative positivism. (See i.a. G.J. Postema, *Bentham and the Common Law Tradition*, op. cit.; Tom D. Campbell, *The Legal Theory of Ethical Positivism*, Aldershot: Dartmouth, 1996; Jeremy Waldron, "Normative (or Ethical) Positivism," in: *Hart's Postscript*, op. cit.). The standpoint of ethical positivism, which I treat as an interesting and inspiring alternative for analytical stream of that tradition, is not the matter of current paper. Still, it may be noted that this variety of positivist theory, with its explicit moral justification of autonomy of law, drives to the very same paradox as described in the next sections. Indeed there are some fragments in Raz's writing that allow him to be read as an ethical positivist as well.

the basic function of law is "providing publicly ascertainable ways of guiding behaviour and regulating aspects of social life," he makes a claim on what he believes to be the desireable point of law in our society. His claim is moral in nature. When he derives from that the mediating conception of authority, this is inevitably a morally justified idea. And, when in the next step he comes to the conclusion that the identification thesis is right, he claims in fact that the law has to be identified without any recourse to 'background' morality if it is to plausibly fulfil its moral point. Thus the autonomy of law from moral considerations is directly justified by considerations of a moral kind.

Before going further with this obvious paradox, let us first consider the point that there is actually no paradox here at all. One may argue that I was wrong while treating claims on function of law as made from theoretical perspective. In fact - one may add in opposition to what has been said before - they are simply reports of participants' convictions and beliefs on that question. These are the statements made "from a detached point of view" in Razian terminology or "by virtual participant" in Dworkinian terms.[41] Thus, they are purely descriptive in nature (even if no longer analytical) and do not require any moral justification.

Let me make two reservations on this argument. Firstly, I don't believe in a purely descriptive theory of social practice (of which a theory of law is a variant). I agree that even a purely normative theory (if the descriptive-normative opposition were correct) may contain some descriptive statements, but not in the core of itself. In fact, I am quite familiar with the idea that all crucial points of a theory are in some way involved in the process of supporting or criticising some practices. This is certainly the case for issues that are the matter of dispute between competing theories, as the problem of the function of law is. Secondly, I have already explained why we cannot treat the theoretical statement about the function of law, if we wish to build further elements of our theoretical construction on it, as a simple report on participants' point of view that is constantly threatened by the

[41] See Stephen R. Perry, "The Varieties of Legal Positivism," *Canadian Journal of Law and Jurisprudence* 1996, vol. IX, no. 2, p. 371.

possibility of change. That does not mean that there are no possible relations between theoretical and practical attitudes. In fact, I believe there are. Still, these relations are much more complex and may by no means be treated as *pure description*. Thus I find the argument examined to be entirely false.

But even if the argument were true - if the theoretical claim made by positivism were a direct report of a practical attitude towards the point of law - it would not eliminate the paradox mentioned above. Statements made from a detached point of view are completely dependent on the perspective that they virtually adopt. This is the moral perspective in the case, as it is set by participants' view on the goals and values, that law should serve. Therefore, the thesis on law's autonomy is even more directly rooted in moral assumptions, those of participants of the practice.

Actually, despite the failures of the argument examined, there is some useful intuition contained within it that warrants our attention. As I have said before, *there is* some relation between a theoretical and practical attitude to the function of law that does not allow us to treat it as solely theoretical problem. As I pointed out in the first section, the autonomy of law is not only an internal issue of positivism, but is also the idea that is widely spread in practice. It is similar to the function of law that justifies its autonomy: the idea of "practical difference" is familiar for most of the members of our society, although they may disagree on another level with respect to the particular goals and interests that law should serve. Thus, the paradox of "moral justification of excluding morality" is even stronger, as it is not a solely theoretical question anymore, but has its own practical weight and consequences as well.

However, there are at least two important differences in that view when comparing it to the preceding argument. A relation between theory and practice should not be seen in terms of a description of the latter by the former, but rather in terms of "double hermeneutics" mentioned in the first section. It is a partly circular relation, in which a theory finds its own justification in specific aspects of the practice it interprets, but at the same time supports the same aspects of practice by justifying them. In other words, a theory gives some interpretation of the practice and modifies the latter in the direction it points. The partial reason for that is the second difference between the preceding argument and my own view: it is impossible to give a neutral description of any social practice because it is always complex, ambiguous and vague. Particular components and aspects of it are often contradictory to each other and do not create a consistent picture. A theoretical interpretation of a practice has no choice but to favour some of its aspects against another.

6. Law and morality: the paradox domesticated?

We may return to the paradox presented in the last section (which I will call the Paradox). Within a positivist view, the autonomy of law from morality is justified on moral grounds. In other words, the exclusion of moral considerations from legal reasoning is an outcome of considerations of a moral nature. The Paradox establishes the internal contradiction in positivist theory, for this theory gives no plausible answer to it. This is one of the weak points of positivism.

But is there any possible solution to the Paradox? One may of course reject the very idea of autonomy as illusionary and internally incoherent. But, as I attempted to show in the first section, that would not be the proper approach. If we want to affirm and protect this idea as an important component of our legal culture (and perhaps of our self-understanding as autonomous agents as well), do we have any choice but to accept its inevitably paradoxical character? I claim that even if it is impossible to solve the problem, there is still a theoretical view that may be helpful in understanding the idea of autonomy as less paradoxical. I will attempt below to give a brief outline of two basic points of such a view.

First of all, we should consider more carefully what we are referring to when discussing "morality" or "moral considerations" within the Paradox. In fact, one may distinguish two different meanings of this term in such a context. Morality may be treated as a part of practical reason that creates a local field of reasoning within the latter. I will describe this kind of morality as "ethics." We may find this method of understanding ethics in Aristotle for instance, when he writes about its relation to politics and describes both as parts of the "philosophy of human affairs."[42] Thus, ethics possesses equal positions as political, economic or legal reasoning, which are themselves other local fields of practical reason. However, that does not yet explain anything about mutual relations between these components. It is possible, for instance, that ethics works as a yardstick of criticism of the law, or that it affects legal argumentation. But these relations should still be seen as a dialogue between more or less equal partners. One thing is thus certain: none of these local fields can be a sufficient foundation for the justification of the others. In other words, the economy cannot give (complete) explanations of the need for politics, politics of the need for ethics, and so on. Nor can ethics explain the need for law.

It should already be clear that in the second sense, morality means a general practical reason. This contains all local kinds of reasoning mentioned above. Nevertheless, we should not treat the practical reason in this sense as a "compilation" of ethics, politics, law, and so forth. It is rather an unstructured integrity, in which various kinds of reasons are not yet differentiated. This is the foundation from which the law might subsequently be separated, and which at the same time justifies the need for law. This description of the relation between the general practical reason and the law remains true not only from an analytical but also historical standpoint, as the history of transforming the customary "pre-legal" orders of early societies to modern, autonomous legal systems teaches us.[43]

Thus, when we are formulating the Paradox of "moral justification of autonomy from morality" we are using the same word in two different senses: morality that justifies the autonomy of law is

---

[42] Aristotle, *Nicomachean Ethics*, 1181b; transl. by Harris Rackham, Harvard: Harvard University Press, 1926 (available at: <http://www.perseus.tufts.edu/hopper/>).

[43] This is the view of H. Hart (*Concept of Law*, op. cit.), but we may find similar in writing of Jürgen Habermas (*Between Facts and Norms. Contributions to a Discourse Theory of Law and Democracy*, transl. by William Rehg, Cambridge, Mass.: The MIT Press, 1996). See also A. Kozak, *Myślenie analityczne w nauce prawa i praktyce prawniczej* [Analytical Thinking in Legal Science and Legal Practice], op. cit. The latter point doesn't mean adopting a perspective of evolutionism in social theory. It refers only to the history of legal order in European societies. Also, the term "pre-legal order" makes sense only from the perspective of particular legal culture.

a "background morality," i.e., general practical reason; and morality as mutually independent from law is ethics as a local field of practical reasoning.

The second point of view offered here states that autonomy is still a related and dependent concept, but based on general practical reasoning rather than on the ethics it ought to exclude. It makes the idea of autonomy possible, even if problematic. Nevertheless, we probably still need such a change in the manner of understanding authority. The authority of law might be exclusionary to ethical, political or economical reason, albeit in a rather weak sense of exclusion. But it cannot create exclusionary reason in relation to general practical reasoning. Opposite to Raz's view, the force of legal reason in this area is a matter of weight rather than exclusion. Law adds reasons of a special kind to practical considerations. We may find such a concept of authority in J. Bentham (as Postema interprets him) or H.-G. Gadamer.[44]

Do these two points give a satisfying basis for a solution to the Paradox? The answer is probably "no." They make the autonomy of law possible, but do not nullify its paradoxical potentiality. Some may see this as the weakness of the view offered. It might be said that my argument did not make any real difference to the positivist perspective. After a long-winded critique of the latter, it finally came to the very same outcome: moral justification of autonomy of law.

Well, I claim that there is a real difference between the views of positivism and mine. The act of distinguishing within morality and the change in understanding authority are not merely irrelevant modifications. They effect in important dissimilarities in practical consequences of theory, but I have no room to explain them here at length.[45] Instead, I will simply note that within a positivist perspective, when taken seriously, the autonomy is in fact impossible. My view tries to explain its possibility but I will not to deny its paradoxical nature.

---

[44] See G.J. Postema, *Bentham and the Common Law Tradition*, op. cit., pp. 324–327; Hans-Georg Gadamer, *Truth and Method*, transl. by Joel Weinsheimer and Donald G. Marshall, 2nd ed., London–New York: Continuum, 1989, pp. 277–285.

[45] See M. Pichlak, *Autonomia argumentacji prawniczej* [The Autonomy of Legal Argumentation], op. cit.

One may pose the question of why anyone should protect such a paradoxical idea. If someone feels uncomfortable with such paradoxes, two solutions are possible. One is to reject the idea of autonomy, and the second is to make it more radical. The first is the solution of Dworkin for instance (or at least of some interpretations of his writing), where morality becomes a part of law. In consequence, there is no clear border between moral and legal reasoning. The second solution is typical of the doctrine of formalism, where the autonomy becomes a complete separation of law and morality. Thus, both these doctrines, regardless of how opposite they are to each other, have one thing in common. Both are trying to "domesticate" the paradox by rejecting its existence on a theoretical and practical level.

But that's not how law works in the real world. Taking a look at actual legal practices, we may often meet contradictions and clashes of legal and moral reasons (in both senses of morality described above), where no 'one right answer' can be given. On the practical level, the idea of autonomy is inevitably paradoxical, which is, incidentally, noted by some positivist scholars as well.[46] Each manner of denying that there is a *real* problem in such cases is fallacious, and probably equally dangerous.

The paradox of autonomy should not be domesticated, but rather treated with the respect it deserves.[47] Instead of denying it, we should remain watchful to it. This is a "general justification through partial critique," to use another Kaarlo Tuori's expression. The existence of unautonomous law would be pointless, and we thus need the autonomy of law as a *general principle* without treating legal reasoning in any *particular case* as *a priori* autonomous. To say it in other words: we have to accept the idea of law's autonomy; but our biggest mistake would be to feel comfortable with this.

---

[46] See Frederick Schauer, *Playing by the Rules: A Philosophical Examination of Rule-Based Decision-Making in Life and Law*, Oxford: Clarendon Press, 1991; Larry Alexander and Emily Sherwin, *The Rule of Rules: Morality, Rules and the Dilemmas of Law*, Durham: Duke University Press, 2001, pp. 53–95.

[47] See Zenon Bańkowski, "In the Judgment Space: the Judge and the Anxiety of the Encounter," in: Z. Bańkowski, James MacLean (eds.), *The Universal and the Particular in Legal Reasoning*, Aldershot: Ashgate, 2006. The beautiful metaphor of a tiger as a wild animal that is emasculated when domesticated is to be mentioned here.

Martin Škop
Masaryk University, Czech Republic

Legal Rules, Moral Norms and Arbitrariness

Abstract: This article deals with possible definitions of legal rules, moral norms and democratic principles as well as the relationships among these. It explores the underlying premise that the contents of legal rules as well as moral norms are defined arbitrarily: the content depends on no principle or even rationality. The content is determined mostly by argumentation that adopts methods beyond legal cognition. In a legal system we can operate with moral norms and in most cases specifying their contents is not necessary. On the contrary, the content of democratic principles should be determined by the concept of democracy and democratic system. This is specified by its content: democratic principles depend entirely on the definition of the concept of democracy and is subject to its variability. Legal rules have a specific content that is defined while the same does not necessarily apply to moral norms. In this article the concepts of legal rules and moral norms is showed as kinds of myths. This does not in any way prevent them from expressing societal value judgements and at the pragmatic level of the perception of law their contents overlap.

Key words: legal norms; legal principle; myths; societal values; legal system

This article focuses on possible definitions of legal rules, moral norms and democratic principles as well as the relationships among these. We explore the underlying premise that the contents of legal rules as well as moral norms are defined arbitrarily. In contrast, the content of democratic principles is determined by the concept of democracy and democratic system. This specifies its content, yet, it depends entirely on the definition of the concept of democracy and is subject to its variability. While teleology does not fully impact on legal rules and moral norms, democratic principles are fully subjected to it.

We will also attempt to demonstrate that legal rules must have a specific content that is defined while the same does not necessarily apply to moral norms. In a legal system we can operate with moral norms and in most cases specifying their contents is not necessary. Hence the concepts of legal rules and moral norms act as kinds of myths that in their bare existence necessarily characterize the legal system. This does not in any way prevent them from expressing societal value judgements and at the pragmatic level of the perception of law their contents overlap. This applies whether we accept either the separation thesis or the connection thesis.[1]

1. The arbitrariness of rules

Moral norms and legal rules closely resemble each other in nature. Their connectedness is expressed by Émile Durkheim:

> The moral and juridical facts – let us say, briefly, just moral facts – consist of rules of conduct that have sanction. Sanction is thus the feature common to all facts of this kind.[2]

In both cases we deal with rules that are supported by sanction and it is insignificant that the sanction differs in the two normative systems – in law and in morals. I believe that the nature of democratic principles is different in this respect. They are not so much characterized by sanction, rather by their nature they act as a requirement to optimisation. They are thus closer to Robert Alexy's understanding: "Constitutional rights as principles are optimisation requirements."[3] That is why it is impossible to insist on a link between democratic principles and sanction. They are mainly characterized by process rather than by sanction and that is why they are indeed principles rather than rules. Although it is possible to imagine principles linked to sanction, I believe it is not one of their characteristic features.

---

[1] Robert Alexy, *Arguments from Injustice*, Oxford: Oxford University Press, 2002, p. 20 ff.

[2] Émile Durkheim, *Professional Ethic and Civic Morals*, London: Routledge, 2003, p. 2.

[3] Robert Alexy, "Constitutional Rights, Balancing, and Rationality," *Ratio Juris* 2003, vol. 16, no. 2, pp. 131–40, here at 135.

Let us concede that the contents of both moral norms as well as legal rules are arbitrary – i.e. their contents are arbitrary and are not subject to any solid and unchanging causal determinants. This fact emerges partly from the authoritative nature of legal rules and also from uncertain content in the case of moral norms. The understanding of moral rules as rules with an objectively uncertain content is also supported by the fact that they are often treated as an image or a symbol. They act similarly as punctuation marks in a sentence – e.g. an exclamation mark. We know what they mean but at the same time we are aware that their meaning can vary according to context etc. It is important that we accept the existence of such a rule without necessarily having to accept a clearly defined content of such a moral norm.

It involves the shared idea that something like moral rules actually exists although we are not convinced whether the content of moral rules would be upheld in a rigorous discussion. Jan-R. Sieckmann suggests that

> … on the basis of the idea of moral autonomy, objective validity of norms can only be achieved in a weak and approximative sense, if at all. … On the other hand, it is necessary in some respects to claim objective validity of a norm even though a consensus does not exist.[4]

Although he refers to the objective validity of norms, he is aware of the necessity to separate the content and the form (formal validation) of the given rule. We can even assume that legal theory or legal philosophy works with the term "moral norm" even though it is primarily unnecessary to strictly define its content. We concede its existence and we do not necessarily need to know its content as it is not significant for its existence. It is, however, impossible to accept the assumption that the term moral norm is empty. The fact that we are unable to define its content, does not mean that content is completely missing. It is certainly inappropriate to characterize this approach as nihilism, as Owen M. Fiss suggests:

---

[4] Jan-R. Sieckmann, "On the Tension between Moral Autonomy and the Rational Justification of Norms," *Ratio Juris* 2003, vol. 16, no. 1, pp. 105–122, here at 108.

> The nihilist would argue that for any text – particularly such a comprehensive text as the Constitution – there are any number of possible meanings, that interpretation consists of choosing one of those meanings, and that in this selection process the judge will inevitably express his own values.[5]

In claiming this, Fiss guards against opening up interpretation but such a defensive stance is useless. If we accepted this viewpoint, any interpretation of legal texts would be nihilistic. Hence such a statement is rather short-sighted.

Nonetheless, at the individual level of the application of law, it is necessary to define the content of moral norms. In a court decision that deals with the potential invalidity of a legal norm due to its immoral content, it is crucial to define the content of the moral norm. It is, however, the individual judge's responsibility to completely uncover the relevant reasons for his decision. Without such reasoning Gustav Radbruch could not arrive at his conclusions about extremely unjust law.[6] When we attempt to support our decision with moral norms, there must exist strong arguments about the inapplicability of legal rules and that on the basis of a moral norm with a precisely defined content.

On the other hand, it is necessary to justify the content of a concrete legal rule. When uncovering legal rules in a normative text, we must define these rules precisely. However, in this case we have an established methodology for uncovering the content of normative texts. That is why it is easier for the judge to cope with this duty. The pragmatic level of reasoning is demonstrated strongly in the legal environment, as Ota Weinberger argues:

> From a pragmatic viewpoint it is not important that arguments are objectively valid, rather the case is to convince the participants in the conversation about the weight of arguments.[7]

---

[5] Owen M. Fiss, "Objectivity and Interpretation," *Stanford Law Review* 1982, issue 4, p. 741.

[6] Gustav Radbruch, "Statutory Lawlessness and Supra-Statutory Law" (1946), *Oxford J Legal Studies* 2006 (Spring), vol. 26 (1), pp. 1–11.

[7] Ota Weinberger, *Základy právní logiky* [Fundamentals of Legal Logic], Brno: Masarykova univerzita v Brně, 1993, p. 221.

Although Weinberger's primary focus is on proving facts and truthfulness, his argument can also be applied to the interpretation of legal texts. Even when judging the existence of legal rules or moral norms, the clash of opinions will have an argumentative character.

According to legal positivism it is possible to agree with the statement that the content of legal rules is determined arbitrarily, it is determined by the creative will of the author of the norm, however, the mutual consistency of rules results in the demand for rationality. The authoritative justification of the validity of legal norms (Alexy) represents the primary reason for the validity of legal norms but this justification must be supplemented with the demands of recognized rationality.

> The results of authoritative decisions would then be indirectly supported by the consent on the institutional procedures. This approach is especially relevant for the justification of the objective validity of legal norms.[8]

Let us concede that the basis of law is truly its purpose as Rudolf von Ihering suggests:

> Purpose is the creator of the entire law; that there is no legal rule which does not owe its origin to a purpose, i.e., to a practical motive.[9]

This leads us to an understanding of law as a social phenomenon which cannot exist outside the needs of society. At the same time, however, it establishes the need to interpret law in line with purposes that society projects into law. A moral norm or a moral rule will then be acceptable as normative quality as long as it possesses a strong enough link with this rational demand. In this respect democratic principles differ somewhat from both of the previous social rules. The aim of democratic principles is to ensure democracy hence they are necessarily determined by their purpose. Their existence is justified only in case they lead to ensuring democracy and its necessary components. Thus in their case their contents need to be taken into ac-

[8] J.-R. Sieckmann, "On the Tension between Moral Autonomy and the Rational Justification of Norms," op. cit., p. 113.

[9] Rudolf von Ihering, *Law as a Means to an End*, Boston: Boston Book Company, 1913, liv.

count along with formal validity. This relative determination of the content of democratic principles is nonetheless also arbitrary to an extent as it devolves from the concept of "democracy." Everyone appears to agree that democracy exists and I believe that many know it. Nonetheless, it is much more complicated to provide its definition at the level of everyday decision making. Democratic principles thus make use of their conditioning by the concept of democracy, yet they can be changed arbitrarily precisely due to changes in the meaning of the concept itself.

A certain arbitrariness of moral norms as well as legal rules also stems from the impossibility of defining objective criteria for the content of moral norms. This fact has been expressed also by the European Court for Human Rights:

> It acknowledges that the national authorities enjoy a wide margin of appreciation in matters of morals, particularly in an area such as the present which touches on matters of belief concerning the nature of human life. As the Court has observed before, it is not possible to find in the legal and social orders of the Contracting States a uniform European conception of morals, and the State authorities are, in principle, in a better position than the international judge to give an opinion on the exact content of the requirements of morals as well as on the "necessity" of a "restriction" or "penalty" intended to meet them (see, inter alia, the Handyside v. the United Kingdom judgment of 7 December 1976, Series A no. 24, p. 22, para. 48, and the Müller and Others v. Switzerland judgment of 24 May 1988, Series A no. 133, p. 22, para. 35).[10]

Thus the court acknowledges the existence of such objective moral norms, it only reminds that these are difficult to identify and that it is extremely difficult to defend their contents at a pan-European level. Ronald Dworkin also expresses similar views on these principles:

> … it is sensible to say that people have moral rights when … it is controversial within the community what moral rights they have.[11]

---

[10] Case of Open Door and Dublin Well Woman v. Ireland, art. 68 (Application no. 14234/88; 14235/88).

[11] Ronald Dworkin, *Taking Rights Seriously*, Cambridge: Harvard University Press, 1977, pp. 263–264.

When assessing legal rules and moral norms, it is not solely their content that matters but also their form. We come across the view that the form is that which can safely distinguish a legal from a moral norm. Yet, the form can - to a certain extent - also be a matter of arbitrary recognition. And that not from a formalist viewpoint when the sovereign's will is expressed but rather from a real and practical viewpoint when the form of legal rules is subject to recognition

> ... whether the apex norm hangs on "habitual obedience" (Austin), "efficaciousness" (Kelsen) or "recognition" (Hart), its support must be something non-legal in nature; it cannot be some other legal norm, nor within the legal system at all.[12]

We recognize the normatively stronger position of legal rules compared to moral norms. This is the standard premise of functioning legal systems and that regardless of the fact that according to some - in particular non-positivistic viewpoints - moral norms influence the validity of legal rules. Here we do not concern ourselves with the legal power but with the ability to influence human behaviour.

2. The myth of rules

Taking all of the above into account, we can assume that legal rules as well as moral norms act as myths. Moral norms embody the myth of correctness, goodness or fairness while legal rules embody the myth of rationality. I do not wish to question the concept of rationality here - it is not my purpose to identify what is or is not rational behaviour and neither do I argue that rationality is only a hypothetical characteristic. The frequent negative understanding of myth does not apply here either. "While the utilization of the term 'myth' has grown almost ubiquitous, today, the negative connotations appear to predominate again."[13] Rather, I attempt to understand myth

---

[12] Julius Stone, *Legal System and Lawyers´ Reasoning*, Stanford: Stanford University Press, 1964, p. 133.

[13] Hubert Rottleuthner, *A Treatise of Legal Philosophy and General Jurisprudence*, vol. 2: *Foundations of Law*, Dordrecht: Springer Verlag, 2005, p. 32.

in a more sociological sense, an understanding of myth as constructed by Roland Barthes. "But what must be firmly established at the start is that myth is a system of communication, that it is a message,"[14] and further "We reach here the very principle of myth: it transforms history into nature."[15] Myth unites society into one whole and hence transforms society into a unified system that operates with a unified thought apparatus.

It is relatively usual to encounter myths in legal theory.[16] Normally we link them to certain schools of thought and their simplified versions can then be treated as easy subjects of criticism. Tomáš Sobek suggests in this respect:

> Theories developed within the social sciences create myths about themselves, these are grand narratives about their origins, development, historical significance and above all the regretful inadequacy of their opponents.[17]

Similarly then, it is very easy to identify some legal theoreticians or legal philosophers as representatives of a certain "hypothetical" school and hence offer a very simple version of their exploration of law or a legal system. Peter Fitzpatrick suggests that "law as a unified entity can only be reconciled with its contradictory existences if we see it as myth."[18] These myths are also transferred onto individual legal institutes or concepts. Most frequently such mythologies involve basic - and hence difficult to define - concepts.

We have argued already that moral norms can exist without having their contents precisely defined. We can thus assume that they form a category that is essential yet in general it is unnecessary to define its content. The same applies in the case of legal rules or moral norms. We can find many definitions, a fact that illustrates the diffi-

---

[14] Roland Barthes, *Mythologies*, New York: The Noonday Press, 1991, p. 107.

[15] Ibidem, p. 128.

[16] Tomáš Sobek, *Nemorální právo* [Immoral Law], Plzeň: Vydavatelství a nakladatelství Aleš Čeněk, 2010; Brian Z. Tamanaha, *Beyond the Formalist - Realist Divide*, Princeton: Princeton University Press, 2010 etc.

[17] Tomáš Sobek, "Radbruchův mýtus a Benthamova formule" [Radbruch´s Myth and Bentham´s Formula], *Právník* 2011, no. 2, pp. 128–165, here at 128.

[18] Peter Fitzpatrick, *The Mythology of Modern Law*, London: Routledge, 1992, p. 1.

culties with defining them in a way that covers all the relevant cases. Yet, there is a significant difference between the two. While a legal rule represents an object of everyday legal practice (and hence its content is manifest in everyday conduct, notwithstanding individual differences), a moral norm also has everyday use but unlike a legal rule, it is not necessary to determine its definite content.

It is very strange that normally works in the fields of legal theory or legal philosophy do not deal with concrete contents of legal rules. Without any doubt this forms part of the normative approach as determined in pure legal doctrine or normative theory (Kelsen, Weyr).[19] Their understanding, however, concentrates solely on the purity of methods that explore law and explicitly not on exploring contents. Nonetheless, František Weyr's statement applies purely to this school, i.e. "anything can form the content of a norm."[20] This definition is generally normological, and hence can apply to legal rules as well as to moral norms. In terms of their nature, taking into account their teleological character, it is very difficult to apply to democratic principles. This purely positivist methodological stream is difficult to apply to the overall nature of law, rather it is a contribution to the mythical foundation of legal rules as well as moral norms. In both cases the content of the norm is removed and hence its nature in society is completely emptied out.

This conceptualization can only lead to the term of a rule or a norm without the necessity of exploring whether such a rule is actually possible in society or at least realistically imaginable. Other approaches that also explore legal rules or moral norms are based on the premise that it is possible to identify an ideal norm whose characteristics we explore. In the same way the mutual ratio of these ideal types is explored, however, without an exhaustive application to real situations or real norms. At most, a theoretically conceived example is chosen or possibly an example that adopts a suitable norm as illustration that confirms the given systematic concepts or theories.

---

[19] František Weyr, *Teorie práva* [Theory of Law], Praha: Orbis, 1936; Hans Kelsen, *Introduction to the Problems of Legal Theory*, Oxford: Clarendon Press 1992; idem, *The Pure Theory of Law*, Clark: The Lawbook Exchange, 2005.

[20] F. Weyr, *Teorie práva* [Theory of Law], op. cit., p. 34.

It is not at all possible to argue that due to this reason theoretical concepts are of no use for the practical interpretation and application of legal norms. In fact the opposite is true. These theories can serve to unify systems of legal rules, ontological relationships between legal rules and moral norms, for appropriate interpretation etc. We cannot ignore their role in defining demands on a functioning legal system. This usability of theoretical knowledge is thus very important for law as such. The above only refers to difficulties with defining legal rules and legal norms and the difficult explanation of their mutual relationships at the individual level of application. The myth of objectively existing legal rules and moral norms is thus confirmed. As a term these institutions can then really exist with any arbitrarily defined content whose nature will depend only on the demands of a concrete changing society.

3. The value coherence of moral norms and legal rules

As we have already suggested, formally it is not necessary to define the content of legal rules or moral norms. On the other hand, it is absolutely necessary to define the content of democratic principles. The theoretical level of the existence of law, respectively of a legal system, is possible wholly independently of moral norms.[21] Nonetheless, the practical level of the impact of law is linked to moral norms. When analysing works of legal realism Brian Z. Tamanaha argues:

> Even Roscoe Pound recognized, in an article he published the year before mechanical Jurisprudence, that judges continued to utilize various interpretive techniques (including legal fictions) to see that the cases are "decided in the long run so as to accord with the moral sense of the community."[22]

---

[21] Kenneth E. Himma, "Final Authority to Bind with Moral Mistakes on the Explanatory Potential of Inclusive Legal Positivism," *Law and Philosophy* 2005, vol. 24, pp. 1–45.

[22] B.Z. Tamanaha, *Beyond the Formalist – Realist Divide*, op. cit., p. 40.

This suggests a coherence between moral norms and legal rules in the process of decision making on the one hand but also a coherence with society.

I think that it is not in contradiction with the above to suggest that both moral norms as well as legal rules are also linked to society, they are actually anchored in society and hence acquire societal relevance, a component of their existence. In the Czech Republic, the value laden character of law is discussed also by the Constitutional Court, for example in the decision Pl. ÚS 19/93, where it links the Constitution directly with certain values:

> Our new Constitution is not founded on neutrality with regard to values, it is not simply a mere demarcation of institutions and processes, rather it incorporates into its text also certain governing ideas, expressing the fundamental, inviolable values of a democratic society.

We will arrive at a very similar conclusion if we accept the chain of connections as constructed by Jeremy Waldron:

> The textuality of legislative measure is thus connected to the conditions under which it may plausibly be regarded as authoritative: authority requires superior expertise; superior expertise comes from deliberation among those who are different from one another; deliberation among those who are different from one another is possible only on the basis of formal rules of order; an agreed text as the focus of discussion is key to formal rules of order.[23]

The value coherence between legal rules and moral norms is also manifest in terms of interpretation. In the process of interpretation a legal rule is deducted from normative sentence. Yet, the process of interpretation is influenced also by other phenomena that have an impact on exploratory and decision making processes. It is thus understandable that a moral norm can also be used as a justification of a legal rule deducted from a normative sentence. The division into legal positivism and legal naturalism appears useless as the interpretation process itself is not subject to such strict limitations. Primary

[23] Jeremy Waldron, *Law and Disagreement*, Oxford: Clarendon Press, 2004, p. 85.

limits are defined by the normative text and the systematic context of the interpreted object.

We have already suggested that it is difficult to agree on a definitive content of a moral norm. Similarly, a legal rule in itself does not represent any content. Neil MacCormick goes as far as to suggest that "...law claims nothing."[24] It is only through values that can be acquired, for example, from moral norms that a legal rule acquires its regulatory potential. It is only through values that law can arrive at a correct content through interpretation. Doubtless, some values that can also be embedded in the principles of democracy are generally shared in a democratic society, however, it is still not necessary to precisely define their contents. If a society opts for a certain understanding of a moral norm, it can also have an impact on a legal rule. Its content can change and although the changes involved will often be very small, they can still have an impact on the final form of law. As society changes,[25] the images of law can also change without its basis undergoing alterations. That is why when exploring law, it is necessary to look into the above mentioned purposes that determine its form and also apply values that fill neutral legal tools with a specific content.

Admittedly, at the level of constitutional law there is a clash between legal rules and moral norms - or at least this is what Robert Alexy argues: "The norm N is authoritatively issued and socially efficacious but not law, for it violates fundamental principles."[26] These cases, however, occur at times of major turning points, fundamental changes that go hand in hand with historical turning points. It is unthinkable that they would have an impact on everyday legal practice. It does not make good sense to deny the legal validity of legal rules at this level, in fact this could lead to the negation of the principle of legal certainty or other purpose that law serves. It is much more appropriate to deal with this imbalance with the help of an adequate

---

[24] Neil MacCormick, "Why Law Makes No Claims," in: George Pavlakos (ed.), *Law, Rights and Discourse. The Legal Philosophy of Robert Alexy*, Portland: Hart Publishing, 2007, p. 59.

[25] Miloš Večeřa, "Diversita a jednota práva" [Diversity and Unity of Law], in: *Dny práva – 2008 – Days of Law*, Brno: Masarykova univerzita, 2008, pp. 1329–1341.

[26] R. Alexy, *Arguments from Injustice*, op. cit., p. 22.

interpretation at individual level. It is possible to embed the interpretation with the individual moral norms of the interpreting subject. The interpreting subject is responsible for the societal coherence of these individual norms, transparency and approximative objectivity.

> We might say in this connection that there are as many forms of morals as there are different callings, and since, in theory, each individual carries on only one calling, the result is that these different forms of morals apply to entirely different groups of individuals.[27]

In their externalization subjective moral norms verge on societal understanding. I just reiterate that not even in this case is it necessary to precisely define the content of moral norms. It cannot be determined by authoritative power, rather its power stems from interpretive communities[28] that guarantee the relative stability and conformity of such an interpretation. It is very close to Durkheim's social determination of moral norms.

> From the very definition just made, it follows that the essential rules of these morals are those determining the relation of individuals to this sovereign authority, to whose control they are subject.[29]

4. Recognition

Hence in order to distinguish legal and moral rules as well as specific democratic principles, it is essential to understand how these are recognized by a community - a community consisting of people dealing with law. What distinguishes legal rules from moral norms is above all that they are recognized as such. Each of these normative elements can be grouped under "law" or "morals" depending on the wishes of the community that applies and interprets a given norm. This brings us back to the consolidated discussion on the nature and

---

[27] É. Durkheim, *Professional Ethic and Civic Morals*, op. cit., p. 5.

[28] Sanford V. Levinson, "Law as Literature," *Texas Law Review* 1982, vol. 60, no. 3, pp. 373–403, here at 383.

[29] É. Durkheim, *Professional Ethic and Civic Morals*, op. cit., p. 47.

content of rules, a discussion that is reflected in the everyday practice of application. In a similar vein Jeremy Waldron describes a

> ... noisy scenario in which men and women of high spirit argue passionately and vociferously about what rights we have, what justice requires, and what the common good amounts to, motivated in their disagreement not by what's in it for them but by a desire to get it right.[30]

In this case it is not necessary to understand recognition as a source of legitimacy of moral norms or legal rules but rather as a necessary pre-requisite of their creation and functioning. Let us understand legitimacy as the subsequent process that assesses the quality of the given norms rather than their existence as such. If we want to have a legitimate rule, it is first and foremost necessary that the rule (whether a moral norm or a legal rule) actually exists. Such recognition is determined not only by the standpoint of legal theory but also that of legal practice. Both standpoints then again intersect in following the above mentioned interpretive communities.[31] This is particularly characteristic of moral norms. Although we assume that they are relative and individual, in the legal system we only encounter those that pass the appropriate tests of the highest subjects that apply them (e.g. the High Court, the Constitutional Court but also the Parliament which is naturally not an organ involved in application, that is tests of "marginal organs" – "Grenzorgans" as described by Alfred Verdross[32]).

> Someone has to have the "last word" on substantive disputes about the content of law; and courts are usually granted that responsibility.[33]

In practice, however, these are really only the organs that occupy the highest ranks of the hierarchy. Their approach becomes established as a recognized source of moral norms. Although these subjects cannot

---

30 J. Waldron, *Law and Disagreement*, op. cit., p. 305.

31 S.V. Levinson, "Law as Literature," op. cit.

32 Alfred Verdross, „Die naturrechtliche Basis der Rechtsgeltung," in: Norbert Hoerster (ed.), *Recht und Moral. Texte zur Rechtsphilosophie*, Ditzingen: Reclam, 1986, pp. 42–46.

33 K.E. Himma, "Final Authority to Bind with Moral Mistakes...," op. cit., p. 3.

act as true sources of moral norms, subjects that apply law respect their approach almost literally. It is not only the already discussed myth of rules that plays a role in this respect but also the pragmatic nature of application and interpretation of law. In this these highest organs not only fulfil their unifying role in decision making practice but also necessarily objectify the nature of institutes (moral and legal norms) whose objectification is always only approximative. This is another reason why we can assume that the nature of legal rules and moral principles continues to be not only arbitrary but also mythical. Hence it does not matter whether we adhere to the separation or to the connection thesis as it is only through the recognition of subjects involved in the application that the above mentioned rules acquire content as well as a nature and a role in the legal system. Whether one way or another, it is impossible for these organs to avoid defining the content of moral rules - unless they refer solely to their mythical presence - as such a definition is expected from them in some cases by the legal system itself but in every case by the public.

The case of democratic principles is somewhat different. It is impossible to claim that their nature is different - in the sense discussed above. Their overarching teleological nature - i.e. the tendency to support democracy or its constitution - lends them their own content. This uncovers their possible conditioning in terms of content but only until the moment when we discover that the concept of democracy is also subject to such a process of recognition. Only thus is the content of the concept of democracy acquired and subsequently also the content of democratic principles. Until then they only involve empty concepts that can, however, have a certain potential for legitimation. We can deal with them within pre-recognized and pre-defined operations, we can place them within anticipated contexts. In all this it is not always necessary to know their content. However, when dealing with a concrete situation, it is necessary to define such content and this should be in line with the whole normative system and should fulfil all the criteria that a given community demands.

Barbara Weber
University of Regensburg, Germany

Between Rationality (Habermas) and Sympathy (Rorty): two Pragmatic Perspectives on Human Rights

Abstract: Although it may seem paradoxical to recognize and respect cultural and ethnical differences while simultaneously guaranteeing equal treatment, this ranks among the most crucial challenges currently facing pluralistic democracies. It results in multiple problems, such as the struggle for recognition of cultural minorities or the actualization of universal human rights.
Jürgen Habermas and Richard Rorty find two seemingly contradicting answers to that question: while the first praises communicative rationality, the latter relies on the power of sympathy. This article explores the pragmatic foundations of both theories and unfolds the consequences for a cultivation of Human Rights. Which will lead to an even more fundamental question: Are rational dialogues with other cultures a requirement for the cultivation of sympathy for their needs or is the reverse true, i.e. that sympathy is the precondition to enter such a rational dialogue in the first place.

Keywords: Communicative Rationality, Facticity and Value, Human Rights, Sympathy, Culture of Human Rights, American Pragmatism

1. Introduction

Today's news, whether in England, Egypt or China, shows that in the course of globalization and with the need for transnational political action, the call for interculturally recognized human rights is becoming ever more urgent. In this fight for the universality of such rights, two discourse modes of global value formation stand in exemplary opposition: Jürgen Habermas's "unforced" discourse based on communicative rationality, and Richard Rorty's "culture of human rights," which relies on sympathy. In this context it has been proclaimed as a problem that rationality and sympathy are often seen as two competing approaches to global value formation and public education.

The "inclusion of the other (the stranger)" plays an essential role here for both approaches, which even Habermas's communicative rationality cannot bypass, insofar as it wishes to engage with the postmodern's critique of reason. For only if communicative rationality withstands the tension between plurality and universality can the discursively won, i.e. the rational, recognition of human rights provide the common ground for solidarity in a post-national society. Communicative reason draws its disruptive force in part from its direct connection with action, which it owes to the two basic phenomenological concepts of intersubjectivity and *lifeworld*.

Rorty on the other hand sees the physical and emotional similarities among humans as the preliminary basis for cultivating human rights: that is to say, I acknowledge the other as a person with feelings like myself. Not rational agreement constitutes solidarity, but only the common striving to avoid cruelty and humiliation. The idea of sympathy thus moves to the center of political affairs because it alone sensitizes us to the presence of an ethical conflict situation.

In its content, this article intends to show that both Habermas and Rorty agree that cultures generate context-specific truths.[1] As the locus of such truths, the public sphere serves as the communal lifeworld shared by language users. As to differences we will show that Habermas draws transculturally valid premises from communicative rationality, whereas Rorty posits "rationality" itself as culture-specific and contingent, and thus proclaims as an alternative a widespread sympathy as culture-transcending element.

In the first section I will contrast the two opposing concepts of human rights in order to then analyze the epistemological premises on which these concepts are based. In conclusion I will show how communicative rationality (Habermas) and sympathy (Rorty) should be understood as not really contradictory but rather complementary theories.

---

[1] See Detlev Horster, *Richard Rorty zur Einführung*, Hamburg: Junius Verlag, 1991, p. 52.

2. Jürgen Habermas: Towards a Cultivation of Human Rights through Communicative Rationality

2.1. Facticity and Value

Habermas takes as his starting point the foundation of human rights in natural law, which states that human rights are based in an inborn and inalienable human dignity.[2] The question, however, is to what extent such a subordination to morality can be seen as a global basis for legitimizing human rights, especially since Habermas surmises here a metaphysical leftover from the foundation of human rights. From this he derives the more fundamental question of how social integration can be achieved in a secularized society, or in other words, how the tension between facticity and value can be reconciled. For in the uniformly structured and consensual lifeworld the tension between facticity and value recedes into the background and disappears in the pale light of the prepredicative, that is, in everyday action's forgotten basis in meaning.

Only with the appearance of the secularized constitutional state do facticity and value move further and further apart. This especially affects the political level: here processes of capitalist modernization encounter the still indivisible unity of facticity and value in more traditional societies. Cultures aware of tradition must confront global validity claims and are thus exposed by necessity to a reflective outside perspective. Such problematics of globalization are fundamentally aggravated by the intensification of worldwide social relations.[3]

Due to this separation, for the first time the question arises, to what extent is that which "is" also recognized as valid, or in other words, whether the social order is also legitimate. Such a process of growing awareness results from the communicative "liquefaction"[4] of

[2] Jürgen Habermas, *Faktizität und Geltung. Beiträge zur Diskurstheorie des Rechts und des demokratischen Rechtsstaat*, Frankfurt am Main: Suhrkamp Verlag, 1994, p. 112.

[3] On this theme cf.: Ulrich Beck, *Was ist Globalisierung? Irrtümer des Globalismus – Antworten auf Globalisierung*, Frankfurt am Main: Suhrkamp Verlag, 1997.

[4] With "liquefaction" Habermas means the increasing linguistic awareness and reflectivity in areas of the cultural lifeworld (*Lebenswelt*).

traditions and life forms as it has progressed in tandem with the secularization, demystification and pluralization of societies. Whereas in traditional societies the right originates in divine authority, in modern societies the question arises how the normative order can be upheld without meta-social guarantees. At this point Habermas introduces the concept of right or justice. It functions as a prism[5] by ensuring the social integration of facticity and value. But here, too, both sides must be integrated: both, the social-factual value as well as the legitimacy or validity of the law. For only through their legitimacy do norms of the right find their factually to be expected acceptance. For Habermas such a socially integrative power is only given insofar as those addressed by the law are also its authors.[6] As a further condition Habermas notes that rights must be derived from intersubjectively recognized normative claims to validity. He calls for the same principle in the application of human rights, which for him are fundamental rights. These must on the one hand be factually secured and on the other hand require transcultural legitimacy or recognition. With this they are in direct correlation with the democratic constitutional state, because only through autonomous legislation do they become positive human *rights*. This means, however, that Habermas requires a compelling (i.e. cross-culturally legalized) character for human rights, although through their universal validity they manifest a feature of moral rights.[7]

2.2. The Coherence between the Constitutional State and Democracy

We see from what has been said so far that due to the splitting apart of facticity and value the law can no longer draw its legitimacy from a higher moral right. Instead laws are only legitimized through the autonomous agreement of the citizens.

---

[5] See Rainer Forst, „Kommentar zu Faktizität und Geltung," in: Manfred Brocker (ed.), *Geschichte des politischen Denkens. Ein Handbuch*, Frankfurt am Main: Suhrkamp Verlag, 2007, p. 759 f.

[6] Here Habermas is of course taking up on Kant's concept of autonomy.

[7] See J. Habermas, *Faktizität und Geltung*, op. cit., p. 135 ff., among others.

> This is why we should not see fundamental rights that take the positive form of constitutional norms as mere representations of moral laws, nor political autonomy only as a mere reflection of moral autonomy.[8]

To the question of the legitimacy of positive law in secular societies Habermas now gives a double response: the interdependence of popular sovereignty and human rights in the modern construct of democracy and constitutional state.

Popular sovereignty designates in principle a democratic process guaranteeing the legitimate positing of rights; that is, it includes rights of communication and participation to secure the public autonomy of citizens. By contrast classical human rights aim to protect the realm of private action or the individual's private sphere from state intrusion. This means that popular sovereignty secures public autonomy, while human rights secure the private autonomy of citizens.[9]

In political philosophy, however, there has traditionally been a certain tension between public and private autonomy. In republicanism precedence is given to public autonomy and thereby to popular sovereignty as opposed to liberalism, which warns against the dangers of such majority resolutions. Thus in order to protect life and private freedom, liberalism stipulates fundamental rights (in the sense of human rights), to which the popular will is subordinated. These constitute legitimate limitations that protect the subject's inviolable autonomous space against the encroachment of the sovereign popular will. In republicanism, on the other hand, human rights draw their legitimacy solely from sovereign self-determination.[10] Habermas is not satisfied with either of these solutions and asks instead:

> Which basic rights must free and equal citizens concede to one another if they wish to legitimately regulate their communal lives together by means of positive law?[11]

---

[8] Ibidem, p. 138.

[9] Regarding this problematization see Jürgen Habermas, *Die postnationale Konstellation. Politische Essays*, Frankfurt am Main: Suhrkamp Verlag, 1998, p. 173 ff.

[10] Regarding this comparison see ibidem, p. 174.

[11] Ibidem, p. 175 and J. Habermas, *Faktizität und Geltung*, op. cit., p. 109.

This question follows from Habermas's fundamental idea that only those principles may claim legitimacy to which participants agree in rational discussion. Such discourses must guarantee the inclusion of all arguments and achieve a balance between the different interests. With the help of discourse ethics, Habermas has described in detail how such a process should look. But for now it is important that Habermas wants to institutionalize in the law a rational process of decision-making that ensures legitimacy by means of corresponding communication forms. From this follows an internal connection between human rights and popular sovereignty, because "Rights that make the practice of human rights and popular sovereignty possible … cannot be imposed as limits from without."[12] Naturally such argumentation is only obvious for the area of communication and participatory rights. Here Habermas concedes only an "intrinsic" and not an "instrumental" value to civil liberties,[13] that is, the status of "Rechtsgenossen" (members of the rights community): Without classical civil liberties the possibility would not exist to demand subjective rights, "there would be no legal institutionalization of those conditions under which citizens are able to participate in the practice of self-determination."[14] That is, private and public autonomy alternately take precedence, since the internal connection of democracy and the constitutional state lies in the fact that citizens can only make appropriate use of their public autonomy if they are sufficiently independent due to an evenly guaranteed private autonomy; but that at the same time they can only enjoy an even-handed private autonomy if they as citizens make appropriate use of their political autonomy.[15] Especially in the "Western-motivated" argument for universally applicable human rights such a reciprocal genesis of civil and political rights is of central importance.

The interconnection between popular sovereignty and human rights then affects in turn the place given to human rights in the context of the constitutional state and democracy. Kant considered the

[12] J. Habermas, *Die postnationale Konstellation*, op. cit., p. 176.

[13] Ibidem, p. 176.

[14] Ibidem, p. 176.

[15] See ibidem, p. 177.

bounds of state sovereignty to be insurmountable, and so he envisioned the cosmopolitan union as a federation of states and not as one of world citizens. However, in such a federation human rights can only be morally "prescribed," but not legally enforced. However, since for Habermas human *rights* can only actualize their democratizing power as positive rights, above all in view of accelerating globalization, he argues, unlike Kant, for universal civil rights. Such jurisprudence, of course, makes determinations over the heads of the collective national subjects and speaks for the direct membership of individual subjects in the association of free and equal world citizens.[16] In a footnote Habermas explains this claim and says:

> Formation of an analogy between state sovereignty recognized by the law of nations and the freedom guaranteed as a basic right to natural legal persons misapprehends not only the fundamental place value of individual subjective rights and the individualistic tailoring of modern legal orders, but also the specifically juridical meaning of human rights as subjective rights of citizens in a cosmopolitan order.[17]

3. Richard Rorty: Towards a Cultivation of Human Rights through Sympathy

3.1. Who or what is a Human?

For Rorty three basic questions arise in his examination of the classical human rights debate. (a) Who is actually recognized as a person? (problem of dehumanization); (b) Do rational arguments really influence moral action? (skepticism about rationality); (c) Is the insistence of Western culture on exclusive and static moral knowledge not more likely to lead to a rejection of human rights culture in other countries than to its implementation? (problem of cultural colonialism).

[16] See Jürgen Habermas, *Die Einbeziehung des Anderen,* Frankfurt am Main: Suhrkamp Verlag, 1996, p. 211.

[17] Ibidem, p. 209.

As an anti-essentialist and neopragmatist, Rorty tries to reformulate the central problems and questions so that they either disappear or can be corrected by concrete instructions for action. For him, unlike for Habermas, it is not a question of whether something is true or false, rational or irrational but rather, of whether a change in perspective helps us to better deal with a problem or minimize suffering. And because Rorty is convinced that the idea of reason harms more than it helps, he tries to free the concept of human rights from its metaphysical baggage.

For this purpose Rorty distinguishes first between three stigmatizations, on the basis of which historically and also more recently others have been stripped of their human dignity: (a) by classification as human animals, as for example the Jews in the eyes of the Nazis; (b) by categorization as ignorant or primitive, as in the cases of women or blacks; and (c) through simple linguistic erasure, as in the case of women, excluded by the predominant usage of masculine forms.

From this Rorty concludes that cultural identity is often mobilized through the principle of exclusion, that is, by defining what a group member is not: not black, but white; not a woman, but a man; no longer a child, but an adult; not a believer, but an atheist, and so on. In this way people can distinguish themselves from other "rudimentary, perverted, or deformed examples of humanity".[18]

On the other hand, the countervailing effort to discover a universal characteristic defining what is human can be seen as the endeavor to overcome cultural exclusions. For instance the distinction between humans and animals is supposed to provide people from different cultures with a reason to develop an identity transcending all cultural differences. Furthermore, the use of such argumentation is supposed to establish why only human beings are entitled to specific rights, but also why such rights pertain to all humans who have this distinctively human attribute: "Respect for this ingredient provides a reason for people to be nice to each other."[19]

---

[18] Jürgen Habermas, *Wahrheit und Rechtfertigung. Philosophische Aufsätze*, Frankfurt am Main: Suhrkamp Verlag, 1999, p. 258 (English as T&F).

[19] Ibidem, p. 244 (T&F, p. 169).

3.2. The Substitution of Sympathy for Reason

Rorty himself might agree completely with the intention of such a project, and thus also with Habermas, only he raises fundamental doubts about the effectiveness of such anthropological and rational-optimistic attempts at legitimation.

> [I]t is not clear why 'respect for human dignity,' – our sense that the differences between Serb and Muslim ..., male and female should not matter – must presuppose the existence of any such attribute.[20]

But if rationality cannot contribute to the cultivation of a universal human dignity, then what is the appropriate role of this concept in relation to the problematics of human rights?

For Rorty rationality never exists in the singular. Wherever it shows itself as practical reason, it is based solely on contingent cultural facts. However, such a view should not be equated with cultural relativism or irrationalism.

> [O]ne need not be irrationalist in the sense of ceasing to make one's web of belief as coherent, and as perspicuously structured, as possible.[21]

And so Rorty goes on to ask what actually influences the moral behavior of the man on the street: the categorical imperative or sentimental narratives about people? He concludes that rationality can be seen neither as an element that transcends cultures and ensures knowledge nor as one that binds people together. For this reason it is replaced on the political level by the idea of sympathy.[22]

But how can sentimentality bridge cultural differences? Must we not then assume, given all the differences, that the world of feeling would also have similar incompatibilities? Rorty counters:

> ... [P]rogress consists in an increasing ability to see the similarities between ourselves and people very unlike us as outweighing the differ-

[20] Ibidem, p. 246 (T&F, p. 171).
[21] Ibidem, p. 246 (T&F, p. 171).
[22] Richard Rorty, *Philosophy and Social Hope*, London 1999, p. 81.

> ences. ... (These) are such little superficial similarities as cherishing our parents and our children - similarities that do not distinguish us in any interesting way from nonhuman animals.[23]

Although this thought may at first sound hopelessly idealistic, Rorty himself acknowledges that such a "sentimental education" is only fruitful when it happens in societies and places where one has the means and leisure to sit down and listen to others.[24] Behind such a demand is the insight that what rapists and Nazi thugs lack is not moral knowledge, but rather security and sympathy. That is, one needs conditions that are secure enough that the difference of others no longer seems a threat to one's self respect and sense of worth.

For here it is not a matter of moral duty - which for Rorty is a sign of immaturity - but rather of whether we can open our hearts, thus extending our sympathy to an ever wider circle of people whose customs and beliefs are alien to ours and who are thus experienced as threats to our own cultural identity.

4. Habermas and Rorty in Dialogue about Truth, Justification and Solidarity

4.1. Transatlantic Convergences between Phenomenology and the Philosophy of Language

But what is actually concealed behind Rorty's determined critique of rationality, and to what extent do Habermas and Rorty really differ? This question arises especially because their philosophical roots (pragmatism) and their intentions (cultivation of human rights through a communicative community) at first may appear very similar. To clarify these questions a brief discussion follows regarding the epistemic premises of both trains of thought so that we may then look into the complex interrelationships of rationality and sympathy.

The anti-essentialist Rorty views truth completely in terms of usefulness, "that which it is best for us to believe." With this statement he

---

[23] WuF, p. 261, T&F, p. 181.

[24] Cf. WuF, p. 260.

simultaneously ushers in neo-pragmatism and dispenses with the distinction between doing and finding, constructing and discovering. Thus the conceptual difference between "true as rationally acceptable in a given context of justification" and the decontextualized statement "true as rationally acceptable" is neither argumentatively nor pragmatically tenable. Habermas - with a side glance at Peirce - warns against such leveling:

> If "truth" is explained in terms of rational acceptability, and if the cautionary use of the truth-predicate reminds us of the fact that what is "justified" by our best available standards might still not be "true," we must not assimilate truth to rational acceptability. We have to build some reservation into the notion of rational acceptability if we want to bridge the gap, but we must not blur the line between "-is true" and "-is justifiably held to be true."[25]

Thus Habermas continues to hold fast to the statement that "what is true is what can be rationally accepted under ideal circumstances."[26] Many have objected to this: some criticize that truth is thus too far removed, others criticize that it is not clearly delineated against what is justifiably held to be true. In response to Rorty's contextually motivated objections, Habermas cautions that in ideal speech situations we not only operate from the basis of our own cultures, but begin from the procedural justification practices actually found in all cultures, which can thus be regarded as transcending culture. An example would be the illocutionary intention: that people who enter into a discussion in order to learn or discover something can only be persuaded by the unforced force of the better argument.[27] In fact, communicative actors always already assume that an interpretation found in this manner is not only valid for 'our' context, but true in all possible contexts. Were that not so they would not even enter into such a discourse. Of course this does not also mean that "p" is actually

---

[25] Jürgen Habermas, "Coping with Contingencies - The Return of Historicism," in: Józef Niżnik and John. T. Sanders (eds.), *Debating the State of Philosophy: Habermas, Rorty, and Kołakowski*, Praeger Publishers, 1996, p. 21.

[26] J. Habermas, *Wahrheit und Rechtfertigung* , op. cit., p. 256.

[27] See ibidem, p. 258 f.

true, since in fact it is not possible to achieve a direct grasp of things that transcend language. In addition, the anticipation of future objections remains beyond us, because for humans time represents a factual limitation of the ontological kind. This unavoidable provinciality of the limited mind requires us to be satisfied with the rational acceptability of statements.[28]

This discussion already makes clear that Habermas and Rorty develop their arguments before fundamentally different backgrounds in the history of philosophy. Habermas's argumentation is rooted in a phenomenologically inspired pre-reflective lifeworld, whereas Rorty's arguments can be traced back to a language-philosophical holism.

As a result Habermas responds to Rorty's critique of the connection between truth and justification with his "Janus-faced" truth concept, in which he tries to connect both sides - absolute truth and pre-reflective certainty in action - by means of rational discourse. That is to say, one end of the vertical dimension remains anchored in the lifeworld context of action. The other end, through the horizontal dimension of discourse, should again be aimed toward "absolute truth". Parallel to this, beliefs validate themselves differently (a) on the level of action than b. in discourse. In the first case a. they remain pre-reflective and unproblematical, but prove themselves in an action's success; in the second (b) they are problematized and validate themselves through the more convincing argument.

> Of course the question of the internal connection between validation and truth poses itself only on this reflective level; but only the interaction between actions and discourses allows an answer.[29]

It is only the combination of success in action (vertical dimension) and rationally conscious justification in dialogue (horizontal dimension) that allows for an adequate orientation toward an absolute truth.

An allusion to this combination of action and discourse (world and language) is only found in Rory in contact with the world by means of certain "pressure points." In this contact it is solely a matter

---

[28] See ibidem, p. 260.

[29] Ibidem, p. 263.

of the "most adaptive coping" with the world. On the surface then there is a certain proximity between Habermas and Rorty, since both are concerned with augmenting the subject-object relationship in conversation and thus with the solidary constitution of a communal living space. The results of such conversation are validated in successful action. However, the role of discourse differs: for Habermas discourse serves to remediate a context of action that has become problematic. The goal is social re-integration. For Rorty, on the other hand, discourse seems to be primary, because it is here that dreams, hopes and fantasies for the future find expression. They validate themselves finally in an adequate coping with the world.

This is of interest because it brings to the fore the respective preferences of Habermas and Rorty: for Habermas the physical-human anchoring in the social context of action, for Rorty the linguistic (re-)construction of reality. With Habermas one aims for the truth concept from a limited human perspective. With Rorty, on the other hand, absolute truth is so far removed from the human sphere that it no longer has any relation to it at all - as a kind of truth concept with no point of view that would have to be equally valid for quarks and for space aliens, gods, giants, and so on. Thus, Rorty carries the epistemization of the truth concept to its logical conclusion and distances it to the point that it indeed appears "useless" or "irrelevant" for our society. After all, the concept of truth is only meaningful if there is a point of view, just as an answer derives its epistemic value from the question asked.[30]

Habermas's truth concept on the other hand tries to embrace both extremes - an absolute abstract truth concept on the one hand which always transcends justification, and another concept of truth in action that is always already operatively effective and proves itself in the success of an action.[31] Thus there is a kind of symmetrical relationship in the vertical dimension between the pre-reflective action context

[30] I'm thinking here of the following episode in *Hitchhikers Guide to the Galaxy*: a computer calculates over many millenia the answer to all questions and arrives at the number "49." It remains meaningless, of course; that is, it tells us nothing because the concretization of the question is missing.

[31] See J. Habermas, *Wahrheit und Rechtfertigung*, op. cit., p. 264.

and absolute truth. The absolute truth influences the physical-factual givenness of the context, and conversely, in our active dealings with the world we experience something of the being-as-it-is of things. An attempt is made to repair the reflective problematization of different interpretations of the action context on the horizontal level and in rational discourse, and this in turn has concrete effects on our action strategies. An intuition of absolute truth is only indirectly possible through rational justification in discourse, which remains, however, anchored in concrete action.

> The value claimed for propositions and norms transcends space and time, but the claim is always made in the here and now, in specific contexts, and accepted or rejected with factual consequences for action.[32]

These three fixed points - action (before language), justification (language), and absolute truth[33] (beyond language) - make it possible to judge when the conversational community has approached or distanced itself from the truth. They thus legitimate adherence to the connection between truth and justification.

Rorty on the other hand stands by his language-transcendent truth concept. For him - following Peirce - beliefs are "habits of action." "A rational discourse is just one more action-context in which a behavioral certainty evinces itself."[34] That is, not even the certainty of action - for Habermas pre-linguistic - is able to approximate the language-transcendent truth concept. Everything - rationality as well as action - remains liquefied in language. As a result he is unpersuaded by the anchoring of the discourse situation in a pre-reflective action context. One can just as well change one's opinion in a rational discourse as in the failed attempt to accomplish something through action. There is no need to differentiate. Thus there neither is nor

---

[32] Jürgen Habermas, *Nachmetaphysisches Denken. Philosophische Aufsätze*, Frankfurt am Main: Suhrkamp Verlag, 1988, p. 79.

[33] I speak here of "absolute truth" (lat. *absolutus* means detached or disconnected) to clarify the claim in Rorty that this truth concept has to be valid beyond all relationships.

[34] Richard Rorty, in: Robert B. Brandom (ed.), *Rorty and his Critics*, Oxford: Blackwell, 2000, p. 57.

needs to be any feat of translation which a Janus-faced truth concept would need to accomplish.[35]

4.2. Political Realist versus Idealist Dreamer?

These epistemic "wrestling matches" have corresponding effects on the different conceptions of political action:

Habermas, despite his insight that in the final analysis absolute truth cannot be attained through discourse, holds fast to the connection between truth and justification. His argument is based on the pragmatic assumption that the concept of absolute truth is indispensable for the functioning of rational discourses - which in fact have a stabilizing function in societies today.

Rorty's language-philosophical holistic interpretation of the public sphere separates the horizontal dimension of discursive reality construction from the vertical poles of, on the one hand, a transcendental-normative reference point and, on the other hand, the unproblematically presumed foundation in a lifeworld. From this follows - independent of the vertical plane - an openness for reality constructions in language. Everything (linguistically) imaginable is possible in principle. The socio-political possibilities and consequences of such contextualism are sounded out in the concepts "fantasy," "hope," and "sympathy." On a political level, then, Habermas can be better described as a political realist, Rorty, on the other hand, as an idealist dreamer.

Also of interest is the fact that a change in perspective is central to both concepts and leads to a chiasma between the poles of rationality and sympathy that can be described as follows: for Habermas the comprehensive acceptance of a new perspective is only necessary on the level of moral-justice-theory, since moral theories, when they follow a cognitivistic beginning, must be agreed to by all possible affected parties in order to be both legal and legitimate. By contrast ethical-existential questions - especially in pluralistic societies - are so struc-

[35] Ibidem.

tured that no single answer can be found for everyone. In response to "an ethical-existential question ... which concerns the identity of certain people or of a particular cultural group … an answer, however reasonable, will only have relative value for the goal of a, or our, good or not misspent life, and will not be able to claim any generally binding legitimacy."[36] And he continues:

> (E)thical questions of self-understanding are oriented around the goal of my, or our, good life, or better yet: not misspent life. … The answers must for this reason relate to the context of a particular life perspective held to be valid by particular persons or particular collectives, that is, they must be answered in such a way that they seem valid to everyone – not only to those directly concerned, from whose perspective the question was posed. … But in relation to a given context; ethical questions can be rationally answered, that is, in such a way that they are clear to everyone – not at all only to those directly affected, from whose perspective the question was asked.[37]

But that means conversely that only theoretical questions of moral justice call for generally binding and universally valid answers. The role of philosophy is now to distinguish whether in a certain circumstance one is dealing with an ethical, moral-theoretical or pragmatic question. The latter does not allow for consensus, but at most for compromise. Correspondingly it is necessary to decide whether moral discourses, self-defining discourses or negotiations are appropriate. The determination of maxims has the function – in the sense of Kant – of helping to minimize the number of decisions required in daily practice.[38]

Naturally objections were raised from many sides that discourse ethics would attend only to rights, not needs. But Habermas responds that his discourse ethics are intersubjectively constructed, that is to say, at stake is the public and communal acceptance of a perspective. Such an adoption of perspective forces each person to examine

---

[36] Jürgen Habermas, „Interview mit T. Hviid Nielsen," in: idem, *Die nachholende Revolution*, Frankfurt am Main: Suhrkamp, 1990, p. 126.

[37] See ibidem, p. 141.

[38] See ibidem.

whether an adjustment also does justice to other understandings of the world and oneself.

> Justice and solidarity are the two sides of the same coin ... Only when the continued existence of the communicative community is secured, which requires of all a selflessly empathetic achievement with the ideal adoption of roles, can those conditions of reciprocal recognition reproduce themselves, without which each individual's identity would also of necessity disintegrate.[39]

Rorty's separation of a private and a public sphere can be seen as parallel (though in no way identical) to this distinction between ethical and moral questions. The private sphere accommodates questions of personal identity and life projects. As in Habermas, such private decisions claim no general validity. Yet for Rorty the private sphere is also the site of intellectual "expansion," or in other words, the acquisition of foreign vocabulary and the experimentation with different worldviews. A change in perspective takes place in the private realm on a relatively abstract level. Here philosophy plays the role of helper because it opens up for us different worldviews. The ironist knows, however, that worldviews relate idiosyncratically to each other.

In the public sphere the goal is minimizing cruelty through sympathy. Here a change in perspective occurs solely on an emotional plane. And so here it is no longer philosophy, but rather literature that plays the role of helper so that we can feel our way emotionally into other life worlds. A liberal, empathetic attitude, however, has no normative obligation to fall back on, but relies only on moral motivation or recommendations and role models.

Naturally the boundaries between private and public and ethical and moral do not run parallel. Here it essentially revolves around the methodical question about the role philosophy or literature takes on in order to cultivate such a change in perspective. From this follow the various nuanced understandings of perspective change between the poles of rationality and sympathy.

---

[39] Ibidem, p. 121 f.

5. Rationality and Sympathy between Incompatibility and Complementarity

Following his differentiated epistemological critique, Rorty declares that what results from free discussion is "true" and "good." As a thoroughgoing liberal he sees the establishment of political freedom as the first priority. The "true" and the "good," on the other hand, will take care of themselves.[40]

> Going all the way with Habermas's project of replacing a subject-centered conception of reason with a communicative conception would, it seems to me, leave us without any need or use for the notion of universal validity. For it would let one think of rational inquiry as having no higher goal than solving the transitory problems of the day.[41]

Rorty has reservations about Habermas's approach because he recognizes in it only "the almost correct" philosophical position, but finds that Habermas does not take the final step (the separation from epistemology).[42] But then since Habermas's concept of communicative reason is irrevocably rooted in the pre-reflective context of action, this last step is conceptually unavailable. Rorty on the other hand consistently follows the political consequences resulting from his epistemological critique. That is, he decouples the horizontal-intersubjective dimension completely from the vertical truth-oriented dimension. It follows from this that there is no other truth aside from the one we intersubjectively agree upon. This public-discursive level is "regulated" by two ideas: fantasy and sympathy. For Rorty fantasy and openness to a "better" future are largely independent of an immediate action context. He does not see (or does not want to see) why, from a language-philosophical perspective, rootedness in an action context

---

[40] Richard Rorty, *Contingency, Irony and Solidarity*, New York: Cambridge University Press, 1989, p. 144 f. See also: Richard Rorty, in: Eduardo Mendieta, *Take Care of Freedom and Truth Will Take Care of Itself.* Interviews with Richard Rorty, Stanford: Stanford University Press, 2006.

[41] Richard Rorty, *Philosophy as Cultural Politics*, Cambridge: Cambridge University Press, 2007, p. 78.

[42] See ibidem, p. 78.

is necessary at all. Thus new ideas have more space in the public realm than they do for Habermas: for fantasy is supposed to guarantee that - in accordance with the Darwinian principle of the most rapid adaptation - we welcome change and experiment with its uses. Accordingly Rorty finds it positive that also for Habermas rational discourse is open to future objections,[43] but at the same time he criticizes Habermas's underestimation of the role of fantasy.

A further finding in Rorty's criticism of philosophy is that the search for truth, or the striving for rationality, is not only futile from an epistemological point of view, but even does harm on the political level because it disrupts the direct relationships among people in order to re-orient them toward something outside the sphere of mortal human activity. Should people nonetheless come to agree through rational discourse about certain human rights, the danger would remain that these rights would only be applied if sanctions could be expected for ignoring them. The much more fundamental problem for Rorty lies in recognizing people as humans (persons capable of suffering), and not on the rational level, but on the emotional one. Here his idea of sympathy bears fruit, representing for him the prerequisite for such public discourses concerning a "better" future. In the sphere of cultivating human rights he even sees it as a "substitute" for their juridical establishment. For as soon as I recognize the other as a person, which for Rorty means a feeling being, I will listen to her, share her suffering, and try to minimize this suffering - regardless of what kind of suffering it may be. Here one starts from the assumption that every person is fundamentally capable of sympathy for every other being, but that such sympathy needs to be cultivated.

Finally the cultivation of human rights is seen as a "liberal" attitude that tries to prevent the specific sufferings of the individual while at the same time allowing for the greatest possible freedom for one's own self-realization. For Rorty the intention to engage discursively with others and plan common future projects follows only from such a fundamental position. Rorty also knows that such a discourse

---

[43] "Your arguments fulfill all our current norms and standards, and nothing occurs to me that I could object to in your thesis, but nevertheless it could be that your statement is not true" (Habermas in the words of Rorty, T&P, p. 89).

can further strengthen solidarity, not as the beginning, but rather as the result of such cultivation: for only the antecedent cultivation of sympathy guarantees that humans everywhere and always recognize and try to avoid suffering. Thus for Rorty sentimental education is primary, while the (also rational) discourse about a better future is secondary. Only when this common ground of mutual sympathy has been secured will human rights be adhered to, even in situations beyond the reach of state sanctions.

With Habermas the argument runs in the other direction. On a philosophical level he continues to hold fast to the connection between justification and truth. Thus for him discourse is primary because he actualizes the problematized truth claims of the communicative actors. Or to put it another way, we must first agree on "what is" (interpretation of reality) before we speak about how we should act (manipulation of reality). The establishment of an intersubjectively shared interpretation of the lifeworld is thus for him the prerequisite for the cultivation of solidarity. And so he tries to replace the "merely wished for" solidarity in communitaristic theories with a content-based rational identification. Such a discourse principle should thus lead to an interconnection between human rights and popular sovereignty, as well as between the parliamentary state and democracy.[44] For only insofar as we are, at the same time, both authors and addressees of the laws is adherence to such laws guaranteed. And therefore rational discourse precedes both the cultivation of human rights and social solidarity. On the empirical level Habermas of course admits that sympathy is necessary in order to even recognize a moral conflict situation, which also means – in relation to human rights – to recognize the humanity of the other and thus grant him these rights. On an international level Habermas finds sympathy alone insufficient because only the establishment of human rights with legal sanctions can guarantee their universal implementation.

The debate between Habermas and Rorty is to some extent analogous to the question of the "chicken or the egg": Habermas and Rorty don't agree whether we must first agree in dialogue in order to culti-

[44] See J. Habermas, *Die Einbeziehung des Anderen*, op. cit., p. 192 f.

vate sympathy for each other, or whether we must first cultivate sympathy in order to engage the other in dialogue.

A harmonization of the two approaches might lie in recognizing communicative rationality and sympathy as two extremes on a continuum at whose center is an alteration of perspective, or in other words, the intelligible role assumption for communicative rationality and an empathetic approach to sympathy. To attempt such a solution, however, would be the task of a project going beyond the scope of this article.

Sebastian Sykuna & Jerzy Zajadło
University of Gdańsk, Poland

Towards a New Theory of Hard Cases

Abstract: In the modern theory and philosophy of law the concept of so called hard cases is often associated with Ronald Dworkin's integral philosophy of law. Authors of the study argue that it should be assumed that this is may be too narrow meaning of the discussed concept as it is limited to the process of application of law and, as a result, also to its interpretation. They claim that hard cases may also refer to other "dimensions" of the phenomenon of law - its creating, application and observing. Moreover, they renounce the absolute acceptance of the need of reasoning in direct connection with applicable law, as it limits the concept of hard case. Thirdly, authors recognize that hard cases occur where there is a clash of law with other normative systems, as well as the conflict of law with itself.

Keywords: Hard cases; Hart; Dworkin; legal reasoning; conflict of law; morality; Teubner

In the modern theory and philosophy of law the concept of so called hard cases is often associated with Anglo-Saxon culture of law, and especially with Ronald Dworkin's integral philosophy of law,[1] which is not a surprising fact. The problem of hard cases is directly proportional to the role played in the system of law by organs applying law, especially by courts. It certainly does not mean that hard

[1] Marek Zirk-Sadowski discussing two most prominent Dworkin's works, *Taking Rights Seriously* and *Law's Empire*, writes: "In *Taking Rights Seriously* the aim of Dworkin's discussion was to demonstrate the way of defining limits of law in so called hard cases *Law's Empire* was dedicated to reconstruction of mechanisms of application of such defined law" - Marek Zirk-Sadowski, "Wprowadzenie" [Introduction], in: Ronald Dworkin, *Imperium prawa* [Law's Empire], transl. by Jan Winczorek, Warszawa: Oficyna Wolters Kluwer Polska, 2006, p. XIV.

cases can be found exclusively in common law model and they are absolutely alien to continental law culture. In authors' opinion, it should be assumed that this is may be too narrow meaning of the discussed concept as it is limited to the process of application of law and, as a result, also to its interpretation. In Polish literature invoking Dworkin's works the following definition can be found:

> Hard case in its most general presentation occurs when a judge does not have at his disposal an explicit norm made by certain authority, but also cases involving decision-making problems resulting from the lack of consent among lawyers.[2]

Accepting the above-mentioned narrow meaning of the discussed concept, it may be considered correct when it is used to talk about especially complex and at the same time appalling for public opinion issues. The most evident may be proceedings in cases of genocide - Stephen Landsman titled his book devoted to the Nuremberg Trials and well-known cases of Adolf Eichmann, John Demianiuk and Imre Finta in a very distinctive way: *Crimes of the Holocaust: The Law Confronts Hard Cases*.[3] Not always the cases must be so spectacular. Daniel E. Lee discusses in this context the question of state's interference into freedom of individuals in such cases as e.g. the issue of obligatory wearing helmets by motorcyclists, euthanasia supported by a doctor, taking marihuana, abortion or parents' refusal concerning medical

---

[2] Bartosz Wojciechowski, "Rozstrzyganie tzw. trudnych przypadków poprzez odwołanie się do odpowiedzialności moralnej" [Adjudication of hard cases through appeal to the moral responsibility], *Studia Prawno-Ekonomiczne* 2004, vol. LXX, p. 11; see also Sebastian Sykuna, Jerzy Zajadło, "'Sprawy konstytucyjne' w integralnej filozofii prawa Ronalda Dworkina" [Constitutional cases in Ronald Dworkin's integral philosophy of law], *Gdańskie Studia Prawnicze* 2004, vol. XII, p. 288 f., and Sebastian Sykuna, "Trudne przypadki" [Hard cases], in: Jerzy Zajadło (ed.), *Leksykon współczesnej teorii i filozofii prawa* [Lexicon of the contemporary theory and philosophy of law], Warszawa: Wydawnictwo C.H. Beck, 2007, pp. 339–340.

[3] Stephan Landsman, *Crimes of the Holocaust: The Law Confronts Hard Cases*, Philadelphia: Pennsylvania University Press, 2005; there are also publications defining in general the issue of prosecuting perpetrators of massive violations of human rights as hard cases, especially in the context of so called universal jurisdiction - see e.g. International Council on Human Rights, *Hard cases: bringing human rights violators to justice abroad*, Versoix (Switzerland) 1999.

treatment of a child.[4] Some authors use the notion 'hard cases' in relation to complicated constitutional issues[5] and complex problems arising in regimes violating human rights and solved later during transition periods with the use of so called transitional justice.[6] The latter seem to be especially interesting as they are connected with the fundamental question concerning limits and possibilities of applying instruments of law (especially of criminal law) in the process of critical review of the past and taking history to court.[7]

A distinction between hard and soft case has been recently made in literature in English language by B.H. Bix. In his opinion, the difference may be considered in three aspects: degree, time and certainty of consensus which may be (or may not be) achieved by well-educated and sensible lawyers in a specific case.[8] Hard cases understood in this way appear in various mutations also in other authors' concepts, who differ not only in understanding their essence but, above all, in the suggested ways of solving them by court applying law and making its interpretation.

For the sake of clarity, it has to be said that originally hard cases, although not literally named as such, appeared in John Austin's positivism and later in its sophisticated version suggested by Hart, whereas Dworkin's concept constituted elaborate criticism of such understood positivism in general, and Hart's concept in particular. Not discussing similar understanding of the essence of the issue, there is no doubt that using the notion of *hard cases* is commonly associated with the name of Dworkin,[9] although Hart in afterword to his basic

---

[4] Daniel E. Lee, *Freedom vs. Intervention: Six Tough Cases: Six Hard Cases*, Lanham: Rowman&Littlefield Publishers, 2005.

[5] See e.g. Lisa A. Kloppenberg, *Playing It Safe: How the Supreme Court Sidesteps Hard Cases and Stunts the Development of Law*, New York: New York University Press, 2002.

[6] See e.g. David Dyzenhaus, *Hard Cases in Wicked Legal Systems: South African Law in the Perspective of Legal Philosophy*, Clarendon Press, 1991; more on this subject: Ruti G. Teitel, *Transitional Justice*, Oxford – New York: Oxford University Press, 2002.

[7] More on this subject in Polish literature: see Jerzy Zajadło, *Odpowiedzialność za Mur. Procesy strzelców przy Murze Berlińskim* [Responsibility for the Wall. The trial of Berlin-Wall shooters], Gdańsk: Wydawnictwo Arche, 2003.

[8] Brian H. Bix, *A Dictionary of Legal Theory*, Oxford: Oxford University Press, 2004, p. 81 f.

[9] As e.g. Raymond Wacks, *Philosophy of Law. A Very Short Introduction*, Oxford: Oxford University Press, 2006, p. 42 f.

work *The Concept of Law* also uses similar expressions.[10] In 1975 Dworkin in pages of Harvard Law Review published an extensive essay entitled: *Hard Cases*.[11] What is characteristic, the work was a changed version of the inaugural lecture given by the author in 1971 while taking the chair in jurisprudence in Oxford after Hart. Both authors differed substantially in their approach to solving the problem of hard cases and to the outcome of the solution.

According to Hart, who believed that system of law consists exclusively of rules, solving hard cases required going beyond the system thanks to, so called, open texture notions. On the grounds of positivism it created certain difficulty connected with potential law-making character of court decision. Abandoning the model of simple subsumption and breaking off the direct relationship between the rule and the settlement causes that

> ... the confidential way and going beyond the system of law is all that a judge has at his disposal. ... Hart tries to circumvent difficulties connected with the position acknowledging court decision made in hard case as a law-making decision. From the point of view of positivism, it is an unacceptable solution. In that case Hart suggests that such decision should be recognized as being within the frame of standard of correct (i.e. in conformity with law) court decision. The standard is outlined by the scope of meaning of the rule containing open texture notions. Going beyond this scope means, according to Hart, going beyond the standard of correctness.[12]

The most elaborate concepts of hard cases were suggested by Ronald Dworkin, who works on completely different assumption.[13] In his opinion, in the system of law there are not only rules but also principles and policies. Unlikely to Hart's approach, a judge who,

---

[10] See Polish edition of Herbert L.A. Hart, *Pojęcie prawa* [The Concept of Law], transl. by Jan Woleński, Warszawa: Wydawnictwo Naukowe PWN, 1998, p. 364 f.

[11] Ronald Dworkin, "Hard Cases," *Harvard Law Review* 1975, vol. 88, pp. 1057–1109.

[12] Małgorzata Król, "Koncepcje trudnych przypadków a prawomocność" [The conceptions of hard cases and legal validity], in: *Teoria prawa. Filozofia prawa. Współczesne prawo i prawoznawstwo* [Theory of law. Philosophy of law. Contemporary law and jurisprudence], Toruń: Wydawnictwo UMK, 1998, p. 99.

[13] More on his concept – Ronald Dworkin, *Taking Rights Seriously*, Cambridge, Mass.: Harvard University Press, 1977.

deciding a case, does not have an explicit regulation in the sense of a rule at his disposal, does not have to go beyond the system of law. On the contrary, he is obliged to search for a solution within the system, on the grounds of principles and/or policies. In accordance with assumptions of positivism, a judge making a ruling on a hard case is obliged to apply legal rules. In this way, he is within frames He cannot go beyond. As a result, he is searching for an optimal solution not in general, but optimal in particular circumstances. According to Dworkin, basing on the grounds of integral philosophy of law, it is inadequate, or even incorrect. Legal rule may turn out to be insufficient for making a right decision - right, using Gustav Radbruch's rhetoric, from a point of view of justice, appropriateness or legal safety. While Hart in such situation granted a judge an authority to make a "free" decision, integral philosophy suggests staying within the system of law and demands referring to legal rules. Dworkin believes that court ruling in hard cases should not mean creating new legal rules *ad infinitum,* the system of law should be searched for "latent" standards which are in the form of principles and policies.

A certain paradox may be noticed here: a positivist Hart searches for solution of hard cases on the grounds extralegal norms, while non-positivist Dworkin - on the grounds of rules and guidelines which are the immanent part of the system of law.

Assuming that the phenomenon of law covers five "dimensions" i.e. creating, applying, interpretation, binding and respecting, the issue of hard cases, on the grounds of philosophy and theory of law, from traditional perspective is present exclusively in the process of applying of law and connected with it its interpretation.

In Polish theory of law the concept of hard cases elaborated in the 80s of the last century by J. Wróblewski deserves particular attention. What is important, also this author restricts his analysis of hard and soft cases only to court- type law application. Noticing fluidity of distinction between hard and soft cases, Wróblewski suggested concentrating on four points of view, which he called: institutional, substantive, institutional-factual and theoretical.[14] First of them consisted in

[14] Kazimierz Opałek, Jerzy Wróblewski, *Prawo. Metodologia, filozofia, teoria prawa* [Law. Methodology, philosophy, theory of law], Warszawa: Wydawnictwo Naukowe PWN, 1991, pp. 273–284.

taking into consideration regulations of procedural law "in procedural model of court law application." Therefore, it could be assumed that taking institutional division of jurisdiction into account, only cases examined by the Supreme Court, as the most important organ of judicial power adjudicating legal disputes, could be recognized as hard cases.[15] The above-mentioned position of the Supreme Court Wróblewski connected both with its institutional importance, in many cases as a kind of final instance, and its competences. As an example of the latter, Wróblewski acknowledged for instance the competence of issuing resolutions concerning legal questions addressed to the High Court, thanks to which doubts emerging in the process of examining cases in lower courts were removed.[16]

Institutional distinction did not have to coincide with substantive criterion. Wróblewski clearly emphasized that taking substantive content of a case into consideration, the High Court also deals with soft cases. When then would it be hard case, distinguished on the basis of factual criterion? In Wróblewski's opinion, the analysis of court records concerning specific case being actually examined would be necessary. From the substantive point of view, only cases in which "divergence in positions of participants in the process or in opinions of court instances expressed in divergent or differently justified decisions is stated"[17] may be recognized as hard cases.

Combining the two criteria above, J. Wróblewski distinguished also the third, institutional-substantive point of view. It was the consequence of the above-mentioned, right claim that not all cases reaching the High Court must be recognized as hard cases considering the substantive criterion. The third point of view allows to treat a certain case as a hard case only when, on the one hand, it is the subject of interest for the High Court and, on the other, it is complex because of divergent decisions of various court instances.[18]

The last criterion of distinction of hard case is the theoretical point of view. As Wróblewski wrote in his work, it is based on "the analysis

[15] Ibidem, p. 274.

[16] Jerzy Wróblewski, "Stosowanie prawa przez Sąd Najwyższy" [Application of law by the Supreme Court], *Nowe Prawo* 1985, no. 5, p. 25.

[17] K. Opałek, J. Wróblewski, op. cit., pp. 274–275.

[18] Ibidem, p. 275.

of part-decisions and final court decision concerning application of law in which crucial issues affecting right justification reasoning are stated."[19] In court model of application of law final decision is justified by several part-decisions. From the theoretical point of view, a case should be recognized as hard case when, beside issues of factual character there is a dispute concerning the relationship between those considered to be proven facts related to the examined case and particular legal rule.[20]

In theory of legal arguments the narrow meaning of hard cases can be found. In Polish literature on the subject, J. Stelmach states that hard cases are the essential element of practical argumentative discourse in general, and legal discourse as its variation in particular. Practical discourse is pointless when it concerns simple, not controversial, explicit cases, not raising doubts:

> We start a discourse only when it concerns a so called hard case, i.e. a case which cannot be adjudicated applying standard methods of interpretation - only theoretical discourse. It was just because of examining such cases that the whole modern theory and philosophy of legal argument developed.[21]

However, just as in Hart's and Dworkin's works, the theory of legal argument uses the category of hard cases exclusively on the grounds of application of law and its interpretation. A legal discourse conducted in the right way should be tightly connected with applicable law:

> If the legal dispute were not in direct relation with applicable law (yet such possibility exists), it would simply be an ethical dispute. Legal discourse, to be legitimate and effective, must therefore have a dogmatic

---

[19] Ibidem.

[20] M. Król, op. cit., p. 107.

[21] Jerzy Stelmach, *Kodeks argumentacyjny dla prawników* [Argumentation code for lawyers], Kraków: Kantor Wydawniczy Zakamycze, 2003, p. 38; and more also see idem, *Współczesna filozofia interpretacji prawniczej* [Contemporary philosophy of legal interpretation], Kraków: Wydawnictwo UJ, 1999; and Jerzy Stelmach, Bartosz Brożek, *Metody prawnicze*, Kraków: Wolters Kluwer Polska, 2006 (English version - *Methods of legal reasoning*, New York: Springer Verlag, 2005).

> character. ... The starting point for legal argument is to determine law applicable in controversial case. Any preliminary findings, made mostly still within the frames of theoretical discourse enabling us to establish factual and legal condition of the case in question, are then findings *de lege lata*. Practical legal discourse transfers us to the sphere of findings *de lege ferenda*, or the postulated law. ... In simple cases findings based on theoretical discourse are enough, and their settlements are essentially of algorithmic (repetitive) character. Entering into practical discourse, we begin to "seek the law", somehow automatically, moving onto the plane of findings *de lege ferenda* which, of course, must always be in "direct connection" (i.e. must be consistent) with applicable law, even when they lead to a precedential decision.[22]

On the grounds of the theory of legal interpretation, another, very important difference in Dworkin's and Hart's concepts is raised. According to Dworkin, there is only one right answer in hard cases,[23] which exemplary judge Hercules should give referring to the principles and guidelines that are the part of law. If this were indeed then: firstly, practical discourse would not be needed and it could be limited to theoretical discourse; and secondly, in fact it would not be considered a hard case but the simple case. So it is exactly the opposite - the essence of a hard case consists in the fact that in the process of argumentative discourse several settlements, which may be justified on the grounds of accepted criteria of rationality and correctness, can be reached. Then, and only then, additional criteria enabling the choice of one settlement, may complement the discourse.[24]

Both Dworkin[25] and theoreticians of legal argument[26] quote a case settled by the Court of Appeal in New York in the late 19th century - *Riggs v. Palmer* (verdict of 8 December 1889) as a classic example of

---

22 Also there, pp. 59–61.

23 Ronald Dworkin, "Is There Really No Right Answer in Hard Cases?" in: idem, *A Matter of Principle*, 9. edition, Cambridge, Mass. - London: Harvard University Press, 2000, pp. 119–145.

24 J. Stelmach, op. cit., p. 15 f. and 20 f.

25 R. Dworkin, *Taking Rights...*, op. cit., passim.

26 J. Stelmach, B. Brożek, op. cit., p. 87 f.; in Polish literature this example, after Dworkin, is referred to also by e.g. Lech Morawski in *Główne problemy współczesnej filozofii prawa. Prawo w toku przemian* [Main problems of the contemporary philosophy of law. Law in the course of change], 3. edition, Warszawa: LexisNexis, 2003, p. 307.

hard case. The case consisted in a problem of answering the question if a murderer could inherit from his victim. Dworkin describes the case in the following way:

> In 1889 a New York court, in the famous case of *Riggs v. Palmer*, had to decide whether an heir named in the will of his grandfather could inherit under that will, even though he had murdered his grandfather to do so. The court began its reasoning with this admission: "It is quite true that statutes regulating the making, proof and effect of wills, and the devolution of property, if literally construed, and if their force and effect can in no way and under no circumstances be controlled or modified, give this property to the murderer." But the court continued to note that "all laws as well as all contracts may be controlled in their operation and effect by general, fundamental maxims of the common law. No one shall be permitted to profit by his own fraud, or to take advantage of his own wrong, or to found any claim upon his own iniquity, or to acquire property by his own crime." The murderer did not receive his inheritance.[27]

According to Dworkin this is a classic example of hard case, where the rules of law do not allow achieving a satisfactory verdict. However, we do not have to look for solutions outside the legal system, on the contrary - the rule *ex iniuria ius non oritur* which allows us to refuse Elmer Palmer the right to inherit from his grandfather, Francis Palmer, despite the content of the will of the latter, may be applied in this case. In other words, "the legal rule that 'nobody can benefit from the evil he had committed' produces an exception to the legal rule according to which Elmer was to inherit from his grandfather."[28] However, it must be added that the verdict was not unanimous. Judge J. Gray enclosed distinct opinion which argued that the case should be decided on the basis of the applicable rules of law which did not exclude Elmer Palmer from inheritance. As a murderer, he had already suffered legal consequences of his criminal act and there is no legal basis to punish him also within the frames of law of succession. Clearly expressed will of the deceased should be crucial. Negative reviews cannot be anticipated as we actually do not know if

[27] R. Dworkin, *Taking Rights...*, op. cit., p. 23.
[28] J. Stelmach, B. Brożek, op. cit., p. 88.

Francis Palmer would disinherit his grandson knowing that he would be his murderer. The possibility that deep feelings towards his grandson and family ties would prevail can not be excluded.

The case would not be treated as hard on the grounds of modern civil law. There is, for example, the following regulation in the Polish Civil Code:

> **Art. 928.** § 1. Successor may be found by the court unworthy, if:
> 1) intentionally committed a crime against the devisor;
> 2) with the use of deceit or threat urged the devisor to draw up or cancel a will or in the same way prevented him from performing any of these operations;
> 3) intentionally concealed or destroyed the will of the devisor, forged or transformed his will, or consciously benefited from the will forged or transformed by a third person.
> § 2. Successor unworthy is excluded from inheritance as if unable to attend the opening of the will.

J. Stelmach and B. Brożek make a detailed logic analysis of *Riggs v. Palmer* case and point out certain practical danger resulting from the verdict of the New York court:

> The rules may "produce" exceptions to the rules in specific cases, and the number of such exceptions is theoretically unpredictable. Thus, a full formalization of any rule of law can never be given as there is always a possibility that in an unforeseen situation a kind of rule would "produce" an exception.[29]

It seems however, that this is the very essence of hard cases.

In English literature, N. MacCormick expressed his criticism concerning R. Dworkin's concept.[30] First of all, it is noteworthy that in his opinion hard cases concern all disputes during court proceedings. Furthermore, according to MacCormick, they also cover both factual and legal issues. The main objection addressed by MacCormick towards Dworkin concerned the fact that the latter, on the grounds of positivism, limited hard cases exclusively to lawmaking situation.

---

[29] Ibidem, p. 89.

[30] Quoted after M. Król, op. cit., p. 103.

MacCormick, referring to the idea of W.D. Ross's "duties *prima facie*", builds definition of hard cases on "rights *prima facie*", and understands them as potential rights of a party in court proceedings. Their potentiality is seen in the fact that only after the conflict between principles and values is settled, specified subjects are granted these rights. In the Polish literature MacCormick's concepts were introduced by M. Król, who stresses that it is the idea of rights and duties *prima facie* that is the basis for defining by MacCormick the concept of hard cases as situations in which "each party has grounds on which they demand their rights of at least right *prima facie* character."[31]

Distinguishing between simple and hard cases MacCormick sees the main difference in justification of court decisions. While in a simple case reasoning of the decision of the body applying law is based on straightforward deduction of clear legal rules, in a hard case, before the deduction, interpretation of those legal rules or sometimes even consideration of other issues is required, which in consequence entails the need of justification of the second level.[32]

Describing the issue of hard cases M. Król also refers to suggestions of A. Peczenik according to whom the concept of hard cases is a developed theory of jumps.[33] Originating from the idea of transformation of law, A. Peczenik considered the role of judge who, in his opinion transforms established sources of law into interpreted "applicable law." This transformation is based on the above-mentioned jumps - not-deductional steps of reasoning.[34] The frames of this article do not allow us to analyse the whole concept of jumps by A. Peczenik.[35] It is noteworthy however, that they were the hard cases which for Peczenik accounted for the reasons of jumps leading to the transformation of law. As it can be guessed, Peczenik referring to

---

[31] Ibidem, p. 104.

[32] Neil MacCormick, *Legal Reasoning and Legal Theory*, Oxford: Oxford University Press, 1978, chapter VIII, p. 198; quoted after M. Król, op. cit., p. 103.

[33] M. Król, op. cit., p. 105. As for the details of A. Peczenik's theory of jumps see also the article by the same author published in 1996 in *Artificial Intelligence and Law* 1996, vol. 4, no. 3–4, pp. 297–329 under the distinctive title "Jumps and Logic in Law. What Can One Expect from Logical Models of Legal Argumentation?"

[34] Ibidem, p. 105.

[35] See also Aleksander Peczenik, *On Law and Reason*, Kluwer Academic Publishers, Dord-recht/Boston/London 1989, pp. 114–118 and 130–131.

judge reasoning analyzed the essence of hard cases exclusively on the grounds of application of law where in the process of reasoning their decisions judges apply this technique of jumps. In fact, we can talk about a hard case when it is not enough to rely only on sources of law while reasoning decision. As M. Król wrote, hard cases for Peczenik "are solved basing on compromise between axiological legal premises and judges' own axiological options."[36]

The above comments were aimed at: firstly, confirming the existence of the phenomenon of hard cases; secondly, determining its conception on the grounds of modern theory and philosophy of law, especially the philosophy of legal reasoning. So we are dealing with a well-established paradigm, from which this article is exception. For its needs we adopt much broader and a little different conception of the essence of both hard cases and scope of practical application of legal discourse. Our goal is to present several examples which are not necessarily within the above definition of hard cases which does not mean that they are not of such character on the basis of conventional assumptions given below.

Firstly, we believe that hard cases occur not only in the process of applying law and associated with it interpretation, but they may also refer to other "dimensions" of the phenomenon of law - its creating, application and observing. In this sense, a factor deciding if the case is hard or easy is recognized the possibility of many various solutions which may be justified in the course of practical legal dispute on the basis of accepted criteria of rationality and fairness. Hard case in this sense is not only domain of the judge seeking solution in a specific case when clear rule of law is not available for him. Similar problems can encounter on the one hand a legislator deciding whether to regulate or to refrain from regulating specific social relations, and on the other for instance, a citizen appealing to the institution of civil disobedience or abstaining from it. It does not change the fact that indeed hard cases concern mainly in judicial practice in the process of application of law and/or its interpretation. It also concerns the sphere of law application, for instance, when a court faces an extremely rare and at the same time highly dramatic choice arising from confronta-

[36] Ibidem, p. 106.

tion between rules *dura lex sed lex* and *lex iniustissima non est lex.* Recent decades clearly show that the choice is not at all, and contrary to all appearances, purely hypothetical fantasy of philosophers of law. We are not so much interested in a specific decision taken in a hard case but rather in more general problems accompanying reaching the decision.

Secondly, we renounce the absolute acceptance of the above-discussed thesis concerning the need of reasoning in direct connection with applicable law. We believe that it limits the concept of hard case as it refers only to its existence on the grounds of application of law and its interpretation. While we confirm that a direct link with applicable law in the process of legal discourse will often be present but extension of hard cases to, for example, lawmaking process may cause that the link will become not necessary. Sometimes a legislator faces a decision which does not have a direct connection with applicable law as it enters the area of *terra incognita.* At the same time we find that the lack of the necessary character of this connection does not automatically determine that practical discourse cannot be called a legal discourse and it will be shifted to the plane of ethical discourse. The essence of legal discourse, for the purpose of this book, is determined not by necessity of direct connection with applicable law, but legally relevant subject of the discourse within the frames of hard cases, understood in this way.

Thirdly, we recognize that hard cases occur mainly where there is a clash of law with other normative systems. Traditionally, it is stressed that it mainly concerns the relationship between law and morality – according to some authors, this is the area where the concept of hard cases should be applied in a much broader sense than this which is accepted in modern theory and philosophy of law. While, for the needs of this chapter, we confirm that the problem of conflict between legal norms with moral norms is of fundamental importance,[37] at the same time we believe that it is worth to point to

[37] For example, D. Lyons generally combines the problem of hard cases with moral decisions – see *Etyka i rządy prawa* [Ethics and the rule of law], transl. Paweł Maciejko, Warszawa: Dom Wydawniczy ABC, 2000, p. 84 f. In Polish literature hard cases have recently been combined with judicial ethics issues – see Teresa Romer, Magdalena Najda, *Etyka dla sędziów. Rozważania* [Ethics for judges. Deliberations],

other areas in which this contrast may have significant effects - in particular: morality, religion, politics, economics, ecology, legal ethics and scientific and technological progress. In each of them, examples of broadly understood hard cases can be found because we are faced with the necessity of choosing between various, rationally justified and right solutions. So this is always a choice between different values - in this sense, argumentative legal discourse is also axiological discourse. And even more than that, moral dilemmas may arise not only in the clash between law and ethics but also in other areas such as media, medicine, morality, politics, etc.[38] Such hard cases which are within the paradigm determined by Hart - Dworkin dispute should not be ignored. In this case however, it is recognized that the problem does not concern the conflict between law and other normative systems, but paradoxically - the conflict of law with itself and therefore the conflict between law and law. Last but not least, we will have to deal with hard cases whose solution would simply require reference to rules of prudence and so called common sense. As a typical example may be given a fierce dispute in modern science of law concerning the issue of legality and legitimacy of humanitarian intervention. Recently it has been indicated that seemingly insoluble conflict between ethics, politics and law requires perhaps reference to commonsense morality.[39] It is all the more important as the reference to the category of common sense is especially popular in the Anglo-Saxon culture of law which the idea of hard cases originates from. An example of humanitarian intervention treated in categories of a hard case implies different understanding of it (hard case). In a specific sense, it may be said that they occur in situations where there is a discrepancy between legality and legitimacy - moral, political, economic, environmental, religious, etc. The essence and methodology of the dispute ongoing even during the Weimar Republic in German philosophy of

---

Warszawa: Wolters Kluwer Polska, 2007. More on the clash between law and morality see Matthew H. Kramer, *Where Law and Morality Meet*, Oxford: Oxford University Press, 2004.

[38] See Ovadia Ezra, *Moral Dilemmas in Real Life. Current Issues in Applied Ethics*, Law and Philosophy Library, vol. 74, Dordrecht: Springer Verlag, 2006.

[39] So e.g. Eric A. Heinze, "Commonsense Morality and the Consequentialist Ethics of Humanitarian Intervention," *Journal of Military Ethics* 2005, vol. 4, no. 3, pp. 168–182.

law under the banner of *Legalität und Legitimität*, is still present,[40] although, what may be understood, the notion of hard case was not used then. Moreover, although the dispute concerned the legality and legitimacy of the political-legal order as a whole, it can be transferred also to the area of individual norms of the system.

Assigning actual states considered to be hard cases to certain kinds of conflicts of law with law and with other normative systems and common sense rules is, to some extent, of symbolic character - sometimes it is difficult to precisely isolate problems appearing at the meeting of, for example, morality and social morals, politics and economics, law and legal ethics, science and religion, etc. It also applies to common sense rules which are not in ethical or political void.

In our opinion, several cases where there is a conflict between law and other normative systems or common sense rules, which allow us to talk about hard cases, can be distinguished. First of all, we accept that the conflict within the law itself is possible which implies the need to identify the situation of law versus law. Next we can talk about a conflict between law and morality, social morals, religion, science, medicine, history, politics, media, economics, ecology, legal ethics, common sense and a human. Some of these distinctions as, for instance, law versus morality seem to be obvious and are described in detail in literature. In our opinion however, they also should be briefly reminded of and supplemented with certain exemplifications. In no case, our aim is to give a thorough and exhaustive presentation of a clash between law and other chosen normative system and consequences resulting from it. This assumption only partly is due to the limitations imposed by publishing frames of this chapter. Above all, we believe that reference to brief but explicit examples would be enough to present our broad understanding of hard cases.

Firstly, considering the conflict of law with itself we do not talk about such situations where conflict rules commonly known among lawyers are applied when dealing with apparent and real contradictions in law. From the point of view of above methodological assumptions concerning hard cases we mean a different type of conflicts. It

[40] More on the subject: David Dyzenhaus, *Legality and Legitimacy*, Oxford: Oxford University Press, 1999.

could be seen in already discussed dispute between Dworkin and Hart, and especially in the way dilemmas in *Riggs v. Palmer* were settled. Above all, Gustav Radbruch's concept of the idea of law was the starting point for us. According to this author, as it is commonly known, it consists of three elements: security, usefulness and justice. The problem, however, is that there may be - to use Radbruch's rhetoric - various kinds of antimonies between individual components of the idea of law. It is not always the clash between law and other normative systems (e.g. morality), but sometimes the conflict of law with law within such expressed concept of law. The most dramatic situations occur on the line security-justice. In easy cases a lawyer will seek the solution in favour of security, sometimes at the cost of justice, guided by a little trite slogan *dura lex sed lex.* In hard cases the issue may turn out to be more complicated. Sometimes justice will win; sometimes however in equally rational way we may defend the immanent value of legal security even if the accepted solution will be in conflict with our sense of justice.

Morality is a classic example of other normative system which clashes with law. In our opinion, a conflict of this type is the core of hard cases. The most numerous examples of such situations on the one hand, and the most complicated problems on the other, can be found in this area. Moral-legal dilemmas have the longest tradition and at the same time they are still relevant today. It is enough to say that the classic dispute between the doctrines of law and legal positivism has now adopted the form of controversy between positivism and non-positivism, whose essence is in defining the relationships between law and morality.

In the literature[41] on this subject four potential theoretical approaches are indicated:

1) ethical and legal nihilism recognizing the lack of any relationship between law and morality (e.g. Scandinavian legal realism),

2) ethical and legal reductionism recognizing that although such relationships exist but they are not of necessary character and are not desirable (e.g. H. Kelsen),

[41] Dietmar von der Pfordten, *Rechtsethik,* München: Verlag C.H. Beck, 2001, pp. 99–209.

3) ethical and legal prescriptivisim (normativism) recognizing that such relationships exist and even if they are not of necessary character, they are desirable (e.g. H.L.A. Hart),

4) ethical and legal essentialism recognizing that such relationships not only exist but they are of necessary character (e.g. R. Dworkin).

In our opinion, other classification covering three distinguished kinds of ethical-legal disputes may be mentioned. The first group may include such dilemmas which are relatively new and therefore not yet solved - they are connected on the one hand, with scientific and technical development (e.g. the issue of genetic engineering), and on the other, with the change in morals (e.g. the issue of legalization of partner relationships of persons of the same sex). The second group includes, in turn, well-known and traditional disputes in which actually everything that has to be said, has already been said and which are, to some extent, insoluble due to different starting points of adversaries - such as issues of abortion, euthanasia or capital punishment. And finally, the third group of ethical-legal disputes concerns such issues which were resolved long ago both in the moral and juridical sense and to which therefore we do not want to revert (e.g. the problem of the ban on slavery and servitude, or the ban on torture and cruel, inhuman and humiliating treatment).

Considering the nature of conflict between law and morality certain regularities may be shown. Firstly, it is extremely difficult to distinguish hard cases occurring on the line law-morality from other areas of potential conflicts, e.g. law and history, law and medicine, law and science, law and morals, law and politics, law and religion, etc. Secondly, continuous and incessant civilization progress causes that ethical-legal disputes regarded as settled long ago, unexpectedly and, at times, paradoxically, turn out to be still relevant today. Thirdly finally, even so called insoluble disputes in which theoretically everything has already been said there was to say, are still the subject of ethical-legal discourse.

Writing about the clash between law and other normative systems we intended to indicate the conflict which may occur on the line law-morals. We are aware however, that equally right would be referring to it as to the conflict "Law and Culture." Deliberately and consciously we adopted however the other terminological convention - at the same time we would like to stress that we use the narrow concept of morals and distinguish them, on the one hand, from custom and customary law and from morality, and on the other, from other elements of culture in its broad sense. We consider mainly some groups of norms which, on the one hand, outline the tradition-honoured rules of specific ways of conduct typical for certain social groups and, on the other, enter a very delicate sphere of human sexuality and sex life. In this sense, morals is the element of culture or even the culture *per se*. We realize that the borderline between moral and customary norms is vague and fluid. Using two examples we will try to prove that In this sphere hard cases may occur.

The first example indicates first of all the clash of certain specific cultural norms characteristic for different kinds of minorities (religious, ethnic, national, racial, etc.) with the law binding in a given society as a whole. One of the basic assumptions concerning modern democratic state of law is the principle of equal rights of all citizens. Even if we find it as a dogma, a question arises whether in practice there would not be situations entailing its verification. Should the minority governed by tradition-honoured rules resign from them and totally submit to the standards accepted by majority, or vice versa – should the law take into account, sometimes at the expense of the principle of equal rights of all citizens, these specific cultural norms? The above questions arise spontaneously when we consider the phenomenon characteristic for common law which takes the form of the institution called cultural defence. It is often assumed that it may be used in situations when the body applying law takes (or does not take) into account specific cultural norms characteristic for a certain social group, norms which differ substantially from accepted standards of society as a whole.[42]

The second example concerns the right to interfere in the privacy of individuals in a very delicate sphere of their sex life (of individuals). In this sense, the difference between morals and morality is blurred although we are aware of its existence and importance. Is sexuality really exclusively a private matter of individuals or perhaps,

[42] Jeroen Van Broeck, "Cultural Defence and Culturally Motivated Crimes (Cultural Offences)," *European Journal of Crime, Criminal Law and Criminal Justice* 2001, vol. 9, no. 1, p. 5.

in some situations, it becomes an element of social life? If the answer to the first question is negative and to the second - positive, then where is the borderline whose crossing justifies legislative *fiat* interference? Should we also in this case take into account (and to what extent?) cultural difference of certain minorities, thinking for example about incest, or may be the standard for society as a whole, or even for humankind should be determined? How to create, apply and interpret law to avoid the trap of false alternative - either moral tolerance within pluralistic and multicultural society or moral imperialism or even paternalism of the majority?

Another conflict, in our opinion, involving hard case may arise on the line law - religion. However, understanding the essence of these hard cases may be especially difficult due to modern, but from historical point of view as a matter of fact only apparent, difference in these two areas. Quoting at this point the title of a known work of Romanian historian and philosopher Mircea Eliade, it can be said that religion still remains in the sphere of *sacrum*, while law is in the sphere of *profanum*.

Four very important things however, should be remembered. Firstly, originally law was closely linked with religion, and indeed religion was its source, and our distant ancestors did not distinguish or oppose the sphere of *sacrum* and *profanum*. Secondly, the process of secularization of the state began only a few centuries ago in Europe and against the long history of civilization constitutes merely a territorially limited episode of modernity and post modernity. Thirdly, many of the modern legal institutions kept their peculiar religious origin while even a secular state tries to regulate at least some spheres of *sacrum* applying legal norms as *profanum*. And finally, we tend to judge modern relationship between law and religion exclusively from the perspective of Western world in its broad meaning, often forgetting that the same problem is perceived differently in different cultures. Characteristic exemplification of the conflict arising at the meeting of law and religion may be the famous Socrates trial which was held in the period when *sacrum* and *profanum* were not distinguished. On the other hand however, specific hard cases may occur when there is a conflict between legally guaranteed freedom of art and legally protected religious feelings.

Contrary to all appearances, finding contemporary examples of existence of another type of conflict, i.e. between law and science caused some difficulties. We would have to point to, for example, such cases in which solutions adopted by legislator (*ergo* - also specific court decisions) go "against the current" of scientific progress, and especially when they contradict laws of nature or proven scientific theories. Besides, even if such examples exist they: firstly, concern the past rather than the present; secondly, are never restricted only to science but concern also, and perhaps above all, other areas described in this article, for example, ecology, economics, medicine, morality or religion. The case, once well-known and on which the famous film of 1960, "Inherit the Wind" was based, concerning the ban on teaching Darwin's theory of evolution in schools in some states in the USA could be named a classic exemplification of such situations. In fact, it was a very unfortunate interference of a legislator and judicial authorities in the conflict between science and religion rather than a conflict of law with science. Moreover, it turned out that the problem is not as outdated as it might seem. In 2005 (*sic!*) one of the courts in Pennsylvania was deciding again which theory - of creationism or evolution - should be taught in schools. And interestingly, another film ("Dover") was based on this case.

Not forgetting these objections, and wanting to show the conflict at the meeting of law and science, some problems are worth noting. They may be expressed in the following questions: does the progress in law keep pace with the progress in science and technology?; Is law an effective instrument of balancing the benefits and risks involved in development of science and technology?; how to combine the access to the latest achievements of human mind with the idea of global distributive justice, on the one hand, and protection of copyrights on the other?

The purpose of this study is to present practical aspects of philosophy of law. Therefore, discussion concerning law and medicine is, to some extent, of specific character: on the one hand, very large number of hard cases occur in this sphere, and on the other, - they are extremely complicated. Today, in legal science even specific trend may be isolated in this area which is sometimes referred to as biojurisprudence. Indeed, hardly any sphere can be more spectacular for hard cases than that concerning fundamental problems of human life - beginning from the moment of conception and ending with death. In this sphere we deal with traditional, eternal and, in a sense, insoluble dispute (e.g. abortion or euthanasia). However, new dilemmas and challenges come with the progress in science and technology (such as genetic engineering) - here in turn we are faced with the need of formulating new, not yet known, ethical-legal standards.

It is hard not to notice that hard cases arising at the meeting of law and medicine are often at the same time the dilemmas on the line law-morality. But not only - in this sense the clash between law and medicine is a multifaceted issue and relates also to other spheres where hard cases are possible to be found, such as law and science, law and economics, law and religion, etc. It must be admitted that choosing exemplifications of a discussed conflict we have to talk about a kind of "oversupply." Beside examples referring to traditional and familiar disputes (e.g. abortion or euthanasia), some new and particularly relevant phenomena, such as issues accompanying the institution of surrogate motherhood or the access to medicines for poor people of the world in connection with protection of intellectual property, may be noticed.

Law comes into conflict with history as well. This same conclusion applies to the whole process of reviewing the past after the fall of communist system in Europe. We mean here application of legal instruments for reviewing the past. Although in such cases you might as well talk about the conflict between law and politics, but nevertheless, in our opinion, history, strictly speaking "policy towards the past" (German *Vergangenheitspolitik*) and so called "transitional justice" (or "retrospective justice") comes to the front.

The collapse of communism revealed that the discussed problem is extremely complicated. Policy towards the past carried out in a rational way should aim to achieve five basic objectives: (1) establishing the truth, (2) inflicting punishment, (3) moral condemnation, (4) restitution and redress for injustice, and (5) cultivating memory. It should not be forgotten however, that the problem of so called historic injustice is not restricted only to the faults of communism within one country and has a much broader dimension. Policy towards the past comprises more than only redress for intergeneration damages but also international (*vide* - effects of wars), and sometimes even intercivilisation (*vide* - legacy of colonialism).

Law is not the only and not always the best instrument for carrying out such understood policy towards the past, as in general "taking history to court" requires extraordinary caution and prudence. Polish vetting and decommunization experience proves how complicated and sensitive matter it is. In this sense, the clash between law and history often leads to hard cases in the broadest meaning of the term. Law, as an instrument of reviewing the past, is very helpful and in achieving objectives No. 2 and 4 it is in fact necessary.

Objective No. 2 refers to criminal law and concerns individual responsibility for crimes committed in the past in the lawless state - therefore it is retrospective justice inflicted by the court in a criminal trial. It should be remembered however, that ultimately it is not history, but individual embroiled in it is who is tried in court. The trials of so called shooters at the Berlin Wall (*Mauerschützenprozesse*) may be given as examples of such cases.

In practice, achieving the objective No. 4 is even more complicated. We deal here with another type of retrospective justice - it is corrective justice aimed primarily at restitution in the field of property as a means of compensation for harms inflicted on people in the previous period. It is accomplished by means of, among other things, legal instruments although these are not instruments characteristic for criminal law but rather for administrative and civil law. As a result law clashes here not only with history, and consequently with politics, but very often with economics which is best demonstrated by the re-privatization process in Poland after 1989.

Another, suggested by us type of hard cases concerns the clash between law and politics. In our conviction, this type of situations are the greatest threat to law, and especially to its idea conceived as a harmony between security, relevance and justice. It is mainly caused by the fact that these are the politicians who practice politics on the one hand, and on the other, in representative democracy they ultimately determine the shape and content of legal norms. Inevitably, as a result, it can create two very serious threats - firstly, sometimes short-term and opportunistic, and sometimes even long-term primacy of politics over law; and secondly, instrumentalization of law for the needs of politics. It concerns both the sphere of international and domestic relations. In the first case it may be still not settled issue of humanitarian intervention, and in the other, native to us, case of late submission by the mayor of Warsaw of financial disclosure of his spouse.

Sometimes the dilemmas on the line law-politics are accompanied by complicated moral problems. The outstanding German expert on international law, Michael Bothe, in the context of NATO military intervention in Kosovo stated that "if the clash between law and ethics occurs, something must be wrong either with the law or the ethics." Paraphrasing this statement it may be noted that there is usually nothing wrong with law, moral intuition is also, as a rule, right and this is so called *Realpolitik* which often disappoints us.

It results from a certain historic paradox. In practically all languages in the world, including Polish, such words as "law" and "ethics" have definitely positive semantic connotations. By contrast, the word "politics" has recently undergone some strange, paradoxical and ambivalent changes. For the average modern man, the term has negative associations, although its ancient prototype had strong positive overtones. May be we should return to Aristotelian understanding of politics as actions for the common good (*ergo* - good) of humanity, mankind) and in this way remove the above-mentioned threats to the idea of law posed by improperly understood *Realpolitik*?

A vast majority of conflicts between law and other normative systems which, in our opinion, may be referred to as hard cases are, in a sense, timeless and are not produced in the present. On the contrary, moral, political or religious dilemmas connected with law have a very long history. This issue is slightly different with reference to such areas as economics, ecology or science as even if hard cases may have occurred earlier, their existence and essence was not always realized. Undoubtedly, in comparison with the past, modern civilization provides many more examples of conflicts on the line law-economics, law-ecology or law-science.

In the case of another type of conflict, which occurs at the meeting of law and media, we are faced with a completely different situation because they never played such important role as they do now, and besides, they are, in a sense and to some extent, exclusively the product of modernity and postmodernity. The number and complexity of questions and doubts arising in modern democratic societies on the line law-media is so big that they are very difficult to be discussed in accordance to the convention adopted in this study. Suffice it to say that the spectrum of problems stretches from constitutional law, administrative, civil, commercial, criminal, international, procedural law as far as financial law and it virtually crosses the whole system of democratic state of law.

Without going into details concerning theoretical considerations of the described conflict, the already famous O.J. Simpson's trial is worth mentioning in this place. In our opinion, it demonstrates well that a confrontation between legally guaranteed freedom of the media and other legally protected interests such as legal guarantee to a fair trial, including especially presumption of innocence, may occur.

Representatives of the younger generation of lawyers, particularly in Western Europe, often do not realize that a few decades ago, quite seriously, disputes under a strange slogan: who is more important – a lawyer or an economist? were held. In socialist economy, the problem was politically significant as – to use Karl Marx's terminology – the economy was a part of social basis and law was only a part of ideological superstructure.

Speaking seriously however, it is hard to ignore potential conflicts that may occur between law and economics, especially in free market economy and European integration and in the face of progressing globalization. Today however, no one treats it as a strong disjunction "either-or" and a completely new methodology of discussion in this area of hard cases has been developed. The fact that a new theoretical-legal trend, which is known as so called law and economy analysis, was born may be regarded as a sign of overcoming this type of – in fact, false – dilemmas. The unquestionable advantage of such modern approach is that a lawyer and an economist ceased to compete with each other and saw the possibilities of creative collaboration.

It does not change the fact however, that at least two fundamental questions regarding the conflict between law and economics still remain in force. The first of them concerns the economic factors of legislative *fiat* – should a legislator, taking his decision, take into consideration its economic effects, or can he arbitrarily disregard them? The second, in turn, is a question of limits - on the one hand, of economic determinism, and on the other autonomy of law.

Writing about another "enemy" of law it enters into a conflict with, we encountered a problem similar to the one discussed above while considering the antagonism on the line law-science. In fact it is not so much a direct conflict between law and issues of protection of environment, but rather rationality of settlements of dilemmas arising on the line ecology-economy-science-politics using legal instruments. Therefore, hard cases in this area consist mainly in the need a legislator or the authority applying law is faced with to balance or choose between different, sometimes difficult to be brought together, arguments which are often of non-legal character. At the same time they must remember to take decision which is in accordance with the norms binding in the system of law, and the latter is not always internally consistent and coherent.

A lawyer is accompanied by extremely important ethical dilemmas not only In connection with the clash between law and morality but also on the grounds of professional ethos. Today, virtually every professional corporation within a very broad scope of legal professions has its own code of ethics - not only judges, attorneys, legal advisers, prosecutors, notaries, bailiffs, civil servants or government advisers but even law students and academics. There may be found problems common to all these professional groups but also specific dilemmas connected with not only practicing as a lawyer but also representing certain attitudes and moral views within each of the groups may be indicated. For the sake of accuracy, it should be added that this includes both ethical norms and pragmatic rules of professionalism. In our view, two examples, which seem to be particularly important and spectacular and at the same time are within methodological assumptions of hard cases adopted by us, should be mentioned.

First of them concerns the problems connected with the relatively little-known in Poland ethics of government advisors. Here we enter the sphere of professional ethos in a very special situation when a lawyer is mandatory of a state. This is not a standard lawyer-client relationship because the effects of faulty interpretation or even instrumentalization of law may turn out to be disastrous not just on an individual but on a global scale. The exceptional moral, political, legal and social responsibility which should accompany this particular form of legal "services" must be stressed. The basic dilemma is included in the answer to the following question: Should a government advisor tell his specific client mainly what he expects and what he wants to hear or only what is in accordance with the law? The best exemplification of the subject problem is the controversy around the now famous *Torture Papers.*

The second example is of more standard, not to say classic character and concerns practicing as a lawyer. Also in this case, the degree of moral responsibility is very high although it relates to the plane other than government advisor's activity. The problem which is raised most often is the issue of the limits of admissibility of defence lawyer's activity in a criminal trial. It concerns the standards determined on the one hand by the law, and by the principles of legal ethics on the other. The issue raises a number of questions which only partly may be suggested here. Among these the most important seems to be the question concerning using lies by a lawyer, i.e. can a lawyer himself tell lies, and also can he urge his client to tell lies? Then, should a lawyer as a defence lawyer in a criminal trial be objective? Should it be a defence "at any cost" or there are limits which must not be crossed (exceeded) even by a lawyer in the interest of his client? If and when can he refuse to take the case on? If and under what circumstances should he denounce the previously accepted power of attorney and relinquish the role of defender? As it has been said, it is only a part of difficult questions which may and should be posed by a lawyer acting as a defence lawyer in a criminal trial - being aware that although not all, but certainly some of them are hard cases and require applying the Kant's practical reason.

Initially, when we started to work on this study whose, as it was mentioned, main purpose was to demonstrate practical aspects of philosophy of law, we intended to show only a few classic areas where hard cases occur. They were to concern mainly the relationships of law-law, law-morality, law-morals or law-politics. But as we were writing we started to notice new fields on which law fiercely clashes with other normative systems. This was how two last cases appeared. The assertion that law may enter into a conflict with common sense and the man may be ventured.

In general philosophy the notion of common sense is usually associated with so called Scottish Enlightenment and the name of Thomas Reid, but it must be stressed that it has much longer and rather ambiguous tradition. Suffice it to say that Aristotle was referring to common sense with great respect while Plato on the contrary - with great contempt. By contrast, philosophers of law devoted relatively little attention to the problem and a rise of modern discursive-argumentative trends (e.g. J. Habermas, R. Alexy) may be considered as a breakthrough in this negative tradition. And yet, it cannot be ignored that in the process of application and interpretation of law as a highly formalized existence, the conflict with common sense may sometimes occur. And a typical example of such are rules of evidence in judicial proceeding.[43]

The last case to which we would like to draw the reader's attention, became, in our opinion, a conflict raising the hardest case - namely a widely discussed issue concerning torture. The exceptional difficulty of this case is manifested in four basic aspects; (1) in the science of law in general and in philosophy of law in particular, this is the issue most widely and most fervently discussed nowadays; (2) virtually all mentioned in the beginning dimensions of law - its creation, application, interpretation, binding and compliance with it - are focused in it; (3) it concerns the problem which yesterday was recognized as belonging to non-disputable imponderables; (4) if the law is to serve primarily the highest value - individual's inherent dignity - is put , not without reason, on the line of the debate.

All the above-cited cases lead to the question which, in fact, has been "tormenting" theorists of law for centuries, i.e. what is actually law in its essence? Is it just a tool which in skilled hands of a "social engineer" would solve every, even the most complicated, hard case? Or perhaps a part of the open, and therefore imperfect humanities that is condemned to reality *per fas et nefas*? What actually is the ultimate purpose of law - efficient management of the system, or the good of an individual.

---

43 See Eugene Borgida (ed.), *Beyond Common Sense. Psychological Science in the Courtroom*, Blackwell Publishing, 2007.

So what is the relevance of hard cases: do hard cases create bad law, or perhaps on the contrary – in the fire of practical discourse a good, wise and responsible lawyer is shaped? And what should be the role of practical mind – *ergo* the philosophy of law - in professional life of a lawyer? Where does its role as a medium necessary for every system of law of axiology end, and unnecessary or even dangerous burden hindering the process of application of law and leading sometimes to interpretation *contra legem* begin?

Oliver Wendell Holmes, a famous judge and one of the founders of American legal realism in his opinion enclosed to the U.S. Supreme Court decision on the case *Northern Securities Co v. United* States of 1904, wrote that "great cases like hard cases make bad law". In American jurisprudence the sentence has been so often quoted that it may be regarded as a kind of legal topic. Holmes's statement that hard cases, being the object of our interest, make bad law, had however, certain meaning *hic et nunc* – it was associated with acknowledgement that the essence of common law is that first the judge decides a particular case and only later, on that basis, he tries to determine a principle. Cases which were on the one hand, great and spectacular, and morally and politically complex on the other, made bad law because they were atypical – principles created on their basis referred to extreme situations and went beyond the standards and the needs of current legal procedure. Holmes's statement may also be associated with the danger indicated above by J. Stelmach and B. Brożek – of "overproduction" of exceptions to the rules by regulations.[44]

Today, more and more frequently the Holmes's argument is either recalled in the context of complex ethical, political and legal issues, or subjected to substantial revision.[45] Or perhaps it is just the opposite, perhaps the hard cases make good judges,[46] or even broader – good lawyers? At the end it is only worth stating that hard cases indicate the teaching value of this part of law which is a function of practical mind in Immanuel Kant's meaning. We assume, after D. v. der

---

[44] J. Stelmach, B. Brożek, op. cit., passim.

[45] Frederick Schauer, "Do Cases Make Bad Law?," *The University of Chicago Law Review* 2006, vol. 73, pp. 883–918.

[46] Suzanna Sherry, "Hard Cases Make Good Judges," *Northwestern University Law Review* 2004, vol. 99, no. 3, pp. 3–31.

Pfordten,[47] that philosophy of law in its broad meaning includes on the one hand, theory of law (theoretical analyzing, generalizing and systematizing mind), and on the other, ethics of law (practical critical mind). Therefore, with some simplification, it may be said that theory of law from this perspective analyzes, generalizes and systematizes the law as it is; while ethics of law criticizes it referring to the law as it should be from the point of view of a certain ideal of law. In deciding hard cases, theory of law is no longer sufficient for a lawyer, he must appeal to practical mind, *ergo* - to philosophy of law *sensu largo*. For purposes of this study it is assumed, as in Polish literature by for example M. Zirk-Sadowski, that philosophy of law may be practiced "from philosophy to law" or "from law to philosophy."[48]

A well-known contemporary theorist of law Günther Teubner often refers in his works to the following anecdote:

> An elderly Bedouin sheikh drew up his will. The whole wealth - a huge herd of camels - was divided among three sons. Achmed, the eldest, was to inherit half of it; Ali, the younger was to get a fourth part of it; and the sixth part should be given to the youngest, Benjamin. After the sheikh's death it turned out that there were only eleven camels in the herd. Achmed demanded six camels and it was opposed by his brothers. Unable to reach an agreement the sheikh's sons asked the Caliph. He decided as follows: "I will give you one of my camels. Give it back to me, for Allah sake, as soon as possible." Dividing the herd of twelve camels was not difficult. Achmed got his half, six camels. Ali received his fourth, three camels. Benjamin inherited the sixth part, that was two camels. Happy brothers fed the twelfth camel, which was left after dividing the herd, and gave it back to the Caliph.[49]

For the law and lawyers very different morals may be drawn from this tale. From the point of view of the main subject of this study we

---

[47] Dietmar von der Pfordten, "Was ist und wozu Rechtsphilosophie?" *Juristenzeitung* 2004, no. 4, pp. 157–166.

[48] Marek Zirk-Sadowski, *Wprowadzenie do filozofii prawa* [Introduction to the philosophy of law], Kraków: Kantor Wydawniczy Zakamycze, 2000.

[49] Günther Teubner, "Sprawiedliwość alienująca. O dodatkowej wartości dwunastego wielbłąda," *Ius et Lex* 2002, no. 1, p. 109 f. (English version - "Alienating Justice: On the Surplus Value of the Twelfth Camel," *Ius et Lex* 2005, no. 1).

would like to point out the following: the work of any lawyer, both theorist and practitioner, consists in searching for the twelfth camel. The law in the sense of positive law is often not perfect and we are faced with the need to find a certain "surplus" (*ius*) enabling rational and right decision. Sometimes, when the norm is unambiguous and the facts do not raise doubts, the process of searching for the twelfth camel is relatively easy. In practice, especially where law comes into contact with other normative systems, hard case may be found. From the point of view of the adopted here definition of hard cases, the collision between *lex* and *ius* may occur not only in the process of applying law and its interpretation, but also in relation to its creation, binding and compliance with it. This "Caliph" who lends us the twelfth camel (*ius*) thus enabling decision in legal equation (*lex*) exemplifies a broadly understood idea of law which is expressed in the harmony of three elements: security, usefulness and justice.

Hard cases show that there is an inherent relationship between *ius* and *lex* – *ius* without *lex* appears to be helpless; and in turn *lex* without *ius* is often coldhearted. A little perversely perhaps, because at the end of this article, we would like to pose some questions and in this way ask the reader for a moment of reflection: What exactly is the relationship between law and humanities in its broad sense[50]? What exactly is law: also a part of humane culture, or just a tool of social engineering[51]? Are the problems forming the basis for hard cases only taboo that can be overcome or may be the archetype we do not want to undermine? And finally, do hard cases in fact make bad law or may be vice versa – hard cases make good lawyer? It is difficult to disagree with the opinion of a well-known Australian judge Michael Kirby that "to judge is to learn" and therefore "formalism and purely mechanical approach to performing the function of a judge makes it impossible to perform the real role of a judge."[52]

---

[50] Jack M. Balkin, Sanford Levinson, "Law and Humanities: An Uneasy Relationship," *Yale Journal of Law & Humanities* 2006, vol. 18, pp. 155–187.

[51] David Howarth, "Is Law a Humanity (or is it more like Engineering)?" *Arts & Humanities in Higher Education* 2004, vol. 3, no. 1, pp. 9–28.

[52] Michael Kirby, "To Judge Is to Learn," *Harvard International Law Journal* 2007, vol. 48, p. 36.

Massimo Leone
University of Torino, Italy

Citizens of a Lesser God – Religious Minorities and the Legal Discourse of Multi-Cultural Democracies: the Case of Canada[1]

Abstract: Global migration flows are changing the socio-cultural fabric of European cities. New issues in the management of public and particularly urban space arise. Countries where cultural diversity is a relatively new phenomenon should learn from countries where it is a long-debated issue. Know-how and good policies should be exported and adapted. Canada is one of the most culturally diverse countries in the world. In the last thirty years, the legal and planning system of Canada has sought to adapt to the needs of new ethno-religious communities. Islamic communities in the Great Toronto Area and in other Canadian metropolises have recurrently faced problems in their attempts of 'making Muslim space'. Major contentious areas are parking and traffic standards, planning compatibility, aesthetic impact, and fiscal regulations. The semiotic analysis of legal controversies about the establishment of new minority (and particularly Islamic) places of worship in Canada reveals socio-cultural tensions concerning the sense of belonging of both majority and minorities. The Canadian legal and planning system is not perfect but is still a model of rationality in comparison with the way in which the issue of minority places of worship is hijacked by media and politics in most 'Western' countries.

Keywords: migration; ethno-religious diversity; minority places of worship; urban planning; law; policy making; Canada; Great Toronto Area; semiotics

---

[1] Research for the preparation of the present paper benefited from a Faculty Research Grant of the International Council for Canadian Studies through the Canadian Embassy in Italy. I thank Paul Bouissac and Marcel Danesi at the University of Toronto (Victoria College) for their support and semiotic insights. Some of the contents of the paper were discussed with Sandeep Kumar Agrawal at the School of Urban and. Regional Planning of Ryerson University, Toronto, with Annick Germain at the Institut National de la Recherche Scientifique – Urbanisation, culture et société, Mont-

1. Global socio-cultural changes and management of public space: reasons for a comparison

As new migration flows increasingly diversify the socio-cultural demography of Europe, new minority religious communities are taking shape in European cities. Both new and old minority religious communities are constantly evolving. Their presence and development in the socio-cultural fabric of European cities are bringing about new issues in the management of public space.[2] How can the space of multi-confessional European cities be handled in order to respect the right to religious freedom of all citizens without jeopardizing the general harmony of urban life? Which new theoretical frameworks, empirical investigations, and urban policies are required in order to make sure that all citizens feel that their religious identity (or their lack of religious identity) fits into the socio-cultural fabric of European cities? How can a lasting equilibrium between expressions of particular religious identities and common societal belonging be reached in European legal, planning, and socio-cultural systems?

In order to answer these questions in the last years I have undertaken a comparative study of legal and planning systems concerning religious minorities in old and new multicultural and multi-confessional societies, focusing in particular on Australia, Canada, Europe, and the USA.[3] The hypothesis behind this comparison is that

réal, with Richard Arteau and Dominique Fortier de la Ville de Montréal, with Richard Smith, Stuart Poyntz, and Gary McCarron at the School of Communication of Simon Fraser University, Vancouver, with W. Wesley Pue at the Faculty of Law and Renisa Mawani at the Department of Sociology of the University of British Columbia. A first version of the paper was presented on September 5, 2010 at the 9th International Roundtable for the Semiotics of Law at the University of Poznań, Poland. A second version of it was presented on September 12, 2010 in Sozopol, Bulgaria, at the Doctoral Summer School in Socio-Semiotics of the New Bulgarian University. I thank the abovementioned colleagues and those who attended the first presentations of the paper for their critiques, comments, and suggestions

[2] Massimo Leone, "Legal controversies about the establishment of new places of worship in multicultural cities: a semiogeographic analysis," in: Anne Wagner, and Jan Broekman (eds), *Prospects in Legal Semiotics*, Berlin and New York: Springer Verlag, 2010, pp. 217–237.

[3] Massimo Leone, "Architectures of transcendence – A trans-cultural analysis of legal processes for the construction, modification, and restoration of places of wor-

societies in which an increasing diversity of religious demography is a relatively new phenomenon might learn from both achievements and failures of societies in which, on the contrary, such diversity has long been a constitutive element and has been addressed through various experiments in the elaboration of legal and planning systems, policies, standards, laws, and bylaws.

2. Focus, method, and purposes of the analysis

The present paper is a study of the ways in which religious minorities in Canada, and specifically in the Great Toronto Area, interact with the Canadian society, as well as with its planning, legal, administrative, and bureaucratic systems in order to exert an impact upon the management of public and particularly urban space, mainly through the establishment of new places of worship.[4] The paper fo-

ship," in: *Trans(l)egalité*, proceedings of the Conference of the Law and Literature Association of Australia, Griffith University in Brisbane, 2-5 December 2009, available in CD-Rom; idem, "Sustainable religions in contemporary cities - A semiotic approach," *International Journal of Environmental, Cultural, Economic, and Social Sustainability* 2009, vol. 5, no. 3, pp. 47-59, Melbourne: Common Ground Publisher; Urbana (IL); idem, "Legal controversies about the establishment of new places of worship in multicultural cities: a semiogeographic analysis," op. cit.; idem, "Invisible frontiers in contemporary cities - An ethno-semiotic approach," *The International Journal of Interdisciplinary Social Sciences* 2010, vol. 4, no. 11, pp. 59-74; idem, "Hearing and Belonging – On Sounds, Faiths, and Laws," in: Vijay K. Bhatia, Anne Wagner, Christoph Haffner, and Lindsay Miller (eds), *Perspectives in Legal Communication*, (Law, Language, and Communication Series), Farnham (Surrey): Ashgate, 2012, pp. 183-198; idem, "The reasonable audience of religious hatred: the semiotic ideology of anti-vilification laws in Australia," in: Nadir Hosen, and Richard Mohr (eds), *Law and Religion in Public Life: The Contemporary Debate*, New York and Oxford: Routledge, 2011, pp. 112-134.

4 Literature on this topic is extensive. As specifically regards Canada, on Montréal cf. Annick Germain, and Bernadette Blanc, "La vie de quartier dans le Montréal multiethnique," *Revue européenne de migrations internationales* 1998, vol. 14, no. 1, pp. 141-158, monographic issue on "La ville destabilisée? Faits et representations" (on neighborhood life in multi-ethnic Montréal with several insights on the role of places of worship); Richard Arteau, *Orientations en matière d'encadrement urbanistique des lieux de culte à Montréal - Implantations de plein droit et dérogations*, Montréal: Ville de Montréal, 2000, Service du développement économique et urbain (a sort of how-to guide for urban planners concerning places of worship in Montréal) and idem, "Les

dieux dans la ville - Diversité religieuse et multiplication des lieux de culte à Montréal - Les défis posés à l'aménagement urbain," paper presented at the Forum Urbain - Centre Canadien d'Architecture on March 20, 2000; Julie Elizabeth Gagnon, and Annick Germain, "Espace urbain et religion: esquisse d'une géographie des lieux de culte minoritaires de la région de Montréal," *Cahiers de géographie du Québec* 2002, vol. 46, no. 128, pp. 143-163 (an overview of the geography of minority places of worship in Montréal); Julie Elizabeth Gagnon, "Cohabitation interculturelle, pratique religieuse et espace urbain: quelques réflexions à partir du cas des communautés hassidiques juives d'Outremont/Mile-End," *Les Cahiers du Gres* 2002, vol. 3, no. 1, pp. 39-53 (on the Hassidic community of Outremont/Mile-End); Annick Germain, "Capital social et vie de quartier en contexte multiethnique," paper presented at the symposium "Les possibilités et les défis de la diversité : un rôle pour le capital social" (séance plénière 4: *Le Capital social dans le contexte de l'immigration et de la diversité : Communautés*), Montréal, November 24-25, 2003 (on the heuristic efficacy of the concept of "social capital" to explain socio-cultural dynamics concerning minority places of worship); Annick Germain *et al.*, *Les Pratiques municipales de gestion de la diversité à Montréal*. Montréal: Institut National de la Recherche Scientifique - Urbanisation, culture et société, 2003 (a survey on the management of diversity, including ethno-religious diversity, in the city of Montréal); Annick Germain, and Julie Elizabeth Gagnon, "Minority places of worship and zoning dilemmas in Montréal," *Planning Theory & Practice* 2003, vol. 4, no. 3, pp. 295-318 (English updated version of A. Gagnon and J.E. Germain, op. cit.); Amélie Billette, "Pratiques municipales de gestion de la diversité ethnoreligieuse à Montréal : le cas des piscines publiques," étude exploratoire sous la direction d'Annick Germain, Institut national de la recherche scientifique Urbanisation, Culture et Société, 2005 (on the issue of the multi-confessional management of swimming pools and other sport facilities in Montréal); Julie Elizabeth Gagnon, and Francine Danserau, "'Ethnic' dilemmas?: Religion, diversity, and multicultural planning in Montréal, Canada," *Canadian Ethnic Studies Journal* 2004, vol. 36, no. 2, pp. 51-75; Julie Elizabeth Gagnon, "L'Aménagement des lieux de culte minoritaires dans la région montréalaise : transactions sociales et enjeux urbains," thèse de doctorat en Études Urbaines, Institut National de la Recherche Scientifique à Montréal - Urbanisation, Culture et Société, under the direction of Annick Germain, soutenue le 24 mars 2005 (with a rich biblio-graphy at pp. 291-314); several interesting articles on the topic are also in the collection Bernard Jouve, and Julie Elizabeth Gagnon (eds), *Les Métropoles et la question de la diversité culturelle : nouveaux enjeux, nouveaux défis*, Grenoble: Presses universitaires de Grenoble, 2006; *Cohabitation urbaine et usages de lieux de culte minoritaires: dynamisme social dans la gestion municipale*, Montréal: Conseil Interculturel de Montréal, 2009 (a sort of 'handbook' prepared by a team of la Ville de Montréal); cf. as well the monographic issue of *Nos diverses cités* devoted to *Québec* (Annick Germain, ed., "Immigration et diversité: au Carrefour des cultures et au Coeur du développement économique," special issue of *Nos diverses cités* 2010, 7). As regards Toronto, one of the first contributions on the topic is Engin F. Isin, and Myer Siemiatycki, "Fate and faith: claiming urban citizenship in immigrant To-

cuses on legal controversies as the epiphenomena of socio-cultural tensions triggered by two seemingly opposite tendencies: on the one hand, the tendency of new religious minorities to increase their pragmatic and symbolic agency in the management of public space through the establishment, enlargement, and/or renovation of places

---

ronto," Toronto: Joint Centre of Excellence for Research on Immigration and Settlement, 1999, working paper n. 8 (followed by Myer Siemiatycki, and Engin F. Isin, "Making Space for Mosques: Struggles for Urban Citizenship in Diasporic Toronto," in: Sherene Razack, ed., *Race, Space and the Law: Unmapping a White Settler Society*, Ottawa: Between the Lines Press, 2002, pp. 185-209); seminal papers on multicultural and multi-confessional urban planning with a specific focus on Toronto are Mohammad Qadeer, "Urban planning and multiculturalism in Ontario, Canada," in: Thomas Huw, and Krishnarajan Vijay (eds), *Race, Equality, and Planning - Policies and Procedures*, Aldershot, Hants (UK), Brookfield (VT): Avebury, 1994, pp. 187-200; idem, "Pluralistic planning for multicultural cities," *Journal of the American Planning Association* 1997, vol. 63, no. 4, pp. 481-494; idem and Maghfoor Chaudry, "The planning system and the development of mosques in the Great Toronto area," *Plan Canada* 2000, vol. 40, no. 2, pp. 17-21; for a survey of the legal controversies concerning minority places of worship in Ontario cf. Lilith Finkler, "Stressing Sacred Space" (2002), available at www.stason.org [last access September 21, 2010]; cf. also Sandeep Kumar Agrawal, "New ethnic places of worship and planning challenges,"*Plan Canada* 2008, vol. 48, Special Edition, pp. 64-67 (on planning issues concerning minority places of worship in the Great Toronto Area) and idem, "Faith-based ethnic residential communities and neighbourliness in Canada," *Planning Practice and Research* 2008, vol. 23, no. 1, pp. 41-56; idem, "Faith-based ethnic residential communities and neighbourliness," CERIS (The Ontario Metropolis Centre), 2008, working paper n. 63; Mohammad Qadeer, Sandeep Kumar Agrawal, and Alexander Lovell, "Evolution of Ethnic Enclaves in the Toronto Metropolitan Area, 2001-2006," *Journal of International Migration and Integration* 2010, vol. 11, no. 3, pp. 315-339 (on the role of religion in shaping neighborhoods in suburban Toronto). Literature on minority places of worship in Vancouver is less developed, but cf. David Ley, "The immigrant church as an urban service hub," *Urban Studies* 2008, vol. 45, no. 10, pp. 2057-2074, and other papers by the same author. On planning and ethno-religious diversity in Canada cf. as well Heidi Hoernig, "Lessons from recent immigrant, minority place of worship development for urban planning amidst cultural diversity" [no date], available at www.canada.metropolis.net [last access September 20, 2010] and the special issue of *Plan Canada* devoted to the topic "Welcoming communities: planning for diverse populations" (Agrawal Sandeep Kumar, Caroline Andrew, and John Biles, *Plan Canada*, special issue on "Welcoming communities: planning for diverse populations," 2009). An extremely important source of information about urban studies in Canada is the *Metropolis* network: http://ceris.metropolis.net/ (as regards Ontario, with links to analogous research clusters in other major Canadian cities).

of worship; on the other hand, the apparently contradictory tendency of old religious majorities (including the case of majorities composed of non-believers) to oppose such projects, considering them capable of decreasing their own pragmatic and symbolic agency in relation to the same space.

Semiotics, that is, the discipline that studies patterns of meaning and communication, is adopted as an epistemological, methodological, and analytical framework for the observation, description, and analysis of two communication processes: on the one hand, the way in which new places of worship are conceived, established, and received as spatial and architectural 'statements' concerning the relation between a religious minority and the territory; on the other hand, the way in which religious majorities, or at least some of their members, seek to counter such 'statements' by producing other communication processes: public demonstrations, media messages, and especially legal arguments.[5]

In other words, the paper aims at studying the spatial, architectural, and symbolic projects through which new religious minorities seek to 'make their own space', as well as the way in which religious majorities react to these projects.[6]

The purpose of such study is twofold. First, a theoretical purpose: social tensions arising from the establishment of new places of worship by religious minorities are an effective vantage point in order to understand that which is increasingly becoming a central element of contemporary societies: the complex interplay between cultural difference and cultural identity, which manifests itself mainly through

---

[5] Such semiotic approach elaborates on a trend of cultural and human geography of religion that has been already developed with promising results; cf. Lily Kong, "Geography and religion: trends and prospects," *Progress in Human Geography* 1990, vol. 14, no. 3, pp. 355–371; Julian Holloway, and Oliver Valins, "Editorial: Placing religion and spirituality in geography," *Social and Cultural Geography* 2002, vol. 3, no. 1, pp. 5–9; Leonie Sandercock, "Spirituality and the urban professions: the paradox at the heart of planning," *Planning Theory & Practice* 2006, vol. 7, no. 1, pp. 65–97.

[6] From this point of view, the paper is deeply influenced by the concept of "spatial justice" as developed by Edward D. Soja, *Seeking Spacial Justice*, Minneapolis and London: University of Minnesota Press, 2010.

the dynamics of belonging.[7] The work-hypothesis of this paper is that the ability of having an impact on the management of public space is an essential factor in determining the sense/feeling of belonging of a social group — especially in the case of a minority — in relation to the territory.

Second, a practical purpose: social tensions are not ineluctable. On the contrary, planning, legal, administrative, and bureaucratic policies can be conceived, engineered, and adopted in order to rationalize the management of public space also as regards its symbolic dimension.[8]

So as to achieve its theoretical goals, the paper relies on the existent literature on the topic as well as on new semiotic analyses of legal controversies in Canada. Research experience accumulated in other socio-cultural contexts, and in particular in Australia, Europe, and the USA, is also used to cast light on the dynamics of belonging in the present-day Canadian society.

3. Cultural diversity and urban planning in Canada

Canada is one of the most culturally diverse countries in the world. The last available census data indicate that Canada, and particularly the three major Canadian cities of Montréal, Toronto, and Vancouver, are characterized by a religious demography that is both extraordinary diverse and diversifying at extraordinary speed.[9] In the last thirty years, and especially since Canada has officially embraced multiculturalism, Canadian planning and legal systems have been constantly adapted in order to suit the pragmatic and symbolic needs

---

[7] Massimo Leone, "On my accent – Signs of belonging in present-day multicultural societies," in: idem (ed.) *Analisi delle culture – Culture dell'analisi, Analysis of Cultures – Cultures of Analysis*, monographic issue of *Lexia* 2010, 5–6, pp. 415–450; idem, "Sémiotique du sentiment d'appartenance", Nouveaux Actes Sémiotiques [online], February 21, 2012, available at revues.unilim.fr/nas/ [last access June 12, 2012].

[8] Massimo Leone, "The Semiotic Therapy of Religious Law," *International Journal for the Semiotics of Law* 2009, vol. 24, no. 3, pp. 293–306.

[9] Cf. www12.statcan.ca [last access September 21, 2010].

of new religious minorities while preserving the overall socio-cultural harmony of the urban fabric.

One of the pioneers in the field of urban planning research on religious minorities in Canada is Mohammad A. Qadeer. In 1994, Qadeer published a seminal article entitled "Urban planning and multiculturalism in Ontario, Canada",[10] later expanded in the 1997 essay "Pluralistic planning for multicultural cities".[11] In a prophetic statement, Qadeer claimed that

> Canada is an appropriate setting for studying these issues. It is an acknowledged multicultural society and is explicitly committed to sustaining the cultural heritage of minorities. Its experiences may hold lessons for other countries with large immigrant populations.[12]

While acknowledging that the post-1960s social consensus against racism had eliminated overt forms of discrimination in the Canadian management of public and particularly urban space, Qadeer also remarked, in his 1997 essay, that historical practices, public policies, administrative procedures, and regulatory standards prevailing in Canada in the late 1990s could be still considered as originating "from social patterns and cultural values of the dominant communities, namely, in Canada, the English or the French".[13]

4. 'Making Muslim space' in the Great Toronto Area

The last part of Qadeer's article, devoted to the pluralistic planning of "Institutions and services", deals with the question of the establishment of new mosques in Canada, triggered, especially from the early 1990s on, by new migratory fluxes from the Middle East, Eastern Europe, and South Asia. Socio-cultural tensions and legal controversies concerning the establishment of new places of worship in Canada do not concern only Islamic communities. However, for reasons that the present paper will seek to account for, no other religious

---

[10] M. Qadeer, "Urban planning and multiculturalism in Ontario, Canada," op. cit.
[11] M. Qadeer, "Pluralistic planning for multicultural cities," op. cit.
[12] Ibidem, pp. 481–482.
[13] Ibidem, p. 482.

communities have faced the same level of hardship in 'making religious space'.[14]

According to Qadeer, the establishment of new mosques in Canadian metropolises typically developed through three phases:

In the beginning, someone's living room serves as the gathering place for weekly prayers, which leads to renting a hall or buying an unused church for congregational gatherings, and finally to the stage of building a new mosque.[15]

Each of these three phases entails an interaction between the Islamic minority and the planning, legal, administrative, and bureaucratic systems established by the majority, with the consequent need of obtaining public approvals and planning permissions. Yet, Qadeer points out that at least up to 1997 – when his essay was written and published –, such systems were modeled after the idea of the establishment of a new Christian church, so that obtaining approvals and permissions for the establishment of a different place of worship would imply a constant need for derogations. The typical example mentioned by Qadeer is the construction of minarets, a delicate issue in most predominantly non-Islamic 'Western' countries.[16] In one famous case, an Islamic community was obliged to apply for the planning and the construction of a new "clock tower", the only planning category that in the Canadian administrative system could analogically apply to a minaret.

The process of adjustment through which planning, legal, administrative, and bureaucratic systems imbued with the socio-cultural identity of the majority are transformed through the impact and interaction with the needs of a new minority is, to a certain extent, physiologically impervious. However, in some cases such process can

---

[14] Literature on social tensions and legal controversies triggered by the establishment of new Islamic places of worship is vast and growing. For an overview, M. Leone, "Architectures of transcendence - A trans-cultural analysis of legal processes for the construction, modification, and restoration of places of worship," op. cit., and idem, "Legal controversies about the establishment of new places of worship in multicultural cities: a semiogeographic analysis," op. cit.

[15] M. Qadeer, "Pluralistic planning for multicultural cities," op. cit., p. 491.

[16] For a survey of the literature on this subject, M. Leone, "Hearing and Belonging – On Sounds, Faiths, and Laws," op. cit.

be so slow as to give rise to countless opportunities for (at times violent) pathological socio-cultural tensions. The lack of appropriate laws, bylaws, and regulations, as well as the lack of predefined procedures to connect socio-cultural needs and regulatory systems brings about a gap of uncertainty, ambiguity, and discretionary decisions, which is often filled by discriminatory phenomena and media and political opportunism.

However, already in his 1997 essay, Qadeer underlined that significant progress in the ability of the Canadian system of public space management to accommodate the needs of new religious minorities, and in particular those of new Islamic minorities, had been made – thanks to the efforts of planners more than to those of their political referents – leading to the establishment of thirty new mosques in the Toronto area.

5. Planning places of worship in the GTA: current procedures and possibilities of improvement

Despite the generally optimistic tone characterizing Qadeer's 1997 essay, its conclusions emphasize a limit of the management of public space in pluralistic (and multi-confessional) Canada that is still a distinctive trait of even the most multicultural and 'superdiverse' 'Western' societies:[17] the spatial needs of religious minorities are mostly accommodated as exceptions to the norm, and not considered as an essential element of the socio-cultural fabric to be preemptively taken into account. Solutions are mostly found *ad hoc*, under the form of derogations, whereas planning per se remains relatively impermeable to cultural and religious diversity. The essay therefore insists on the fact that multicultural planning requires a formulation of "policies, programs, and standards ... beyond simply advocacy for the disadvantaged",[18] a requirement that, according to the author, can be fulfilled only through the representation of minorities in planning bodies.

[17] Steven Vertovec, "Super-diversity and its implications," *Ethnic & Racial Studies* 2007, vol. 30, no. 6, pp. 1024–1054.

[18] M. Qadeer, "Pluralistic planning for multicultural cities," op. cit., p. 493.

As it will be pointed out in the present essay, the role that religious minorities can play in the management of public space, especially in multi-cultural cities, is directly proportional to their capacity to turn into an active political agent capable of influencing regulations and decisions not only according to a bottom-up logic (minorities manifest their needs, majorities seek to accommodate them) but according to a top-down logic (representatives of minorities seek to exert their socio-cultural sensibility already at the stage of planning, or even at the previous stage of elaboration of policies, programs, standards, and regulations).[19]

Each Canadian province adopts different legal and planning systems for the management of public space. As regards the city of Toronto and the Great Toronto Area, where the largest Canadian Islamic communities live, the administrative and political agencies involved are essentially the City Planning Division of Toronto [CPDT] (set up by district - Etobicoke, York, North York, Toronto & East York and Scarborough), municipal councils, municipal planning committees, interest groups and individual citizens, and the Ontario Municipal Board (the quasi-judicial appellate body).[20]

The proposal to establish a new place of worship is first submitted to the CPDT, which reviews it on the basis of official plan policies and zoning criteria. The recommendations of the CPDT are presented to local municipal councils that, taking into account input from citizens and local interest groups, make the final deliberation, approving or rejecting policies and zoning amendments when required. In Ontario, decisions by local municipal councils can be subsequently appealed through the Ontario Municipal Board.

As the present article will point out, several passages in this procedure are interesting from the perspective of the semiotics of law:

---

[19] Cf. Myer Siemiatycki, "Urban citizenship for immigrant cities: One Resident, One Vote in municipal elections," in: Sandeep Kumar Agrawal, Caroline Andrew, and John Biles, *Plan Canada* 2009, special issue on "Welcoming communities: planning for diverse populations," pp. 75–78, on the "One Resident, One Vote" movement.

[20] For an excellent analysis of the efficacy of the Ontario Municipal Board cf. Sandeep Kumar Agrawal, "Urban design decision-making: a study of Ontario Municipal Board decisions in Toronto," *Canadian Journal of Urban Research* 2005, vol. 14, no. 2, pp. 209–237.

(a) the way in which the structure of the procedure as a whole as well as the internal organization of the CPDT and the official plan policies and zoning criteria signify a certain 'forma mentis', which is the epiphenomenon of the historical and socio-cultural context of Toronto; (b) the interplay between this 'planning system', the socio-cultural legacy it embodies, and bottom-up inputs from citizens and groups of interest. Such inputs constitute a sort of 'natural corpus' for any research on the semiotics of religious space planning, especially as they are embodied in media messages and records and transcripts of legal controversies; (c) the internal structure, formal procedures, and final deliberations of the Ontario Municipal Board.

The relation between Islamic communities in the GTA and the planning system of this territory has not always been idyllic. On the one hand, Islamic communities have often lacked the political agency required to be effective at the legal, administrative, and bureaucratic level in order to have a significant impact on the planning system of the GTA and its socio-cultural presuppositions.

On the other hand, this 'minority status' has frequently brought about a vicious circle where the hypersensitivity of Islamic communities in the GTA started to play a major role. Given that *some* negative feedback from the planning system was motivated by discriminatory rationales imbued with Islamophobic prejudices, *every* negative feedback from the same planning system was interpreted by the Islamic communities of the GTA as a further demonstration of the presence and role of such rationales.[21]

As the present article will point out, one of the major tasks planning policies will have to face in the future of Toronto as well as in that of other 'Western' metropolises around the world is to break the vicious circle of mistrust between religious minorities and the planning system. The planning system of the GTA has already rapidly

[21] For a lucid study of this process in the Montréal area cf. Ali Daher, *La Construction de l'islamité et l'intégration sociale des musulmans selon la perspective des leaders musulmans au Québec* (1999), available at www.bibliotheque.uqac.uquebec.ca [last access September 21, 2010]; cf. also Chantal Goyette, "L'établissement résidentiel des nouveaux immigrants arabes - Un processus de regroupement ethnique" (2000), mémoire présenté à la faculté des études supérieures en vue de l'obtention du grade de maître ès sciences (M.Sc.) en sociologie, under the direction of Jean Reneaud.

moved several steps forward in such direction. One of them is the way in which the semantic of religious space is conceived and 'lexicalised.' In 1988, Toronto City deleted the term "church" from planning regulation documents in favor of the term "place of worship." Analogously, the former City of Etobicoke in its 1990 Official Plan started to designate places of worship in its territory as "religious assembly with other related uses."

A neutralized 'religiously correct' planning lexicon is not per se a guarantee for a pluralistic, non-discriminatory planning system. It does not matter whether a planning system does not use the term "church" when deliberating on the establishment of a synagogue or a mosque, if agents involved in such deliberation (city planning officials, for instance) still conceive of a synagogue or a mosque as if it was a church. The cultural specificity of the space 'made' by different religions must be taken into account in order to achieve a substantially pluralistic planning. However, the neutralization of the lexicon of planning is also an important element in developing mutual trust between religious minorities and the planning system.

Planning regulations concerning places of worship vary considerably in the different municipalities of the GTA, although local conditions do not always change accordingly. Although plans for the establishment of new mosques in the GTA have been generally approved, most of them have implied presentations and negotiations with local Councils, few cases have required approval of the Ontario Municipal Board, and one case was contested up to the Ontario Court of Appeal.

6. Common contentious areas

The existent literature identifies four major areas of contention involved in the establishment of new mosques in the GTA: traffic and parking issues, compatibility with surrounding land uses, architectural design, and fiscal impact.

The first area recurs quite often around the world in socio-cultural tensions and legal controversies about the establishment of new places of worship by religious minorities, and especially by Islamic communities in predominantly non-Islamic 'Western' countries. Such area apparently entails a mere matter of calculus and is of no interest from a semiotic perspective. However, this is far from being true. First of all, regulations that determine the traffic and parking conditions, which new places of worship must fulfill, are extremely various and, to a certain extent, quite arbitrary, even in a single territory such as the GTA.

Second, as several studies have underlined, methods for the calculation of such requirements often stem from a specific *imaginaire* concerning the proxemics of religious space. For instance, the potential attendance of planned non-Christian places of worship in Canada has been sometimes estimated in relation to the number of seats, without taking into account that seats are a specific feature of the religious proxemics of Christian places of worship.

Third, as it has been emphasized by several scholars, it is sometimes difficult not to suspect that traffic and parking matters are used as an acceptable legal, administrative, and bureaucratic argument to thwart the establishment of religious minorities in a certain territory. However, discriminatory intents are not behind every parking and traffic regulation contention. Affirming it would be tantamount to reinforce the vicious circle of mistrust described above.

The semiotic analysis of legal controversies can give a precious contribution to uncover the discriminatory rationale potentially at work in administrative contentions. Some cases are so evident that they do not even need the intervention of a semiotic analyst. Consider, for instance, the case of the Islamic Foundation's mosque in Scarborough, where parking turned out to be a convenient planning argument after the plaintiff, a neighboring restaurateur, had "failed to convince the city that the mosque would 'adversely affect his liquor sales'."[22]

Fourth, there is an aspect of this contentious area that has been rarely dealt with by the existent literature on the topic: the priority by which the logistics of traffic and parking is considered as more important than any other value (including the freedom of religion of a community) is never questioned. Nobody would like to be a resident of an urban area in which attendance to the local place of wor-

[22] M. Qadeer, M. Chaudry, "The planning system and the development of mosques in the Great Toronto area," op. cit., p. 18.

ship regularly brings about massive traffic congestion and severe shortage of parking space. However, if the priority above was rediscussed, or at least, not considered as a dogma, urban planners would probably find that in many circumstances there would be room for a certain amount of negotiation and compromise: residents could perhaps be encouraged to accept a certain increase in traffic and decrease in parking space for the sake of creating a more equitable urban socio-cultural fabric.[23]

The second contentious area is compatibility. This area too shows a great amount of disparity in terms of which zones are considered by the municipalities of the GTA as suitable in order to host new places of worship. The interest of this issue for a semiotics of planning resides not only in such apparently arbitrary variety of regulations, but also in the way in which such variety interacts with the religious *imaginaire* behind urban planning.[24] For instance, when plans for the establishments of new mosques are rejected – in Canada as well as elsewhere – because they seem to attract believers from different areas of a city, and therefore are not judged to comply with the traditional definition of "neighborhood institution", planners are actually projecting the usual logistics of a church on that of a mosque.

Given the different 'temporality of praying' in Islam as compared with Christianity, most practicing believers are inclined to attend mosques which are close to where they work, and not to where they live. Furthermore, sometimes believers are ready to travel great distances from their places of residence in order to attend mosques where religious functions are held in their mother tongue, or where they can assembly with those belonging to the same Islamic denomination and/or ethnic background.

---

[23] Cf. Maurice Blanc, "La transaction, un processus de production et d'apprentissage du 'vivre ensemble'," in: Marie-France Freynet, Maurice Blanc, and Gaston Pineau (eds), *Les Transactions aux frontières du social – Formation, travail social, développement local*, Lyon: Éd. Chronique Sociale, 1998, pp. 219–237, on the concept of "social transaction" (which has inspired much Canadian scholarship on the management of minority places of worship).

[24] Cf. Massimo Leone, "Praying and planning – Advances in the semiogeography of the religious imaginaire," presented at the Summer School of the New Bulgarian University on September 12, 2010; available at www.unito.academia.edu/MassimoLeone

The third area of contention is of distinctive semiotic concern: architectural design. In many cases, in Canada as well as in other 'Western' countries, plans for the establishment of new places of worship by minorities have been opposed and sometimes rejected because of 'aesthetic' reasons. This area too involves two dimensions: a properly aesthetic dimension and a 'political' one. As regards the first, a semiotics of planning should inquire into the way in which aesthetic projects in a territory interact with the patterns of feeling /sense of belonging characterizing a socio-cultural fabric: why do religious minorities care about building places of worship according to specific aesthetics, for instance, those 'recreating' the architectural flavor of a certain ethno-religious background and/or historical period? And why do these projects of architectural design, which are also projects of symbolic belonging, so often trigger the hostility of the 'aesthetic majority'? How are the concepts of 'character' and 'amenity', so frequent in legal controversies about these issues, involved in this contentious area?

The second dimension is political: as in the logistic area of traffic and parking, is it not the case that aesthetic arguments too become the legally, administratively, and bureaucratically acceptable alibi through which discriminatory logics take place in the management of public space? And if this is so, why is the acceptability of these arguments not even a matter of debate? Why is it not acceptable to claim in the courts of most 'Western' countries that, for instance, Muslims should not be present in a certain area, whereas it is acceptable to claim that, for instance, Islamic architecture should not be present in a certain area?

The fourth and last area of contention is rapidly becoming one of the most heated ones in Canada as well as in other countries with similar planning and legal systems: since places of worship usually benefit from the status of being totally or partially tax-exempt, permitting the establishment of a new place of worship implicitly entails a decrease of revenues for the municipality within which such establishment takes place.

This area concerns not only fiscal studies but also social studies, and particularly, a socio-semiotics of planning: either an urban community finds that all places of worship are advantageous for the socio-cultural fabric as a whole and, therefore, the community itself is willing to face a cost for their establishment in the urban territory, or, on the contrary, the urban community considers that places of worship do not represent a benefit for the social fabric and, therefore, their establishment must not entail any relevant fiscal externalities.

In both cases, though, a management of both public space and fiscal revenues as equitable as possible is necessary. Allowing the status of partial or total tax-exemption to the places of worship of the majority, while denying the establishment of places of worship by minorities with the argument that they would reduce the revenues of a municipality, smells of covert discrimination.

Furthermore, as it was pointed out in relation to the contentious area of traffic/parking, there is no reason for which the priority fiscal needs are given over needs of symbolic belonging should not be rediscussed in order to encourage a more pluralistic and equitable management of public space. That places of worship are an anti-economic luxury implying nothing but fiscal externalities for an urban community is the contention of a narrowly materialistic point of view on society, which does not take into account, for instance, the extremely relevant role places of worship may play as social institutions mediating between new migrant communities and the established urban socio-cultural fabric.

7. Conclusions: the Canadian lesson

Given the limits of the present paper, only some aspects of the legal and planning systems of Canada and their interaction with the pragmatic and symbolic needs of religious minorities could be dealt with. The paper could not expand on differences existing between the legal and planning systems of Ontario and those of other provinces, and in particular on the remarkable divergences between predominantly Anglophone and predominantly Francophone Canada. Neither could the paper analyze in-depth all the achievements and failures of the way in which the legal and planning system of the GTA seeks to adapt to the needs of new religious minorities.

However, even such a sketchy inquiry into the legal and planning implications of the establishment of minority places of worship in Canada prompts some final observations. The legal and planning system of Canada is not perfect. Under several aspects, religious minorities, and especially new Islamic communities, are 'citizens of a lesser God', meaning that their 'projects of belonging', as well as their consequent impact on the management of public space, entails facing legal, administrative, and bureaucratic obstacles that are rarely confronted by the religious majority or by politically more established religious minorities.

On the other hand, probably no country more than Canada has been characterized by a constant effort to strike a balance between pragmatic and symbolic needs of religious minorities and preservation of an harmonious socio-cultural urban fabric. If one compares the way in which Canadian law and policy makers, urban planners, officials, and scholars have tackled these issues with the way in which the same problems have been dealt with not only in Europe, and especially in continental Europe, but also in multicultural societies such as Australia and Great Britain, not to speak of present-day USA, a difference is particularly striking. With few exceptions, mostly concerning the particular religious demography of Québec,[25] socio-cultural tensions and even controversies concerning religious minorities have not become a main issue in the agenda of mediatic and political opinion leaders. No *Lega* or *Tea Party* in Canada, at least thus far, seems to have been able to poison the rationality of legal and planning discourse concerning the establishment of new non-Christian places of worship.[26]

The reasons for which Canada seems to be, at least to a certain extent, immune to the rampant xenophobia that distorts the perception of inter-confessional relations in both Europe and the USA have roots

---

[25] Cf. the recent "Soeur grises affaire," Phyllis Lambert, and Serge Joyal, "Couvent des soeurs grises de Montréal - Détournement de pouvoir inacceptable," *Le Dévoir*, July 13, 2010; available at www.ledevoir.com [last access September 22, 2010].

[26] For a critique of the discourse of the xenophobe Italian political party *Lega* about the establishment of new Islamic places of worship in Italy cf. M. Leone, "Architectures of transcendence - A trans-cultural analysis of legal processes for the construction, modification, and restoration of places of worship," op. cit.

in the history of Canada and cannot be investigated in-depth on this occasion. One lesson, though, can be drawn from this rapid survey of the planning and legal systems of Canada: issues concerning the relation between religious minorities and the management of public space should be protected as much as possible from the discretional and at times discriminatory rhetoric of the media and political discourse and should be addressed from the point of view of a calm and lucid knowledge of the planning and legal systems of a country, their characteristics, their limits, and their possibilities of improvement.

Part II

Rights and Citizenship in the Legal Practice

Marta Soniewicka
Jagiellonian University in Kraków, Poland

How Dangerous Can the Sterilized Needle Be? Torture, Terrorism, and the Self-Refutation of the Liberal-Democratic State*

Abstract: The paper addresses the problem of the justification, legitimization or authorization of torture as a method of interrogation in an emergency state. The paper starts with the analysis of ambiguities of the definitions of torture and terrorism. There are discussed the arguments used in favor of moral justification of torture in the emergency state based on the ticking time bomb scenario. The paper discusses also the argument from necessity used in the post facto authorization of torture in the "Dirty Harry case." Finally, the paper poses the question about legalization of torture. The main thesis of the paper is that the idea of the justification or legitimization of torture corrupts the rule of law and undermines the main values of the liberal state, and therefore is unacceptable in any form and in any circumstances.

Keywords: torture, ticking time bomb scenario, terrorism, liberalism, life-saving torture, salvation torture, necessity, Daschner, Gäfgen, liberal-democratic state, rule of law

> *Ach, wie übel ihnen das Wort ,Tugend' aus dem Munde läuft! Und wenn sie sagen ,ich bin gerecht,' so klingt es immer gleich wie: ,ich bin gerächt!'.*
>
> Friedrich Nietzsche[1]

---

* The first version of the paper was presented at the seminar "Health Law, Bioethics and Human Rights" at Boston University School of Public Health in April 2011 during my Fulbright post-doc fellowship. I owe special thanks to Professor George Annas, whose seminar inspired me to work on the topic and to Professor Reiner Schmidt, from whom I received valuable comments and encouragement; I am grateful to Aeddan Shaw for editing the text.

[1] Friedrich Nietzsche, *Also Sprach Zarathustra*, die Digitale Kritische Gesamtausgabe Werke und Briefe (eKGWB) von Friedrich Nietzsche auf der Grundlage der *Kriti-*

Introduction: intellectually dirty hands?

For a long time there was a sort of consensus in liberal-democratic societies concerning the legal prohibition and moral condemnation of torture. The imperative "do not torture" seemed to be the only one which did not allow any exceptions, in contrast with such imperatives as "do not kill" or "agreements must be kept." Thus, the successful "return" of torture in the USA is perplexing. It is difficult to understand how the ticking time bomb scenario, which was originally used to discuss the limits of morality with first year philosophy students, has left the classroom and infiltrated serious political and legal debate on the justification of torture.[2] In the shadow of the collapsing twin towers and in light of the horrifying new threat of global terror, something has changed in the debate in liberal political philosophy - and this change is alarming. Thus, some philosophers refuse even to discuss such problems as the justification of torture since they do not to get their "hands intellectually dirty." Slavoj Žižek argues that introducing torture as a legitimate topic for philosophical debate is even more dangerous than introducing it in practice.[3] Jeremy Waldron expresses his critical attitude to contemplating torture by saying that "It is dispiriting as well as shameful to have to turn our attention to this issue."[4] La Torre adds that: "Torture is morally objectionable not only in itself but also as a subject of

---

schen Gesamtausgabe Werke, herausgegeben von Giorgio Colli und Mazzino Montinari, Berlin/New York, Walter de Gruyter, 1967 ff. und *Nietzsche Briefwechsel Kritische Gesamtausgabe*, Berlin/New York, Walter de Gruyter, 1975ff., herausgegeben von Paolo D'Iorio, available at <http://www.nietzschesource.org/texts/eKGWB>; in English: "Ah! how ineptly cometh the word ‚virtue' out of their mouths! And when they say: 'I am just,' it always soundeth like: 'I am just-revenged!'" (Friedrich Nietzsche, *Thus Spake Zarathustra*, transl. by Thomas Common, New York: Modern Library, 1925, p. 111).

[2] See: George Annas, *Worst Case Bioethics. Death, Disaster, and Public Health*, Oxford: Oxford University Press, 2010, p. 49.

[3] Slavoj Žižek, *Welcome to the Desert of the Real*, London: Verso, 2002, p. 103.

[4] Jeremy Waldron, "Torture and Positive Law: Jurisprudence for the White House," *Columbia Law Review* 2005, vol. 105, pp. 1681–1750, here at p. 1683.

discussion."[5] Although I regard the shift from an absolutist objection to relativist consent in the debate over torture in liberal societies as distressing, I do not believe that making torture a taboo-topic would solve or remove the problem. It could only make us think that the problem of torture does not exist and this is exactly what we should try to avoid by discussing it and making people aware of all of its bitter consequences.

In this paper I shall analyze some of the lines of argumentation used in favor of the justification, legitimization or authorization of torture as a means of interrogation in an emergency state. The main aim of my analysis is to show that the argumentation for torture is a dangerous double edged sword which is used for the sake of the survival of liberal societies and yet brings about quite the opposite result. I claim that the idea of the justification or legitimization of torture in the war on terror produces terror itself, undermining the main values of the liberal state, and therefore supports the main purpose of its own enemies.

1. Torture and terrorism – problem with definitions and applications

I shall start with presenting briefly two notions crucial for my considerations: torture and terrorism. Both notions are controversial, ambiguous and far from clear. Nevertheless, we will try to understand them since it is necessary not only for legal regulations but also for a fruitful discussion. When we do not agree about the concepts, we usually do not agree about the facts.

1.1. Torture

According to the definition provided by the United Nations Convention Against Torture and Other Cruel, Inhuman or Degrading Treatment or Punishment (CAT):

[5] Massimo La Torre, "'Jurists, Bad Christians': Torture and the Rule of Law," in: Bev Clucas, Gerry Johnstone and Tony Ward (eds), *Torture: Moral Absolutes and Ambiguities*, Baden-Baden: Nomos Verlag, 2009, p. 20.

> ... torture means any act by which severe pain or suffering, whether physical or mental, is intentionally inflicted on a person for such purposes as obtaining from him or a third person information or a confession, punishing him for an act he or a third person has committed or is suspected of having committed, or intimidating or coercing him or a third person, or for any reason based on discrimination of any kind, when such pain or suffering is inflicted by or at the instigation of or with the consent or acquiescence of a public official or other person acting in an official capacity. It does not include pain or suffering arising only from, inherent in or incidental to lawful sanctions.[6]

To avoid criticism that this definition is too broad, since any kind of punishment or interrogation may produce suffering, it provides a provision of exception for "lawful actions." However, this provision makes the prohibition of torture problematic. On one hand, the CAT provides an absolute prohibition of torture, stating in the Art. 2 para. 2 that:

> No exceptional circumstances whatsoever, whether a state of war or a threat of war, internal political instability or any other public emergency, may be invoked as a justification of torture.[7]

On the other, it leaves a door open for any kind of torture which is sanctioned by law. Taking advantage of this loophole, some kinds of torture may become non-torture from the legal point of view, gaining the new name of coercive interrogation techniques etc. To avoid such situations, Christopher Tindale offers a corrected version of this definition, by which he understands torture as:

> ... any act by which severe pain or suffering, whether physical or mental, is intentionally inflicted on a person for such purposes as obtaining from that person or a third person information or confession, punishing that person for an act committed or suspected to have been committed, or intimidating or dehumanizing that person or other persons.[8]

---

[6] Art. 1 of the United Nations Convention Against Torture and Other Cruel, Inhuman or Degrading Treatment or Punishment (1984), available online.

[7] Ibidem.

[8] Quoted in Bob Brecher, *Torture and the Ticking Bomb*, Blackwell Publishing, 2007, p. 5.

However, this definition is not free from further controversy either since one can argue that this definition is too narrow since it assumes that torture is inflicted only for certain purposes like obtaining information or punishment. It means that the definition of torture does not apply to a case in which a sadist tortures his victim for pleasure. On the other hand, this definition can be criticized as too broad and applicable to any kind of punishment which is often understood as a sort of intentional infliction of suffering on a punished person. It could also be criticized as too vague by using such ambiguous terms as "severe pain."

To challenge all these difficulties arising from each definition of torture, I shall make two crucial points. First of all, we should rethink the idea of punishment based on classical retributivism. In my opinion, the idea of punishment in a liberal society should not imply producing suffering as its aim and part of its definition. Appealing to John Rawls's rule of fair play or Herbert L. Hart's idea of the reciprocity of obligations in a society,[9] one should understand a punishment as a means of taking away undue benefits which a perpetrator gains from not obeying legal norms. It can include taking away or suspending some of the rights of that person, such as the right to her property or the right to freedom of movement. The question which arises here is whether there are any rights that cannot be taken away or suspended by a society, such as the right to life or the right to the integrity of one's body.

The main role of justice in the liberal society is to guarantee a *status quo* based on legal norms and social values and to restore *status quo ante* when somebody questions these values and violates the norms. Justice demands punishment for a murderer not because that person killed somebody's wife or sister but because one must not kill anybody (even if this person is not anybody's wife or sister). This makes a significant difference between a legal punishment and mere revenge or vengeance. Aristotle, in his insightful analysis of justice, strongly refused to identify justice with any kind of revenge and reciprocity.[10]

---

[9] See: Herbert L.A. Hart, *Punishment and Responsibility*, Oxford: Oxford University Press, 2008, pp. 1–27, 210–237.

[10] Aristotle, *Ethica Nicomachea*, transl. by W.D. Ross, Oxford: Clarendon Press, 1925, Book V, 1132b.

Revenge is always destructive for a community since it deepens existing conflicts opening the never-ending chain of revenges. Justice, on the other hand, in its equalizing (compensatory) role has to bring back and preserve the unsettled equilibrium in the community. Thus, enforcing a law by the state cannot be understood as taking revenge in the name of victims. The main aim of the just state is to use law as an instrument for restoring in a society *trust* to infringed values and violated norms.

The liberal approach to justice and punishment can help us to distinguish legal punishment from torture since the latter always implies the infliction of suffering and pain which is for torture both a means to achieve an end and an end in itself. Producing suffering and pain is a necessary condition of torture but not a sufficient one. Inflicting suffering or pain has to be intentional (not accidental) and also systematic (if one hits somebody out of rage it would not count as torture). Torture infringes upon human dignity by treating a tortured person not as a person, but as a subject, a means to an end which the torturer has in mind. By giving the conditions which torture must meet, I am not attempting any legal definition but rather striving to make this phenomenon clearer. Not every phenomenon regulated by law (protected or prohibited) has its legal definition; for instance we do not define such abstract and general terms as human dignity or define such empirical states as "causing pain" or "inflicting suffering." What is more, we do not define many practices, nevertheless we understand what they are when we describe them or give examples of them. Therefore, I argue, and this is the second point, that it is not necessary to construct a legal definition of torture when we can instead work out our intuitive meaning of this phenomenon and describe it by giving examples.[11] No definition of torture would be perfect and distinguishing between different methods of torturing people, as well as providing a distinction between such notions as torture and coercive interrogation,[12] would only bring about a softening of the notion and the deprivation of its force.

---

[11] I follow here the line of argumentation presented by B. Brecher, *Torture and the Ticking Bomb*, op. cit., pp. 5–6.

[12] See: Jean B. Elshtain, "Reflection on the Problem of 'Dirty Hands,'" in: Sanford Levinson (ed.), *Torture: A Collection*, Oxford University Press, 2004, pp. 77–91, here at p. 77.

The manipulation of the definition of torture is one of the most common political and legal practices which are aimed at giving the green light for this practice. One tries to *restrict the scope of the meaning of the term "torture"* so as it does not cover already used methods, such as waterboarding (simulation of drowning), sensory deprivation etc.[13] A perfect example of this practice gives an overview of the US legal documents on torture in the last decade, like the Bybee memorandum.[14] Narrowing the definition of torture to only inflicting physical harm threatening life (short of the killing of the detainee), causing organ failure or the permanent impairment of a significant body function, seems inadequate to the common intuitions regarding the word "torture" where the pain and suffering of a tortured person are the essential part of the procedure. Measuring pain and suffering is always subjective and too vague to make it a criterion of distinguishing between torture and non-torture. One can be tortured in a more or less cruel way, but it still constitutes torture.

Another frequently used line of argumentation to enforce torture as a legitimate means of interrogation rests on *restricting application of the term only to some agents*, excluding some other agents to whom the definition does not apply. It means applying a double-standard procedure, where some people are protected against torture, while some others are deprived of such protection. For instance, the US government invented the term "Unlawful Enemy Combatants," who are not designated as Prisoners of War, to deprive them of the legal protection of the Geneva Convention.[15] The President of the USA has the

---

13 More about different methods of torture which are not always recognized as torture by the authorities can be found in: "Broken Laws, Broken Lives. Medical Evidence of Torture by US Personnel and Its Impact. A Report by Physicians for Human Rights," June 2008, p. 73 ff.

14 Jay S. Bybee, Memorandum for A. Gonzales, "Standards of Conduct for Interrogation under 18 U.S. C. §§ 240-2340A," of 1 August 2002, available online; see: Augustin J. Menéndez, "Bush II's Constitutional and Legal Theory: The Constitution of Emergency between Law and Propaganda," in: B. Clucas, G. Johnstone and T. Ward (eds), *Torture: Moral Absolutes and Ambiguities*, op. cit., p. 125 ff.; M. La Torre, "'Jurists, Bad Christians': Torture and the Rule of Law," op. cit., p. 15 ff.

15 The denial of habeas corpus act to detainees in Guantanamo Delta Camp was questioned by the Supreme Court in the Boumediene v. Bush decision (128 S. Ct. 229, issued on June 12, 2008).

power to decide who is a threat to US national security and who constitutes an enemy combatant to be deprived of habeas corpus and the protection of the Geneva Convention.[16] As it has been argued, the protection of US law is refused to those who aim to undermine it, and the Geneva Convention is not applicable to "uncivilized nations" or "failed states."[17] This brought about a dual constitutional theory which provides a distinction between the ordinary constitution and the emergency constitution.[18] A similar idea was also discussed in Germany in the debate about security and anti-terror legislation, when some scholars proposed a distinction between two kinds of penal law: one for citizens and a different one for enemies, but this idea was never introduced to the legal system.[19] This kind of distinction can be defended by the claim, made by a legal philosopher Burton Leiser, that the "enemies of mankind" (*hostes humani generis*) who refuse to abide by the laws of society put themselves outside of society (in the state before the law); thus the law does not apply to them.[20] This argument, rooted in Hobbesian philosophy, is based on an assumption of reciprocity. If the terrorists refuse to accept and violate the fundamental principles of a liberal society such as the moral equality of every person and human dignity, they also refuse to be protected by these principles, so the argument goes. This argumentation is very striking in all situations in which we face such devastating wrongs, such as genocide, war crimes or terrorist acts that our laws seem to be helpless in challenging them. Yet this argumentation remains inconsistent with one of the essential parts of liberal thought which is also seen as its biggest achievement, namely the assumption that *all* human beings are free and equal, irrespective of their status. It

---

[16] The Military Commissions Act of 2006, public law 109-366 – Oct. 17, 2006, Sect. 3930, available online; see also: A.J. Menéndez, "Bush II's Constitutional and Legal Theory," op. cit., pp. 119-126; M. La Torre, "'Jurists, Bad Christians': Torture and the Rule of Law," op. cit., p. 14, pp. 21-22.

[17] John Yoo, *War by Other Means*, New York: Atlantic Press, 2006, p. 33.

[18] A.J. Menéndez, "Bush II's Constitutional and Legal Theory," op. cit., pp. 127-129.

[19] Günter Jakobs, "Bürgerstrafrecht und Feindstrafrecht," *HRRS* 2004, Nr. 3, pp. 88-95, here at p. 89.

[20] Burton Leiser, "The Catastrophe of September 11 and its Aftermath," in: Igor Primoratz (ed.), *Terrorism. The Philosophical Issues*, Palgrave Macmillian, 2004, pp. 192-208, here at p. 203.

means that we cannot refuse to recognize somebody as a human being even if that person refuses to recognize oneself as a human being or refuses to recognize other people as human beings. This assumption is unconditional. Thus, if we agree that torture rejects the recognition of someone's dignity by treating a tortured person like a subject (a means to an end) not a person (an end itself), we also have to agree that the right to be free from torture applies to *every* human being.

Finally one can *restrict application of the term "torture" with regard to some special emergency, situations.* This line of argumentation in favor of torture rests on an assumption that there can be such circumstances that make the use of torture necessary and therefore permissible. In his lecture delivered in 1992, Niklas Luhmann argued that there are no unrenounceable norms in our societies anymore. Therefore he claimed that in cases of the massive violation of human dignity, effective protection may require some violation of the dignity of the perpetrators.[21] This is the only line of argumentation which I will discuss further. Challenging the idea of the moral justification, legitimization and legal authorization of torture, I shall concentrate on two general positions:

(a) The moral justification of torture in special circumstances;

(b) The legitimization or authorization of morally unacceptable torture out of necessity.

1.2. Terrorism

Considerable controversy surrounds the term "terrorism" and the international community has failed to provide a comprehensive, generally accepted definition. However, we can find many "operational definitions" adopted in many international conventions and European legal acts. One of the most frequently cited definitions comes from the United Nations Security Council Resolution 1566 introduced in 2004, where the Security Council:

---

[21] Niklas Luhmann, *Gibt es in unserer Gesellschaft noch unverzichtbare Normen?* Heidelberg: Müller, 1993, pp. 8–16; see also: Francesco Belvisi, "The Ticking Bomb Scenario as a Moral Scandal," in: B. Clucas, G. Johnstone and T. Ward (eds), *Torture: Moral Absolutes and Ambiguities*, op. cit., p. 63.

> *Recalls* that criminal acts, including against civilians, committed with the intent to cause death or serious bodily injury, or taking of hostages, with the purpose to provoke a state of terror in the general public or in a group of persons or particular persons, intimidate a population or compel a government or an international organization to do or to abstain from doing any act, which constitute offences within the scope of and as defined in the international conventions and protocols relating to terrorism, are under no circumstances justifiable by considerations of a political, philosophical, ideological, racial, ethnic, religious or other similar nature, and *calls upon* all States to prevent such acts and, if not prevented, to ensure that such acts are punished by penalties consistent with their grave nature…[22]

The controversy about the definition surrounds elements such as: agents, purpose, victims, and methods. According to the above mentioned definition, an act of terror may be committed by all kinds of actors - private individuals, members of associations and organizations, as well as states. Thus, on the basis of this definition, we could not distinguish between a mere kidnapper who takes hostages for the purpose of blackmail and a terrorist. We would also not know how to distinguish between a terrorist and an assassin. However, we do provide such distinctions and they seem significant in challenging terrorism. It seems that we have to appeal to the purpose of such an action. The essential part of this definition, which rests on the etymology of the word "terror" (which from Latin means "great fear") could be expressed as inflicting a state of fear on a group of people or the general public. We should add here that it must be an *intentionally* provoked state of fear. The state of fear is an aim and a means to achieve further aims by a terrorist act. But still, one can argue that a kidnapper who takes a hostage to achieve a financial benefit, also intentionally creates a state of fear (for instance in the family of kidnapped person) to enforce his or her will. Similar problems appear when we focus on the victims of a terrorist act. Some people argue that we should distinguish between direct casualties (who died or were injured in a terrorist act) and indirect casualties - all those who were put in a state of fear in the consequence of the act. The direct casual-

[22] S/RES/1566 (2004); <http://www.unhcr.org/refworld/docid/42c39b6d4.html>.

ties are usually not the final purpose of the terrorist act, which is directed against some other actors (governments or nations put under the pressure and forced to meet demands of terrorists). There are some who stress that the characteristic feature of terrorism is that its casualties are innocent civilians. Yet placing such a restriction on the definition would cause further controversies and rule out many acts that are seen as acts of terror, such as the kidnapping of Italian Prime Minister Aldo Moro by terrorists or an attempt to blow up the Russian tsar in the 19th century by revolutionaries. Even terrorist acts against civilians (like Palestinian terrorist acts against Israelis or IRA attacks on British citizens) could be put in question, if we start to discuss whether members of a democratic society who support their government are "innocent." Finally, concerning methods, we simply cannot give the full catalog or name all possible means that could be used in acts of terror. The development of technology and human creativity, also in killing or injuring, has no limits. Just as with torture, we can see that any definition of terrorism is either too narrow or too broad. It means that we should probably be satisfied with some sort of intuitive description of this concept[23] and stop arguing about the words.

Although after 9/11 there has been no mainstream philosophical, legal or political discussion about justifying terrorism, to advocate terrorism one could use similar "tricks" as those used by defenders of torture. One can restrict the scope of the meaning of the notion "terror," for instance by naming which methods count as terrorist and which not; or by making the definition dependent on the final purpose of an act so to exclude for instance freedom fighters aimed at independence of their nation. One can also, just like in the discussion on torture, claim that the term "terrorism" does not apply to everybody. Finally, one can argue that there are some emergency situations where acts of terror performed by people or the state are permissible out of necessity. In my further considerations I shall come back to the latter argument.

---

[23] See: Robert Young, "Political Terrorism as a Weapon of the Politically Powerless," in: I. Primoratz (ed.), *Terrorism. The Philosophical Issues*, op. cit., pp. 55–64.

1.3. Torture and terrorism - common features

I started with introducing torture and terrorism since both are treated as necessary means of war, and share some essential features. The most important one is that both torture and terrorism treat their victims not as persons but as subjects and thus they always infringe human dignity. What is also common to both torture and terrorism is that they are aimed at threatening people - putting their victims in a state of anxiety or fear by using violence or threatening of using it, depriving them of trust to the world in which they live (breaking them, their will, their self-confidence) and depriving them of control over their own lives (violating their autonomy).[24] One of the most moving testimonies of torture comes from the Holocaust survivor, Jean Améry, who said that as a result of the torture he experienced he could no longer feel at home in the world; he had lost his trust in the world and could never regain it.[25] I think that the same feeling of the breakdown and loss of trust in the world in which one lives may come from being exposed to a terrorist attack. I claim that these features make both torture and terrorism morally objectionable in any situation and for any purpose.

2. The ticking time bomb scenario and what is wrong with it

The moral justification of torture in some exceptional emergency situations is usually based on a utilitarian reasoning illustrated by the thought experiment called the ticking time bomb scenario. The ticking time bomb scenario was constructed to show the limits of moral absolutist thinking and is rooted in the considerations of Jeremy Bentham.

Let me invoke the ticking time bomb scenario in the Jean Bethke Elshtain's version:

---

[24] B. Brecher, *Torture and the Ticking Bomb*, op. cit., pp. 84-85.

[25] Jean Améry, *At the Mind's Limit*, transl. by Sidney and Stella P. Rosenfeld, Bloomington: Indiana University Press, 1980, p. 40.

A bomb has been planted in an elementary school building. There are several such buildings in the city in question. A known member of a terrorist criminal gang has been apprehended. The authorities are as close to 100 percent certain as human beings can be in such circumstances that the man apprehended has specific knowledge of which school contains the deadly bomb, due to go off within the hour. He refuses to divulge the information as to which school, and officials know they cannot evacuate all of the schools, thereby guaranteeing the safety of thousands of school children. It follows that some four hundred children will soon die unless the bomb is disarmed. Are you permitted to torture a suspect in order to gain the information that might spare the lives of so many innocents?[26]

2.1. Premises of the scenario - unrealistic realism

The above presented scenario consists of some important premises that must be met; however they are very unlikely to be all met in one case. Let me name them:

(1) Certainty of knowledge - we know that that person knows;
(2) Certainty concerning methods - torture will work;
(3) Guilt of that person;
(4) The scarcity of time;
(5) No other choice - torture are the only alternative;
(6) Easy calculation - pain and suffering of one person vs. suffering and life of hundreds.

As Alan Dershowitz writes, since 9/11 almost everybody asked whether non-lethal torture *should* be applied in the case of the ticking time bomb scenario answers positively to this question. No one, in his opinion, has any doubt as to whether torture *would* actually be used in such a case.[27] Claiming a realistic position, Dershowitz argues for the legalization of torture in emergency situations. The strongest objection given against Dershowitz's argumentation is that his "realism" seems to be in fact unrealistic. I do not mean here the assumption that states do practice torture; this is a fact, a shameful fact. But Dershowitz does not argue that we should legalize torture just be-

---

[26] J.B. Elshtain, "Reflection on the Problem of 'Dirty Hands,'" op. cit., p. 78.

[27] Alan M. Dershowitz, *Why Terrorism Works. Understanding the Threat, Responding to the Challenge*, Yale University Press, 2002, p. 150.

cause they are practiced and it would be an absurd to think so. He argues that non-lethal torture (like for instance a sterilized needle being shoved under the fingernails)[28] should be legalized only if we have to deal with an emergency situation like in the ticking time bomb scenario. This is an unrealistic assumption since the ticking time bomb scenario can hardly ever be true. It is rather more of a pure fantasy than a scenario,[29] a political-fiction with the stress placed on fiction. Let me consider the premises of the ticking time bomb scenario to make this point clear.

The first deep controversy arises when we take the premise of certainty, either of knowledge or concerning methods. Of course one can argue that a human being cannot be certain about anything but nevertheless we have to assume certainty for the sake of making plans, giving promises etc. This is true and that is why in the scenario discussed we assume certainty close to 100 percent (not full certainty) yet it still remains problematic.[30] We have to assume that we are sure that there is a bomb; that we are sure that the detainee knows where the bomb is; that we are sure that by torturing him we will get the information about the location of bomb; that we are sure that we would make use of the information and save the children. No known case of torturing people can meet such a high level of certainty concerning all these matters. The most powerful part of the ticking time bomb scenario, which speaks directly to our emotions and imagination, is that there is limited time and that the decisions must be taken quickly. The scenario falls apart when we begin to add any new conditions that must be met, such as proofs for our knowledge. We have to remember that thought experiments work perfectly in our thoughts but much less so in reality. This is something which many of those who rest their argumentation in favor of torture upon the ticking time bomb rationale seem to forget. Life is much more complex and uncertain than such imaginary scenarios. As Dershowitz himself admits, "in a democracy there is always a *choice*."[31] What is more, the choice is

[28] Ibidem, p. 148.

[29] B. Brecher, *Torture and the Ticking Bomb*, op. cit., pp. 14–39.

[30] Ibidem, pp. 31–38. G. Annas, *Worst Case Bioethics. Death, Disaster, and Public Health*, op. cit., p. 49.

[31] A.M. Dershowitz, *Why Terrorism Works*, op. cit., p. 134.

usually broader than between two bad alternatives given in the scenario. In real life, we can consider evacuating all schools or only those which could be presumably most endangered; we can investigate carefully all information about the detainee and his or her life and surrounding to get the information etc.

Another premise which has proved controversial is that the tortured person is guilty. Again, we come back to the problem of certainty and proof. In our western legal culture, the presumption of innocence belongs to the most fundamental principles on which modern law is based. This presumption means that one cannot be treated as a guilty without being proven guilty. What is more, the burden of proof, as we assume according to another fundamental principle of law, rests on who asserts, not on who denies. If there are any doubts about someone's guilt left, a defendant may not be convicted by the court. This is the role of law and of legal trials to prove if somebody is guilty or not. It means that detaining people without charge and treating them as guilty without proving it, is absolutely unacceptable.

A premise about guilt is a psychological trick, which is actually completely irrelevant from the utilitarian point of view presented in the ticking time bomb scenario. The knowledge of guilt of the person being tortured for the noble end of saving life seems to comfort people who have to solve the moral dilemma. Suppose we have to torture a wife or a child of a terrorist to get the information about the location of a bomb. More people who accept torture in the former scenario would have serious moral doubts in the latter. Whatever we say about our "civilized" societies, people can feel in many situations some kind of desire for revenge. So if a terrorist is tortured to force him to reveal the life-saving information, the feeling is that this person deserves what he gets simply helps people accept the unacceptable. We have no compassion for murderers, sadists, psychopaths, pedophiles, terrorists etc. So in fact, justifying the torture of terrorists or turning a blind eye to such practices in our countries leads to the acceptance of torture as a part of punishment which was a common practice in our societies, even if it was abandoned in recent years.[32] As

---

32 About the history and sociology of punishment see: Michel Foucault, *Discipline and Punish, The Birth of the Prison*, New York: Vintage Books, 1995.

I have mentioned at the beginning of this essay, the role of law and justice is not to satisfy people's desires but to solve conflicts and to enable cooperation in a community based on norms.

2.2. Preemptive justice and its discontents

The basic idea of law rests on an assumption that people's actions can be to some degree calculable and predictable. To make this idea feasible, law has been based on two crucial concepts – that of the concept of responsibility and the concept of obligation. The former assumes that people can be held responsible for their wrongful previous deeds. The concept of responsibility overcomes a problem of the past and its irrevocability by binding us with our previous actions and punishing our previous wrongs. The latter assumes that people can oblige themselves, i.e., they are able to keep promises, which overcomes the problem of the future and its unpredictability.[33]

What seems innovative and particularly interesting in the argumentation of Dershowitz is that he argues for the transformation of our legal (especially penal) systems from punishing into preemptive ones.[34] In other words, he argues for the transformation from a deterrent state based on the paradigm of after-the-fact punishment into a preventive state based on a paradigm before-the-fact prevention. Though traditional penal justice which looks back on what we have done and what could have been predicted and prevented is far from perfect, preemptive justice seems to be even more problematic. The biggest problem of preventive actions which require moral costs is the uncertainty of the future. This is one of the weak points of utilitarian thinking. We know all of the consequences of our actions *post factum*. We do not act in a void; our actions are affected by the actions of other people, as well as by miscellaneous and often unpredicted factors. The Chinese monk who first invented a certain powder while searching for an elixir for immortality did not know the consequences of his discovery and its use for quite the opposite aim. Hitler or Stalin's par-

[33] See: Hannah Arendt, *The Human Condition*, New York: Anchor Book, 1959, p. 219.

[34] Alan M. Dershowitz, *Is There a Right to Remain Silent? Coercive Interrogation and the Fifth Amendment After 9/11*, Oxford University Press, 2008, p. 19.

ents did not know what monsters they had brought into the world. Suppose we can travel in time and therefore know about the consequences of these events. Could we morally accept killing the parents to prevent the monster-child being born? Even if one answers yes, hardly anybody would like to live in a state which pursues a preemptive politics of such a sort. What is more, even those who believe in "numbers ethics" would not be able to calculate all the costs and benefits of such preventive actions. Our knowledge about the consequences of our actions, even supposing time travel, would never be perfect. Thus, it seems deeply unconvincing that preemptive justice would ever work in concert with our moral intuitions.

2.3. Taking utilitarian argumentation seriously – the problem of the calculation of costs and benefits

From the utilitarian point of view, which is based on a mere calculation of costs and benefits, we are not only permitted to torture that person to extract life-saving information in the scenario, but we are also *morally obliged* to do so. One may argue that the calculation in the discussed scenario is easy since non-lethal torture is always better than death. Numerous moving testimonies of torture victims could undermine this assumption but those who would not be convinced can be confronted with the question, asked by Ivan in his moving dialogue with Alosha in Dostoyevsky's book *The Brothers Karamazov*:

> Imagine that you are creating a fabric of human destiny with the object of making men happy in the end, giving them peace and rest at last, but that it was essential and inevitable to torture to death only one tiny creature – that baby beating its breast with its fist, for instance – and to found that edifice on its unavenged tears, would you consent to be the architect on those conditions? Tell me, and tell the truth.[35]

It would be very hard to admit that it is morally good to sacrifice one baby, torturing her to death, to guarantee the happiness of the

[35] Fyodor Dostoyevsky, *The Karamazov Brothers*, transl. by Constance Garnett, New York: W.W. Norton & Company, Inc., 1976, p. 226.

rest of humanity. What sort of happiness would it be, should we ask; and I am sure that many of us do not long for such happiness.

The most disturbing part of utilitarian argumentation, which can also be illustrated by another famous thought experiment, the trolley dilemma, is that it requires us to calculate something which is incalculable such as human life, suffering or pain. I think that we cannot accept any morality which requires us to sacrifice somebody's life for any noble end. We cannot sacrifice something that does not belong to us. We could only sacrifice our own life to save the life of somebody else but I deeply believe that it should be our own choice and not a moral or a legal obligation.

What is more, utilitarian reasoning invoking the ticking time bomb rationale is a double-edged sword since one may apply the same calculation to considerations on the justification of terrorist acts. Suppose we live in a country which is under the occupation of a foreign army which makes the people in our country suffer and systematically kills them. A terrorist attack to stop the occupation is the only alternative we have since our country has been defeated. Just like in a torture scenario, we do not know for sure if our method will result in what we want to achieve. Perhaps it will only escalate the terror of the occupation. Neither will we know whether the object of our attack guarantees our success. The only thing that we do know is that from our subjective point of view it is worth trying to stop suffering of our fellow citizens. So we decide to blow up either some barracks with enemy soldiers inside or an embassy with people who work for the enemy government to produce a state of fear and put pressure on the government. We can go one step further and blow up a train full of civilians in the country of our enemies to stop them from killing our compatriots. Are we morally justified, or even morally obliged, to do so?

This is a well-known moral dilemma discussed in political philosophy with regards to such examples as the bombing of Dresden during World War II by the British and American airforces or the dropping of the atom bombs on Hiroshima and Nagasaki by the Americans.[36] It is frequently argued that these were necessary steps to de-

[36] Michael Walzer, *Just and Unjust Wars: A Moral Argument with Historical Illustrations*, New York: Basic Books, 2000, pp. 251–268; John Rawls, "Fifty years after

feat the Nazis and their allies in WWII and to stop the horrible threat which they brought to the world. In both cases thousands of civilians were killed and suffered unspeakable harm but the most controversial part of this argumentation is whether these acts were in fact necessary, i.e., whether they were the only alternative to win the war and to stop the killing. Taking into account the moment of war in which they were undertaken, it is implausible and very unconvincing to say that there were in fact necessary steps.[37] Were they rather a kind of revenge or a lesson for the future given to the enemies? What makes these examples speak to people's imagination and ask for some kind of their approval is that, as I said, people do not have compassion for their enemies.[38] Considering these situations, one does not calculate suffering and lives, but rather thinks that the enemies were *guilty* for an incredible evil which had to be stopped. And thinking of this in the scenarios mentioned above, one must assume the collective guilt of the nation which created such evil. However, this assumption is deeply inconsistent with common moral beliefs in the liberal state, which are based on personal guilt and individual responsibility.

Yet even if somebody does not find it morally disturbing at all, let us turn to a more difficult case of a terrorist act aimed at a kindergarten to make the moral dilemma more vivid. One may assume that in the democratic society, all citizens who may vote share responsibility of its government actions but this argument does not cover children

---

Hiroshima," in: idem, *Collected Papers*, ed. by Samuel Freeman, Cambridge, Mass.: Harvard University Press, 1999, pp. 565–572. However, to make the picture full, it is worth adding, after Timothy Snyder, that „About as many Poles were killed in the bombing of Warsaw in 1939 as Germans were killed in the bombing of Dresden in 1945 ... More Poles were killed during the Warsaw Uprising alone than Japanese died in the atomic bombing of Hiroshima and Nagasaki." (Timothy Snyder, *Bloodlands: Europe between Hitler and Stalin*, Basic Books, 2010, p. 317, pp. 405–406). Nevertheless, suffering and loss of life are not comparable and cannot be compensated by revenge.

37 C.A.J. (Tony) Coady, "Terrorism, Morality, and Supreme Emergency," in: I. Primoratz (ed.), *Terrorism. The Philosophical Issues*, op. cit., pp. 80–96, here at pp. 85–87.

38 It is quite remarkable that in the end of WWII Germans were frequently seen by the allies as inhuman (T. Snyder, *Bloodlands: Europe between Hitler and Stalin*, op. cit., p. 317, p. 400).

who cannot vote. Let us imagine a situation, given by Dershowitz, in which the relatives of inmates in a Nazi death camp blow up a German kindergarten and threaten to repeat this unless the death camps are shut down.[39] Is it morally right to do so? If we want to claim that this situation does not imply vengeance, why do we insist that the terrorists are relatives of Nazi victims and that the kindergarten be German? If we want to argue that it is only about the pure calculation of lives, we, any person like you and I, should be ready to blow up any kindergarten if only it could force the Nazis to shut their death camps. We are in a thought experiment so we do not have to worry about counterfactual elements of our imaginary situation and this leads us back to the moral dilemma captured by Dostoyevsky in the above mentioned quotation. These examples show, in fact, the limits of morality which cannot be solved by any calculation.

There are two points that I would like to make to conclude these considerations. First of all, decisions in such situations as described in last two sections are based rather on our intuitions and emotional feelings than on any sort of calculation. The rationalization of our emotional decisions usually comes *ex post-facto*, when we have to face its consequences and this sort of rationalization remains deeply controversial. Secondly, in such moral dilemmas, unrealistic though they are, there are no morally right choices, I think, but only tragic ones.[40] A tragic moral choice is a choice between two morally *equivalent* values which contradict each other in a particular conflict situation, which means that by choosing one of them, we have to reject another. Thus, whatever we chose we would lose something equally important. Therefore, I shall argue that when we face tragic moral dilemma and are brave enough to choose one of the values, we also have to be brave enough to bear the full moral responsibility of our choice. Whoever decides to make her hands dirty by breaking moral

---

[39] A.M. Dershowitz, *Why Terrorism Works*, op. cit., p. 146. About similar actions which took place in reality and which were undertaken by Jewish partisnats (who also wanted to continue their fight after the war by taking revange on the Nazis), see: Rich Cohen, *The Avengers. A Jewish War Story*, New York: Vintage Books, 2001.

[40] Many philosophers would agree with this statement. Also Dershowitz claims that torturing in an emergency situation is not a moral, but a tragic choice (A.M. Dershowitz, *Why Terrorism Works*, op. cit., pp. 131–163).

rules for reasons of state should be ready for punishment just as those who break the laws of the state for moral reasons.[41]

3. Can it ever be right to do wrong? - life-saving torture and the argument from necessity (Dirty Harry Case)

So far I have argued that torture, even in an emergency situation, cannot be morally justified. Nevertheless, we can argue that although torture is always morally wrong, there can be situations in which we are forced to use it. Being forced to act is not the same as being morally obliged to act. Acting out of force does not have to be and usually is not morally praiseworthy. As Shakespeare insightfully pointed out, "There is no virtue like necessity."[42] Being fully aware of the fact that we are forced to choose between two evils, we should never forget that the chosen lesser evil remains evil.

The ticking bomb scenario which is very unlikely to happen is a frequently misused argument, a striking rhetorical argument which is applied to situations which it does not cover. All real cases given to illustrate the scenario, like the Philippine case mentioned by Dershowitz or often quoted Israeli cases[43] are based on *post-facto*

---

[41] Michael Walzer, "Political Action: The Problem of Dirty Hands," *Philosophy and Public Affairs* 1973 (Winter), vol. 2, no. 2, pp. 160–180, here at p. 179. See also Max Weber, "Politics as Vocation," in: *From Max Weber: Essays in Sociology*, ed. and transl. by H.H. Gerth and C. Wright Mills, New York: Oxford University Press, 1946, pp. 77–128. Weber argues that a politician who is a good man with dirty hands could be a hero, but a tragic one. A similar position is defended by Allen and Shue who both argue for holding a torturer responsible for torture even if it was performed for the good of the society (Henry Shue, "Torture," in: S. Levinson (ed.), *Torture: A Collection*, op. cit., pp. 47–60, here at p. 58; Jonathan Allen, "Warrant to torture? A critique of Dershowitz and Levinson," *ACDIS Occasional Paper, Program in Arms Control, Disarmament, and International Security*, University of Illinois at Urbana-Champaign, 2005, p. 13). However, the emergency circumstances may be used as arguments to suspend or minimize the penalties, as I will argue in the next section.

[42] William Shakespeare, *King Richard II*, transl. by Peter Ure, London–New York: Routledge, 1994, Act I, Scene 3, p. 37.

[43] A.M. Dershowitz, *Why Terrorism Works*, op. cit., p. 137 ff.

knowledge. We do not exactly know how many cases prove the opposite. As Bob Brecher points accurately out, "In the real world, necessity is always retrospective."[44] Thus, I shall now turn to the question of whether we can give authorization *ex post facto* to torture or threaten to torture in the case of life-saving necessity.

These considerations can be illustrated by the Dirty Harry Case, which also has its exemplifications in real life. One can name here the broadly discussed Daschner case which was concerned with the threat of torture used by police against a kidnapper Magnus Gäfgen in Germany. In 2002 Gäfgen, a 27-year old law student, kidnapped 11-year old Jakob von Metzler, son of a prominent banking family. The kidnapper demanded a one million Euro ransom from the parents. Having picked up the ransom, he was followed by the police and arrested at the airport in Frankfurt am Main. He refused to tell the police where the kidnapped boy was kept. After hours of nterrogation, assuming that "Jakob's life had been in great danger, if he was still alive at all," the deputy police chief of Frankfurt, Wolfgang Daschner, ordered the detainee to be interrogated by a police officer under the threat of torture.[45] The police officer told Gäfgen "that he would suffer considerable pain at the hands of a person specially trained for such purposes if he did not disclose the child's whereabouts."[46] After minutes of questioning under the threat of those measures, he revealed the place where the boy was kept, though the boy was already dead.

During the further proceedings the kidnapper claimed that he remained a victim of torture prohibited by Article 3 of the European Convention on Human Rights (ECHR), as well as by German law. Thus, he maintained that all of the statements which he had made to the authorities should not have been used as evidence in his trial (according to a right to fair trial of Article 6 of the ECHR, which comprises a right not to incriminate himself and a right to defend himself effectively), including all items of evidence, such as the child's corpse,

---

[44] B. Brecher, *Torture and the Ticking Bomb*, op. cit., p. 37.

[45] The Judgment of the Chamber of the European Court of Human Rights, the case of Gäfgen v. Germany (application no. 22978/05), Strasbourg, 30 June 2008, available online.

[46] Ibidem.

which had been found by police as a result of the illegally extracted information. The Frankfurt am Main Regional Court admitted that in accordance with the Code of Criminal Procedure (Article 136a § 3) all confessions and statements of the detainee were inadmissible as evidence in the criminal proceedings since they were obtained through the use of prohibited methods of interrogation. Nevertheless, the court did not exclude from the proceeding all other items of evidence which had become known in the investigation in consequence of excluded statements.[47]

Gäfgen was sentenced to life imprisonment and appealed to the Federal Court of Justice, to the Constitutional Court of Justice, as well as to the European Court of Human Rights. In 2004 the Federal Court of Justice held that the use of prohibited methods of interrogation did not lead to an impediment to the criminal proceedings but led only to the exclusion of such evidence as confession under threat of torture. The Constitutional Court of Justice held that the applicant's constitutional complaint was inadmissible, stating that

> However, the violation of fundamental rights outside the trial did not necessarily warrant the conclusion that the judgment delivered by a criminal court, which was based on the findings made during the trial, breached constitutional law.[48]

Gäfgen also claimed that he was traumatized by the methods of investigation and needed psychological treatment and wanted to bring official liability proceedings against the Land of Hesse for the payment of compensation. The Frankfurt am Main Regional Court refused him legal aid for it and this decision was upheld by the Frankfurt am Main Court of Appeal which found that "the officers' threat was negligible compared to the traumatisation caused by the fact of having killed a child"[49] and that the exclusion of his statements from evidence was the sufficient satisfaction for the violation of his human dignity. He was refused further recognition as a "victim" of torture. The Federal Constitutional Court rejected the decision of the

47 Ibidem.

48 Ibidem.

49 Ibidem.

Court of Appeal and remitted the case to that court, claiming that the Court of Appeal violated the principle of equal access to court by its speculations.

The Grand Chamber of the European Court of Human Rights made its final judgment in 2010, holding (by eleven votes to six) that there was a violation of Article 3 of the Convention (ECHR) and that the applicant might claim to be the "victim" of torture; as well as holding (by ten votes to seven) that the State was to pay the applicant 1,723.40 euros in respect of *some* costs and expenses of the proceedings. The Court unanimously dismissed the remainder of the applicant's claim for just satisfaction.

There were also charges brought against the deputy chief of the police as well as his subordinate who made the threat of torture.

According to German law, one can use any necessary measures in self-defense against unlawful attacks (§ 32 of the German Penal Code).[50] So if killing in self-defense is not an act against the law, the question is whether self-defensive torture is. One may argue that since killing is worse than torturing, and since self-defensive killing does not violate human dignity, *a fortiori* neither does self-defensive torturing.[51] Though the *a fortiori* reasoning seems plausible, it is questionable, as are the premises of the reasoning. What is more important, we cannot apply this reasoning to the authorization of a procedure with the same force as to an act of self-defense. Inflicting severe pain and suffering on an offender in self-defense is something distinct from a special procedure of inflicting pain and suffering by the official authorities. The difference is significant. The aim of the self-defense law is to give an individual legal protection when she is forced to defend herself or others in a situation when the authorities failed to defend them. But when the authorities defend us in our name, the argument of necessity has to meet higher standards, where the prohibition of torture must be recognized. Besides, any regulation legalizing torture as a procedure in interrogation would require the

---

[50] According to the Polish law, on the other hand, one can use measures only *proportionate* to a threat (Art. 25 of the Polish Penal Code).

[51] Uwe Steinhoff, "Justifying Defensive Torture," in: B. Clucas, G. Johnstone and T. Ward (eds), *Torture: Moral Absolutes and Ambiguities*, op. cit., p. 52.

institutionalization of such a questionable practice as torture which is very difficult to accept.[52] Agreeing that some sort of action was necessary in some circumstances is different from institutionalizing that practice. Moreover institutionalizing torture would mean making a torturer a profession, which also seems very controversial.[53]

In the discussed case, the Court rejected the use of the argument of "necessity," even in life-saving situations, to authorize torture or a threat of torture since such methods violate the protection of inviolable human dignity, guaranteed by the Article 1 of the Basic Law (German Constitution). The protection of human dignity is absolute and no exceptions or the balancing of interests is allowed. However, in determining the sentence the Court took into account "significant mitigating factors," such as the fact that police officers were acting out of concern for saving the life of Jakob, which was the exclusive aim of the threat of torture, and under the huge pressure of public opinion which was horrified by the crime. As a result, the Court cautioned the defendants with symbolic fines. The Court found

> ... that the preservation of the legal order did not warrant the enforcement of the fines imposed. Through the defendants' criminal conviction it had been made clear that an order by a State agent to use force to obtain information was illegal.[54]

I think that we can draw a very important lesson from the German case and the aforementioned judicial statements. It was explicitly held by all of the instances of judicial procedure that torture constitutes a violation of human dignity, that it is inconsistent with the rule of law and therefore cannot be authorized or justified by the "necessity argument." Still, this very clear position did not exclude the taking the argument of necessity into account as a mitigating factor in determining the legal consequences of violation of prohibition of torture by the

---

[52] B. Brecher, *Torture and the Ticking Bomb*, op. cit., pp. 43–44.

[53] Ibidem, p. 68 ff. As Ignatieff argues, torture violates basic commitments to human dignity, harming both the tortured person, as well as the torturer, Michael Ignatieff, *The Lesser Evil: Political Ethics in the Age of Terror*, Princeton: Princeton University Press, 2004, p. 140.

[54] The final Judgment of the Grand Chamber of the European Court of Human Rights (2010), available online.

police officers in that particular case.[55] There are many who argue that "symbolic" sentencing is worth nothing but actually, every sentencing in criminal procedure is to some degree "symbolic" since no verdict can reverse time, i.e., no verdict can bring back what was lost by the wrongful act. One of the crucial aims of sentencing is not punishing itself, but restoring the violated norms and trust in them.

One may pose the question of whether any new regulation is needed to respond to that case. Quoting the famous sentence of Justice Oliver Wendell Holmes that "great cases like hard cases make bad law," I would answer this question in the negative.[56] By hard cases I mean cases that concern situations that cannot or hardly can be generalizable, which means that they cannot be addressed by any general legal norms.

The idea of the legalization of torture was discussed in Germany long before the Daschner case appeared when one of the German law professors, Winfried Brugger, introduced the term "Rettungsfolter" (salvation torture).[57] He argued for the legalization of torture in certain emergency situations concerning terror suspects and hijackers but his proposition was never introduced in German law. The aforementioned Harvard professor of law, Alan Dershowitz, who believes that torture is morally wrong also pushed for its legalization in emergency situations. To make the use of torture limited to the really rare situations in which they are really necessary, Dershowitz argues that the judicial warrant should be required to inflict non-lethal torture. He claims that the legalization of torture would in fact protect people from illegal torture made under a retrospective excuse of necessity. Dershowitz's position was frequently objected to by many scholars who questioned the assumption that such a warrant would really

---

[55] The same point is argued by Jonathan Allen, "Warrant to torture? op. cit., p. 13.

[56] Olivier Wendel Holmes, Northern Securities Co. v. U.S., 1904.

[57] Winfried Brugger, "Würde gegen Würde," *Verwaltungsblätter Badden-Württemberg* 1995, p. 414 ff.; idem, "Vom unbedingten Verbot der Folter zum bedingten Recht auf Folter?," *Juristen-Zeitung* 2000, 55, pp. 165-173; idem, "Das andere Auge: Folter als zweitschlechteste Lösung," in: Peter Nitschke (ed.), *Rettungsfolter im modernen Rechtsstaat: Eine Verortung*, Bochum: Kamp, 2005, pp. 107–117; M. La Torre, "'Jurists, Bad Christians': Torture and the Rule of Law," op. cit., p. 24; Hanke Brunkhorst, "Torture and Democracy," in: B. Clucas, G. Johnstone and T. Ward (eds), *Torture: Moral Absolutes and Ambiguities*, op. cit., p. 76 ff.

limit the practicing of torture. They usually argued that the consequence of legalization of torture would be its routinisation. I object to the legalization of torture on normative grounds, claiming that introducing torture (in any kind and in any circumstances) to law is inconsistent with the fundamental principle of the liberal state on which the concept of law is based. The idea of the liberal society is based on an assumption that the state has a monopoly for using violence in a society. What is more, the state's violence is limited by a set of rights and liberties based on the notion of moral equality (which could be also expressed by the concept of human dignity) of all human beings, which means all, including our enemies, "unlawful combatants," non-citizens etc.

Even if the sterilized needle is safer than the non-sterilized needle, and even if sleep deprivation is less painful than rape, all of these practices belong to methods of torture which infringe upon human dignity. "It is difficult to torture just a little,"[58] as Pokempner accurately points out and what Brecher claims asking rhetorically: "how many fingernails; for how long?"[59] And therefore, even if they are "safe" for the life of a tortured person, they are not safe for liberal-democratic society. For a society, any wrongful practice is less dangerous as its legalization which corrupts the rule of law and destroys the most fragile fibre of each society – the trust in the world which is based on the norms accepted by society.

Conclusions

My conclusions could be summed up in Michael Ignatieff's accurate point: "We cannot torture ... because of who we are."[60] Is it hypocritical to argue so? It is rather idealistic but in my opinion political

[58] Dinah Pokempner, "Command responsibility for torture," in: Kenneth Roth, Minky Worden, Amy D. Bernstein (eds), *Torture. Does It Make Us Safer? Is It Ever OK? A Human Rights Perspective,* London – New York: The New Press, 2005, pp. 158–172, here at p. 167.

[59] B. Brecher, *Torture and the Ticking Bomb,* op. cit., p. 83.

[60] Michael Ignatieff, "Moral Prohibition at a Price," in: K. Roth, M. Worden, A.D. Bernstein (eds), *Torture. Does It Make Us Safer? Is It Ever OK? A Human Rights Perspective,* op. cit., pp. 18-27, here at p. 27.

philosophy must be idealistic when we assume a kind of ideal to which we should aspire and from which we judge the real imperfect world.

According to what was written in *The National Defense Strategy of the United States of America*, the Americans are the strong ones and Al Qaeda members the weak in the conflict.[61] If it were true, Americans should be seen as the Athenians in the Peloponnesian war who have power to enforce their rules and their vision of "justice" on their enemies. Yet if we define strength as an ability to play the game by your own rules we have to be clear what rules we actually have in mind. If we talk about "necessity" and "terrorist pressure" which have forced our "civilized" societies to practice "uncivilized" methods (such as torturing suspects, detaining them without charge, refusing them the right to due trial, assassinating them etc.), it means that we are in fact in a position of defense, suspending (i.e., betraying) our liberal values. If we want to remain strong, by which I mean faithful to our own values, we should refuse any kind of methods in this war by which we are forced by our enemies and which distort our culture based on liberal values. Accepting such unacceptable methods makes us, paradoxically, supporters of our enemies whose main aim is to destroy everything what we believe in and who we are. In other words, accepting torture means the self-refutation of the liberal state. We should keep in mind that the survival of nations is not only the survival of their subjects, but foremost the survival of their values. As pointed out by Carlo Della Chiesa, a General of the Italian State Police who refused to inflict torture on a prisoner who had kidnapped former Italian Prime Minister Aldo Moro to force him to disclose his whereabouts: "Italy can survive the loss of Aldo Moro, but it cannot survive the introduction of torture."[62]

---

[61] Donald H. Rumsfeld, *The National Defense Strategy of the United States of America*, Washington, DC: U.S. Department of Defence 2005, p. 5.

[62] Quoted in A.M. Dershowitz, *Why Terrorism Works*, op. cit., p. 134.

Paul Bouissac
University of Toronto, Canada

The Moral and Legal Status of Animals: from Perpetrators of Wrongs to Victims of Abuses

Abstract: The moral and legal status of animals has undergone drastic changes during the last few decades. In many countries laws have been voted by parliaments, notably in Europe and North America, to protect animals from abuses. It is implied the animals cannot be the perpetrators of wrongs. This paper reviews some of the evidence which show that in the past animals were considered as potential criminals which could be tried and condemned whenever they were causing harms to humans. This change of attitude and the legal consequences it entails can be understood in the broader context of ideological shifts. This paper addresses the issues raised by the semiotic transformations which have construed animals as necessary victims to the extent that when they happen to cause harm or even death, the blame is cast on their human victims. This constitutes a challenging problem for legal semioticians who are confronted to this dissymmetry all the more so since, at the same time, some animals continue to be credited with moral virtues, if not in the court room, at least in the media where public judgments nowadays often take place.

Keywords: animal, semiotics, actantial structures, ideology, cultural evolution, morality, responsibility

1. Introduction: animal classifications

The categorization of animals and their differential integration in, or exclusion from human social structures has been the object of intense anthropological research. Each culture evolved its own way of distinguishing various statuses among species and of assigning them to particular places in its cosmology. Those animals which share an ecological niche with humans expectedly are the objects of more refined categorical and semantic distinctions in the particular languages of the populations concerned than those which are lumped in the less precise category of "exotic" animals. Distinctions among the latter are driven by a different logic which often mimics the classification of alien human populations with respect to their geographic locations. Descriptions and explanations of the ways in which animals are cognitively and symbolically treated in cultures are found in the works of anthropologists such as Claude Lévi-Strauss,[1] Edmund Leach,[2] and Stanley Tambiah,[3] to name only a few, who have elaborated comparative systems of animal classifications and scrutinized their pragmatic consequences for human behavior with respect to hunting, consumption, use, and ritual. Tim Ingold,[4] Eugenia Shanklin,[5] and Roy Willis[6] have summarized and further discussed the issues involved in animal categorizations. Animal species can be endowed by religions and philosophies with a vast range of meanings and values as preys or predators, evil or holy, edible or non-edible, useful or dangerous, pets or pests, reincarnated humans or mere instinctual machines, among other oppositional values. These distinctions are not purely abstract but have definite practical and institutional consequences in the cultures which foster them and which are, to a great extent, defined by them.

The advent of Cartesianism imposed on Western modernity a model of the animal as a mere machine deprived of consciousness and feelings. Animal suffering was considered to be non-existent. We know for instance, from the record of complaints which neighbors lodged with the police at the end of the 19th century, that horses were skinned alive at the veterinary school in Paris in order to demonstrate

[1] e.g., Claude Lévi-Strauss, *The Savage Mind*, London: Weidenfeld and Nicolson, 1966.

[2] e.g., Edmund Leach, "Anthropological aspects of language: animal categories and verbal abuse," in: Eric H. Lenneberg (ed.), *New Directions in the Study of Language*, Cambridge: The MIT Press, 1964, pp. 23–63.

[3] e.g., Stanley J. Tambiah, "Animals are good to think and good to prohibit," *Ethnology* 1969, vol. 8, no. 4, pp. 423–259.

[4] Tim Ingold (ed.), *What is an Animal?* London: Unwin Hyman, 1988.

[5] Eugenia Shanklin, "Sustenance and symbols: anthropological studies of domesticated animals," *Annual Review of Anthropology* 1985, vol. 14, pp. 375–403.

[6] Roy Willis (ed.), *Signifying Animals: Human Meaning in the Natural World*, London: Routledge, 1974.

their muscular anatomy to the students. The complainants, though, were not concerned with the cruelty of the process but with the disturbance caused by the noise. Darwinism contributed to bridging this ontological gap between animals and humans but provided at the same time a strong rationale for the distinction between the two, at least from the point of view of its popular interpretation which comforted the perception of their differences conceived as incommensurable degrees of evolution.

By contrast, in Antiquity and Mediaeval Europe, animals were conceptualized in complex semiotic webs rife with ambiguities as messengers of the god(s), embodiment of witchcraft power, objects of worship, or vehicles of curses and blessings. For example, the number of birds which appeared in the sky and the direction of their flight were interpreted by the Roman priests as providing divine answers to questions concerning future events. During the reign of the Inquisition, witches were identified among other signs by their familiarizing with particular animals. But there were also cases of elevating some dogs to quasi sainthood such as the greyhound Guignefort who had saved a child from a snake but was unjustly killed by the boy's father, and became the object of a popular cult sanctioned by the Catholic Church. There were shrines and pilgrimages dedicated to Saint Guignefort, a word whose etymology means "strong dog".[7] Still nowadays, in the European countryside, owls are feared as harbingers of death whereas swallows nesting in a human dwelling are considered to be a blessing for its inhabitants. These customs and the attitudes they reveal have persisted in spite of the strength of Cartesianism among the European intellectual and scientific elite inspired by the Enlightenment.

2. Animal agencies: the legal context

In contexts in which animals were construed as agencies living within human groups or at the interface between human settlements

[7] David G. White, *Myths of the Dog-Man*, Chicago: The University of Chicago Press, 1991; Claude Gaignebet, *A plus hault sens: l' esoterisme spiritual et charnel de Rabelais*, 2 vols, Paris: Maisonneuve, 1986.

and outside wilderness, their actions had necessary impacts on the populations and these actions had to be interpreted in view of the current legal rules and moral norms. Their occasional abnormal or destructive behaviors marked individual animals as responsible agencies whose actions were subject to categorizations in terms of transgressions which could be assessed on grounds similar to some extents to those applying to the population at large. The normal behavior of cattle for example is a set of behavioral expectations not necessarily identical with, but preferably compatible with the safety of their human keepers. Bernard S. Jackson[8] has documented through his early historical research and his more recent semiotic interpretation, the legal status of animal in the Ancient Near East and the Bible, in rabbinic law, Roman law, English law, and other European legal systems. As perpetrators of wrongs animals were held responsible in various degrees, with or without intent, and punished accordingly. The historical record shows that trials of animals were a rather common occurrence in Western civilization.[9] Juridical procedures against animals are well documented in Mediaeval and Modern times.[10] Even in more recent history, trials of animals took place in the United States.[11]

The assumed interference of supernatural powers can endow destructive animal actions with a meaning which require a different redress involving religious norms and rituals. In Mediaeval times the Catholic Church was prone to prosecuting animals which were accused of being manifestations or instruments of diabolic power. As

---

[8] Bernard S. Jackson, "Liability for animals; An Historico-Structural Comparison", *International Journal for the Semiotics of Law / Revue Internationale de Sémiotique Juridique* 24/3 (2011), pp. 259–289 (Special Issue, ed. Deborah Cao).

[9] Jen Girgen, "The historical and contemporary prosecution and punishment of animals," *Animal Law* 2003, vol. 9, pp. 97–133.

[10] Bernard S. Jackson, "The goring ox," in: idem, *Essays in Jewish and comparative legal history*, Leiden: Brill, 1975, pp. 108–152; Jacob J. Finkelstein, "The Goring ox: some historical perspectives on deodands, forfeitures, wrongful death and the western notion of sovereignty," *Temple Law Quarterly* 1973, vol. 46, pp. 169–290.

[11] Jacob J. Finkelstein, "The Ox that Gored?" *Transactions of the American Philosophical Society* 1981, vol. 71, no. 2, Philadelphia: American Philosophical Society, 1981, pp. 48–85.

dreaded manifestations of magic they were treated as the witches with whom they were usually associated. The story of a Scot named Banks and his educated horse Marocco has been chronicled by several writers.[12] The performance was observed in Paris in 1601 and thoroughly described by Pierre de l'Estoile.[13] Following a pattern that can still be witnessed today in circuses, a horse is prompted to nod or shake his head on discreet cues as if he were understanding the questions he is asked and responded appropriately by a gestural "yes" or "no". Other cues signal when he should start and stop other routines. The clever framing of this controlled behavior in the social context created by the performer can convey an uncanny sense of magic. Eventually the man and the horse were tried for witchcraft in Rome and were condemned to be burnt alive.

3. Animals as moral agencies

The notion of guilt presupposes the capability of making choices. If animals are construed as responsible agents who may be punished for their crimes or sins, they must also be endowed with the possibility of choosing good rather than evil, the respect of the norm over its transgression. Although animal behavior has been stigmatized in Western cultures and languages in opposition to civilized and moral conduct as it is obvious from the numerous expressions and common metaphors which mark humanity as non-animal, there are celebrated exceptions which show that animals are also capable of reaching an exemplary moral status in some cultures. There are indeed individual animals which have been construed as "symbolic types" in the sense proposed by Grathoff,[14] that is, embodiments of values which transcend the relativism and inconsistencies of social norms and behaviors. These animals survived their physical deaths by being "immortal-

[12] For a bibliography see R. Toole Stott, *Circus and Allied Arts. A World Biography 1500–1957*, Harpur & Sons, 1958, p. 30.

[13] Pierre de l'Estoile, « Moraco, le cheval de l'écossais » [1601], *Le cirque dans l'univers* 1978, vol. 110, pp. 11–12.

[14] Richard Grathoff, *The Structure of Social Inconsistencies : A Contribution to a Unified Theory of Play, Game, and Social Action*, The Hague: Martinus Nijhoff, 1970.

ized" through literature or art, in particular by having their commemorative statues set in prominent locations in town squares, temples, and shrines. The case of the greyhound Guignefort was mentioned above. But a more recent example is the Japanese Akita dog Hachiko whose statue stands in Tokyo in front of Shibuya train station. An autochthonous pure breed, a detail which is not without relevance, this animal was born on November 10, 1923, and soon became the pet dog of a man who was teaching at the University of Tokyo. Every day, this man was walking with his dog to Shibuya station on his way to work, and the dog had developed the habit of waiting for him to come back every day in front of the station. Two years later, the professor died suddenly while he was at the university. For the next ten years, Hachiko faithfully came back to the station each evening waiting for his master until he himself died in 1935. His loyalty had by then become famous and a campaign was organized to raise money for immortalizing this icon of national virtue. There are several statues of Hachiko in Japan and his story was publicized in various literary forms including children books in which this dog is celebrated as a moral example of loyalty.

In addition to exceptional anecdotes concerning pets, the semiotic foundation of the social construction of animals as responsible and liable agents rests in part on the traditional performances of trained animals which were framed by interpretative narratives as we saw above in the case of Banks's educated horse. The story of the Androcles's lion provides another good example. The Roman chroniclers reported the story of a slave being thrown to the lions in the amphitheater and being saved by one of the animals which came to his defense and protected him. The audience was then told that this man who was from Africa had once removed a crippling thorn from the lion's paw. Both were separately captured later on and sent to Rome for the entertainment of the crowd. The story goes that the lion recognized his savior and reciprocated the favor by saving him. Any contemporary lion trainer can replicate the staging of this performance with a properly trained young animal. Androcles's lion has become a literary icon which embodies virtuous gratitude in most trying circumstances even though there is ample evidence that the story was fabricated in order to frame an instance of skilled wild animal training.

Folktales and fables have also contributed to the attribution of a sense of moral norms to animals, a quality which justifies the accusation of a deliberate intent to transgress these norms. The celebrated Bremen's four animals (the donkey, dog, cat, and rooster) whose statue adorns one of the main squares of this German city, exemplify the virtue of cooperation and innovativeness as opposed to the wickedness of the criminal humans these animals are credited to have overcome.

The emergence of a global culture has exposed the West to Asian attitudes toward animals that blur the ontological distinction grounded in theological thinking. When elephants in an Indian circus ring are trained to perform a Hindu ritual (the *puja*) focused on a Shiva Lingam, the audience accompanies them with religious songs. There is no hint of sacrilegious behavior because these animals participate in a divine status. So do the mischievous monkeys which harass people in Indian cities. There are not eliminated as pests but are captured by specialists who release them with all due regards in distant parts of the countryside. They are often causing fatal accidents but their agency as proxy of Hanuman is considered sacred and righting their wrongs too radically would constitute a still bigger wrong in the context of Hindu cosmology. There has been in human history and probably prehistory a consistent semiotic drive to endow animals with *actantial* status as subjects, helpers or opponents rather than as mere passive objects of a quest. This semiotic status was a prerequisite for their legal status as punishable perpetrators of wrongs. But, more importantly, it construed them as moral agencies confronted to the universal choice between good and evil. Although elephants are considered holy animals by Hinduism, their husbandry exposes their keepers to many unfortunate accidents. An obedient and fully cooperative elephant is very rare. This is why there exists in a temple near Trichur in Kerala the statue of an animal which had shown perfect consistency of friendliness and cooperation during all his long life. Like the Japanese dog Hachiko, this elephant's moral status is immortalized as an icon to be worshipped.

4. A cultural paradigm shift: animals as non-human persons

The moral status of animals in the West provided for a long time the legal grounds for their prosecutions and eventual punishments. But a semiotic sea change has occurred during the 20th century to the point that an animal trial would be unthinkable today in any part of the civil global society. A regular monitoring of human deaths caused by tigers in India during the last decade, notably but not exclusively in the Sundarban mangroves in Bengal, show that elimination is considered a last resort for confirmed man eaters. The official doctrine is that rehabilitation should be the first line of defense. The same reasoning can be observed with respect to urban dogs which behave aggressively toward people. In all the cases involving tigers and other wild animals or pets, the animals are not blamed but the responsibility is ascribed to deforestation or encroachment on their natural habitat for the former or lack of proper attitudes for the latter. The guilt ultimately falls on the victims of these attacks because they are often illegal fishermen, hunters, poachers, or simply foresters who happened to be at the wrong place at the wrong time. Problem pets' owners are considered to be guilty of abuse or neglect and their victims are assumed to have indulged in provocative behavior. More generally, in contemporary civil and democratic global society, the legal status of animals has switched from perpetrators to victims of wrongs. And a corresponding legislation has emerged. It is interesting to identify the conditions of possibility for such a cognitive and moral change of attitude.

The discourses which sustain a legal semiotic landscape - let us call "landscape" the set of laws and court cases which define a norm with respect to a certain cultural area at a certain period of time - can be metaphorically conceived as tectonic plates in geology. All discourses are not necessarily logically coherent but their particular semiotic consistencies compete with each other. The Darwinian discourse has normalized the notion that the ultimate *destinateur* of animal behavior is Nature in the form of natural selection. This discourse still competes with the notion of the ladder of beings that had been previously elaborated by Natural Philosophy. Another underlying discourse is the Rousseauist argument for the fundamental goodness of nature and its perversion by society. All these discourses collide at many points of their semiotic interfaces but they concur to exonerate animals from deliberate wrongdoings and to put the blame on those who interfere with nature whenever animals cause harm to humans or their properties. In addition, being at the top of the great chain of beings (whether in a creationist or evolutionist perspective), should imply a moral grandstand that should not stoop to litigating with lower beings.

Modernity has developed a kind of pervasive anxiety of anthropomorphism conceived as an epistemological sin and, from this point of view, construing animals as victims even when they are the perpetrators of wrongs, allows the human subject to transcend their own animality. The fear of anthropomorphism is a consequence of the discourse of denial and resistance to the naturalization of humans confronted to evolutionary biology and evolutionary psychology or socio-biology, two discourses which tend to blur the distinction between humans and animals. In contemporary society, the legal status of animals rests at the nexus of several semiotic regimes which exercise contradictory pressures for the definition of norms and their translation into legal rules. It is not the purpose of this paper to analyze the legislative texts bearing on animals, nor to scrutinize the court proceedings in which animals were the subjects of litigations. Its goal is to document the much broader semiotic net of relations which sustains the public consensus regarding the moral and civil status of animals in our society, and which grounds any new legislations on a virtual public will for which references are not rooted in mere anecdotes but in the contemporary scientific culture and its spreading in the media.

There have been indeed, during the last few decades, several high profile publications which spilled over to the mass media from the scientific literature and molded the public perception of animals. Primates, especially chimpanzees and gorillas, have been the focus of passionate reports and documentaries on their cognitive capacities, intense social lives, and meaningful interactions with dedicated humans.

But the scope of awareness of animals' commonalities with humans has extended beyond primates. Extreme cases of empathy have taken center stage with unlikely subjects such as the love story between psychologist Irene Peperberg and Alex, an African grey parrot with which she claimed to have developed by an appropriate educational training a code through which verbal communication could occur between the two. Whether the parrot was actually understanding the questions she asked him in English or was simply engaging in mimicking duets with variations as many birds do was debated among the scientific community. But the media coverage foregrounded the news value of the claim irrespective of the serious debates it had triggered. When it was reported that Alex had said "I love you" before dying, tears were shed and obituaries were published.

This general attitude is reinforced by credible scientific investigations of the emotions of animals[15] and the transformation of data gathered by empirical inquiries into rationale for a political agenda. Marc Bekoff, for instance, published an *Animal Manifesto*[16] advocating the recognition of animals as beings endowed with personal feelings and values, as did John Sorenson in a publication squarely titled *Animal Rights*.[17] We are witnessing the cultural emergence of a moral and legal definition of animal rights which raises the issue of how to set the boundary between humans and animals within a civil society. Even in the animal advocacy literature, arbitrary distinctions are made between rabbits and mice when it comes to medical experiments.[18] The extermination of bed bugs, flies, or mosquitoes does not raise any legal or moral objections in Western countries as it does in some Asian religions. The Jains of India, for instance, wear gauze-masks on their mouths lest they would kill a gnat inadvertently when they breathe. But the defense of animals in Europe sometimes goes beyond the advocacy and implementation of lawful protection such as extreme cases in which circus animals were poisoned on the

---

[15] e.g., Marc Bekoff, *The Emotional Lives of Animals*, New York: New World Library, 2007.

[16] Marc Bekoff, *The Animal Manifesto*, New York: The New World Library, 2010.

[17] John Sorenson, *About Canada: Animal Rights*, Fernwood Publishing, 2010.

[18] e.g., M. Bekoff, *The Animal Manifesto*, op. cit.

ground that they were bound to be happier dead than alive in a circus. In 2010, the primatologist and media celebrity Jane Goodall has pleaded for the recognition of the rights of chimpanzees,[19] and, in the same year, during a special session at the American Association for the Advancement of Science's annual meeting, researchers have proposed to redefine dolphins (and some other animals endowed with human-like cognitive and emotional competencies) as "non-human persons".[20] This new state of mind accounts for the facts that, in 2010, a political party whose main agenda is the protection of animals has some elected members in the Dutch parliament and that, in Switzerland, citizens were asked to vote in a referendum proposing to officially assign in each canton a lawyer in charge of litigating on the behalf of animals (who lack language for doing so themselves). Had the referendum been won, all regions in the Swiss Confederation would have been forced to assign lawyers to abused animals. Interestingly, the goal was to defend their rights as victims and, assumedly, argue for the punishments for their abusers, and the nature and levels of compensations rather than represent them as defendants. These high profile moves are symptoms of a deep shift of attitude toward animal life which ultimately tends to integrate animals into the democratic process of the civil, and, probably, specifically urban society which projects its views and values toward the rest of the world in the name of globalization. Thus animal legislations have emerged in many countries as a result of the actantial transformation of animals in the public discourse of the media and the moral credit their behavior enjoys among a global society which mostly experiences animals as pets or protagonists of narratives displayed in virtual reality. However, it should not be forgotten that pets are tailored to the needs of their owners, and that even scientific documentaries are heavily edited with a view not to transgress what is considered to be community standards as far violence and sexuality are concerned. The legal and moral status of animals in the current century and the corresponding

[19] Jane Goodall, and Lilian Pintea, "Securing a future for chimpanzees," *Nature*, 2010, 8 July, vol. 466, pp. 180–181.

[20] David Grimm, "Is a Dolphin a Person?", *Science* 2010, 26 February, vol. 327, pp. 1070–1071.

legislations which attempt to regulate human behaviors toward them are semiotic phenomena which selectively involve a limited range of species and situations. The categorical constructions of animals as *dramatis personae* within actantial structures and the psychological and legal consequences it entails, are fascinating domains of inquiry which semioticians should further explore.

Piotr W. Juchacz
Adam Mickiewicz University, Poland

Public Hearing: on the Dangers of Adversarial Participation

Abstract: An article falls into the area of reflection called *public philosophy* and it is an example of normative analysis of functioning of *the institution of public hearing* introduced to Polish democratic order in 2006. Public hearing is presented as a *dynamic process* which consists of the three phases, with different methods, scope and purpose. The analysis focuses on *the second phase – the public hearing during the parliamentary committee meeting*: a key issue related to the second phase is *discourse structure* that dominates during the public hearing. In particular, the following aspects are considered: A) lack of opportunities of undertaking a discussion and referring to the statements made by others; B) the professional language vs. everyday language, C) psychological challenges associated with performing in public; D) the problem of formulating the conclusions of the public hearing; E) the phenomenon of 'three circles of participation and influence', namely the lack of equal access of the participants of the public hearing to the legislative process; F) the political context, G) the conditions of an effective public hearing. Finally, after careful consideration of it's flaws and good points the public hearing is identified as an example of the adversarial participation.

Keywords: the process of public hearing, adversarial participation, equal access to legislative process, deliberative democracy, citizens' participation

1. Introduction

1.1. On the importance of civic participation

Disappointment with insufficient civic participation in decision-making processes at all levels of governance in modern liberal democracies and with the inefficiency of traditional methods of civic participation in cases in which the authorities attempted, either spontaneously or under legal regulations, the task of a broader inclusion of the citizens in the processes of co-determination of the development of a specific political community has resulted in extensive research, experiments, and proposals regarding the implementation of new deliberative methods of civic participation.

John Gaventa, when analyzing the various initiatives undertaken in Great Britain in order to broaden the public participation of citizens, draws attention to four features that they have in common: (1) the development of active and participatory forms of citizenship should be linked with (2) the inclusion of such social groups as were previously marginalized in decision-making processes, e.g., young people, the elderly, etc., (3) the involvement of multiple stakeholders, which entails the development of new forms of partnership between them and the authorities and citizens, and ultimately results in the broader legitimacy of the decisions and implemented projects, and an emphasis on (4) extending the forms of accountability of politicians and decision-makers (let us keep in mind that a majority of decisions having a considerable impact on the daily lives of citizens are undertaken by the officials in the local and state governments, which are not verified in democratic processes) by going beyond solely legal, fiscal, and political accountability and widening the scope of social accountability *vis-à-vis* the citizens and the organizations of civic society.[1]

1.2. The idea of collaborative participation

One of the most interesting proposals in mainstream research regarding the expansion of civic participation was presented by American researchers from California, namely Judith E. Innes and David E. Booher. They developed the idea of *collaborative participation*, which "should be seen as a multi-way interaction in which citizens and other players work and talk in formal and informal ways to influence action in the public arena before it is virtually a foregone conclusion."[2]

---

[1] John Gaventa, *Representation, Community Leadership and Participation: Citizen Involvement in Neighbourhood Renewal and Local Governance*, Prepared for Neighbourhood Renewal Unit Office of Deputy Prime Minister, July 2004, p. 7, see the website: http://www.dfid.gov.uk/r4d/PDF/Outputs/CentreOnCitizenship/JGNRU.pdf (available as of 23-08-2012).

[2] Judith E. Innes, David E. Booher, "Reframing Public Participation: Strategies for the 21st Century," *Planning Theory & Practice* 2004, December, vol. 5, no. 4, p. 429.

The starting point of their considerations is the answer to the question about the tasks and objectives of civic participation. J. Innes and D. Booher identify seven objectives of participation, among which the first five, in their opinion, are usually indicated in order to justify this participation, while the last two are added in the context of applying, in recent years, some new collaborative methods of engaging citizens in decision-making processes. This allows the expansion of the spectrum of the justification for broadly understood civic participation. In fact, participation primarily allows the meeting of the following seven goals[3]:

1) decision-makers can learn about citizens' preferences;
2) decisions can be improved by taking into account the local knowledge of citizens;
3) public participation advances fairness and justice; it helps the least advantaged social groups to be better recognized to a greater extent than traditional methods;
4) public participation constitutes evidence of the democracy of decision-making processes and is the source of their public legitimacy;
5) participation of citizens in decision-making processes is often required by law, and although it mostly assumes only the traditional form of public consultations, it increases the citizens' influence on the authority that bears the obligation of conducting such consultations;
6) participation helps to build civil society;
7) participation helps to generate an adaptive and self-organizing polity capable of approaching even the most difficult problems in a conscious and efficient manner.

As an alternative to traditional methods of civic participation, Innes and Booher propose and develop the idea of *collaborative public engagement*, or *collaborative participation*, treating these terms synonymously. According to them:

> ... participation must be collaborative and it should incorporate not only citizens, but also organized interests, profit-making and non-profit organizations, planners and public administrators in a common framework where all are interacting and influencing one another and all are acting

[3] Ibidem, pp. 422–423.

> independently in the world as well. ... It is a multi-dimensional model where communication, learning and action are joined together and where the polity, interests and citizenry co-evolve. The central contention is that effective participatory methods involve collaboration, dialogue and interaction. They are inclusive. ... focused on anticipating and defining future actions. They are self-organizing both in content and membership. They challenge the status quo and ask hard questions about things otherwise taken for granted. They seek agreement or at least build shared knowledge and heuristics for collaborative action. This framework is ... based on the complex systems imagery of a fluid network of interacting agents, gathering information from each other and the environment and acting autonomously based on their needs, understandings, and shared heuristics ... This system ... can build societal capacity and produce innovative responses to seemingly intractable problems.[4]

The concept of collaborative participation has the characteristic features of a broadly understood type of deliberative model of public engagement of citizens. Its authors, trying to bring out the fundamental difference between this approach and the traditional methods, list six major differences[5]:

1) a dialogue instead of a one-way conversation,
2) a representative diversity of participants instead of elites or volunteers,
3) the involvement of citizens from the beginning instead of reactive activity (attenuating the arising tension),
4) mutually sharing knowledge instead of top-down education,
5) continuous involvement of citizens instead of one-shot activity,
6) non-standard choices instead of routine actions.

The concept of collaborative participation undoubtedly opens us to new opportunities to transform the existing democracy, which is paternalistically oriented at citizens, into such a political system as is closer to the ideals of autonomy and the empowerment of citizens as active members of political community, who involved in its life by being able to influence and determine the directions of its develop-

---

[4] Ibidem, p. 422.
[5] Ibidem, p. 430.

ment, the selection of the measures needed to achieve those objectives and to monitor the current exercise of power by elected representatives, thus enhancing the existing representative democracy with an additional dimension of a profound, mature, participatory citizenship.[6]

1.3. The idea of adversarial participation

After having indicated what objectives should be pursued within the framework of civic participation and after elaborating the idea of collaborative participation, Innes and Booher draw attention to the pathologies of the traditional forms of participation. To my mind, the deliberations that are most interesting and undoubtedly worth a closer look are those in which the authors in question warn against the possibility of falling into the fallacy of *adversarial participation*,[7] which may take two forms.

First of all, in the framework of adversarial participation, we can deal with publicly involved citizens who are opposed to the representatives of the authority. This duality exaggerates, in a harmful way, the tension between the legitimacy behind the citizens integrated in the decision-making processes and the effectiveness of elected officials. Why? Because on the one hand, the participation of citizens often allows the implementation of more favourable, yet previously unforeseen, solutions to the debates and thus contributes to making better decisions (so citizens turned out to be effective), and on the other hand, officials, democratically elected to their positions or appointed by other elected representatives of political community, also already have political legitimacy.

---

[6] See more: Piotr W. Juchacz, *Demokracja – Deliberacja – Partycypacja. Szkice z teorii demokracji ateńskiej i współczesnej* [Democracy – Deliberation – Participation. Essays in the Theory of Athenian and Modern Democracy], Poznań: Wydawnictwo Naukowe IF UAM, 2006.

[7] Innes and Booher use the term *adversarial participation* only once (p. 421), yet I do believe it is worth a more common and frequent application, since it excellently captures the essence of the form of participation which is created by the traditional methods of civic participation.

Secondly, *adversarial participation* may take a form in which it mutually antagonizes publicly engaged citizens. This is usually the case when using traditional methods of public consultation, which "... often antagonize the members of the public who do try to work with them. The methods often pit citizens against each other, as they feel compelled to speak of the issues in polarizing terms to get their points across,"[8] rather than jointly seek solutions acceptable to all the parties.

A typical example of the traditional method of increasing the impact of citizens on decision-making processes, while actually antagonizing its participants, is public hearing, which have been widely used for years in many countries in Western Europe and the U.S.

1.4. Public hearing as the institution of public consultations

The institution of public hearing was introduced in Poland relatively recently as part of the *Act on lobbying activities in the legislative process* of July 7, 2005,[9] and by the "Directive of the Council of Ministers of 7 February 2006 on the public hearings concerning the proposed regulations"[10] and by Article 1 Point 2 of the "Resolution of the Polish Sejm of 24 February 2006, on the amendment to the Rules of the Polish Sejm," which added Chapter 1a in Section II, entitled "Public Hearing."[11] During the past six years, the Sejm of the Republic of Poland has decided to hold 22 public hearings: seven in the Sejm of

[8] J.E. Innes, D. E. Booher, *Reframing Public Participation...*, op. cit., p. 419.

[9] See Chapter II, Article 8 (bills) and Article 9 (directives); the entire text of the "Act on lobbying in the legislative process" is included in the *Journal of Laws* of 2005, no. 169, item 1414; Article 3 of the "Act of 29 January 2009 amending the Act on the Council of Ministers and certain other acts" has introduced several changes to supplement the aforementioned Act (see the *Journal of Laws* 2009, no. 42, item 337), yet they do not relate to the institution of public hearing.

[10] *Journal of Laws* 2006, no. 30, item 207. Detailed rules governing the process of conducting public hearing by a specific government department on the draft directive have been governed by this directive.

[11] See *Polish Monitor* 2006, no. 15, item 194. Detailed rules for conducting public hearing by a specific Sejm Commission on a bill have been set forth in the "Rules of the Polish Sejm," Section II, Chapter 1a.

5th tenure (2005–2007, of which one was cancelled), twelve in the Sejm of 6th tenure (2007–2011), and, so far, three in the Sejm of 7th tenure.[12]

A public hearing is a typical example of a traditional method of public consultation with the aim to increase the transparency of law-making processes and their legitimacy in the eyes of citizens. A six-year period of presence in the Polish legal system allows us to make preliminary analyses of its usefulness, to look closer at its structure in the Polish legislative system, and to consider whether it lived up to expectations.

2. The analysis of the second phase of the process of public hearing – public hearings during the parliamentary committee

2.1. Three phases of the process of public hearing

I believe that the analysis of public hearings *as a dynamic process* is of a fundamental importance for a proper understanding of their character. I propose distinguishing three phases in the process of public hearing, each of which is equally important to assess its success or failure. In my opinion, the process of public hearing consists of the following three phases, each having different methods, scope and purpose.

A. The first phase – before the public hearing.[13] The primary cause of concern regarding the first phase of a public hearing relates to the formal and legal arrangements adopted in the *Rules of the Sejm* of the Republic of Poland, primarily the fundamental *issue of convening the public hearing*, in which we can distinguish seven problem areas that, in my opinion, require special attention and a detailed analysis: A) who

[12] See the information on the recently conducted public hearings on the website of the Polish Sejm: http://www.sejm.gov.pl/Sejm7.nsf/page/inf_wys_pub.

[13] I will brood upon the analysis of the first phase of public hearing in a separate article which should be published forthwith. See Piotr W. Juchacz, "*Ab ovo*, i.e. on the issue of convening the public hearing," *Principia* 2012, Kraków: Wydawnictwo UJ.

should be allowed to present the proposal to convene the public hearing; B) the facultative vs. arbitrary nature of convening the public hearing; C) the moment of convening the public hearing; D) the problem of publicizing the decision to convene the public hearing; E) the contents of the application form; F) the possibility of reducing the number of participants; G) the issue of cancelling the public hearing.

B. The second phase – the public hearing during the parliamentary committee meeting. The key issue related to the second phase is the *discourse structure* that dominates during the public hearing; in particular, the following aspects should be considered: A) the lack of opportunities to undertake a discussion and refer to statements made by others; B) the problem of using of the proper language: the bureaucratic and scientific language of professionals vs. the everyday language of ordinary citizens; C) the psychological challenges associated with performing in public; D) the problem of formulating the conclusions of the public hearing; E) the phenomenon of 'three circles of participation and influence,' namely the lack of equal access of the participants in the public hearing to the legislative process; F) the political context; G) the conditions of an effective public hearing.

C. The third phase – after the public hearing. The key issue regarding this phase concerns the impact that the public hearing has on the further work on the bill in parliamentary committee and information about that for ordinary citizens; the fundamental issues to be considered relates to the publication of transcripts from the public hearing in the bulletin of the Sejm and the need to provide a summary, as well as to the fundamental importance of reliable information in the media about the course of a particular public hearing.

The following discussion, because of the modest frames of this article, will focus on a detailed analysis of the second phase of the public hearing, thus paying particular attention to the contentious issues and the problems that are, on the one hand, characteristic for this form of public consultation and, on the other hand, are related to the pattern according to which this institution functions in Poland.

2.2. The basic principles of the second phase of the public hearing

Let us start our discussion on the second phase of the public hearing, namely the very act of the public hearing being convened by the Parliamentary Committee, by reminding ourselves of some brief records in the Rules of the Sejm that relate to it. According to these rules, the public hearing is held only at one committee meeting, and the agenda for the meeting cannot include other items (Article 70f); the chairman of the committee shall determine the order and the speaking time of the people involved in the public hearing, and each participant may take the floor only once, although the chairman may extend the speaking time of a specific person (Article 70g); in justified cases, the chairman may interrupt the meeting, and he decides the date, time, and place of its resumption, either immediately informing all those present or placing such information in the Information System of the Sejm (Article 70h); in the course of the public hearing, each reported participant may note to the protocol the text of a speech that has not been delivered, for instance, due to an insufficient amount of time (it will be marked in a way that will help to distinguish it from the texts delivered), and the same opportunity is granted to those who expressed their willingness to participate, yet did not take part in the public hearing, provided that the submission of the text will take place by the date of the hearing (Article 70i). If more than one person is willing to deliver a speech in the name of the same legal entity, then the speeches of all the people representing the entity in question must fit within the prescribed time; the proportion of the distributed time shall be arranged between them. After the speeches of all the participants whose applications were submitted in the prescribed time and manner, the chairman may allow the speeches of those whose applications do not meet all the requirements of the Rules of the Sejm.

As we can see from the above description, the formal structure of the public hearing is precisely specified because the indicated stipulations generally refer to some formal regulations, which do not raise major controversies. They essentially provide for equal and fair participation in the public hearing. When describing the second phase of the public hearing, we will focus on the nature of this institution of public consultation by undertaking a detailed analysis of the discourse structure that dominates in the course of the public hearing.

2.3. False hopes?

The supporters and advocates of implementing the institution of the public hearing into the Polish legal system harbour considerable hopes in relation to this issue. According to Paweł Dobrowolski and Łukasz Gorywoda, the authors of the report for the Sobieski Institute as of 2004, who promote this method of engaging citizens, the public hearing aims at "reducing corruption by providing citizens with full knowledge of the arguments for and against the proposed bills, providing the legislators with the arguments and opinions of all the parties, and balancing the conflicting interests of citizens in order to maximize the common good."[14] In the opinion of the above authors, the most crucial benefits of implementing public hearings are the following: publicizing the law-making process, enabling citizens to engage in public life, systematizing public debate, hindering manipulation, civilizing lobbying, democratizing access to the Sejm, introducing the need for a public justification for controversial legislation, and avoiding a law-making process that takes place behind the backs of citizens in closed groups of experts.[15] The objectives and benefits that should result from implementing the institution of public hearing seem, therefore, to be very important and extensive.

2.4. Reasonable doubts and the real threats

However, prior to the introduction of public hearings to the Polish democratic system, there appeared serious allegations and concerns regarding this institution. We will nevertheless narrow down our discussion to one example, namely the speech delivered by Danuta

[14] Paweł Dobrowolski, Łukasz Gorywoda, *Publiczne Wysłuchanie. Kontrola stanowienia prawa przez obywateli* [Public Hearing. Citizens' Control over Law-Making Process], Raport Instytutu Sobieskiego [The Sobieski Institute Report], Warszawa 2004, p. 2.

[15] Ibidem, pp. 13–19.

Przywara, the representative of the Helsinki Foundation for Human Rights, who drew attention to the one-sidedness of public hearings and lack of possibilities for deliberation between the participants of the public hearing as opposed to the possibilities present during the discussions in parliamentary committees, to which the representatives of NGOs are sometimes invited:

> I have strongly mixed feelings because both the public hearing as well as submitting one's comments in writing are somehow one-sided acts. There are no dialogue, no answers, no debate. It is much like throwing the idea into the box. The legislator will either make use of it or not, but it is his ruthless law. Indeed, the legislator always behaves in this way, except that in the course of the work in the committees, one can additionally answer some questions, and that is not the case here.[16]

This statement, so characteristic of sceptics, goes to the heart of the objections that can be raised *vis-à-vis* the public hearing institution.

Unfortunately, long-standing practice reveals that the reality of applying this method can considerably differ from the optimistic hopes. Most practitioners of public participation take a negative attitude towards this method and they warn against its application. For example, James L. Creighton, in his well-known work *The Public Participation Handbook*, writes as follows:

> Normally, except where legally required, avoid public hearings. ... The one positive value of public hearings is that everybody gets to hear whatever anybody else says. But hearings also *tend to exaggerate differences*: leaders of organized groups have to be seen defending their group's interests and *have to take more extreme positions than they would in private*. Public hearings are also easily dominated by organized groups. People who simply want information have to sit through hours of speeches in order to get that information - and may never get it.[17]

[16] To quote the words of Danuta Przywara (Helsinki Foundation for Human Rights), see the transcript of the seminar: "Lobbying and advocacy activities of NGOs in the light of new regulations," Warszawa, 10th January 2006, pp. 16–17, cf. at: http://www.isp.org.pl/kompas/files/6779439460236719001182100907.pdf.

[17] James L. Creighton, *The Public Participation Handbook. Making Decisions Through Citizen Involvement*, San Francisco: Jossey-Bass, 2005, p. 130 [emphasis - P.W.J.].

An excellent example of the dangers entailed in this method of public consultations was a pioneering use of the method, before public hearings had been even officially introduced into the Polish legal system, which took place in February 2005 in the Ministry of Health, concerning the commencement of legislative work on the "Drug Abuse Prevention Act."[18] There were over one hundred people who came forward to participate, as a result of which the speaking time was limited to three minutes. Accordingly, everyone had to quickly present their positions, and additionally, in order to be noticed, their conduct had to be quite strident, which resulted in the polarity and rigidity of their standpoints. This was aptly pointed out by Wiktor Osiatyński, who participated in the meeting. He observed that this public hearing "took the form of a forum for the exchanging of the different ideas of the representatives of two diverse, often radical points of view, yet there were no specific proposals of solutions or of a compromise."[19]

It is indeed the lack of the possibilities of deliberation, mutual persuasion, or changing standpoints and finding compromise solutions acceptable to all citizens in a pluralistic democratic state that suggests the doubtful value of this method of public involvement. This method does not meet the basic function of common reflection and exploration of solutions, thus reducing the citizens' participation to the possibility of expressing their opinion. This is a far too small an achievement, which is unfortunately quite characteristic of the traditional methods of civic participation.[20] What also turns out to be illu-

[18] "Ustawa o przeciwdziałaniu narkomanii" [Drug Prevention Act] has been enacted on 29th July 2005. See the *Journal of Laws* as of 19th September 2005, no. 179, item 1485.

[19] More information on the public hearing in the Ministry of Health can be found in the article by Justyna Rutkowska, "Public hearing - wysłuchanie publiczne - studium przypadku" [Public hearing - a case study], *Trzeci Sektor* 2006, Summer, no. 6, pp. 41–46. This article was also the source of the abovementioned quote taken from the interview carried out by the author of the article with W. Osiatyński, ibidem, p. 45.

[20] Further on the new deliberative methods of public engagement of citizens, see John Gastil, Peter Levine (eds.), *The Deliberative Democracy Handbook. Strategies of Effective Civic Engagement in the Twenty-First Century*, San Francisco: Jossey-Bass, 2005.

sory is the belief in the broad involvement of ordinary citizens in the public hearing. Its participants are mostly the representatives of interested non-governmental organizations and public institutions, focusing mostly on the impact of the proposed regulations on their direct activities and less on the long-term consequences for ordinary citizens.

The researchers of the pathologies associated with the public hearing cite numerous arguments against the use of this method. However, the fundamental objections can be reduced to the following: merely discussing the already-proposed solutions, one-way communication, the lack of the possibilities for the citizens to develop a discussion and pose questions, promoting adversarial language, and even the use of metaphors of combat and battle between the opposing standpoints.[21] As a result, we have a pathological form of civic participation, devoid of a genuine transformational power of civic deliberation. It is indeed only

> ... when an inclusive set of citizens can engage in authentic dialogue where all are equally empowered and informed and where they listen and are heard respectfully and when they are working on a task of interest to all, following their own agendas, everyone is changed. They learn new ideas and they often come to recognize that others' views are legitimate. They can work through issues and create shared meanings as well as the possibility of joint action. They can learn new heuristics. ... They also came to see themselves as people who could make a difference ...[22]

Let us add that the interaction of citizens affects not only the development of their participatory abilities, mutual respect, and recognition, but also the common construction of public institutions in a specific form: institutions open for the cooperation and dialogue. And only through such transformed institutions influencing various areas of the public sphere and political reality.

---

[21] J.E. Innes, D.E. Booher, *Reframing Public Participation...*, op. cit., p. 424.
[22] Ibidem, p. 428.

2.5. Discourse structure that dominates during the public hearing

When analyzing the discourse structure that dominates during the public hearing, we can perceive its four characteristics:

A. Lack of any discussion or the possibility of referring to statements made by others (polemics)

A public hearing is of a non-deliberative character because it eliminates both the discussions between citizens and the representatives of legislative bodies as well as between the citizens themselves by limiting the possibility of making statements to merely few minute-long presentations. Additionally, there exists the problem, observed by the researchers of this issue, of pathological behaviour on the side of the representatives of the authorities, such as ostentatious disparaging of the speakers by reading papers, having discussions with other participants during speeches, etc.[23]

The lack of any possibility of discussion is reflected in the rules provided by the chairmen of particular public hearings, such as the Chairman of the Committee on Justice and Human Rights, Ryszard

---

[23] It is worth quoting a loudly applauded scathing remark made by one of the participants in the public hearing on the government bill concerning the principles of unpaid acquisition of Treasury shares by eligible employees in the process of consolidating the companies within the energy sector, the principles of changing their shares and the amendment to the Personal Income Tax Act: "I do hope that the fact that a large part of our official guests and MPs sit with their backs to the speakers, does not reflect their attitude to what is being said here". In response, A. Grad, the MP who chaired the hearing, awkwardly tried to justify the government representatives and the MPs in the following words: "I want to point out that no one is sitting with their back to anyone. It is just the way that the room is arranged .... " [See: the "Transcript of the meeting of the Economy Committee (no. 160) and the Treasury Committee" (no. 98), *Bulletin* no. 2283/V term, 23rd August, 2007, the Chancellery of the Sejm – Sejm Commissions Office, Warsaw 2007, p. 12, available at: http://orka.sejm.gov.pl/Biuletyn.nsf/0/24AFA4D06D1702C3C125735A0029AD7B/$file/0228305. pdf]. After all, such arrangement of the seats is an unforgivable failure of the organizers of the public hearing, thus demonstrating the arrogance of the authority *vis-à-vis* the citizens, or it is at least usually perceived in this way by the participants of the public hearings and therefore neither the mentioned remark nor the applause of the participants should come as a surprise.

Kalisz, the MP who expressly warned the participants at the beginning of the public hearing concerning the bill introduced by the Polish President amending the Personal Data Protection Act (July 2008) with the following words:

> The person referred to in paragraph 1 can stand only once during the meeting organized for the purpose of the public hearing. Accordingly, there are no *ad vocem* speeches. There is no possibility of taking a stance on the speeches delivered by other participants.[24]

Similarly, when concluding the public hearing on a bill amending the Law on the National Judicial Council (September 2006), the chairman and MP Cezary Garbarczyk said,

> The Rules of the Sejm are very categorical at this point, and they do not allow to take a stance again by any person, who has already delivered a speech. I cannot, therefore, give the floor to anyone...[25]

Nevertheless, I would like to note that despite the lack of polemics assumed in the course of the public hearing, it is to some extent present in the form of comments made by further speakers. This results in a certain imbalance and exposes another weakness of this institution of public consultations. We can often observe a situation, or, as some may say, a peculiar social engineering game, in which a representative of a specific organization who was to make his presentation earlier resign from delivering his speech in favour of a person from the same organization who was to make a presentation in the subsequent part of the public hearing. This allows, in addition to presenting their own position, for at least a short comment on the earlier proposals on an on-going basis. In this context, it is probably worth taking a closer look at this phenomenon during subsequent public

[24] The stenographic record: "From the Session of the Committee on Justice and Human Rights" (no. 50), *Bulletin* no. 914/VI term of office, 9 July 2008, the Chancellery of the Sejm - Sejm Commissions Office, p. 3. See: http://orka.sejm.gov.pl/Biuletyn.nsf/0/21D852F718DDF6F5C125749D0025FEA7/$file/0091406.pdf.

[25] "The stenographic record of the meeting of the Committee on Justice and Human Rights" (no. 68), *Bulletin* no. 1144/V term, 28 September 2006, the Chancellery of the Sejm - Sejm Commissions Office, Warsaw 2006, p. 28. See: http://orka.sejm.gov.pl/Biuletyn.nsf/0/19262711A6D14543C1257218004CC81E/$file/0114405.pdf.

hearings, and if it becomes clear that the habit of commenting on the statements of the previous speakers or the habit of providing a specific summary of the already-presented proposals by those who take their stance in the subsequent part of the public hearing is being more and more established and used as a kind of advantage, introducing an imbalance between the participants of the public hearing, then it would be advisable to consider applying a rule demanding a random order in taking the floor, rather than following the rule of the alphabetical order, which should not pose a problem given today's technical capabilities.

B. Bureaucracy and scientific language vs. the everyday language of citizens

Those who conduct the public hearings very often use and prefer to use, on the one hand, a considerably bureaucratic language (which is a kind of combination of bureaucratic newspeak and legal language), and on the other hand an academic language, often full of specialist terms, especially when the issue under consideration draws the attention of non-governmental organizations represented by people who come from the scientific community (sometimes they only help to prepare the speech of a particular representative of the NGO). Both these jargons, bureaucratic and academic, are usually difficult to understand for the average citizen, and thus, they blur the transparency of the law-making process. The use of such jargons also results in the fact that the average citizen, who speaks everyday, non-professional language, can, on the one hand, have a depressing sense of being excluded from the "specialist" discourse dominant in the course of the public hearing, while on the other hand, his arguments, despite their possible aptness, may be underestimated by the other participants in the public hearing on account of the colloquial language. I believe that the crucial issue in the course of the hearing, which is to be public, open both to all citizens wishing to listen to it as well as accessible and open for the participation of all those concerned, is to use language that is understandable for the average citizen, manifesting both respect of the legislators for those who chose them as their representatives as well as the mutual respect of the entities that represent the public. This respect takes the form of recognizing all the participants as equals capable of rational deliberation in the public domain for the common good.

C. The psychological challenges associated with public speeches

A separate issue that can be only signalled here is the mental challenges faced by the participants of the public hearing. For those without experience in public speaking, taking part in the public hearing undoubtedly entails considerable psychological stress, which is related firstly to the necessity of speaking in front of a group of MPs, before the representatives of the executive, and typically before a large number of other participants of the public hearing, which can be undoubtedly intimidating for the average citizen, and secondly, with the inevitable situation of entering into public dispute with other citizens. Due to the fact that the people who have already gained proficiency in public speaking, like politicians, local government representatives, scientists, lawyers, experienced representatives of NGOs, journalists, etc., are in a much more comfortable situation than the average citizens and that they often have advantages resulting both from their social position and education (see: the previous paragraph), it seems essential for the chairman to conduct a proper inclusive hearing. On the one hand, this is for the purpose of emphasizing the equality of all the entities participating therein, and on the other hand, it is for responding to *ad personam* statements that disturb the speeches delivered by others. The problem of the acceptable forms of emotional expression during public hearings constitutes a separate and, at the same time, very interesting issue, which cannot be touched upon here due to the modest frames of this article. Let us not forget that the said mental challenges may constitute a nuisance for some citizens and thus affect their decisions to participate in the public hearing. One may naturally say that any form of public engagement exposes us to the need of dealing with mental challenges associated with the activity among other citizens and the inevitable diversity of opinions and proposed action, however, we should perceive significant differences between the various methods of public engagement of citizens, some of which, like public hearings, take the form of adversarial participation, while others, such as – for example – *citizens' juries*, which have been successfully developed for years, have a more deliberative and consensual nature.

D. The need to formulate a summary

The problem of formulating a summary of the public hearing should be considered on two mutually complementary levels:

a) a summary of the deliberations during the public hearing, which take place in the second phase of the public hearing, undertaken by the chairman or by the representatives of the authors of the bill;

b) a summary of the comments made by the participants in the public hearing, drawing up the theses made by the participants together with their reasons as well as a substantive response to them, accompanied by the presentation of the standpoint of the petitioners in the final report of the public hearing (the third phase of the public hearing).

The current discussion of the second phase of the public hearing will focus on the first of the above areas. When analyzing the public hearings that took place in last six years in the Polish Sejm, we can perceive a significant problem, namely that the "Regulations of the Sejm" lack the requirement of any substantive summary of the public hearings conducted by Parliamentary Committees. Such a loophole in the form of the absence of provisions regarding necessary summaries after public hearings concerning draft legislation (bills) comes as a surprise because the Regulations of the Sejm were set forth more or less at the same time as the said "Regulation of the Council of Ministers of 7 February 2006 on the public hearing concerning the draft directives,"[26] which is much more precise in relation to this issue. The

[26] Detailed rules governing the manner of conducting the public hearing by the respective ministry on the draft directive have been set forth in the "Regulations of the Council of Ministers of 7 February 2006 on the public hearing concerning the draft directive," cf. *Journal of Laws* of 2006, no. 30, item 207. Article 8 of these Regulations provides, inter alia, that "the process of the public hearing is documented in the minutes" (paragraph 1) and it can be also "recorded by means of sound recording devices *or* image recording devices" (paragraph 2) – it is interesting that if someone wanted to read this provision verbatim, it could result either in a silent movie or in a record with a mere sound. Paragraph 3 indicates, inter alia, that the minutes of the public hearing includes, in particular, the main theses of the opinions presented by the participants (paragraph 3, point 2), and "the standpoint of the chairman of the public hearing in respect to the presented opinions" (paragraph 3, point 3). In accordance with paragraph 4, "the minutes of the public hearing is published in the Bulletin of

provisions of the regulations impose much heavier duties on the chairmen of the public hearings concerning the draft directives than those specified in the Regulations of the Sejm concerning bills, because they stipulate that the chairman of the public hearing or "the people who participated in preparing the draft directive in substantive and legal terms" (§ 5, section 2) "systematically address the reasons and arguments presented by the participants of the public hearing" (§ 6). None of these provisions has been reflected in the provisions concerning the public hearing in the Sejm, which were adopted 17 days later.

What is the current practice? When comparing the twenty one public hearings that have already taken place, we typically deal with a short summary provided by the drafters or the chairmen of the public hearings, yet they are quite general, often rhetorical, and sometimes casual in nature. Typically, they do not constitute substantive discussions regarding the demands, but are rather treated as a promise of reviewing these demands in the subsequent stages in the parliamentary subcommittees.

Nevertheless, a systematic summary does not seem to be an overwhelming task for the people who work on specific draft legislation. In the course of the public hearing, arguments are often repeated and the speakers generally refer to specific provisions in the bill, many of which were probably already discussed at the earlier stages of the legislative process. What can be provided as an interesting example is the statement made by Jakub Wygnański in the course of the public hearing concerning the government bill on the government bill on the amendment to public benefit and voluntary work act, and on other acts. He delivered his speech as the last of the participants, not counting the MPs and the representatives of the drafters, and he summarized the issues raised by dividing them into three categories: uncontroversial, ambivalent, and those that raise resistance from the circles potentially influenced by the act. The details are not presented here, because the content of the act is not of our interest now. Even such a simple distinction introduced a certain order into the debate

Public Information, on the website of the body responsible for drawing up the draft regulation."

and showed that the public hearing may, by the mere indication of the three areas for further work, bring some positive effects. Wygnański concluded his speech by addressing the MPs as those who are the decision makers regarding the final statutory solutions:

> I do hope that you will inform us how much time we have to work on this issue because from the perspective of my speech, it can be seen that there are things that can be dealt with tomorrow and that there are matters so fundamental that we need to work together and come up with a solution for them. It is up to you to decide whether there is time to do this.[27]

Naturally, in order to provide a complete summary, the most important part is missing, namely a direct reference by the drafters to the presented comments.

To recapitulate this part of the considerations, I would like to emphasize that making a summary of the key findings, the postulates, the justifications and the rationale behind them constitutes *an essential element* of the public hearing, enabling the participants: firstly, to obtain the initial information on the attitude of the drafters toward their comments; secondly, to determine, in the context of convergence and divergence, on the one hand, with other citizens and, on the other, with the applicants, their standpoint, the arguments used by them, and the justification provided by them; thirdly, (this is difficult to overestimate from the perspective of developing the public participation of citizens) to gain the sense that citizens' participation in the public hearing is important for the legislative process and it translates into the legislators perceiving the contribution made by their proposals. In our opinion, there is no doubt that making a substantive summary along with the comments on the arguments and their justifications provided by the citizens should become the responsibility of the drafters of a given bill and that the current legal solution should be improved in the spirit of the abovementioned proposals and postulates.

---

[27] See the stenographic record: "From the meeting of Social Policy and Family Committee" (no. 145), *Bulletin* no. 2125/VI term, 21 April 2009, the Chancellery of the Sejm – Sejm Commissions Office, Warsaw 2009, p. 22, available at: http://orka. sejm. gov.pl/Biuletyn.nsf/0/BA3C99494059AE67C12575AE004661D6/$file/0212506.pdf.

2.6. Three circles of participation and influence: the lack of equal access for the participants in public hearings to the legislative process

When analyzing the statements made by the participants in the public hearings, we can observe and isolate a phenomenon that could be described as the presence of *'three circles of participation and influence'* in the legislative process.

The first and the most obvious *circle of participation and influence* consists of the representatives of the executive branch, who often initiate a given bill, and the representatives of the legislative branch, primarily the members of the parliamentary committee in which the bill is being debated. They are, after all, the main recipients of public contributions, namely all the statements, justifications, observations, and comments made by citizens during the public hearing. Their presence, which is sometimes unfortunately under-represented, is of fundamental importance for assessing the reasonableness of conducting a given public hearing. The participants in the public hearing often refer to them. Therefore, it can be stated that they are fully aware that they constitute a collective decision-making entity. They decide whether the proposals of particular changes and the arguments supporting them, made by the citizens in the course of the public hearing, will be taken into consideration in the further legislative work. The Rules of the Sejm, in their current form, do not require the drafters to refer to the demands made by the citizens by means of publicly providing the justification, in the minutes of the public hearing, for their adoption or rejection of those demands. The current form of the public hearing is entirely one-sided. However, even in the case of this institution, one could implement the mechanisms of at least an indirect dialogue, thereby enhancing its relevance and legitimacy among the citizens.

After all, what should draw our attention is the ability to separate the two circles of acquaintance among the representatives of the public: one that constitutes, so to speak, *'the second circle of participation and influence,'* consisting of a group of the representatives of such NGOs, which are both kept informed about the work on a given act and take part as guests in discussions during the meetings of parliamentary committees and subcommittees (let us recall that according to many specialists, the crucial decisions in the Polish law-making system are made at the stage of the parliamentary sub-committees) as well as those entities and those citizens comprising *'the third circle of participation and influence,'* for whom the ability to take the floor during the public hearing is often the first and only opportunity to express their viewpoint and provide justifications for their views.

We can observe that the representatives of the abovementioned two groups have utterly diverse ways of expressing their viewpoints. Firstly, the representatives of *'the second circle of participation and influence'* often cite either their own statements and arguments provided during the work of the parliamentary subcommittees or the discussions and disputes that took place there. Secondly, they have a clear awareness of the non-repeatable nature of the public hearing, which manifested in the belief that although it is worth presenting their standpoint, it does not merit going into details, because those details will indeed be discussed during the further work in the parliamentary subcommittee, which they will also participate in.[28]

In contrast to the second circle, the citizens who comprise *'the third circle of participation and influence,'* firstly, are often aware of being excluded from the current work and circumvented in the public consultation. Secondly, in their speeches, they raise the issues crucial to a given act and sometimes very detailed ones. By doing so, it is as if they are sharing with the previous group the awareness of the non-repeatable nature of the public hearing. Thus, they understand it differently, and they feel that if they do not utter something at precisely a given moment during the public hearing, it will be lost, it will go unnoticed, and it will never be uttered in public. Thirdly, it seems that they more often directly address the MPs for taking their postulates into consideration in the course of the further work in the parliamentary subcommittees and committees,[29] as if the abovementioned sense

---

[28] See, e.g. the words – cited on the previous page – uttered by Jakub Wygnański, which allow to unambiguously refer to him as a typical representative of *'the second circle of influence and participation.'*

[29] Here are some examples of the statements made during the public hearing concerning the bill on Veteran Corps of the Fight for Polish Independence, which we refer to in this part of the discussion as being a characteristic example: J. Kacprzak:

of the non-repeatable nature of the public hearing was combined, in their case, with a lack of faith that they will have the opportunity to participate in further stages of the legislative process. Moreover, they frequently try to somehow make up for their current and usually prospective absence in the work on a draft of a given act by adding their standpoint to the minutes of the public hearing, thus believing that their comments will be taken into consideration in the further work on the bill.

In order to illustrate the above comments with an example, let us provide a few statements made by the representatives of war veterans that participated in the public hearing concerning the bill on the Veteran Corps of the Fight for Polish Independence. The first two were made by the representatives of the associations, which can be included to 'the third circle of participation and influence' on account of the above division. Let us begin with the statement made by the secretary general of the board of the Association of Polish Veterans and Former Political Prisoners, Stanisław Całka, who said that

> There are about 200 veterans' organizations active in the country. This number consists of 80 significant organizations. The bill was sent only to a few such organizations. Our Association, which has about 100,000 [sic! – P.W.J.] veterans of World War II, did not receive this bill. We had to obtain it using our private means and contacts.[30]

"On behalf of three thousand veterans who are the members of our Association, I would like to ask you to pay attention to indicated by us legal aspects during the work on this project in the Sejm and the Senate" (p. 7); H. Strzelecki: "I would like to ask the MPs to reflect on it when working on this law in committees. ... Therefore, I appeal to you that the committees should take this matter into account when they consider this draft" (p. 9); D. Kubas: "I hope that during the Committee's work you will pay attention to..." (p. 11); one could cite many similar observations made by the citizens and the representatives of independent associations also at other public hearings. See: "The meeting of the National Defence Committee (57) and the Committee on Social Policy and Family (no. 160)," *Bulletin* no. 2347 / VI term, June 18, 2009, Chancellery of the Sejm – Sejm Commissions Office, Warsaw 2009, available at: http://orka.sejm.gov.pl/Biuletyn.nsf/0/5F1D5FD60C026F40C12575E100305694/$file/0234706.pdf.

30 "The meeting of the National Defence Committee (57) and the Committee on Social Policy and Family (no. 160)," *Bulletin* no. 2347 / VI term, June 18, 2009, op. cit., p. 4.

This statement is supported by that made by Jan Kacprzak, the secretary general of a smaller association, which still has 3,000 members, namely the Association of Former Professional Soldiers and Reserve Officers of the Polish Army: "I would like to point out that we, as an association, have not received this bill [from officials]. We obtained it by means of our personal contacts."[31] What echoes in both these statements is the abovementioned sense of exclusion from the current work on the bill, manifested in the lack of consultations with the organizations represented by these speakers.

The above opinions can be contrasted with a quite characteristic statement made by the representative of the association, which can be included among the 'second circle of participation and influence' in the case of the work on this bill. The president of the board of the World Association of National Army Soldiers, Czesław Cywiński, said, when referring to one of the postulates made by the preceding speaker, S. Całka, that "It seems that this is a matter that can be considered in the course of the committee's work on a bill. We do not need to discuss it today."[32] One moment later, with respect to the next issue, he added that

> This is possible by calling a subcommittee that will commence the work on the bill. It will be the place where we could settle all the issues. This is what subcommittees are for. There is no denying it. ... As for the other issues concerning this bill, these are minor matters. Please believe me, it is a waste of time to deal with these issues at this point. I talked earlier about the people who have been awarded the Military Cross. It is one of the issues that can be settled in a due course.[33]

There is no doubt in this case that the speaker is not only familiarized (competent) in the area of law-making process in Poland, but we assume that he participated in the previous work on the bill, thus having the opportunity to exert some influence on its shape. He believes that he will have the opportunity to participate and influence its content in the next stage of the legislative work in the parliamentary subcommittee.

---

[31] Ibidem, p. 6.
[32] Ibidem, p. 5.
[33] Ibidem, p. 6.

It must be expressly emphasized at the same time that, firstly, the existence of the second and third *circle of participation and influence* is unavoidable in the legislative process because one can never invite all the interested parties to participate at the earlier stages of preparing a bill. However, it is the responsibility of the drafters and legislators to select the most representative non-governmental organizations potentially interested in a given legal regulation. Leaving aside certain organizations and favouring others undermines the credibility of the entire lawmaking process. Secondly, there is no doubt that introducing the institution of the public hearing, despite both a number of imperfections in the adopted legal solutions and the objections raised against the public hearing itself as a form of public consultations, can be vital even for a single inclusion of previously absent bodies thus providing them with the exclusive possibility of having a certain influence, though to a limited extent, by means of an explicit and distinct existence in the public sphere, on the shape of the drafted legislation.

This part of our deliberations can be summarized in the words uttered by Sławomir Piechota, an MP who chaired the public hearing concerning the bill on the Veterans' Corps of the Fight for Polish Independence:

> We can provide many examples of cases which – as we believe – do not aim to solve a problem, but rather serve to create the appearances that there is an intention to solve the problem. Yet, today's public hearing on this bill does not serve the latter purpose. As can be clearly seen from the standpoints presented in this discussion, today's public hearing was needed primarily so that everyone who wished to take part in this discussion on an equal footing, could present their opinion in the course of the debate.[34]

Leaving aside the question, substantively doubtful and decidedly rhetorical in nature, of referring to the public hearing as a debate or discussion, it should be noted that S. Piechota rightly highlighted one of the most important advantages of this institution of public consultations, provided relevant conditions are met: its open and inclusive character.

---

[34] Ibidem, p. 13.

2.7. Political Context

A public hearing is embedded in a broader political context, which is of fundamental importance for its effects, namely taking into consideration the postulates of its participants in the legislative process. Let us cite two statements summarizing the public hearing concerning the government bill to amend the act on public benefit activity and voluntary work (April 2009), which will shed some light on the issues of our interest. Tadeusz Tomaszewski, an MP representing the parliamentary opposition (left-wing) said:

> I hope that a majority of your postulates will be taken into consideration in the course of the work in subcommittees, yet *I would like to note that these good ideas must also be granted the government's consent in the course of work because without such a consent we will simply enter a large room* [here: a plenary session hall] *and start a small war and it is not our aim here.* I think we need to seek such solutions that are acceptable to the partners of the legislative process as quickly as possible, but without haste, with the participation of those of you who wish to continue the substantive work in the subcommittees, and if the Committee decides so, we will take this into account. In particular, you have made a number of mutually contradictory observations. ... It is typical in the legislative process that at some point, firstly in the subcommittees and then in the parliamentary committees, we will have to settle these issues, while listening once more to your arguments. ... If some of these arguments are considered well-thought and mature and *if they have a preliminary consent of the government* then we will take them into account, in addition to the points included in the bill. However, if it is not the case, then in my opinion in order to facilitate this process for the public authority and for the NGOs, they will not be taken into account.[35]

The second quote comes from the speech made by the Secretary of State in the Ministry of Labour and Social Policy – Jarosław Duda:

> I would like to make a declaration that there are no such principles in that matter on the part of the government which could not be changed in the course of work and I have the intention of refining and developing

[35] "From the meeting of Social Policy and Family Committee" (no. 145), *Bulletin* no. 2125/VI term, op. cit., p. 23 [the emphasis in the text added by P.W.J.].

> the consensus in this area. At the same time, I would like to emphasize clearly that *this is a government bill which has undergone the entire process of inter-ministerial consultations*, and some problems presented today have been unfortunately already challenged by other ministries, or it was not possible to force through the arguments raised by you.[36]

What can be perceived in both these statements is the convergence that aims at drawing the attention of the participants in the public hearing that the hearing is by no means an institution detached from the entire legislative process, but is an inseparable part of it, determined in time and place. Thus, although after the first reading in parliament there is still the possibility of introducing even most substantial amendments, as pointed out clearly by the Secretary of State, J. Duda, significant settlements, crucial for the context of the frames of further possible work on the draft legislation, have already been made in the course of inter-ministerial consultations and in the adopted position of the government. As indicated by T. Tomaszewski, introducing such amendments to the draft legislation during the work in the subcommittees, which have not been granted the consent of the government, does not make sense and leads to a 'small war,' which does not lead to success. Both statements indicate a need to develop solutions acceptable to all the partners in the legislative process as well as the fact that the latter cannot be done during the public hearing when, as noted by T. Tomaszewski, "[the participants] have made a number of mutually contradictory observations" (see above). J. Duda, the Secretary of State, adds that "it is impossible to relate in detail to all these comments. It is the task of the permanent subcommittee, which will reflect on this issue."[37] Both of them indicate that the parliamentary subcommittee is the appropriate place for further, already deliberative, work on a bill.

2.8. Four conditions of an effective public hearing

The characteristic features of the public hearing, described in the above considerations, indicate that this institution can trigger frustra-

---

[36] Ibidem, p. 22 [the emphasis added by P.W.J.].

[37] Ibidem.

tion and a sense of disappointment in the participating citizens. John Gastil quotes the words of the former member of the county of Maryland, Bruce Adams, who summed up his experience with public hearings, which are required by law in many cases in the U.S., in the following words:

> I figure I spent nearly 2,000 hours in formal public hearings over the last eight years. It was not time well spent. Public hearings may give the appearance of public involvement, but they are unsatisfactory to citizens and officials alike.[38]

It should be added that the mediocre results of the public hearings can rarely be attributed to the fault of their organizers. They stem from the very nature of this method of public involvement.

J. Gastil lists four conditions that should be met in the course of a public hearing so that it could fulfil its aim, but he emphasizes at the same time that they rarely take place in practice.

These four features, which ensure the effectiveness of a good public hearing, are as follows: *deliberativeness, influence, representativeness,* and *clarity*. In practice, there are problems with each of them. As we have already emphasized, the public hearing is essentially a method constructed in such a way that it lacks room for a substantive (one might say, any) debate and exchange of arguments between, on the one hand, participating citizens who represent different positions and, on the other hand, between citizens and the representatives of public authorities. This method is, as a rule, non-deliberative. The researchers of civic participation note that paradoxically, an authentic debate and exchange of views occurs only if the public hearing is not of interest to citizens, because of the undertaken subject or problem. In such a case, there are a small number of participants, they are not strongly antagonized, and the moderator can allow them to present longer speeches and even exchange arguments. Therefore, there is more time and also the respective officials can at least partially refer to the comments of participants on an on-going basis. In this case, we can also observe the greatest clarity of the public hearing. Unfortu-

[38] John Gastil, *By Popular Demand. Revitalizing Representative Democracy through Deliberative Elections*, Berkeley: University of California Press, 2000, p. 99.

nately, the fulfilment of these two conditions is not sufficient, and it should be noted that such a public hearing has two fundamental drawbacks, namely that it is unrepresentative of a given political community and that it usually does not affect the decisions of the officials. Therefore, it does not meet the remaining two conditions. What is also paradoxical is that the fulfilment of the condition of representativeness (let us keep in mind, however, that having a large number of participants in the public hearing does not guarantee their sociological representativeness), which could lead to the actual impact of the public hearing on further public policy, eliminates the deliberativeness and sometimes even the clarity of the expressed public opinions.

To summarize this part of our discussion, let us quote Gastil:

> Careful discussion and debate can cause people to critically examine the problem they face, their own perspectives, and the views of their opponents. This leads citizens toward a more enlightened understanding of their interests and a more accurate understanding of the policy problem under discussion. This, in turn, can lead to an articulate presentation of the public's shared and divergent interests. In practice, public hearings routinely fail to resemble even a crude form of deliberation.[39]

3. Summary - advantages and drawbacks of the public hearing

The institution of the public hearing has functioned in the Polish legal system for six years. During this period, 21 public hearings took place before parliamentary committees, and they concerned the bills introduced to the Sejm by the President of the Republic of Poland, by the Polish government, and by the Members of Parliament. Taking into account the total number of acts passed by the parliament at that time, this number is not considerable. However, the awareness that this form of public consultation is being used rarely seems to be discernible among politicians. The MP and the chairman of the Social

---

[39] John Gastil, *Political Communication and Deliberation*, Los Angeles: SAGE Publications, 2008, p. 189.

Policy and Family Committee, Sławomir Piechota (from the political party Citizens' Platform), pointed out, when launching a public hearing in April 2009 on the government bill to amend the act on public benefit activity and voluntary work, that "this institution is still inadequately propagated and grounded in the legislative order."[40]

The reasons for this state of things may be various. Nevertheless, the small number of public hearings comes as a surprise, especially if one takes into account and treats seriously the generally positive reviews of the participating MPs and officials who perceive the importance and usefulness of this institution. Let us quote a few of them. The Secretary of State in the Ministry of Labour and Social Policy, Jarosław Duda, said when summing up the public hearing on the government bill to amend the act on public benefit activity and voluntary work: "It is clear that the institution of the public hearing is very useful, given a number of fundamental proposals made here."[41] When making a summary of the public hearing on a draft of a law on the Veteran Corps of the Fight for Polish Independence (June 2009), S. Piechota, the chairman said:

> ... Yet, today's public hearing was needed primarily so that everyone who wished to take part in this discussion on an equal footing, could present their opinion in the course of the debate. ... That is why a public debate is needed. However, what is necessary in this public debate are balanced, rational and honest arguments. Everyone who joins this debate in such way undoubtedly contributes to aiming to a common goal.[42]

The above statements may naturally be collated with many standpoints expressing scepticism about the institution of the public hearing. Such doubts are also expressed during short conclusions of public hearings which have been already held. For example, the representative of the Chancellery of the President of the Republic of Po-

---

[40] "From the meeting of Social Policy and Family Committee" (no. 145), *Bulletin* no. 2125/VI term, op. cit., p. 3.

[41] Ibidem, p. 22.

[42] From "The meeting of the National Defence Committee" (57) and "the Committee on Social Policy and Family (no. 160)," *Bulletin* no. 2347 / VI term, June 18, 2009, op. cit., pp. 13–14.

land, Krzysztof Kondrat noted, when summarizing the public hearing on a draft law amending the personal data protection act (July 2008):

> I regret to say that the speeches delivered lacked substantive proposals which would provide new solutions. ... I hope that the debate held during the subcommittee meeting will be of a more concrete and substantive character.[43]

We could give multiple examples of both the positive and sceptical attitudes to the institution of the public hearing. Our goal in this article was to highlight the potential dangers posed by the public hearing, especially the risk of highly polarized standpoints, which is characteristic for this form of public consultation. When analyzing public hearings that took place in the Polish Sejm, some caused real emotions among their participants, which certainly did not help to improve the quality of the public debate or to understand the views of the opposing groups of citizens. Nevertheless, these public hearings have undoubtedly helped to raise and articulate in the public sphere some competitive arguments in the context of the analyzed draft legislation. Yet, is this not insufficient? Law-making differs from the usual public debate in that in the case of the latter, a plurality of views is not only a possible beginning, but even the most acceptable conclusion. We can be different, and in a democratic state based on the idea of mutual tolerance and respect for distinct perceptions of the world and ways of life, such differences entail the enriching diversity of attitudes and beliefs. After all, these differences are sometimes hard to reconcile in the law-making process. It is equally difficult to afford the luxury of not making any decisions. Accordingly, what seems the best solution in order to enact rational law is to search for consensus, and if the latter is impossible to achieve in a particular case, which is quite common in a pluralistic society, to search for a compromise that is acceptable to most citizens.

---

43 "From the meeting of the Committee on Justice and Human Rights (no. 50)," *Bulletin* no. 914/VI term, 9 July 2008, the Chancellery of the Sejm – Sejm Commissions Office, pp. 25–26. See: http://orka.sejm.gov.pl/Biuletyn.nsf/0/21D852F718DDF6F5C125749D0025FEA7/$file/0091406.pdf.

In this context, how can we determine the usefulness of the institution of the public hearing, which is by its nature devoid of the advantages of the common deliberative settlement of difficult issues in public policy? If we analyze the course of the previous public hearings in the Polish Sejm, we can observe an interesting pattern. When we deal with a bill that is important for the citizens in a specific environment and yet uncontroversial for society and thus devoid of social controversy, the institution of the public hearing allows its participants to explicitly articulate the concerns and expectations *vis-à-vis* the drafters, and it may, at the same time, contribute to improving the enacted law. What can serve as an example are the public hearings on the bill amending the act on public benefit activity and voluntary work, which constitutes the only case so far of conducting two public hearings on a draft of the same legislation and which were essentially constructive in nature. Quite the opposite is true in the case of draft laws on issues creating strong conflict for society. Then, the polarization of the standpoints is even greater, mutual hostility escalates, and reaching a compromise through a rational discussion becomes an impossible task, e.g., the public hearing on the government bill for the law on genetically modified organisms. While the public hearing, despite all the objections raised in this article *vis-à-vis* this institution of public consultation, may occasionally be a good solution in certain situations, in the latter case, it would be advisable to turn to other methods that are more deliberative and thus focused on the search of a possible compromise.

At the end of each legislative process, it is necessary to decide on the final shape of legislation: adversarial participation seems to be of little benefit for the MPs who undertake it.

José Manuel Aroso Linhares
University of Coimbra, Portugal

Law in/as Literature as an Alternative *Humanistic* Discourse

The Unavoidable Resistance to Legal *Scientific* Pragmatism or the Fertile Promise of a *Communitas* Without Law?*

Abstract: This paper tries to identify a certain "common ground" explored by different interlocutors in *Law and Literature*'s debate and this "ground" as a specific construction of meaning: a construction of meaning which, resisting simultaneously to rule formalism and legal *scientific* instrumentalism (and its *calculating forms of reason*), demands not only an alternative type of discourse or rationality —concentrated in the possibilities of narrative and/or performance (if not conducted by an emancipation of praxis-*prattein* and a plausible return to *phronesis*)— but also a renewed experience of *community*.

Keywords: Law and Literature - Community - Phronêsis - Narrative - Interdisciplinarity - *open area* - *humanistic* approaches - indeterminacy

The purpose of this essay is not only to recognise (and identify) a *certain* "common ground" explored by different (exemplary) interlocutors in the *Law and Literature* debate —a "ground" which, with its interpretative assumptions and practices, constitutes a specific (and

* This text was first published *on line* as an *ISLL Papers Special Issue*, available at: <http://www.lawandliterature.org/index.php?channel=PAPERS> [Dossier on *Law and Literature. A Discussion on Purposes and Method*. Proceedings of the Special WS on *Law and Literature* held at 24th IVR World Conference in Beijing, September 2009. Edited by M. Paola Mittica. Published in September 16, 2010, pp. 22–42].

unintentionally overlapping) construction of meaning– but also to pursue (to illuminate) this identification under the reflexive (aggregative) impulse of a well-known formulation by Klaus Lüderssen's (preserved here in its *original* interrogative form[1]): "Is the *Law and Literature Movement* a challenge posed by *Law and Economics*?" ("*The Law and Literature Movement* – eine Herausforderung von *Law and Economics*?").

Stimulated by the possibilities of this interpellation, my intention is not, however, to insist on the primary *methodological* (*interpretative* or *adjudicative*) opposition between a quantitative (supposedly rigorous) translation of comparability (or expectations of legal comparability) and a deconstructive celebration of casuistic singularity (and *différance*) – the opposition that constitutes the core of Lüderssen´s reflection.[2] Neither is it to explore the *anthropological* programmatic and polarised contrast developed by Robin West (herself the well-known protagonist of a devastating debate with Posner): the contrast between a certain "economic *man*" and a certain "literary *person*," or better put, between the „excesses of an *economic man* run wild", which "emerge from economic legal analysis", and the possibilities of a "literary person," if not even of a "literary woman," that emerge (or are beginning to emerge) from literary legal analysis.[3]

Besides these two major specifications of the *Law and Literature* enterprise –with its emphases on the possibilities of *law as literature* and *law in literature*, respectively, or more accurately, on *interpretive* and

---

[1] The first version of "Literatur – gesteigerte Realität" (Klaus Lüderssen, *Produktive Spiegelungen. Recht und Kriminalität in der Literatur*, Frankfurt am Main: Suhrkamp Verlag, 1991, pp. 11–25) includes an explicit reference to a future essay identified as "*The Law and Literature Movement* – eine Herausforderung von *Law and Economics*?" (ibidem, p. 24, note 39). The interrogative form disappears however when this essay is finally published in the second edition-*version* of *Produktive Spiegelungen* (Klaus Lüderssen, "Law and Literature als Herausforderung von Law and Economics", in: idem, *Produktive Spiegelungen. Recht in Literatur, Theater und Film*. Zweite erweiterte Auflage, Baden-Baden: Nomos Verlag, 2002, pp. 32–47).

[2] K. Lüderssen, *Produktive Spiegelungen. Recht in Literatur, Theater und Film*, op. cit., pp. 37–41.

[3] Robin West, *Narrative, Authority and Law (Law, Meaning & Violence)*, Michigan: The University of Michigan Press, 1993, chapter 5, pp. 251–264 ("Economic Man and Literary Woman: One Contrast").

literary jurisprudences,[4] if not indeed on *hermeneutic* and *literary interdisciplinary projects*[5]—, I should also insist that my aim is not even to reproduce or to reconstruct the (so many times already reconstructed!) global "cognitive dissonance"[6] (we could even say *différend*!) between *Law and Economics* and *Law and Literature* —if it is possible to reconstruct it globally (abstracting from its multifarious internal developments)!— ...but rather to face (to revisit) the Lüderssen's challenge by replacing its two explicit interlocutors.

But what does replacing (purposely and meaningfully) the involved interlocutors mean? It means not only expanding the question, but also causing an explicit turn in its dynamic accentuation. The main problem would thus be the resistance offered by a certain view of interdisciplinarity —the one which sees Law as a part of the "noble republic of letters", "not complete unless it draws nourishment" ("assistance" and "edification") from the "sources of *external* knowledge" that "the humanities" (including philosophy and literary criticism) as such provide— to another view of interdisciplinarity —the one which is determined by the hegemony of the social sciences and by empirically explanatory models (if not explicitly by the prediction that the future of the "rational study of law" demands as protagonist "the man of statistics and the master of economics"): as if the path could be cleared by remembering the disagreement between Learned Hand and Oliver Holmes Jr. about the "future direction of Law" (an exemplary "*tale* of two speeches" told by Balkin and Levison[7]), without forgetting that to expand these plausible *interlocutors* means now to enlarge either the targets of resistance (viewed as exemplary opponents), or the possibilities (the *front*) of resistance itself.

---

4 Gary Minda, *Postmodern Legal Movements. Law and Jurisprudence at Century's End*, New York / London: New York University Press, 1995, pp. 153–159.

5 Robin West, "Literature, Culture, and Law — at Duke University," *Georgetown Law Faculty Working Papers* 2008, paper 75, p. 1, available at <http://scholarship.law.georgetown.edu/fwps_papers/75>.

6 Anthony D'Amato, "Pragmatic Indeterminacy," *Northwestern Law Review* 1990, vol. 85, pp. 148–189 ("Legal scholarship today is characterized by massive cognitive dissonance...", ibidem, p. 164).

7 Jack Balkin, Sanford Levinson, "Law and Humanities: An Uneasy Relationship," *Yale Journal of Law & the Humanities* 2006, vol. 18, pp. 155–187, here at 155–160 ("Introduction: Is Law Part of the Humanities? A Tale of Two Speeches").

(a) To enlarge the *opponents'* axis... in what sense? So that this axis may include (and overlap with) all the possible *positive* answers to a maximizing *intertwined* challenge between effective social (macroscopic) strategies and (microscopic) tactics... and these answers under the unifying *mask* of a basic (generalized) bet *(-pari!)* on a scientifically informed *Zweckrationalität* (and *Zweckprogramm*). As if we could recognize a manifold *legal instrumentalism* or *pragmatism* coherently assumed (seriously taken as an ultimate model of integration)... and this recognition might include (and absorb) Pound's *social engineering* and Posner's *pragmatic judge,* but also Hans Albert's *technological teleologism,* and Vermeule's pragmatic justification of a *New Textualism,* without excluding some (overtly ideological) representations of the *political judge* (as the tactic executor of a certain constitutional strategy or as the tactic performer of alternative emancipatory strategies) still informed by a "scientific" (or "pseudo-scientific") concept of *public reason*[8], basing his choices on the social empirical effects that alternative decisions are likely to have.

(b) To enlarge and unify the targets means however, as I have already said, to grant a meaningful development to the possibilities of the promised resistance, to the point that these, at last identified (justified) as *humanistic approaches* (or "humanistic" interdisciplinary projects), may recognize themselves not only as immediate (productive) outgrowths of the *linguistic literary turn* (and *The Law and Literature Movement*) but also as participants in other complementary (sometimes supposedly alternative) trends such as *narrative critical jurisprudences, law as musical and dramatic performance, legal iconology* or *ars legis, law and film, law and emotions* and *law and culture movements.* A meaningful outgrowth, I insist, and a no less meaningful *spectrum*: from Boyd White's *"communitarian" narrativism* (and *communal lawyer*) to Balkin's *transcendental deconstruction* (and *performative triangle);*

[8] The formulation is by Martha Nussbaum's, in *Poetic Justice* (Martha Nussbaum, *Poetic Justice. The Literary Imagination and Public Life,* Boston: Beacon Press Books, 1995): "The aim of this book is ... to present a vivid conception of public reasoning that is humanistic and not pseudo-scientific, to show how a certain type of narrative literature expresses and develops such a conception, and to show some of the benefits this conception might have to offer in the public sphere..." (ibidem, "Preface," pp. xviii–xix).

from Martha Nussbaum's *poetic judging* (and *literary judicious spectator*) to Costa Douzinas' *ethical diké* (and *momentary principle of Justice*); from John Denvir's *jurisprudence of comedy* (and *comic view of Law)* to Richard Delgado's *legal counter-storytelling* (sustained by a specific *voice-of-colour thesis*); from Martin Jay's iconic creative tension between *alterity* and *commensurability* (as a "call for a compromise [between] *seeing* and *unseeing* justice"[9]) to David A. Black's reconstitution of legal and cinematic *narrative regimes* (and its productive interactions); from Richard Weisberg's (morally relevant) deconstruction and "reconstruction" of specific *procedural narratives* to Naomi Mezey's defense of a particular intertwinement between *law as culture* and *culture as law*.

Although certain that this is a „common ground" (a kind of a defensive front) from which we *should not* exclude Robin West's approach —even though she expressly teaches us that "adjudication" ("despite a superficial resemblance to literary interpretation") "is not primarily an interpretative act"[10]—, it is also a "common ground" from which we *have* (good reasons) *to exclude* Dworkin – even though his fidelity to the *aesthetic hypothesis* (to the "use of literary interpretation as a model for the central method of legal analysis")[11] and, more clearly still, his representation of *hard cases* (and *hard cases deciding*) determined by the *chain novel* example, seem at first sight to recommend the opposite *integrative* solution. But we shall return (however briefly) to this apparently paradoxical parallelism and its *differentiation* nucleus: a differentiation, we shall see, that is far from being irrelevant.

Once exposed to this crude resistance *story* —or at least to the promise of a *concertatto* involving such heterogeneous protagonists (different voices that address themselves to shared unified targets!)—,

[9] Martin Jay, "Must Justice Be Blind? The Challenge of Images to the Law," in: Costas Douzinas, and Lynda Nead (eds), *Law and the Image. The Authority of Art and the Aesthetics of Law*, Chicago/London: The University of Chicago Press, 1999, pp. 19-35 here at 33-34. See also Costas Douzinas, and Lynda Nead, "Introduction," ibidem, pp. 1-15, here at 12.

[10] R. West, *Narrative, Authority and Law*, op. cit., pp. 92-93. "Adjudication is in form interpretive, but in substance it is an exercise of power in a way that truly interpretive acts, such as literary interpretation, are not..." (ibidem, p. 93).

[11] Ronald Dworkin, *A Matter of Principle*, Oxford: Clarendon Press, 1986, p. 158.

it behooves us immediately to ask (using a formulation by Rorty's) if it is productive or "interesting" to identify such a *common ground* and its parallel *interdisciplinary claims* (and these concentrated in a plausible *front*)—with the inclusion and exclusion processes that configure this *ground*, and the reduction of complexity that its axis of intelligibility necessary engenders. The sequence that follows is an attempt to specify and answer this question, or at least to privilege it as a leading thematic choice.

1.

Let us begin by beating a path through shared territory: as if scouting it around meant, here and now, to pay attention to the *different* voices that inhabit it (to ear them, privileging their explicit formulations). As we might expect from a resistance front story, it is a *negative* feature —i.e., an explicit convergence (or even consensus) still about the opponents (about the law's typical conceptions we have *to reject*) – that constitutes the main (the most unequivocally reproduced) *topos*. Invoking the binomial *society/community (societas/communitas, Gesellschaft, Gemeinschaft)*, we could say that this permanently revisited *topos* corresponds to the conclusion-claim that the experience of *societas* (and the collective identity that this experience constructs as *totality* and *artifact*) is *one* perspective or *one* interpretative "tradition" among others, with its own understandings of "person, nature and *the* good" and a specific *catalogue of virtues*.[12] To see this experience as *one* among others means, as a matter of fact, to reject exemplarily all the conceptions of Law that, assuming the exclusivity of *society*'s approach (and its "acultural way of understanding the rise of modernity"[13]), project (or specify) this exclusivity onto (or as) a dogmatically

[12] Charles Taylor, "Inwardness and the Culture of Modernity", in: Honneth McCarthy, Offe Wellmer (eds.), *Zwischenbetrachtungen im Prozess der Aufklärung. Jürgen Habermas zum 60. Geburtstag*, Frankfurt am Main: Suhrkamp, 1989, p. 601.

[13] "A 'cultural' theory of modernity is one that characterizes the transformations that have issued in the modern West mainly in terms of the rise of a new culture. The contemporary Atlantic world is seen as one culture (or group of related cultures) among others, with its own specific understandings, for example, of person, nature, the good, to be contrasted to all others, including its own predecessor civilization

pre-determined search of a *unique* language. Which *unique* language? To say it with Boyd White, the *one* that *formalism* sustains (reducing law to a set of self-sufficient rules, and the legal enterprise to an internal use of textual materials and traditional skills), but also the *one* that instrumentalism or pragmatism justify ("imagining" law as a "branch of public policy, in which legal questions are collapsed into questions of social or political preference").[14] A *unique* language nevertheless that, in any of these poles (independently of the different institutional stages where it is performed), addresses itself always to us (*et pour cause!*) as an explicit *nonnarrative mode of speaking* (Hayden White[15]): a *nonnarrative mode* which, condemning its implicit addressees to the story of an "*ex nihilo* creation" ("begining in the state of nature or the original position")[16]—if not to the model of a consummated contractuality (Goodrich[17]), constructed through a selective conver-

---

(with which it obviously also has a lot in common). By contrast, an 'acultural' theory is one that describes these transformations in terms of some culture-neutral operation. ... [The] changes are not defined by their end point in a specific constellation of understandings of, say, person, society, good, they are rather described as a type of transformation to which any culture in principle serve as 'input'..." (Ch. Taylor, "Inwardness and the Culture of Modernity", op. cit., pp. 601–602). „[The] project of founding a form of social order in which individuals could emancipate themselves from the contingency and particularity of tradition by appealing to genuinely universal, tradition-independent norms was and is not only, and not principally, a project of philosophers. It was and is the project of modern liberal, individualist society..." (Alisdair MacIntyre, *Whose Justice? Which Rationality?* London: Duckworth, 1988, p. 335).

[14] James Boyd White, *From Expectation to Experience. Essays on Law and Legal Imagination*, Michigan: The University of Michigan Press, 1999, p. 103. See also idem, *Justice as Translation. An Essay in Cultural and Legal Criticism*, Chicago / London: The University of Chicago Press, 1990, pp. 22–45 ("The Language of concepts"), pp. 46–85 ("The Language and Culture of Economics").

[15] Hayden White, *The Content of the Form. Narrative Discourse and Historical Representation*, Baltimore/London: The Johns Hopkins University Press, 1987, p. 1 ff. ("The Value of Narrativity in the Representation of Reality"), 39 ff., 56–57.

[16] Michael Walzer, "The Communitarian Critique of Liberalism," in: Amitai Etzioni (ed.), *New Communitarian Thinking. Persons, Virtues, Institutions, and Communities*, Virginia: University Press of Virginia, 1995, pp. 52–70 here at 54.

[17] Peter Goodrich, *Languages of Law. From Logics of Memory to Nomadic Masks*, London: Weidenfels and Nicolson, 1990, pp. 149–175 ("Contractions: A Linguistic Philosophy of the Postal Rule"), 319–323 ("The Contract").

gence of Kant's and Bentham's *arguments*[18] –, justifies (legitimises) not only a unilateral experience of democratic citizenship (radically obfuscated by a supposedly scientific conception of public reason) [Nussbaum[19]], but also a self-repressing jurisprudential enterprise (a "legal discourse" which, as "literature" and as "rhetoric", is unavoidably committed to the repressing of its "literary quality" or to the forgetting of its "textual organization and aesthetic arrangement").[20]

2.

Be that as it may, to resist simultaneously rule-centered formalism and legal *scientific* instrumentalism (brought together as *calculating forms of reason*), demands not only an alternative type of discourse or rationality but also a renewed experience of *community*.

Stimulated by this *new* reformulation of our basic challenge – a reformulation that expands a step further the circle of the plausible opponents, bringing together *formalistic internal* and *pragmatic external* attitudes (to the point of allowing Boyd White to denounce them as two possible specifications of an *outside view*![21]) –, we should immediately ask if our draft of a *common ground* can in fact globally (and positively) reveal *anything else* of relevance about the alternative ways and their institutional background. Which means of course asking if we are in a position to show these alternatives meaningfully as a real shared ground, before the effective exploration of the correlative paths (conducted by each of the possible convergent voices) gives rise to an unavoidable emergence of differences (the differences that will fragment and destroy the promised unity). Taking this question seriously, I would risk answering that it is possible to recognize some

---

18 A. MacIntyre, *Whose Justice? Which Rationality?* op. cit., p. 353 („the Enlightenment invoked the arguments of Kant or Bentham…»).

19 See *supra*, note 8.

20 C. Douzinas, and L. Nead, "Introduction," op. cit., p. 10.

21 "Of course the law can be imagined, sometimes usefully, in each of these ways … – as a set of rules (to be obeyed or desobeyed) … and as a branch of public policy, in which legal questions are collapsed into questions of social science or political preference … – …, especially when viewed from the outside…" (J.B. White, *From Expectation to Experience*, op. cit., p. 103).

other common features, even though not *positively* as many as we might expect.

2.1. The call to this facet of *interdisciplinarity*, which we may qualify as *a cultural (or humanistic)* one, involves as a matter of fact two basic complementary common challenges: the first one committed to the return-reinvention of a *communitarian context* **(α)**, the second one concentrated in the possibilities of an autonomous praxis-*prattein* and its rationality types **(β)**. The articulation of these challenges favours, in turn, a sequence of other relevant convergences **(γ)**.

(α) That commitment corresponds, *on one hand,* to the shared claim of freeing the communitarian context (or its interpretative enterprise) from the necessity of an ontological (or onto-anthropological) a-historical representation – saying it *positively,* to the demand of reinventing the experience of *communitas,* assuming (for once) the plenitude of its symbolic-cultural attributes; *on the other hand,* to the search of a constitutive (dialectic) equilibrium between *community* and *society.*

The first attempt justifies the community's horizon as a specific cultural project: not only revealing a determinant bond with an explicit experience of *historicity* (as a radical *constitutive historicity*) but also recognizing the *positive* circularity that makes this experience possible, so that this communitarian project –nuclearly incompatible with an abstract predetermination– may offer itself always inescapably (and simultaneously) either as the foundational *context* or as the reinvented *correlate* (the correlate-*ordinans*) of a changeable stabilizing *praxis*. What kind of *praxis*? A historically open *praxis*, which may only aspire to be recognized as a plausible (and valid) actualisation of the project's intentions when submitting them to specific contexts or to pragmatically or rhetorically precise situations (i.e., when constituting and transforming these intentions).

The second (complementary) claim establishes an exemplary counterpoint between two unmistakable cultural projects of collective identity, which are also two irreducible typical faces of a certain *teleological turn* (both of them responsive to the present circumstance, both of them facing the claims of pluralism, fragmentation, difference): so that the *society project* may be the one which assumes the basic equivalence (if not the quantitative commensurability) of all the subjective needs, ends and interests, and treats them as preference claims... and imposes the exclusive answer of a possible set of hierarchizing decisions (but also the social-political artefact that legitimises collectively these decisions); so that the so-called *community project* may open up our experience (and our possibilities of practical deliberation) to the consideration of an integrative horizon of shared practical commitments and responsibilities, in order to sustain (and to explore) an insurmountable dualism between *subjective goals* and *human goods*, between *ends* and *values* – or at least to reveal the importance of "non-commensurable" ("qualitatively distinct and separate") *ultimate ends*, each one pursued "for its own sake" (demanding as such a set of plausible specifications).[22]

(β) What about the rationality types? We may say that the resistance to the dominant axis of the *episteme-techné* or *techné-episteme*—which is also a resistance to the exclusivity and unilaterality of the *society project* (and to this one as the regulatory nucleus of an historically insurmountable evolutionary stage) – affords us the privileged *occasio* of reinventing the equilibrium of Aristotelian *intellectual virtues* as a major experience of *plurality* (a paradigmatic consecration of plural rational types, if not of a certain *plurality theorem*[23]): here and now as the opportunity to pursue the interrupted emancipation of *praxis-prattein* (for once radically freed from the theoretical predominance of *sophia*), which is also the opportunity to reformulate the challenge of *phronêsis*. What kind of reformulation? A very specific one. Certainly not the reformulation which bets on the radical autonomy of *phronêsis* (and explores its internal hermeneutic and/or argumentative possibil-

---

[22] The quoted formulations are by Martha Nussbaum, "Virtue Ethics: A Misleading Category?" *The Journal of Ethics* 1999, vol. 3, pp. 163–201. See specifically pp. 182–183 ("The Anti-Utilitarians. Expanding Reason's Domain") and 179-188 ("Virtue Ethics...").

[23] Wolfgang Welsch, *Unsere Postmoderne Moderne*, dritte durschgesehene Auflage, Weinheim: Acta Humaniora, 1991, pp. 277–284 ("Aristoteles oder die Selbständichkeit von Vielfalt").

ities), but the one which, reappraising the concern with "the ultimate and the particular",[24] brings *phronêsis* and *poiesis* together through the specific mediation of *aisthesis or aesthesis*: a reformulation that explores the possibilities and promises of a certain *"perception" or "sense-perception"'s analogy* as a productive reconciliation of normative and aesthetic arenas (made possible by the return of law and legal thought to rhetoric and its "imagistic language"[25] or by "literary imagination's interpretative sense of life"[26])... but also as the opportunity (the only one that today remains for us!) to "awake the jurisprudential enterprise from its positivistic slumber and make jurisprudence again the prudence or *phronêsis* of law."[27] Which means recognizing a very specific *path*, followed by such different interlocutors as Boyd White and Douzinas, Nussbaum and Balkin, without forgetting that this path is made possible by an eloquent (selective) dialectic convergence of Aristotelian and Kantian arguments (the latter certainly recomposed on the basis of a *new* hard nucleus, named *Kritik der Urteilskraft*) ...

(γ) Once one recognizes the convergence of these two challenges and the alternative *pathos* they invoke, a few words are enough to catalogue the steps-*topoi* they justify. These involve, as a matter of a fact, a sequence a possible "landings," to be successively accessed (and more or less intensely inhabited) as one presents and explores certain assumptions: the normative and regulatory (if not the *subver-*

---

[24] Aristoteles, *Nicomachean Ethics*, VI, 9, 1142a 25 [see *Nikomachische Ethik VI (Sechstes Buch)*, herausgegeben und übersetzt von Hans-Georg Gadamer, Frankfurt am Main: Vittorio Klostermann, 1998, pp. 42–43].

[25] C. Douzinas, and L. Nead, "Introduction," op. cit., p. 8.

[26] M. Nussbaum, *Poetic Justice*, op. cit., pp. 1–12 ("The Literary Imagination").

[27] C. Douzinas, and L. Nead, "Introduction," op. cit., p. 11. "The aims of literary jurisprudence and of legal iconology are not dissimilar; but while the former closes the eyes to open the ear to the *ars legis* the latter insists that law's captures the soul by addressing the totality of the senses..." (ibidem). "In acknowledging the *ars legis*, the aesthetic dimension of law, we open the institution to the ethics of otherness and the justice of the senses or of Justitia, the feminine principle of transcendence that challenges the patriarchy of sublime Law..." (Costas Douzinas, "Prosopon and Antiprosopon: Prolegomena for a Legal Iconology," in: C. Douzinas, and L. Nead (eds), *Law and the Image*, op. cit., pp. 36–67, here at 67).

sive[28]) potential of the *linguistic-literary turn (we must read law as a kind of literature, we must read literature as a kind of law*[29]); the defense of *narrative* as the archetypal form of practice (*the narrative as the archetypal legal and rhetoric form …, as the archetypal form of human thought in ordinary life*[30]); the assumption that the construction of meaning and the circulation of signs have either stabilized or been transformed through the interpretative communities' *decisions* of *writing* and *rewriting* (decisions that, invoking the "promise" of a critical reconstitution of "topics,"[31] include a kind of basic *rhetoricization of narratives*[32]) – the assumption at least that interpretative pragmatics and/or performance involve the methodological priority not so much of a *reading situation* as of a microscopic *rhetoric circumstance* (experienced as the possibility of "establishing or losing community"[33]); last but not least (we'll see why), the representation that legal textual materials are constitutively wounded by *indeterminacy*.

---

[28] "La littérature est peut-être venue, dans des conditions historiques qui ne sont pas simplement linguistiques, occuper une place toujours ouverte à une sorte de juridicité sub-versive …, une juridicité [qui] suppose que l'identité à soi ne soit jamais assurée ou rassurante. Elle suppose aussi un pouvoir de produire performativement les énoncés de la loi, de la loi que peut être la littérature et non seulement de la loi à laquelle elle s'assujetit. Alors elle fait la loi, elle surgit en ce lieu où la loi se fait…" (Jacques Derrida, "Préjugés. Devant la loi," in: J. Derrida et al., *La faculté de juger*, Paris: Les éditions de Minuit, 1985, pp. 87–139 here at 134). See also M. Nussbaum, *Poetic Justice*, op. cit., pp. 1 and 9 (reading Dickens's *Hard Times*).

[29] James Boyd White, *Heracles' Bow. Essays on the Rethoric and Poetics of the Law*, Madison: The University of Wisconsin Press, 1985, pp. 122–123, 131; idem, *Justice as Translation*, op. cit., pp. 16–20; idem, *Acts of Hope. Creating Authority in Literature, Law and Politics*, Chicago: The University of Chicago Press, 1994, p. 275 ff. ("Reconstituting Self And World: The Creation Of Authority As An Act Of Hope»); idem, *From Expectation to Experience*, op. cit., pp. 52–72 ("'Law and Literature': No Manifesto"), 89–110 ("Meaning in the Humanities and in the Law").

[30] J.B. White, *Heracles' Bow*, op. cit., p. 175.

[31] Jack Balkin, "The Promise of Legal Semiotics," *University of Texas Law Review* 1991, vol. 69, pp. 1831–1852; idem, "A Night in the Topics: The Reason of Legal Rhetoric and the Rhetoric of Legal Reason" (1996), in: *Jack Balkin Home Page*, available at: <http://www.yale.edu/lawweb/jbalkin/articles/topics1.htm>.

[32] Costas Douzinas, and Ronnie Warrington (with McVeigh), *Postmodern Jurisprudence: the Law of Text in the Texts of Law*, London: Routledge, 1991, pp. 92–110 ("Law's Tales. Semiotics and Narratology as Storytelling").

[33] J.B. White, *Heracles' Bow*, op. cit., pp. 3–5.

2.2. If I've just said that a few words would be enough to recognize these common positions, I must add that, as far as the several plausible *answers* are concerned, *only* a few words will be ultimately *possible*. As a matter of fact, every specification, being indispensable to construct a supposedly conclusive answer, exposes the shared ground to an explosion of different irreconcilable voices – differences we cannot pass over in silence, certainly because they present our *humanistic approaches* as separated (divided) between distinct (exemplarily distinct) ways of experiencing the interpretative enterprise.

To characterize this enterprise and its conception of literary language, we are certainly still allowed to go on speaking about a *dialectic constitution of meaning* (Jauss), justified by the irreducibility of the *artistic* (authorial or creative) *pole* and the *aesthetic* (interpretative or performative) *one* (Iser), and supported by the presupposition (the endorsed reconstructed *modus operandi*) of an *implicit "reading" judge*. This call to the categories of *reception aesthetics* (even though taken in *latissimo sensu*) does not, however, avoid the *internal* tension between the discursive strategies of the *intentio lectoris* and the *intentio operis* (the latter disregarding the constitutive *différance* between *effects* and *reading reception processes*), as it does not avoid the oppositions between *narration* and *performance*, between the stabilizing possibilities (and the integrative strength) of a *narrative-text* and the contextual demands of an open *textual notation (as a text that requires performance)*,[34] or even between different ways of understanding the internalist or externalist attitudes about the enterprise of law.

Besides, to recognize an exemplary concentration of all these binominal (polarised) tensions, it would be enough to invoke (and contrast) Boyd White' and Balkin's *implicit judges*: the former presenting himself/herself as a *communal lawyer* engaged in a specific

[34] "Law and music require transforming the ink on the page into the enacted behavior of others. In an important sense, there is *only* 'law (or music, or drama) in action,' in contrast to poetry or fiction, whose texts do not require public performance but can be read silently to one's self..." (Jack Balkin, Sanford Levinson, "Interpreting Law and Music: Performance Notes on 'The Banjo Serenader' and 'The Lying Crowd Of Jews,'" *Cardozo Law Review* 1999, vol. 20, pp. 1513–1568, here at 1518).

way of life – telling a "shared story" in a "shared language,"[35] but also viewing law *from the inside* as a *culture of argument* and carrying out a compositional and literary process of translation that entails an ethical commitment (*justice as translation*[36]);[37] the latter justifying himself/herself as a *performer* or as a *performance director* —understanding the limitations and interests of her co-performers and her audiences and "tailoring her interpretation accordingly" to correspond to a certain "duty of fidelity and responsiveness" (both to the author or composer of the text and to the audience or community in which he or she performs),[38] a duty that is experienced as a kind of *indefinite* (rather

[35] J.B. White, *Heracles' Bow*, op. cit., p. 172. "The law is a way of creating a rhetorical community over time ...: [it is] a culture that makes us members of a common world. This culture is not reducible to rules, but it is objective, in the sense that it can be found and mastered and in the sense as well that it cannot be disregarded or unilateraly changed. Like the text produced by a single mind, the text produced by the culture has a genuine force and reality notwithstanding its irreducibility to rules or to scientific 'knowledge'..." (ibidem, p. 98).

[36] J.B. White, *Justice as Translation*, op. cit., p. 229 ff. ("Translation, Interpretation, and Law"), 257 ff. ("Justice as Translation"); idem, *From Expectation to Experience*, op. cit., pp. 69–71 (V), 97–102 (II). "For whatever the merits of the social sciences as methods for making and informing social policy, they cannot be applied to what is more distinctive about what lawyers and judges actually do, which is to discover, determine, interpret and compose legal texts ... [Scientific] 'methods' cannot simply be applied to the law, any more than its 'findings' can. There must be a process of translation ... [which] is at heart compositional and literary, in fact a form of writing ... Humanistic work can thus be seen as a species of 'translation'" (ibidem, p. 70, 102).

[37] "As an ethics of tentativeness and respect for the other, arising out of the recognition that one's statements and gestures can never have universal validity ... but also as the paradoxical duty, impossible to discharge with perfection, of simultaneously affirming respect for the other – the other language, the other culture, the other person – and asserting the value of one's own experience and judgement, and one's culture too..." (ibidem, p. 84). "A world of difference is thus created; it is kept from the prison-house of 'single meanings' – of thinking that meanings translate directly from text to text – by honest attention to language, to particularity of phrase and context; it is kept from the chaos of indifferent relativism – of thinking that nothing can be known or understood, no common values held – by a principle of humility and sincerity, or what I would call the ethic of the translator..." (J.B. White, *Justice as Translation*, op. cit., p. 268).

[38] Jack Balkin, Sanford Levinson, "Law as Performance" (1998), in: *Jack Balkin Home Page*, p. 1, available at: <http://www.yale.edu/lawweb/jbalkin/articles/london 21.htm>.

than *infinite*) *duty*, presupposing the intelligibility horizon of an *ethics of Otherness* (and the *external* mediation of Deconstruction, as *transcendental Deconstruction*[39]).[40] We are aware, however, that the interpretative *spectrum* is far from being reduced to these poles. Isn't our shared ground also inhabited by a political judge who wants to be a privileged listener of narratives (paying attention to stories of marginal identities and contributing to the microscopic destabilization of hierarchies),[41] and by a judge who wants to become a *literary judicious spectator* (going behind "empathy" to focus our attention on "individual singularity," to treat the other "as a unique person with one's own narrative history"),[42] or even by a judge who wounds us

---

[39] Jack Balkin, "Transcendental Deconstruction, Transcendent Justice" (1994), in: *Jack Balkin Home Page*, available at: <http://www.yale.edu/lawweb/jbalkin/articles/trans01.htm>; idem, *Cultural Software. A Theory of Ideology*, New Haven and London: Yale University Press, 1998, p. 99 ff. ("Ideology"), 142 ff. ("Transcendence"). "The encounter between deconstruction and justice has changed both parties; yet, of the two, deconstruction appears to be the more transformed. If deconstructive practice is to be of any use to the question of justice, it must become a transcendental deconstruction. It must exchange the logic of the infinite for that of the infinite. It must act in the service of human values that go beyond culture, convention and law. It must recognize the chasm that differentiates human values from articulated conceptions of it, and it must identify Deconstruction with that chasm..." (J. Balkin, "Transcendental Deconstruction, Transcendent Justice," op. cit., part III, p. 5).

[40] "Thus, the scope of the duty owed to speak in the language of the Other depends on our definition of the roles of the parties – as victim or injurer, strong or weak – but this definition will in turn be affected by the scope of the duty to speak in the language of the Other. ... The scope of our duty to speak in the language of the Other does not exist before we decide what their respective roles are, but the roles each plays cannot fully be determined before we fix the scope of the duty; each feature of the situation provides the proper context in which the other feature is to be judge. Because of the mutual dependence and differentiation of these contexts, the scope of the duty toward the Other is indefinite...." (J. Balkin, "Transcendental Deconstruction, Transcendent Justice," op. cit., part II (III, "Speaking in the Language of the Other"), pp. 7–8).

[41] I mean a political judge sensitive to *Critical Race Scholars*'s arguments: See Richard Delgado, and Jean Stefancic, *Critical Race Theory. An Introduction*, New York and London: New York University Press, 2001, p. 37 ff. ("Legal Storytelling and Narrative Analysis").

[42] M. Nussbaum, *Poetic Justice*, op. cit., pp. 72–78, 79 ff., 90 ff., 99–118 ("Poetic Judging").

as a spinner of alternative tales, answering aesthetically and ethically to the call of the suffering Other, assuming the task of a specific *justice as diké* (as a *momentary principle of Justice*)[43]?

When one gets to this degree of differentiation, the opposition is no longer played out only between different ways of experiencing the interpretative enterprise or the literary turn – or between different ways of understanding rhetorics and the practical *continuum* (justified by the intertwinement of *prhronêsis* and *aesthesis*, law and ethics), or even between different "evaluations" of modernity's heritage (including the need of identifying a *postmodern path*) –, but between radical different conceptions of *community* (and of the *return to community*).

On one hand, with Boyd White and Martha Nussbaum (but with different outcomes), we have communitarian meaning stabilized in the collective identities of a *community of memory* and a *community of ideas,*[44] or in the (unequal) dialectic process these *communities* construct. Boyd White oscillates, as a matter of fact, between the foundational share of common stories (and a common narrative pragmatics)[45] and the care-*Sorge* with intercultural dialogue (which is also the "bet" on an *ethics of translation*);[46] while Martha Nussbaum invokes the integrative horizon of a democratically participatory and republican citizenship (a typical *community of ideas*!), claiming that this experience of citizenship finds its constitutive experience in a kind of *concrete* universalism or cosmopolitanism (a cosmopolitanism which values the presupposed horizon as a patrimony of incommensurable

[43] Costas Douzinas and Ronnie Warrington, "A Well-Founded Fear of Justice: Law and Ethics in Postmodernity," *Law and Critique* 1991, vol. II, nº 2, pp. 115–147, here at 117–120, 142–147; Costas Douzinas, and Ronnie Warrington, *Justice Miscarried. Ethics, Aesthetics and the Law,* New York/London: Harvester Wheatsheaf, 1994, pp. 132–185 ("Another Justice"), 211–241 ("A Well-Founded Fear of the Other: the Momentary Principle of Justice").

[44] To say it invoking the *ideal types* proposed by Robert Booth Fowler, "Community. Reflections on Definition," in: A. Etzioni (ed.), *New Communitarian Thinking,* op. cit., pp. 88–95, here at 88 ff.

[45] "By communities of memory I mean current ideas of community that derive from long established belief-systems that link the present and the past…" (ibidem, p. 91).

[46] See *supra,* notes 35–37.

goods, still opening itself to the emotions and singularity of difference).[47]

On the other hand (with *Cls* and *postmodern jurisprudence* scholars), one experiences community as a microscopic reinvented *promise* (a promise which is permanently sought and *deferred*) – as the construction of meaning (the cultural articulation and the integrative order-*ordinans*) that a specific *praxis* pursues (and recognizes) when invoking the (reunited or separated) spells of a certain *political morality* (based on the Foucaultian experience of a capillary immanent tissue of *powers* and *resistances*), of an *aesthetics / anesthetics of the sublime* (justified through a Lyotardian reinvention of Kant's *reflexive judgment*) and of a radically autonomous *ethics of alterity* (committed to the Derridian translation of Levinas's *infinite responsibility*).[48]

3.

But let us go back to our leading question. When differences are so overwhelming, is it productive or „interesting" to identify such a *common ground*? I would insist it is. Certainly because it's only when one pays attention to the diversity of the implicated voices, assuming

---

[47] See an exemplary synthesis in Martha Nussbaum, "Patriotism and Cosmopolitanism" (1994), available at <http://www.soci.niu.edu/~phildept/Kapitan/nussbaum 1.html>. Without forgetting the *corrections* introduced in Martha Nussbaum, "Toward a Globally Sensitive Patriotism," *Daedalus* 2008 (Summer), vol. 137, n° 3, American Academy of Arts & Sciences, pp. 78–93.

[48] I have systematically explored some possibilities-trends of these *promises of community*, specially in: J.M. Aroso Linhares, *Entre a reescrita pós-moderna da juridicidade e o tratamento narrativo da diferença*, Coimbra: Coimbra Editora, 2001, pp. 92 ff. and 181–211 (the Foucaultian contribution), 221 ff. and 462–507 (the Lyotardian's *aesthetics of sublime*); and idem, "Autotranscendentalidade, desconstrução e responsabilidade infinita. Os enigmas de *Force de loi* (2004)," in: *Ars Iudicandi. Estudos em Homenagem ao Professor Doutor Castanheira Neves (Boletim da Faculdade de Direito da Universidade de Coimbra,* special number), vol. I. Coimbra, Coimbra Editora, 2008, pp. 551–667 (the Derridian trend). See also idem, "Dekonstruktion als philosophische (gegenphilosophische) Reflexion über das Recht. Betrachtungen zu Derrida" (2005), *Archiv für Rechts- und Sozialphilosophie (ARSP)* 2007, Bd. 93, H. 1, pp. 39–66; idem, "O *dito* do direito e o *dizer* da justiça. Diálogos com Levinas e Derrida" (2006), *Themis – Revista da Faculdade de Direito da Universidade Nova de Lisboa* 2007, VIII, n° 14, pp. 5–56.

the *need* of going beyond a basic (crude) diagnosis of connections and affinities, that the character and the limits of the sought *human alternative* become at last clear. One may even add that this is so because the awareness of an irreducible *pragmatics of plurality* (sometimes clearly the celebration of an invincible *différend*) paradoxically opens up the way for us to discover (to experience) *other* troubling (not to be confessed) affinities (between the reunited voices) —affinities which, in turn, contribute to the structural perpetuation of the differences!

3.1. As a matter of fact, all the *humanistic approaches* that we have brought together reproduce a-problematically what we may denominate (with the unexpected help of Kelsen's and Posner's formulations) a conception of *law as frame (Rahmen)*[49] or an *open area* discursive strategy.[50] Not only because all of them treat law as an ensemble of textual materials (to be read or to be performed), but also because all of them (without exception) wound these materials (standards, policies, rules, canons) with an a-problematic *indeterminacy thesis* (justifying indeterminacy as a decisive parameter of the interpretative enterprise). Which means recognizing that the juridically autonomous (internal) treatment of these *wounds* and *blind spots* (if not *points of rhetorical or argumentative loosening or condensation)*[51]— i.e., the juridically relevant "capacity" of dealing with this situation of *uncertainty*[52] — stops (ar-

[49] „Das Ergebnis einer Rechtsinterpretation (…) kann (…) nur die Feststellung des Rahmens sein, den das zu interpretierende Recht darstellt und damit die Erkenntnis mehrerer Möglichkeiten, die innerhalb dieses Rahmens gegeben sind" (Hans Kelsen, *Reine Rechtslehre*, zweite Auflage, Wien: Deuticke, 1960, p. 349).

[50] "Legalism's inability in many cases to decide the outcome … and the related difficulty, often impossibility, of verifying the correctness of the outcome, whether by its consequences or its logic …, create an open area in which judges have decisional discretion—a blank slate on which to inscribe their decisions—rather than being compelled to a particular decision by 'the law.' How [the judges] … fill in the open area is the fundamental question that this book addresses, though lurking in the background and occasionally coming to the fore is the question how they should fill it in…" (Richard Posner, *How Judges Think*, Cambridge Mass.: Harvard University Press, 2008, p. 9).

[51] See the development proposed in C. Douzinas, and R. Warrington (with McVeigh), *Postmodern Jurisprudence*, op. cit., pp. 55–73 ("Hermes versus Hercules"), 183–196 ("The Books of Judges"), 238–243 [«Suspended sentences», part (e)].

[52] J.B. White, *Heracles' Bow*, op. cit., pp. 21–23, 25–26, 42, 192–212; idem, *Justice as Translation*, op. cit., pp. 84–86.

rests itself) drastically with a process of determination of *limits*: a process that —with more or less meaningful stabilizing effects (those will be minimal in deconstructive semiotics)— is, so to speak, already predetermined in the abstract representation of these materials, and consummates itself without remission in the construction of the *frame*, the frame that confines (allows) an ensemble of (virtually) plausible (legally equivalent) alternatives, simultaneously renouncing interference with the *open area* or the *blank slate* it contains. Thus the choice between those alternatives must be pursued through decisional jurisdictional discretion (taking seriously a *decision paradigm*), which means invoking different foreseeable effects, but also an evaluation of these effects justified by an horizon of intentions, expectations and possibilities of determination which are explicitly *non-juridical* — those that the literary or performative imagination justifies (with the constitutive aid of *humanistic arenas* such as literary and ideology criticism, moral and political philosophy, ethical and ecological studies, semiotics and... *grammatology*).

Without forgetting that this *indeterminacy thesis* specifies itself in a sequence-chain of exemplary positions, such as:

(a) the reproduction of the binomial *easy / hard cases* (the first ones corresponding to the exceptional methodological situation of a frame which allows only one possible decision)[53]...

(b) the rejection of the intelligibility category of the *legal system* (whose possibilities are reduced to those justified by *formalistic understanding*)[54]...

---

53 "Does literary judging make a difference? Not in all imaginable cases, obviously. Sometimes the legal issues tell clearly one way or another; sometimes the facts are so simple and uncontroversial that literary imagining is not important..." (M. Nussbaum, *Poetic Justice*, op. cit., p. 117).

54 "At least until recently the image of law most widely accepted among legal academics ... was that of a set of rules passed by the legislature or articulated in judicial opinions ... perhaps coupled with the more general rules called 'principles' that inform the lesser ones..." (J.B. White, *Justice as Translation*, op. cit., XIII). "So that law is in this sense objectified and made a structure ... and the question 'what is law?' is answered by defining what its rules are, by analysing the kinds of rules that characterize it" (idem, *Heracles' Bow*, op. cit., p. 29).

(c) the complementary assumption of a *continuum* between *legal materials,* which is also a deliberate *confusion* between *principles* and *rules, principles* and *policies* as "standard forms of legal justification"[55] ...

(d) a consequent impossibility of justifying an autonomous methodological problem.

Let's add two words *only* about the third item. It is in fact surprising that all these discursive strategies assume constitutively a *community* project (as a return to values or human goods, or at least to "non-commensurable" *ultimate ends*) without paying attention to the specificity of legal principles (without at least discussing this specificity). There is in them even an explicit hostility to an autonomous mobilization of *arguments of principle,* which we could exemplify invoking once again the exemplary polarised proposals of Boyd White and Costas Douzinas: Boyd White as he confines the relevance of the assumption of the legal system to a rule-oriented formalistic approach (named *law as rules plus principles theory*) —which means also reducing principles to "more general rules;"[56] Douzinas[57] as he denounces the violence against *singularity* and *difference* that *arguments of principle* (and the interpretative presupposition of *law-worked-by-principle*) radically aggravate —which means also denouncing Dworkin and Drucilla Cornell as hermeneutical positivists (the first one, besides, "motivated by the desire to answer positivism's embarrassment," if not to "purify positivism's scandal").[58]

3.2. The conclusion seems unavoidable. Shouldn't we recognize after all that *our* humanistic approaches only get to generate an effective alternative to legal instrumentalisms or pragmatisms when they partially (but no less paradoxically) converge with these privileged opponents, that is to say, when they a-problematically reproduce an *indeterminacy thesis* and an *open area* conception (concentrated in

---

[55] J. Balkin, "A Night in the Topics: The Reason of Legal Rhetoric and the Rhetoric of Legal Reason," op. cit., pp. 8–11.

[56] See *supra,* note 54.

[57] C. Douzinas, and R. Warrington, *Justice Miscarried,* op. cit., p. 237.

[58] C. Douzinas, and R. Warrington (with McVeigh), *Postmodern Jurisprudence,* op. cit., pp. 23–24, 55 ff.; C. Douzinas, and R. Warrington, *Justice Miscarried,* op. cit., p. 199 ff. (III).

a certain *hard cases* theory)? I would say that there are two different *problems* that converge here.

3.2.1. The first one concerns the efficiency of *resistance* itself. Is the resistance to *Zweckrationalität*, that these reunited interlocutors are in a position to oppose, a fragile one? I would say it is... because of the reinvention of *praxis* and *practical thinking* they offer (if not because of the *practical world* they presuppose). This fragility does not however reside in the more or less happily explicit renunciation to an order-*ordinata* of Being (and its ontological *mirror*). As we have already seen, it is the circumstance of this renunciation that opens up, on the contrary, the opportunity for an unique (for once constitutively autonomous) practical philosophy! This fragility resides rather in the specific *paths* or *routes* that, in the name of that autonomous status, *praxis* and its *intellectual virtue* (*phronêsis*) seem here constrained to follow. As if the loss of *sophias*'s theoretical predominance has condemned contingence and mutability —those existences whose causes can be otherwise than they are"[59]— to a practical *continuum*, and this one involved an holistic ethical commitment where *energeia* and *kinesis*, *praxis* and *poiesis*, but also *êthos (ήθος)* and *éthos (έθος)*, *ethos* and *pathos*, would be definitively reconciliated and undifferentiatedly melted. But also as if this holistic experience justified an immediate rejection of all the persistent attempts that —persuasively projected in several legal thinking trends (not certainly by chance to sustain some well-known *internalist attitudes*) — accentuate either a praxis of hermeneutical recontextualisation, or a topical (problematically committed) conception of *pratical arguments*... and either one or the other of these poles searches for and justifies an autonomous (*prudential*) *subject/ subject*'s rationality.

These options shape (constrain) our *humanistic approaches*, not only preventing the possibility of establishing a clear counterpoint between *moral* and *intellectual* virtues,[60] but also favouring a certain con-

---

[59] *Nicomachean Ethics*, VI, 1, 1139a 5 [see *Nikomachische Ethik VI (Sechstes Buch)*, herausgegeben und übersetzt von H.-G. Gadamer, op. cit., p. 27].

[60] See the well-known reconstitution of Aristotle's „practical wisdom» ("akin to sense-perception") proposed in Martha Nussbaum, *The Fragility of Goodness. Luck and*

cept of *ultimate goods*: a concept that —thanks either to the persistence of a selective dialogue with Aristostelian *onto-teleologism* (White, Nussbaum), or to the protagonism of an emancipatory *critic of ideology* (Balkin, Douzinas)— cannot really avoid a very troubling *continuum* with *means-ends rationality*. As if the problem was still only *one* of competitive uncertainty, developed in the immanence of pure *ends*, and the single positive difference to be found might be that of mitigating the rigid equivalence of these ends with the introduction of some plausible hierarchies (*commensurable/ non-commensurable ends*, ends instrumentally pursued / ends pursued for their own sake). Not certainly arbitrary hierarchies, but those sustained by *altruistic ideological convictions* (Balkin) or practical-existential-aesthetic bets (Douzinas), but also recognized thanks to the restitution of *subjective ends* to cultural systems and horizons[61] —the cultural contexts from whose possibilities they were supposedly extirpated (White, Nussbaum).

3.2.2. The other *problem* to pay attention to has to do with a kind of a *misjudgement* (if not with *the* misjudgement *par excellence*) that all the open area discourses cultivate. I mean the kind of misjudgement that inscribes the *claim of legal autonomy* (whatever mask it puts on) exclusively in the prescriptive realm of normativism and formalism (and formalistic legal thinking), reducing the possibilities of an *internal juridical attitude* (the experience of law as an autonomous dimension of practice and an autonomous field of knowledge) to the corresponding *program* of *isolation* of an abstract self-sufficient normative cosmos (freed from the dynamics of social reality or reducing it to an ensemble of discrete *facts*, as such foreseen in the rules' *hypothesis*).

Ethics in Greek Tragedy and Philosophy, Cambridge Mass.: Harvard University Press, 1986, pp. 291-306 ("Non-scientific Deliberation").

[61] "Our motives and values are not on this view to be taken as exogenous to the system (as they are taken to be exogenous to an economic system) but are in fact its subject. The law should take as its most central question what kind of community we should be, with what values, motives and aims; it is a process by which we make ourselves by making our language" (J.B. White, *Heracles' Bow*, op. cit., p. 42). "The only rational 'ends,' the only ends we can confidently use as guides to conduct, are conceptions of ourselves and of our relations with others, not materially describable states of affairs" (ibidem, pp. 21-23).

It is this reductive *misjudgement* that allows our *humanist front* to treat Dworkin as a more or less overt formalist, and that after all imposes that the alternative to *legal pragmatism* and its *interdisciplinary choice* has to be sought (and found!) thanks to the propulsive impetus of another *interdisciplinary claim*: a claim that preserves the *framing task* of legal materials, also plunging into the *open area* and choosing one of the consented alternatives... merely substituting the explanatory dominance of the social sciences by the privileged contribution of *humanistic* arenas (and literary or performative invention). Thus the transitive decision *alternative* to be chosen may be the one whose effects better contribute to defend the judgement's authority in the „language of community itself,"[62] if not also to the creation of meaning of a *communitarian ethics of translation* (Boyd White), to the singular celebration of „emotions" as „forms of intentionality"[63] (Martha Nussbaum), to the microscopic pursuit of an *indefinite duty toward the Other*[64] (Balkin), to a plausible „ethical acting against the grain of the pure interpretative moment"[65] (Douzinas/Warrington)... even to the political authoritative performance of a "jurisprudence of empathy," if not a „jurisprudence unmodified"[66] (Robin West).

This last accentuation confronts us as a matter of fact with the explicit or implicit *need* to search for the *homo humanus* (*or the* humani-

---

[62] J.B. White, *Heracles' Bow*, op. cit., p. 191.

[63] "Emotion and desire are not simply mindless pushes, but complex forms of intentionality infused with object-directed thought; they can be significantly shaped by reasoning about the good..." (M. Nussbaum, "Virtue Ethics: A Misleading Category?" op. cit., p. 180).

[64] See *supra*, note 40.

[65] Costas Douzinas, and Ronnie Warrington, "A Well-Founded Fear of Justice: Law and Ethics in Postmodernity," *Law and Critique* 1991, vol. II, no. 2, pp. 115–147, here at 146.

[66] "A perfect legal system will protect against harms sustained by all forms of life, and will recognize life affirming values generated by all forms of being. Feminist jurisprudence must aim to bring this about and, to do so, it must aim to transform the images as well as the power. Masculine jurisprudence must become humanist jurisprudence, and humanist jurisprudence must become a jurisprudence unmodified..." [Robin West, "Jurisprudence and Gender," in: Hilaire Barnett (ed.), *Sourcebook on Feminist Jurisprudence*, London: Routledge - Cavendish, 1996, pp. 243–244 ("Conclusion: Toward a Jurisprudence Unmodified")].

ty's project) that our circumstance demands... *beyond Law* or at least renouncing Law' specific "thirdness" *(tértialité)* [Levinas] and its comparison claim (its dialectics of personal autonomy and *limited* communitarian responsibility). To justify this need is indeed to assume a kind of constitutive paradox: the one which strikes us when we notice that... if it is true that all these reunited voices are eloquently committed, *in the name* of Law or at least *because* of Law's relevance, to a specific urgent reinvention of praxis and practical discourse – a reinvention which may be able to resist *Zweckrationalität*'s hypertrophy –, it is not less true that all the different parallel answers that these attempts construct only get to impose themselves as plausible (more or less successful) alternatives when they renounce Law –or when they dilute Law in a practical holistic *continuum*, where its project loses sense and autonomy.

Is this all we have to say about the presumed *common ground* and its constructive endeavour? Isn't this a disappointingly aporetic conclusion? Or at least a conclusion which, in its best light, condemns us to the *alternative*-call of an *ethical* answer...or perhaps better, to the challenge of a *certain* political contingent institutionalization (the *one* which may be able to *ear* attentively this call)? I wouldn't say it is. Certainly because to insist on this conclusion does not constrain us either to accept or to reject outright these parallel attempts, even less to forget their meaningful reflective patrimony (or the problems' diagnosis they contribute to *unveil*). The awareness of this paradox rather invites us to *ear* carefully these proposals, recognizing however that we should not so promptly renounce, as they do, *betting* on Law's autonomy... or *reinventing* this autonomy claim in our specific circumstance (to give it the *chance* of an indispensable continuous practical renovation). To go on *betting on law* as an autonomous *task* or an autonomous *way of life* means today either paying attention to plural multifarious contexts of realization, or rejecting the *open area discretion* (with all the presuppositions this discretion invokes). Without forgetting that to reject this area (to admit the *need* of an autonomous juridically plausible answer) means, in turn, to explore the possibilities of a multidimensional open *legal system*: a system of *principles and rules*, in permanent constitutive dialectics with singular, unrepeatable practical controversies, where normative principles (experienced as autonomous *jus*) are (luminously!) seriously taken (and circularly reconstituted) as an irreducible foundational *stratum*.[67]

Now this bet *inverts* the emphasis that the drawing of our *common ground* has presupposed since the beginning. It inverts it, *on one hand*, to receive (to welcome) the experience of narrativity and performance (and its imaginative respect for singularity and difference) as a precious "informative" input (among other interdisciplinarily constructed informative inputs) – a contribution which is indispensable to recognize our practical circumstance and its cultural articulations, but also and in particular to pay attention to the specific sensitivity to singularity that these cultural articulations experience (and to assume the possibilities and the relevance of the different realization contexts). It inverts it, *on the other hand*, to free the *legal materials* from their exclusive framing task, i.e., to make them (and their constitutive realisation) *responsible* for plausible successful answers to concrete inter-subjective controversies, which also means assuming a specific *humanitas* project – a project which is to be pursued in an historical context, and which is as such conditioned by all the involved (political, economic, cultural) *contextual* factors, a project however that is not necessarily (rather on the contrary!) condemned to lose its identity or its distinctiveness.

Does not this mean concluding that the way of combining the specific contributions of *law* and *literature*, legal thinking and literary criticism, legal practice and literary realization, seems to be much more adequately assumed by Dworkin (who never forgets the *distinctiveness* of the legal enterprise) than by all the voices that we have selected as *exemplary frequenters* of a certain *common ground*? I would say it does. To agree on the path to be taken (where literary *stimuli* are mainly used as resources to expose and defend the law's fidelity to

---

[67] I invoke here the specific *legal system*'s conception proposed by Castanheira Neves: see specially António Castanheira Neves, *Metodologia Jurídica. Problemas Fundamentais*, Coimbra: Coimbra Editora, 1993, pp. 78–81, 152–157, 188–196, 278–283 (ßß); idem, "A unidade de sistema jurídico: o seu problema e o seu sentido" (1981), in: idem, *Digesta. Estudos acerca do direito, do pensamento jurídico, da sua metodologia e outros*, Coimbra: Coimbra Editora, vol. II, 1995, pp. 95–180, here at 155 ff., 167–180.

arguments of principle) does not however mean to agree entirely and unconditionally on the proposed answers and the mobilized resources (to begin certainly with the argument that defends the centrality of interpretation in the adjudicative process). But this is naturally another discussion!

Coimbra and Beijing, July and September 2009

Leszek Leszczyński
Maria Curie-Skłodowska University, Poland

Legal Certainty and Judicial Discretion in the Statutory Legal Order

Abstract: Legal certainty is a standard for the law to be achieved through the various activities of all subjects operating in the legal order. The question of the role of the judiciary, in addition to the legislators, in gaining legal certainty must therefore be crucial in the statutory legal culture.
Taking the fact that judicial discretion is an inevitable feature of legal practice, one should raise questions around a conditions making the contribution of the judiciary in legal certainty more effective, even if sometimes jurisdiction might be different in content from what has been enacted as the letter of the law. It is the uniformity of jurisdiction resulting from various activities that seems to be the initial term. The uniform judicial practice, however, vis-à-vis legislation, plays an even more decisive role in shaping the new image of legal certainty: it makes legal argumentation more juridical than political, it dynamizes legal order, shifting it from a formal concept of rule of law to the adaptive discourse in the implementation of law, it strengthens the functional and value-oriented approach to the law, it substantializes and polycentralizes legal certainty, shifting the legal order from instrumental to deliberative and communicative discourse. Finally, uniform judicial practice brings legal certainty (certainty of law) to the certainty of rights being effectively guaranteed in front of courts.

Keywords: legal certainty and uniformity, judicial discretion, statutory law

1. Legal certainty

1.1. Concept of legal certainty (in general)

The concept of legal certainty seems to be the core of the law itself, as seen from the perspective of the creation of one clear standard of human behavior and its control as well as of the predictability of the law in action. Legal certainty as a real feature is important both for law practitioners and law addressees. Perhaps it is even more important for society and social expectations, since its members are not always ready to conduct and develop detailed reasoning in order to bring what is not (entirely) clear to the status of clarity, making at least legal decisions (both judicial and administrative) workable and functional.

Legal certainty does not seem, however, to be the kind of legal principle that is usually discussed in legal sciences as the kind of standard or policy, and sometimes a rule, derived from the legal text or other source of law, accepted in the frames of a legal culture.[1] It is, rather, a standard for the law to be achieved through the various activities of all subjects operating in the legal circulation (in a broader sense of this word). In this number, the legislation and judicial practice, if we take into consideration mainly the statutory legal culture, must play the most crucial role in achieving this principle or feature and, what is decisive, these two actors cannot act separately. The various types of relations between them, among which the conflicting ones must be also considered, define and determine the type and scope of the certainty the legal order may reach.

It is no wonder that, among the terms that legal certainty depends on, clarity, predictability, accessibility, and stability are among the most frequently raised as the vital ones. And, when we start to analyze all of them, we will see that none of them can rely exclusively on legislative processes and their results. Obviously, clarity of law begins more decidedly from the features of the legal text and systematic ties between the rules than from the other terms, but it does not mean that clarity of law equals clarity of the legal text or the legal system. The features of predictability and stability depend on the visibility and accessibility of the law being tied more closely with judicial practice than with legislative works.

---

[1] Ronald Dworkin, *Taking Rights Seriously*, Harvard University Press, 1978, Chapters 2 and 3; Robert Alexy, *A Theory of Constitutional Rights*, transl. by Julian Rivers, 2nd ed., Oxford: Oxford University Press, 2002, at 47 ff., esp. 48, 50, 54. See also Zygmunt Ziembiński, *Wstęp do aksjologii dla prawników* [Introduction to the Axiology for Jurists], Warszawa: Wydawnictwo Prawnicze, 1990, at 199 ff.; Sławomira Wronkowska, Maciej Zieliński, Zygmunt Ziembiński: *Zasady prawa. Zagadnienia podstawowe* [Principles of Law: Basic Problems], Warszawa: Wydawnictwo Prawnicze 1974, *passim*.

1.2. Legal certainty in the implementation of law

The question of the role of the judiciary in gaining legal certainty must therefore be at the top of the analysis, and before answering this question, the question of the certainty of judicial practice must somehow be discussed. The discussion should start from a short consideration of the axiology of judicial decision-making processes.

It is quite well rooted in legal theory that the judicial implementation of law has been determined by both internal and external values, having an impact on the decisions and on the process itself as a result.[2]

Among the external values of the implementation of law, rightness and justice are considered the ones that have the greatest impact on the process of decision-making and on the content of decisions. It should be stated that this impact is definitely more visible in the judicial process, since in administrative decisions both of the above-mentioned values are "filtered" through the political purposes that might influence - and in some types of decisions, i.e., influence as a rule - the contents of them. They act in the implementation of law as a result of a conviction that the law should be certain but at the same time flexible, according to the actual social situation in which the implementation takes place.

There are, however, internal values of the implementation of law, bringing the process and the decision closer to the criteria of legality, uniformity, certainty, and effectiveness of the application of law.[3] What is really interesting for our consideration, if we separate the value of legality - as a value demanding that the judicial and administrative decisions be based on the letter of law (statutes and other normative acts) - from all others, all of them are connected somehow with the value of the certainty of law, in spite of the fact that, in the above-presented catalog, certainty of implementation of law is "only" one of them.

[2] See Jerzy Wróblewski, *Wartości a decyzja sądowa* [Values and Judicial Decision], Wrocław: Ossolineum, 1973, at 183 ff.

[3] See ibidem, Chapters 3, 4, 5 and 6.

Let us see what the certainty of the application of law means. According to Wróblewski, legal certainty has three aspects: (1) certainty of making a legal decision, (2) certainty of the contents of this decision, and (3) certainty of the execution of the decision.

All features are connected with both types of application of law (judicial and administrative), though the links to the judicial practice decide on evaluation and qualification of the legal practice as a whole. One of the reasons for that is the judicial control of the administrative activities (mainly decisions), making the review of their contents and the process of their making it to the courts (usually special administrative courts) possible.

It is clear that the procedural order of making decisions of the process, if initiated properly, makes the first of the aspects of the certainty of implementation of law a rather regular and observed standard of judicial practice in democratic and rule-of-law states. The possible competence disputes between various state organs do not eliminate this value from being widely applied and binding as a base for procedural rule.

Certainty of the execution of the decisions is a rather functional and praxeological value, connected not only with the adequacy of the legal rules but also with the operational effectiveness of the administrative and judicial machinery. Thus the value of certainty of execution of decisions, tied too with the speed of the implementation process, is as a matter of fact a somewhat different type of value than the others. It is, however, strictly connected with them.

Finally, the certainty of the contents of decisions is the most complex and the most involved value of the implementation of law. It might be seen as the result or continuation of the legality of implementation, in the sense that the contents of the decision is based on substantial law (the letter of the law). It might, however, also be treated as a result of the stable "line of jurisdiction," making the contents of the decisions taken on similar types of cases predictable for the audience. This second aspect of certainty, focused on uniformity and connected strictly with the predictability of the law itself, opens the problem of the relation between the judiciary and legislation in the context of judicial discretion.

2. Judicial discretion

2.1. The essence and the sources

The presence of the margin of decision (in any of its form) by entities (subjects) implementing law is taken for granted in every process of law-making. It seems to be an indispensable element of every law-making policy. It is only the scope of the margin as accepted by the lawmaker and its role as specified that can vary.

This means from the one side that, in reality, none of legislators can believe that, thanks to their activities, discretion might be eliminated and, from the other side, that neither courts nor administrative agencies can escape from exercising this discretion in their decision-making processes.

We might define discretion in the implementation of law as the state of things in which more than one solution can be reasonably justified with arguments taken from the legal order. It might also be defined as a activity leading to results that can be justified in the above-noted way. It is important in both aspects that the results do not weaken the value of the rule of law and do not make the order dysfunctional.

Such discretion deals with both types of implementation of law – judicial (by courts) and administrative (by administrative agencies). Since judicial review of the administrative decisions became the model solution in contemporary rule-of-law states (even if the details of this control decisively differ from each other), judicial discretion finally forms the model of the discretion that the law deals with. In addition, in connection with its role in the sphere of politics, the administrative implementation of law brings so many specific problems of administrative purposefulness in deciding the various forms of responsibility for the content of decisions, etc., that a closer elaboration of only some of them would surpass the focus of this paper.

Remarks on the sources of judicial discretion might bring some additional indications dealing with the essence of it and, what is more important, with the relation between the judiciary and the legislature.

The presence of the margin of decision is connected with the diversity of its sources. As a general and immanent characteristic of processes of making decisions around law application irrespective of all other factors, the margin of decision appears independently from the constructions that create it. It may be generated on the basis of purposeful and consciously (intentionally) created constructs as well as on the basis of "natural" sources. The former depend more or less on legislative policy; the latter, being independent of the details of such policy, make the presence of judicial discretion indispensable.

The natural sources of judicial discretion deal with the nature of the legal language, with the characteristics of the decision-making-process based on the general legal norms and with the feature of the dynamics of the legal environment, while the letter of law remains unchanged.[4]

The natural source of the margin is primarily constituted by the characteristics of the language of law itself which, as regards semantics, is somewhere at the border between natural and artificial languages. Moreover, the "activity" of decoding a norm from a legal regulation, i.e., reconstructing a general and "complete" pattern of behavior on the basis of various elements included in a legal text (situations when the pattern of behavior must be compiled from elements not included in the regulations are beyond the scope of our interest), is naturally connected with the margins of decision, as it is not possible for every entity decoding such a pattern to take into consideration the same elements from the same fragments of the system of legal regulations. Also, building the links between various elements of the system, especially in its horizontal structure, belongs in the visible scope of the legal doctrine and practice.

Going further, the source of discretion comes from the process of applying legal norms, consisting in creating the general pattern of behavior included in the norm, which is gradually more and more specified as the process progresses, so that at the end a behavior pattern specific enough to "match" the norm with the actual state of things (facts of the case) can be established. It is connected with the characteristics of specifying general patterns of behavior and elimi-

[4] Leszek Leszczyński, *Zagadnienia teorii stosowania prawa. Doktryna i tezy orzecznictwa* [Problems of the Theory of Implementation of Law: Doctrine and Theses of Jurisdiction], Kraków: Zakamycze, 2001, pp. 41–45.

nating from the general pattern the elements that are simply not necessary for a given decision in the application of law.

Another source is connected with the relation between the letter of law, established at the given date, but binding in a changing world. Harmonization of the actual state of the legal environment with the letter of law, if not accomplished by a legislative change in the statute, must be exercised by the judicial practice. Perception of this actual state of things in light of the facts of the case impacts the way that the rules are treated by the judiciary.

There is no one model of the scope of discretion rooted in these sources. Its scale, in addition to the type of implementation of law (administrative vs. judicial), depends on the type of political regime, the intensiveness of the social changes, the branch of law, the level of organization of the judiciary dealing with discretion, etc.

2.2. The legislative approach to discretion

Taking into account the fact that one of undisputed requirements of regulations by law and, at the same time, one of the legal values is the flexibility of law and the processes of its application, the lawmaker might be interested not only in accepting the above-mentioned sources and making them work for his aims and values, but also in extending the margin of decisions arising from natural sources.[5]

Making law and the processes of its application flexible is sometimes regarded as the necessary individualization of the processes of the application of law, and is frequently claimed to be the most general legislative aim that is attained by various normative constructions. The flexibility of applying law means establishing such a relation between the internal values of the application of law (legality, dependability, and uniformity) and the values and criteria that are external to strictly legal arguments (fairness, rightness, and political appraisals) that would make it possible for the latter to be applied, providing the regulation by law itself allows it and features of the

[5] Tadeusz Biernat, "Law making policy," in: T. Biernat, Marek Zirk-Sadowski (eds), *Politics of Law and Legal Policy. Between Modern and Post-modern Jurisprudence*, transl. by Małgorzata Kiełtyka, Warszawa: Wolters Kluwer Polska, 2008, p. 75 ff.

material of the decision justify it. Depending on the concept of the decision of the application of law that is adopted in a given legal practice, the margin of decision may be unlimited or slightly limited (in the case of a discrete decision regarding the application of law), or it may be subject to "control" as regards the guideline of law-abiding and rational application of these criteria (the concept of rational and law-abiding decision).[6] The consideration of relevant guidelines, the expectations of the lawmaker, the actual discretion of the decision, and the interference of various non-legal criteria with the content of the decisions that are made appears to be a complex issue.

Adopting the thesis that the ultimate goal of creating the margin of discretion is to make the application of law flexible does not explain the possible detailed aims of the lawmaker. Generally speaking, the lawmaker may have two detailed goals in mind as regards the creation of the margin. Regarding the first, the lawmaker may aim for the actual and direct "opening" of the legal system to autonomous evaluations and social norms and "saturating" the content of the law with the values that are considered by the lawmaker as precious, but that are not suitable to be expressed in legal texts. In consequence, the foregoing intentions may result in a more socialized process of establishing new legal values, which may gradually turn into rules of law, even without the necessity of changing specific legal regulations. This corresponds to the attitude of cautious legislative inference where autonomous appraisals and norms operate efficiently enough, and in relation to which detailed regulation by law could weaken these features (e.g., family relations or economic relations and processes).

The other detailed goal may be totally different. Namely, the intention of making the application of law flexible may stem from the desire to make the content of the law dependent on current political trends, systems or aims, or to create an atmosphere of virtual "hand steering" of the processes of the application of law with the application of temporary political directives, which may be formulated in various forms (politicization of the application of law).

---

[6] Max Weber, *On Law in Economy and Society*, New York: Simon and Schuster, 1965, p. 65, 224–225; Jerzy Wróblewski, *Sądowe stosowanie prawa* [The Judicial Application of Law], Warszawa: PWN, 1988, pp. 383–396.

Political criteria would be primarily applied here, as it is these criteria that most affect the application of law even when they are not pointed to directly. The results of the foregoing influence within the sphere of economic relations in a centrally directed economy, with strict guidelines for the official political ideology being additionally invoked, lead up to the weakening, or even annihilation, of the operation of so-called economic laws.

The above-mentioned detailed goals are mutually opposing. They cannot be adopted simultaneously. Nonetheless, what is not excluded is a peculiar compromise, which enables a fragmentary application of both of them, e.g., with reference to various spheres of social relations or the action of various subjects applying law. Additionally, these actions may be subject to modification depending on the intensity of authoritarian or democratic elements over various periods of time. Therefore, the execution of these detailed goals will depend on the utilization of the factors coming from the features of the social surroundings of law.

2.3. The point of the legislator

The effective creation of a margin of decision as an element of rational legislative policy depends on some initial conditions. Leaving aside, for the time being, the question of the form of the model of lawmaking (democratic vs. authoritarian, imperious vs. negotiating, etc.), the lawmaker cannot opt for promoting the margin if there are some factors that do not encourage it. Among these factors, one should mention the methods of regulation of social relations by law prevailing in a given legal practice. Then the executive machinery, according to the lawmaker, should work properly, be mature, and be ready to solve "hard cases," and the features of regulated legislative matters (particular branches of law) and specified conditions of the social surroundings of law (cultural, political, or economic) have another impact on the options. All of them make up a certain concept of the policy of law and, in fact, the part of it that concerns possibilities, needs, and chances to succeed in accomplishing legislative aims by means of utilizing the construction of the discretion of decision. Moreover, all of them are gradable.

What seems to be the condition precedent here is a departure from the casuistic method of norm-setting, which precluded not only creating the margin, but also setting general norms, as understood contemporarily.

Since the margin of decision is anticipated or programmed by the lawmaker in the processes of law-making, we will be concerned mainly with the conditions of its creation that are present in the culture of statutory law. The most significant role, strengthening the security of utilizing the constructions, is bound to be played by political and legal guidelines, usually stemming from the prevailing line of legal doctrine, which accept the possibility of correcting strictly legal criteria on the basis of social norms or natural-law principles that are, however, correlated with the importance of the idea of the state of law. The latter should be confirmed by the existence of formal guarantees of the law-observing activity of agencies, as well as doctrinal and practical acceptance of such a concept of the decision of law application that would exclude the postulate of total discretion of competence and procedure, as well as the material discretion of these subjects (i.e., the postulate allowing for *contra legem* decisions). In light of the expectations of a rational and responsible lawmaker, these three conditions combined would enable the proper establishment of proportions regarding the consideration of legal and non-legal criteria, which facilitate the efficient functioning of legal norms.

However, these conditions do not operate by themselves. For a more thorough analysis, they need to be correlated with the goals that the lawmaker aims to accomplish by means of creating non-legal reference norms. Obviously, what must be ruled out from the very beginning (in the case of the rationality of the lawmaker) is the situation when the lawmaker would create the margin of decision in order to obscure the processes of law application as much as possible, or in order to bring about a state of virtual legal anarchy. However, what cannot be ruled out is the situation that, in principle, does not go along with the requirements of the rationality of law-making, where the lawmaker aims to accomplish, in detailed rather than basic regulations, goals that are not always in conformity with the official system of values declared and protected by law and expressed in the principles of the legal system.

Assuming that the lawmaker's basic formal goal is the establishment of a rational system of norms that would constitute the bases of ordinary addressees' behaviors and the bases of decision-making by state agencies, it may be claimed that the acceptance of the margin may in some circumstances actually bring the accomplishment of this goal nearer. From the point of view of the flexibility of law and its application, it will be, in many cases, more convenient to let the subjects applying law have the margin of decision, e.g., in the form of reference clauses, rather than to lay down regulations and, in fact, attempt to lay down strict content criteria for the decision of the application of the law. In such cases, the value of flexibility goes along with the value of the rationality of the legal system and functionally facilitates the achievement of the effectiveness of law. This is even more soothe case if the requirements concerning the maturity of legal practice are met and the lawmaker has indispensable confidence, stemming from the qualification of the merits as well as from the axiological uniformity, in this practice.

Thus, the condition precedent, residing within the sphere of the features of the legal practice, is the indispensable degree of the lawmaker's confidence in the executive machinery. What is primarily meant here is the efficiency of the machinery (skillful utilization of reference clauses), although the degree of political confidence in subjects applying law will also be of significance. The formulation of general reference clauses will be subject to the operation of the foregoing feature in particular. Such features as: the complex machinery of jurisdiction, broad legal course, genuine independence of decision-making, good organization of work, content-related preparation, the ability to work out hard-and-fast rules, establishment of the indispensable uniformity of legal practice and the dependability of application of law, reasonable use of the discretion granted, etc. are undoubtedly bound to be the factors that will facilitate, from the point of view of the lawmaker, warding off the dangers stemming not so much from the absence of the implementation of his "political line," but from potentially inefficient, i.e., incorrect, decision-making on the basis of constructions creating discretion.

In the case of strong uniformity of the political axiology of the lawmaker and the judicial practice, the degree of the lawmaker's confidence increases, which facilitates the promotion of the margin of decision at the level of lawmaking on an even larger scale. *A rebours*, the absence of such uniformity (i.e., softening the political appraisals incorporated into the legal order by the lawmaker by means of independent practice, i.e., by the agency of reference clauses) may not boost the lawmaker's will as to the acceptance of a broader margin of decision, even if organization-related and content-related conditions on the part of the practice cannot raise any doubts.

2.4. Discretion and uniformity of judicial practice

Once the legislator has extended the scale of discretion through special constructs such as the general clauses (rules of rightness, good customs, social interest, etc.), inexact evaluational legal expressions (important reasons, necessary conditions), or general notions (necessary self-defense),[7] or through the systemic structure of law, legal principles,[8] etc., the impact on the way the discretion is being exercised narrows. Other factors touching the legal culture, the social environment, the way the judiciary decides, etc. start to shape the real scale of the discretion in the decisional processes.

The judiciary does not have any interest in opposing legislature without specific reasons. The scope of discretion, however, may cause a kind of tension or pressure felt between these two branches of state authority. This also happens in statutory legal cultures, though the intensity here cannot be compared with that existing in the common law systems. It may, however, for example, in a situation of deep so-

[7] On the controversy between casuistic methods and the presence of general clauses, see Karl Engisch, *Einfuhrung in das juristische Denken*, Stuttgart: Kohlhammer, 1975, p. 119, 121.

[8] Mark Van Hoecke, *Law as Communication*, Oxford: Hart Publishing, 2002, p. 73 ff.

cial change, lead to a situation in which the judiciary, using its discretion, introduces more liberal and democratic values or solutions that can be implemented faster and easier than the legislation means.

Such a situation on one side shows the role of the judiciary as a kind of opposition to the legislation that, in general measures, weakens the legal certainty as seen from the point of the whole of the legal system, shaped in statutory legal cultures by normative acts (regulations). From the other point, however, such practice does not have to be dysfunctional for the legal order itself. It may sometimes work to establish temporary, more stable measures that are definitely more coherent for the social needs, expectations, and activities. In effect, it may lend order to another type of certainty, coming from the judicial practice.

There are some initial conditions to be achieved to make this practice really work for such a goal. The first and most important one deals with the uniformity of judicial practice. One may say that we are coming back to one of the contexts of the certainty of the implementation of law (see 1.2 above) contributing to the certainty of the law as a whole in the situation of judicial discretion.

Uniformity seems to be an initial condition for the perception of judicial practice as a regulatory measure, even if this practice is placed beside or in some opposition to the legislatures. Uniformity should cooperate with the feature of the visibility of this practice, making the knowledge of it quite easily attainable by the future addressees of judicial decisions.

Uniformity of judicial practice means the stable practice of deciding in the same way and with the same results in the same types of decisional processes and with the same types of legal problems as the subjects of these processes. It obviously does not mean the absolute identity of the content of decisions even if the facts of the case are very similar.[9]

There are various means to achieve a state of uniformity of judicial practice. One of them deals with the same methodology and the

[9] See J. Wróblewski, *Wartości a decyzja sądowa* [Values and Judicial Decision], op. cit., pp. 130–133.

same results of the interpretation of legislative regulations that would bring the legislation and judicial practice much closer to each other. Due to the natural sources of discretion and to the legislative constructs enlarging their scale (see 2.1 and 2.2 above), this situation cannot exhaust possible alternatives. Uniformity must be connected with the efforts of the judicial practice itself to bring the value of uniformity to the real point and to be ready to take responsibility for the legal order if the legislative work fails to achieve its goal of effective regulation of social affairs.

Therefore, other ways of reaching uniformity should be taken into consideration. Among the most important, one might point out the official interpretation coming from the higher judicial instances both through judicial control in the framing of appeal procedures and through the abstract interpretative decisions of constitutional and supreme courts (at the country and supranational level). The precedential practice should not only be noticed here but should also be treated as the most natural and autonomic, shaped independently by the judicial practice way of making the practice uniform.

It is obvious that the *stare decisis* rule does not exist in the statutory legal system in the same manner as in common law cultures. But it is also obvious that if this system's courts use other courts' decisions as a basis for their verdicts and the scale of this practice grows more and more, the courts may not always be ready to develop in their opinions (motives) all arguments dealing with the reason or way the other earlier decision has been implemented to the content of their decision. The courts may even feel quite free in choosing some decisions and omitting other ones, according to their concept of the content of decision. That is why the notions of "soft precedent" or "quasi-precedential practice" are raised in legal discussion. But, and that seems to be important, one may say that in the situation of the lack of *stare decisis* rule, the implementation of the other decisions shows care of the courts for uniformity more visibly. The other decisions are implemented not because of *stare decisis*, but because of the utility of these decisions and the intention to place one's own decision in the "line of jurisdiction." To the same extent, the legalistic approach has been replaced by the pragmatic one.

3. Judicial discretion and legal certainty

Uniformity of jurisdiction brings the feature of maturity to the judicial practice. The judiciary may contribute to the certainty of law (legal certainty) only if it is mature. Stability and uniformity help not only to predict the court's concrete solutions (which is important for the addressees of decisions) but also the attitude of the judiciary to the particular normative solutions adapted by the legislatures. These features bring the discourse between the legislature and the judiciary to a deeper and at the same time more effective level. They may shape the discourse as a communicative one, which in contemporary multicentral law seems to be necessary from the practical side.

Judicial discretion's having these characteristics in effect strengthens the legal certainty as a whole, even if at the same time it weakens this aspect of the certainty, that is connected exclusively with legislative regulation. It brings legal certainty, through the exchange of measures with legislation, into the deeper structure of law, placing it closer to actual social needs and expectations.

Among the general consequences of taking judicial practice into consideration while speaking about the legal certainty one may mention, among others, are several of the most important ones:

1. The juridization of legal certainty, meaning the shift from the political discourse playing a decisive role in the legislation and the content of its results (legal regulations) to the juridical argumentation, as the core of judicial decisions in the democratic and rule-of-law state.

2. The dynamization of legal certainty, meaning the shift from the stability of the rule of law to the adaptive theory of implementation of law, using dynamic interpretation of the letter of the law and bringing the content of the law to the actual state of social affairs.

3. The functionalization of legal certainty, meaning the shift from a positivistic attitude to the functional and value-oriented approach, thus being able to place the essence of law much closer to the actual social axiology.

4. The substantialization of legal certainty, meaning the shift from the formal to the substantial concept of the idea of rule-of-law, allow-

ing for the connection of the content of law with the legal and social axiology undefined in legislative regulations.

5. The "polycentrization" of the content of legal certainty, meaning the shift from the monocratic and instrumental thinking connected exclusively with the legislation and its output to the deliberative, communicative, and polycentric legal order and its certainty.

One may ask whether the above-mentioned effects do not switch the legal certainty from the certainty of law which may be guaranteed to the same extent at the legislation level to the certainty of rights that are connected with the effectiveness of the claims brought in front of courts. Even if the assumption is a little too direct and may go too far, it says something about the legal order in action.

Another question, attached to the problem noticed above, might deal with the meanings of the English and French terms dealing with certainty. The English term "legal certainty" might be connected more with the legislative way of thinking and the certainty of law, while the French term "*securite juridique*" might put the accent on the certainty of rights in the sense of the effective legal protection of legal entities, which is exercised finally through the judicial practice.

It would make the proof that if we deliver the discussion on legal certainty in the statutory legal system as well, we should take into account judicial practice as an important actor contributing in the process of achieving it. This practice, in the situation of inevitable discretion in deciding, if it fulfills the necessary measure of uniformity and maturity, enlarges the perspective of legal certainty, making it more juridical, dynamic, functional, substantial, multicentral, and rights-oriented.

Lin Yuchuan
Sun Yat-sen University, China

Confucianism and the Localization of Chinese Political Democracy

Abstract: Confucianism encountered a severe crisis of cultural identity in modern China. Most Chinese believed that Confucianism needed to be creatively transformed in order to be compatible with modern democracy. There were several movements to push forward such transformations. In analyzing these movements, we arrive at the following conclusions: first, Confucianism's relationship with modern democracy was like that of a double-edged sword, and such a feature continued throughout the process of Confucianism's transformation; second, Confucianism alone cannot provide the solid ground for a modern democratic system; third, the role that Confucianism will play in China's future political system should be judged with regard to the local context of Chinese political democracy.

Keywords: Confucianism, Liberal Democracy, Institutionalization of Confucianism

In modern China, Confucianism encountered a severe crisis of cultural identity, which was caused by its clash with modern democracy. Most Chinese argued that Confucianism needed to undergo a creative transformation in order to be compatible with modern democracy. This article (1) examines the movements that attempted to achieve such a transformation; (2) evaluates the success of the transformation; and (3) reappraises the role of Confucianism in China's future political system in the context of how Chinese political democracy will be locally implemented.

The Crisis of Confucianism in Modern China

In the late 19th century and the beginning of the 20th century, many Chinese experienced a great crisis in Confucianism. Liang Shuming, a prominent cultural conservative, and Chen Duxiu, the founder of the Chinese Communist Party, both reflected deeply on the conflicts between Confucianism and modern democracy at the beginning of the 20th Century.

Liang believed that the conflicts between Confucianism and modern Western democracy could be traced back to the cultural differences between China and Western societies. First, in his view, Westerners actively pursued something external: they were always asking for their personal rights. In contrast, the Chinese were mellow, self-restrained, cooperative and peaceful. Second, Western politicians were good at political competition and selling themselves, while the Chinese were more courteous and self-effacing, and lacked the ethos of competition. Third, in Western countries, political institutions were based on the presumption of an evil human nature. Thus in Western democratic countries the balance among different powers is expected in terms of legal constraints put on the political power and a constant supervision of political institutions, while the ethos of Confucianism was based on the presumption of a good human nature, and stressed trust and cooperation among people. Fourth, in Liang reflections, the conception of Western democratic politics was built on the idea of "desire." This means that both legal law and politics were concerned by the satisfaction of individual desires. In contrast the history of China was full of debates about the contradictions between "Yi" (merit) and "Li" (interest), between "Li" (righteousness) and "Yu" (desire). The traditional Chinese usually didn't take personal interest (such as position and reputation) and material desire (such as the love of money and commodities, etc.) as the goal of their lives.[1]

Taking into account such analysis, Liang Shuming argued:

> I don't believe that it's a temporal phenomenon that the Chinese cannot make use of Western political systems. I am afraid that Chinese and modern political systems are two different things that can never link with each other.[2]

---

[1] He Xinquan, *Confucianism and Modern Democracy*, Beijing: China Social Science Press, 2001, pp. 17–18.

[2] Ibidem, p. 26.

Chen Duxiu pointed out that the conception of "minben" (taking people as the basis) and "renzheng" (humane governance) were essentially different from the leading ideas of modern Western democracy.

> According to Western democracy, people are taken as the subject. That is the meaning expressed by Lincoln when he described rule "by the people" instead of "for the people." In Chinese traditional culture, such statements as "heaven hears what we people hear, and sees what we see," "people are more important than the king," and "people are the root of the state," actually take the king as the root of the state.[3]

Chen believed that the Chinese needed to abandon the Confucian tradition completely if they were interested in introducing democratic solutions in the Western style.

> If we want to build up a new Western-style country, to organize a new Western-style society, and to live a suitable modern life, the fundamental problem is for us to introduce the basic principles of Western society into China, that is, the new belief of equality and human rights. And as for Confucianism, which is incompatible with the new society, new country, new beliefs, we need to have a thoroughly understanding of its defects and a strong will to break with it. We have to abandon something; otherwise we cannot get anything.[4]

After the May Fourth Movement, that lead to the rejection of traditional Confucian culture and the possibility of combining Confucian tradition and modern democracy either, Confucianism retreated from the sphere of political institutions, and stepped back into the sphere of individual life. As Yu Yingshi put it, Confucianism became a "ghost," and got started to function as a kind of philosophy of mind. However, Chinese Confucians never gave up their efforts to revive Confucianism. Representatives of New Confucian, such as Xiong Shili, Mou Zongsan, Tan Junyi, Xu Fuguan and Zhang Junmai, re-examined the Confucianism traditions from different approaches, and discussed the possibility of combining Confucianism and modern Western democracy.

---

[3] *Selected Edition of Chen Duxiu's Works*, vol. 1, Shanghai: Sanlian bookstore, 1984, p. 98.

[4] *New Youth*, vol. 2, no. 3, p. 4.

Examining the Modern Transformation of Confucianism

In 1958, the *Manifesto to the World on Behalf of Chinese Culture* was published in Hong Kong and Taiwan by Tang Junyi, Mou Zongsan, Xu Fuguan, and Zhang Junmai. The Manifesto argued about the possibility and necessity of combining Confucianism and Western democracy. First, it was hold that Confucianism didn't lack certain seeds of democracy. On the contrary, it was raised that Confucianism required the king not to abuse his power and to rule with virtue. Authors of the Manifesto emphasized that it was Confucianism that encouraged crown abdication, and "the revolutions of Tangwu" (the violent revolutions of "Cheng Tang" and "Emperor Zhouwu" against tyrannies) with the claim that the kingdom didn't belong to a person, but belonged to the people within the kingdom. The Confucianism formulated also ideas of "public ethos" and "equality of personality," etc., which seemed to be compatible with the spirit of modern democracy. As to the institutional aspects, the censorial system,[5] the official historian system, and electoral system played a crucial role in restraining the power of the king and the government. Second, the authors believed that modern democracy was actually the inner requirement of the development of Chinese culture:

> The capacity for self-determination by the moral agent requires the possibility of his/her political participation. Here we see a fundamental contradiction between the moral spirit in Chinese culture and the emperor system. The contradiction can only be resolved by a constitutional democracy that affirms that all are equal political agents (*zhuti*). Thus constitutional democracy is required for the internal development of the moral spirit in Chinese culture.[6]

---

[5] The censorial system is part of the government which is responsible for accusation of bribery or other illegal behaviors of government officers. It also has the duty to exhort the king to abide by laws which were set up by his ancestors or himself. In ancient China, there were many cases that officers of the censorial system who strictly accused the king of his wrong doings were killed by the king, but then they were usually praised for their heroic deeds by the people and the king's successors. In this sense, the censorial system isn't effective on restraining the power of the king, but it does function as an institutional tool to restrict the king from doing whatever he wants.

[6] *Manifesto to the World on Behalf of Chinese Culture.*

New Confucianism's standpoint concerning the compatibility of Confucianism and modern democracy has endured an influence of the late Confucians. Under such an influence, the second wave of modern transformation of Confucianism took place in the 1980s and 1990s. In the era of the economic prosperity of South Korea, Singapore, Hong Kong, and Taiwan, scholars around the world were attracted to the discussion about Asia values (i.e. Confucian values). They challenged Max Weber's view about the incompatibility of Confucian tradition and modernity and finally abandoned his view. According to those scholars who advocated the revival of Confucianism, the prosperity of East Asia demonstrated the positive role of Confucianism. Lee Kuan Yew once remarked,

> We were lucky to have this cultural backdrop, the belief in thrift, hard work, filial piety, and loyalty in the extended family … the respect for scholarship and learning.[7]

Even at the level of firm management, the success of some East Asian economies was also alleged to depend upon the Confucian values of harmony, loyalty, and deference between workers and employers.[8] Based on the same logic, Confucianism was taken to be an important resource for the construction of Chinese political democracy.

In this wave of discussion, the Confucianism ideas, such as the ruler's benevolence toward subjects, the stress on fostering personal virtue, the ruler's acceptance of critiques, and the right to revolt against the tyranny, was taken as main themes of its compatibility with modern democracy. In addition, there were further discussions about elements that could help figure out a better political system compared to Western liberal democracy. However, it seems that the value and impact of these elements to modern democracy is not yet clear.

Now let us take a quick look at these elements.

---

[7] F. Zakaria, "Culture Is Destiny—A Conversation with Lee Kuan Yew", *Foreign Affairs* 1994 (March/April), vol. 73, no. 2, p. 114.

[8] Shaun O'Dwyer, "Democracy and Confucian Values", *Philosophy East & West* 2003, January, vol. 53, no. 1, p. 45.

(1) The idea of "Datong" (Grand Union)

According to Samuel P. Huntington, the word "democracy" has two different connotations in the context of Western countries: on the one hand it refers to the rationalist, utopian, and idealistic idea of democracy, and on the other hand it refers to the empirical, descriptive, institutional, and procedural comprehension of democracy.[9] In my understanding, the former formulation of the idea of democracy refers to no less important idea of the autonomy of the people which indicates, in fact, real aspirations and a normative content of the idea of democracy in general. Therefore, the latter formulation refers to the way the democratic normative framework operates in practice, or to the systematization of democratic ideas about institutional settings. Naturally, these two dimensions of the concept of democracy are both indispensable in modern democratic politics. Without the normative guidance of the democratic idea none would be capable to answer whether any actual political system still functions in line with the idea of democracy ("the rule by the people"). And at the same time the idea of democracy cannot be implemented in the real political world without operative and applicable democratic settings according to a specific political and cultural context. The idea of "Datong" in Confucianism provides us with such an ideal democratic situation. In *Liji*, we can read the description of the idea of "Datong" where: "A public spirit will rule all under the sky when the great Way prevails. The sages and talented are elected, and sincerity and harmonious prevails." From this statement emerges an ideal social situation in which everyone receives the right position and the self-determination of each is clearly revealed. This picture of a social condition is quite alike to what Jean-Jacques Rousseau and Karl Marx described in their ideal societies. In that type of social state the conflicts between public good and individual private interests become weaker and weaker. People subjected to the common will are no different from being subjected to their own will.

Unfortunately, the "Datong" idea does not provide us with a feasible political system; on the contrary, Confucians always present us

[9] Samuel P. Huntington, *The Third Wave : Democratization in the late Twentieth century*, London: University of Oklahoma Press, 1991, p. 5.

with an elitist political system in reality: this is the limitation that we must keep in mind in our effort to reveal the value of the "Datong" idea to modern democracy.

(2) "The Rule by Virtue" or "The Humane Governance"

As is known to all, Confucius calls for the "rule by virtue" in *The Analects*. Mencius developed Confucius' theory into the concept of "humane governance." According to Mencius, "humane governance" has two complementary meanings. On the one hand, he proposed "the politics of Wangdao," which required the ruler to rule by virtue, to be benevolent to the people, and to abide by the regulation of "the people are most important, the state is less important, and the king is the least important." On the other hand, due to the limitation of people's education in his time period, Mencius also talked about the social division of labour between "intelligentsia" and "laborers," and argued that the duty of the former is to rule, while that of the latter is to "be ruled." The first aspect is usually understood as a tendency of "Minben" (taking people as the root), while the second aspect is taken as a tendency toward elitism in Confucianism. The contradiction between these two meanings is overcome with Mencius' thesis of a good human nature. Owing to the presupposition that man has innately "four beginnings," that is, "a sense of pity," "a sense of good or evil," "a sense of respectful," and "a sense of right or wrong," he can be such a sage as Yao or Shun by fostering his four beginnings. In society everyone is guided and regulated by Confucian ethics, and conflict between the ruler and the ruled will decrease gradually because the former will be kind to the latter, and the latter will respect the former.

In the view of some Confucians, the thought of the "rule by virtue" of Confucianism is compatible with Montesquieu and Rousseau's thought that "virtue is the principle for the Republic." The "rule by virtue" of Confucianism is taken as a resource to overcome the disadvantages of liberal democracy's overestimation of the importance of people's will. In a democratic system revised with the "rule by virtue," a balance between universal suffrage and the idea of "rule by the sages" can be built. However, taking for granted the dominance of the pluralism of personal interests and conceptions of values, the Confucian ethics as well as the harmony between the 'ruler' and the 'ruled' are gravely challenged in modern society. The elitism brought about by the thought of the 'rule by virtue' in Confucianism finally loses its rational power to reconcile the said diversity in terms of ethical fostering the four 'beginnings' as they appear to be implausible in face of basic descriptive notions of the modern society.

(3) The communitarian propensity

Some Confucians argued that communitarian aspects of Confucianism could provide a social capital for the modern society, which certainly plays a vital role in the modern concept of democracy. In their analysis of the economic development of East Asian countries, Confucians stressed that the conception of "humaneness, righteousness, propriety, wisdom and trust" in Confucianism benefited the harmonious relationship between modern enterprises and its members. Thus, it is believed that from the family and clan concepts of Confucianism, we would develop a certain Confucian idea of social capital, which could be used further to rectify the defects of individualism in modern liberal democracy.

Undoubtedly, social capital is very important to democratic countries. Robert A. Dahl once clearly stated:

> Independent social organizations are dearly needed in a democratic system, at least as some large scale democratic system. The emergence of such organizations is not only a direct result of the democratization of the sovereign of nation-state, but what is needed in the procedure of democratization, and its function is to minimize coercion of government, protect political liberty and improve the quality of people's life.[10]

We find that Tocqueville held such opinions as well when he used the phrase, "art of association," to describe Americans' propensity for civil association. However, the communities of family and clan do not actually work primarily for the public good. Just as Francis Fukuyama has pointed out,

---

10 Robert A. Dahl, *Dilemmas of Pluralist Democracy: Autonomy vs. Control*, New Haven: Yale University Press, 1982, p. 1.

> In the Chinese parts of East Asia and much of Latin America, social capital resides largely in families and a rather narrow circle of personal friends. It is difficult for people to trust those outside of these narrow circles. Strangers fall into a different category than kin. A lower standard of moral behavior applies when one becomes, for example, a public official. This provides cultural reinforcement for corruption: in such societies, one feels entitled to steal on behalf of one's family.[11]

It is true that we can discover the seeds of modern democracy in Confucianism by creative reinterpretation, and we can also reveal the conditions for democracy created in East Asian society, but no matter how vigorous these seeds may be and how important these conditions may be, they cannot substitute basic premises and fundamental features of the modern democracy itself that clearly points at more abstract form of social integration obtained in terms of political participation basically. If a society is related to a particular political power blind to any form of political competition and therefore the members of the society are deprived of their rights to participate in consultation and policy-making in public affairs, then such a society does not meet the paramount requirements of modern democracy. As to its relationship with modern democracy, Confucianism is like a two-edged sword that has both positive and negative aspects. We cannot discard democracy itself in order to give prominence to the characteristics of Confucianism, but must probe the possibilities of constructing a kind of Confucian democracy on the basis of modern democracy that would fit both the Chinese self-understanding and current demands that are put forward by the idea of the modern strongly participatory self-government.

The Institutionalization of Confucianism and its Problems

In recent years, with the rise of cultural confidence brought about by China's economic miracle, a new wave of Confucianism renais-

[11] Francis Fukuyama, "Social Capital and Civil Society," *IMF Working Paper* 2000, April, p. 5.

sance has occurred accordingly. This time people are paying more attention to the idea of institutionalization of Confucianism. The advocates of this proposal are dissatisfied with new Confucianism's approval of modern western democracy. They have criticized advocates of the latter for "they tried to prove the compatibility of Confucianism with Western democratic ideas,"[12] and that "they embraced Western-style science and democracy too quickly, and lacked critical and constructive reflection on such a framework (Western-style science and democracy). The result was that Confucianism could not have an independent contribution to the construction of a fundamental political system."[13] They argued that the legitimacy of a Chinese constitution should be based on Confucianism. Due to their different understandings of the degree and manner of the function of Confucianism in China's constitution system, they proposed different approaches to the institutionalization of Confucianism.

Among these approaches, Jiang Qing takes the most advantage of the resources of Confucianism and attracts the most attention.[14] Jiang Qing believes that, the direction of Chinese political development is toward "Politics of Wangdao," rather than a Western-style liberal democratic system. In his explanation, the purpose of "Politics of Wangdao" is to solve the problem of "Zhengdao" (legitimacy of political power) instead of "Zhidao" (the concrete arrangement of political system). The core connotation of "Politics of Wangdao" is the concept of the "triple legitimacy" of political power. "Political power needs to have triple legitimacy (the legitimacy of 'Tian,' 'Di,' and 'Ren') to attain the power of rule. The legitimacy of 'Tian' (heaven) represents the legitimacy of the transcendental or the divine; the legitimacy of 'Di' (mother earth) represents the legitimacy of historical culture; and the legitimacy of 'Ren' (human beings) represents the legitimacy of

---

[12] Gan Chunsong, *Institutionization Confucianism*, Shanghai: Shanghai People's Publishing House, 2006, p. 10.

[13] Bai Tongdong, "Ideal Confucianism or Political Confucianism? New State old Mission or Old State New Mission?: Considerations about Confucianism Renaissance," *Open Times* 2010.11.

[14] Jiang Qing actually uses phrases such as "political Confucianism" to express his idea about a Confucian Constitutional system. But he is viewed as an advocate for the institutionalization of Confucianism as well.

the people's will."[15] As one may see, the concept of the "triple legitimacy" refers to its certain divine (ethical) source, to the specific and in some ways unique historical culture and eventually to the will of the people.

Jiang argues that because the legitimacy of political power in Western liberal democracy is one-dimensional, because it is founded only on the idea of the "people's sovereignty", hence the political power is downplayed to serve as a tool for the private desires of ordinary people. At the same time, as the moral aspect is missing in the legitimacy of political power, a modern democratic system cannot do anything to protect our environment. Besides, this one-dimensional understanding of the modern democracy would also break one day the link between Chinese politics and Chinese historical culture, and thus cause a crisis in the "legitimacy of historical culture" in terms of the Chinese specific identity (self-understanding).

For Jiang, "Politics of Wangdao" has the following advantages compared to Western democratic politics. First, as "Politics of Wangdao" contains "the legitimacy of divinity or transcendentalism," it helps to overcome the defects of Western democracy, such as the expansion of human desire and extreme secularity, and to solve the environmental problems from the height of "Zhengdao." Second, as "Politics of Wangdao" contains "the legitimacy of historical culture," it provides traditional legitimacy in supporting the political development of non-Western countries, especially that of China, and helps to improve the legitimacy, solidarity, and durability of political authority.

As to the design of political institutions, Jiang has a detailed presupposition:

> In "Politics of Wangdao," the constitutional system takes the form of a parliament. The administration system is generated by parliament and responsible for the latter. The parliament has three houses and each house represents one type of legitimacy. These three houses are "Tongru," "Sumin," and "Guoti." The "Tongru" house represents the legitimacy of transcendentalism or divinity; the "Sumin" house represents the legiti-

[15] Jiang Qing, *On Political Confucianism Again*, Shanghai: East China Normal University Press, 2011, pp. 9–10.

> macy of people's will; and the "Guoti" house represents the legitimacy of historical culture. Members of the "Tongru" house are generated by recommendation and accreditation, members of the "Sumin" house by universal suffrage or community election, and those of the "Guoti" house by heredity or appointment.[16]

According to Jiang's design, the head of the "Tongru" house should be a famous Confucian who was recommended, and its members were usually sages or the gifted. The head of the "Guoti" house should be the offspring of Confucius, and its members should be the descendants of either the sages, kings, famous historical and cultural figures, national martyrs of different dynasties, or university professors of national history, retired former administration and diplomatic higher officials, social sages, or famous figures from Buddhism, Daoism, Islamism, Lamaism, and Christianity. The highest administration and judicial officials have to be approved by all these three houses, and bills have to be approved by two or three houses. In addition, the "Tongru" house had a veto right over bills.

Jiang Qing's theory of the "Politics of Wangdao" and its institutional designs were severely criticized. Scholars criticized Jiang for degradation of the significance of the legitimacy of people's will, his elitist proposals, and for providing Confucius' offspring with special political positions. Among these opponents, there were other advocators for the institutionalization of Confucianism too. Bai Tongdong revealed the fatal drawback of Jiang's approach:

> Both his consideration about western political problems and the Confucian constitution framework he proposed are short of careful and profound reflection. He never demonstrates the rationality and justification thoroughly, but only resorts to the dogma and its divinity of Confucianism he identifies with, and his simple understandings about Western social problems.[17]

Now we can turn to Bai Tongdong's approach. Bai does not provide a set of detailed analysis and proposals for Confucian Constitu-

---

[16] Jiang Qing, *On Political Confucianism Again*, op. cit., p. 23.

[17] Bai Tongdong, "Ideal Confucianism or Political Confucianism?", op. cit.

tions.[18] What he focuses on is the value of Confucianism as a conservative traditional resource to examine and revise the defects of Western liberal democracy. He makes some basic statements, such as human beings have moral claims beyond material desires and private interests, and he claims that the rule by elites is needed in political affairs because people have different moral and intelligent endowments. As one may see, Bai argues for a Confucian limited democracy. First, Confucianism accepts most institutions of Western democracy (such as responsible government, negative freedoms, and the rule of law), and asks for the government to provide adequate conditions (such as civil education, consultation, and arrangement for discussion) for citizens' political participation. Second, the Confucian democracy does not take the model of "one-person-one-vote" as its end. Bai believes that, as most social members under the modern social division of labour are "ignorant of knowledge" and lack political wisdom and special talent, it is unrealistic for them to fully participate in politics. On the one hand, he proposes the elitist system of Confucianism, and on the other hand he stresses that the elitist system should be open to all and constrained by the rule of law. In order to make his argument more clearly understood, Bai even borrows Rawls' difference principle to describe his own idea: "political or electoral inequality is acceptable, if it is good for the lowest people."[19]

Even though Bai accepts some basic values of the liberal democratic system, such as limited rights of freedom of speech, the spirit of tolerance, fair and free discussion among citizens, the principle of the

---

[18] Bai actually talked about the design of Confucian parliament briefly. He expressed his agreement with Daniel Bell's proposal of "a bicameral legislature, with a democratically elected lower house and an upper house composed of representatives selected on the basis of competitive examinations," which he describes as a "House of Scholars." According to Daniel Bell, the upper house ("House of Scholars"), composed of persons possessed of general intellectual and ethical insight, would probably be subordinate to the elected lower house, and act as a house of review and policy debate in a similar manner to that of the British House of Lords. See, Bai Tongdong, *New Mission of an Old State: Classical Confucian Political Philosophy in a Contemporary and Comparative Relevance Context,* Beijing: Peking University Press, 2009, pp. 60–61. Daniel A. Bell, "Democracy with Chinese Characteristics: A Political Proposal for the Post Communist Era," *Philosophy East and West* 1999 (October), vol. 49, no. 4, pp. 451–493.

[19] Bai Tongdong, *New Mission of an Old State,* op. cit., p. 74.

rule of law, the democratic procedure for election and supervising leaders, etc., at the same time it is not enough for Bai to take liberal democracy merely as a political instrument: he is too pessimistic about popular participation in political affairs. On the other hand, he is quite optimistic as he believes in processes of recommendation, elections within small groups, and that competitive examinations can generate a ruling elite free of misguidance compared to that of ordinary people.[20]

By analyzing the representative institutionalization approaches, we can sketch the main problems generated by efforts oriented at a construction of a modern Chinese constitution that would be rooted in Confucian ethics. That is, the advocators of institutionalization are suspicious of people's ability and interest in participating in political affairs, and thus hold a profound elitist perspective. Just as one scholar puts it,

> We already have the tradition of republican revolution and people's democracy of the 20th Century, and now that we further encounter global competition among a pluralist civilization, the most important thing we need to pay attention to is the context of political culture, within which it is difficult for political states to develop. According to this context, the Rawls approach, which takes freedom and equality, pluralism and justice, as the fundamental political values, should be the dominant approach rather than a 'thin' basis. Thus setting up electoral democracy as the basis of political aims, and patiently fostering the public rationality of modern society, should be a reasonable and acceptable approach.[21]

The Localization of China's Political Democracy

There is a consensus that China needs to undergo processes of democratization. There are two reasons linked to such a conviction: one is that more and more people accept the concept of democracy

---

[20] Ren Feng, "When Rawls meets Confucius: Review on Bai Tongdong's Old State New Mission: Political Philosophy of Classical Confucianism in the Context of Ancient and Today, Chinese and Western", *Open Times* 2010.11.

[21] Ibidem.

based on the principle of popular sovereignty under the market economy; the other is that people realize that a democratic constitution will provide an effective tool kit in order to visibly and efficiently decrease an acute political corruption phenomenon. Not only ordinary Chinese highly esteem the value of democratically functioning political institutions, but also political leaders emphasize the importance and significance of carrying on further democratic changes to institutional settings on diverse levels and in a wide range of an exercise of the political authority. Deng Xiaoping, the former General Secretary of the CCP Central Committee, talked many times about the significance of democracy in China's political development, and he was the first leader in the CCP who declared his own retirement when he became old. In the 17th National People's Congress of the CCP, the idea of democracy became a hot topic. Hu Jintao, the incumbent General Secretary of the CCP Central Committee, used the word "democracy" more than 60 times in his report. However, both Chinese political leaders and most people agreed that China was going to take a different democratization trajectory from that of Western countries. China's political system should not take a form of a simple resemblance to the Western-style democratic governance. Thus, these above investigated, different approaches to processes of institutionalization of Confucianism were triggered by the discussions dedicated to the complex problem of application democratic ideas and principles into the specific Chinese political context. And there is no doubt that our political self-understanding that refers on the one hand to general - or world-wide - democratic principles and on the other hand that takes into account our specific, even peculiar cultural and historical embedding should be taken as a precondition for assessing the feasibility of institutionalizing Confucianism.

I will discuss briefly my position on this political self-understanding referred to the problem of China's political democracy and the future of institutionalization of Confucianism below. First of all, a thesis on a peculiar trajectory of processes of democratization political institutions in Chine does not imply a conviction that is necessary neither needed to introduce such a set of institutions that are totally different from that already functioning in the West. Discussions over the issue of the best form of the democratic government for the Chinese polity cannot aim solely at any exaggeration of differences in comparison with other polities, because the main goal here is to peacefully come to an agreement acceptable to as huge amount of Chinese people as it is possible. Therefore, the constant emphasizing differences between China and the West is simply out of scope. The focal point should be these debates that may introduce such solutions concerning processes of political democratization in China that take into account that there are differences concerning political systems even within Western countries. Actually, due to different processes of democratization throughout history, Western countries such as the United States, Great Britain, France, Scandinavian countries, Poland, etc., have different democratic systems, in which the power of the government and the rights of the people are regulated differently. In short, the political systems of Western countries are the result of competition by different political powers in history, rather than the simple result of institutional designs in advance. From the experience of Western countries, we have learned that our political systems cannot rely too much - or just exclusively - on theoretical models; on the contrary, we must pay more attention to the reality of competing political powers and we should search for institutional designs tailored specifically for them. I am not here to deny the significance of theoretical concepts or models, but just to reveal their limitations.

Frankly speaking, theoretical designs can sometimes provide us with an ideal or desirable political system. However, there are still gaps between the ideal of democracy and its actual functioning. The first gap results from the real respond whether or not this ideal model appears to be acceptable to those people it is addressed to. The second gap is dug by human expectations because democracy is not the only thing we expect from a government. Robert D. Putnam once argued that, we should not only care about whether a government is democratic, but also about how a democratic government works in reality. That is, what are the results of its performance? From this perspective, by making attempts to form a peculiar trajectory of processes of Chinese political democratization, we cannot get satisfied solely with setting up a theoretically feasible democratic system, but rather we should explore a democratic system that benefits also its people in practice. Moreover, our critical attitude toward Western liberal democracy does not mean that we are confident that we can find a better democratic system of a Chinese style. The right thing to do is to absorb the successful experience of Western liberal democracy and to modify it the way it could work under Chinese circumstances taking into account their specific practices. A reasonable and stable democratic system must therefore benefit its people and foremost be supported by its people as this very thought forms the crux of a real democratic thinking. It should be the result of practical wisdom instead of an institutional engineering.

Second, as to today's China, the requirements of democratization are raised by the society itself. However, we still need to make it clear what this democratization means and to what kind of institutional as well as social changes it would aspire. What kind of democratization are the Chinese people actually looking for? In order to respond these demands, we need to know more about the political culture that influences the political thinking of modern Chinese people. According to the political culture of modern China, we cannot overestimate the importance of Confucianism because there are also traditions of Marxism and liberalism that have greatly influenced Chinese people's political convictions and beliefs. Even if we agree that the Confucian thought of a good human nature, the rule by virtue, and harmony play a prominent role in shaping Chinese people's political thinking, we must admit that liberalism is another important tradition in China and that it dominates ordinary people's thinking and expectations nowadays. Especially after China's Open and Reform Policy since 1978, due to the influence of economic competition brought about by the market economy, there are requirements for more political openness accordingly. The liberal ideas of freedom, democracy, and human rights have deeply influenced the Chinese people's political thinking. And the necessity for deeper and wider democratization of China's politics has become a part of ordinary people's consensus. Marxism, on the contrary, is a philosophical and political thought known for its critique of liberal premises. It has a very radical claim for social equality and democracy. Compared to liberalism, which advocates democratic political institutional settings, Marxism tries to overcome the conservative features of liberalism and asks for the equality within the social sphere, emancipation of the masses and taking them as fundaments to interpret the sovereignty of the people. And in Mao Zedong's era, Chinese people have already built up a strong consciousness of equality.

As analyzed above, Chinese people's thinking about the democratization of politics has been influenced by these three kinds of thought. Among them, liberalism seems to have the most fruitful ideas concerning democracy, and its pivotal role on the current Chinese political stage is sustained by strong claims for democratization of political institutions. At the same time influences from the part of Marxism and Confucianism are guaranteed as they provide the resources to rectify the defects of liberal democracy. In my view, according to the reality of today's Chinese economic and social development, the theory of liberal democracy seems to have a sufficient support to take a dominant position, while Marxism and Confucianism appear to form yet a complement to these dominant liberal ideas.

Third, based on the analysis of the role of Confucianism in modern Chinese society, efforts to construct a Confucian Constitution through the institutionalization of Confucianism need to be postponed. The recent revelation of shortcomings of individualism and of pluralistic values brought about by liberalism, together with the rise in the self-identifying with native Chinese culture due to China's economic miracle, all of that strengthens the role of Confucianism that becomes increasingly important. However, compared to deeply rooted in the market economy liberalism, Confucianism is relegated to second place, namely to a private sector. In this context, it is still crucial that we work to revive Confucianism in Chinese people's personal lives. Such efforts in enlightening children to Confucianism and teaching Confucianism to college students will be critical for this purpose. As to me, the most important presupposition for the institutionalization of Confucianism is to make values and theories of Confucianism be spontaneously and autonomously accepted by ordinary people. Only after the masses understand and accept the modern value of Confucianism can it be institutionalized easily and legally. As Joseph Chan (Chen Zuwei) put it,

> The institutionalization of Confucianism should be understood as the following: some feasible and desirable Confucian values and principles, af-

> ter having been openly and rationally discussed, are accepted by the masses, and then were raised to be the foundation of laws, institutions, and policies in this country.[22]

We thus need to abandon the illusion that China will set up a totally different political system modeled on the West, but instead follow the approach of 'piecemeal social engineering,' and take Confucianism as the resource to supplement and rectify the theory of liberal democracy.

In reality, China is gradually pushing forward political democratization. Even though China does not resemble a Western-style system of multi-parties and the separation of legislative, judicial, and executive powers, it still maintains its own framework of a political system, uttered in terms of the multi-party cooperation system and the balance of powers among the National People's Congress (NPC), the Chinese People's Political Consultative Conference (CPPCC), and the government. During processes of democratization core values of Western liberal politics (i.e. competition mechanism) were introduced into China's politics. In order to avoid a monopolization of the political power by very few elites, the CCP has figured out some feasible strategies in recent years. First, political power turned open to more economic, social, and cultural elites. The owners of private enterprises are allowed to be members of the CCP. Leaders of business spheres and famous cultural celebrities are encouraged to join the NPC and CPPCC. Second, competitive elections are implemented into the election of higher leaders in the CCP. In recent years, the election of the central committee and the central politburo has begun to introduce competitive elections. Third, China organizes large scale entrance examinations for civil servants every year. Excellent students who have graduated from universities are selected to be civil servants through an open, fair, and just procedure. Many young people from lower social statuses enter the political sphere in this way. Fourth, China requires political leaders to retired when they reach a certain age, even though they are at the highest level of government.

---

22 Fan Ruiping, *Confucian Society and the Renaissance of Dao Lineage: Dialogue with Jiang Qing*, East China Normal University Press, 2008, p. 38.

In conclusion, the localization of China's democratic politics is on its way, and this direction cannot be reversed as history will make evident. However, its speed and quality will be greatly influenced by the balance of powers between the masses who are implementing the process of democratization, as well as the conservative groups who have a vested interest in maintaining the former political order. It is an important issue to explore a more desirable, stable, and effective Chinese model of political democracy by taking advantages of the resources of Confucianism on the one hand, but on the other hand, to also avoid using Confucianism to protect the interests of the conservatives, as well as to put an end to the countercurrent of anti-democracy.

Agnieszka Choduń
Szczecin University, Poland

Influence of Internationalisms on Communicativeness of a Legal Discourse

Abstract: Modern lexical cognates occuring in the Polish legal discourse are in a lot of cases internationalisms. There may be two categories of internationalisms differentiated in the Polish legal discourse. The first relates to those international words, which have been introduced to the Polish legal discourse for practical reasons. The other category of internationalisms are those, which apart from the function mentioned above, play also the role of carrying certain values. This type of internationalisms is of special character as it triggers mental changes in society.
Internationalisms in the legal discourse lead to the similarities in the linguistic depictions of the legal world also the world of values protected by law. An example of such integration is introduction of the legal term 'mobbing' into the Polish legal discourse.

Keywords: lexis in texts of legal acts, internationalisms, legal discourse, mobbing

Introduction

Continual compenetration of languages, cultures and ideas is determined by human relationships. Nowadays these processes have streamlined, undoubtedly due to technological progress and dynamics of particular political processes, which take on particular institutional forms. Processes of the free flow of foods, persons, services, and capital within the European Union are accompanied also by convergence of the legal systems. It is reflected both in the institutional solutions and in the languages these solutions are formulated, that is in the language of the law and in the legal language.

Both the language of the law, understood as a language of the legal acts texts, as well, as the legal language that is a language about the law, are characterized by huge lexical diversity. Both registers include terms belonging to various fields of science or knowledge as well as general lexis.

This terminological diversity, concerns strictly legal or law terms, as well, as terms, belonging to other fields of science or knowledge.

Research, that I have carried out on Polish texts of legal acts[1] shows, that this is, among others, terminology of the following fields: economy, banking, trade, geography, geology, geodesy, farming, zootechnics, biology, anatomy, physics, chemistry, psychology, marine, sailing, hunting, building industry, airborne or military.

Influence of foreign languages, mainly as far as lexical cognates are concerned, may be observed in the strictly law terminology and terminology referring to other fields of science or knowledge.

This phenomenon is related to the existence of the so called cultural and linguistic asymmetry,[2] which is domination of certain languages and cultures over other languages and cultures with simultaneous creation of a certain cultural community. Historically in our cultural zone such a European cultural community started forming a long time ago, taking more or less institutionalized form. Changes in lexis of national languages including specialized registers in them prove this.

1. Influence on Polish legal terminology

Lexis in Polish texts of the acts of law has been from the beginning, similarly like the language of law in other European countries, under the strong influence of Latin. The traces of Latin in the legal

---

[1] Agnieszka Choduń, „Leksyka tekstów aktów prawnych" [Lexis of legal acts], *Ruch Prawniczy, Ekonomiczny i Socjologiczny* 2006, no. 4, pp. 19–30; eadem, „Słownictwo tekstów aktów prawnych w zasobie leksykalnym współczesnej polszczyzny" [Lexis in texts of the acts of law in the varieties of the Polish language lexis], Warszawa: TRIO, 2007.

[2] Anna Jopek-Bosiacka, „Niektóre problemy 'europeizacji' polskich tekstów prawnych," [Some problems of 'Europeisation' of Polish legislative texts], in: Andrzej Kopczyński, Urszula Zielińska-Okrutna (eds), *Język rodzimy a język obcy: komunikacja, przekład, dydaktyka* [Domestic language and foreign language: communications, translation, teaching], Warszawa: Wydawnictwo UW, 2001, pp. 161–162.

discourse are visible till today, which is exemplified by the following terms: apelacja (*appelatio*), alimentacja (*alimentatio*), cesja (cessio), kasacja (*cassatio*), kodeks (*codex*), legislacja (*legislation*), nowacja (*novatio*), posesor (*possessor*), obligacja (*obligatio*), *vacatio legis*. The same about the following words and phrases in the legal language: *ab initio, corpus delicti, ex contractu, ex delicto, ex post facto, expressiss verbis, in personam, in rem,* jurysdykcja (*iurisdictio), per facta concludentia, prima facie, pro forma, res iudicata, quasi, vis maior*. These cognates are historically connected with the adoption of the Roman law into the Polish legal order. Names of the majority of legal institutions have Latin etymology.

Moreover, there are strong French and German influence on Polish legal terminology, which can be exemplified by the following: abandon (French *abandon*), arbitraż (French *arbitrage*), dyspaszer (French *dispacheur*), indosat, indosariusz (German *Indossat, Indossator*), konosament (German *Konnossement* or French *connaissement*), protokolant (German *Protokollant*), prokurator (German *Prokuratur*).[3]

Modern lexical cognates, occuring in the Polish legal discourse concern mainly terms from certain scientific fields. Computer technology terms are good example of that. These are e.g.: CD-ROM, interfejs (*interface*), skaner (*scanner*), *trackball, tuchball*, etc. These words have no Polish counterparts since they refer to previously unknown referents, which got their names in English. Similar situation appears in economic terminology related to the processes going on in economy. Polish texts of the acts of law contain a big number from that field that are internationalisms. This group of words appeared in the Polish legal discourse following Polish political transformation of year 1990, which resulted in the possibility of taking part in particular economic processes. Due to the fact that these actions required legal regulations, it was necessary to use proper names. Specialized terminology was used, and in a lot of cases it means internationalisms. These are, e.g.: titles of contracts: *factoring, franchising, know-how, leasing,* names of professions: *dealer, developer, manager, broker,* but also such words as: *euro, holding, lobbing, logo, marketing, monitoring, recycling, infolinia.* Acronyms appearing in the legal discourse also belong to internation-

3 Anna Jopek-Bosiacka, *Przekład prawny i sądowy* [Legal and judicial translation], Warszawa: Wydawnictwo Naukowe PWN, 2006, p. 35.

alisms, e.g.: PIN - *Personal Identificaton Number,* PIT - *Personal Income Trade,* VAT - *Value Added Tax* (an interesting thing to mention is that there were attempts at replacing foreign VAT with Polish PTU - from: Podatek od Towarów i Usług; however this didn't catch on). The same applies to acronyms specifying terms of delivery in trade documentation (contracts) in foreign trade (in compliance with the International Commercial Trade Terms INCOTERMS 2000).

Particularly intensified enrichment of the lexis of Polish legal discourse with cognates from other languages, including internationalisms understood as language elements - words - appearing in at least three languages belonging to at least two language groups/families, which are similar in form and meaning facilitating communication between people using different languages[4] took place with reference to Polish accession to the European Union. This process started, however, in the pre-accession period, when Polish law was being adjusted to the EU law. It turned out then, that together with the necessity of adjusting Polish law to the EU law, the necessity to introduce some legal institutions not provided for by the Polish law arose. It meant also introducing new names for these new institutions. Due to the normative character of a legal discourse legal terms in a natural way lead to (cause) particular legal effects within the given legal system. Introducing new terms into the texts of law is equal to introducing new legal solutions and as a consequence leads to certain results in domestic law.

Together with some political processes there have occurred intensified processes of language integration on the field of law. The phenomenon of linguistic integration is nothing new in the unifying Europe, though. These processes form the inseparable element of the intellectual activity of a human being as such. Continuity of changes that characterizes our reality is reflected in language itself as a tool for communicating, but also in unifying means of interpreting the surrounding world, adopting cultural patterns and ways of thinking.

In the field of law

[4] Jolanta Maćkiewicz, „Co to są internacjonalizmy?" [What are the internationalisms?], *Język Polski* 1984, no. 3, p. 181.

> ... this includes the trend towards the **internalisations to law** involving, inter alia, the establishment of compatible solutions to legal problems in various states, the popularisation and even unification of many legal norms, the implementation of 'foreign' models of regulation in the internal legal systems of states.[5]

With reference to this there may be two categories of internationalisms differentiated in the Polish legal discourse. The first relates to those international words, which have been introduced to the language of law (language of the acts of law texts) or to the legal language for practical reasons, connected with the necessity to name phenomena, situations or institutions not known to Polish law and Polish reality and having no counterparts in domestic lexis. The other category of internationalisms appearing in the discourse of the language of law and legal discourse are internationalisms which, apart from the function mentioned above, play also the role of carrying certain values. They implement certain patterns of acting and thinking from their country of origin into the field of Polish culture in general and into the Polish legal culture in particular. This type of internationalisms is of special character as it triggers mental changes in society.

An example of such integration not only on the linguistic level but also in the field of law and in the broader social field is introduction of the legal term of 'mobbing' into the Polish legal system. Changes in the Polish Labour Code initiated at the end of year 2003 were aimed at adjusting Polish legal regulations to the law of the European Union. Settling the issues relating to the equal treatment of persons in employment, prohibition of discrimination in the work relationship and introduction to the Polish law a concept of mobbing was an important element of this amendment. Polish legislator included at this point in the regulations of the Polish Labour Code the definition of 'mobbing' and by this defined its character as a term of the Polish language of law.

Although protection of employees against mobbing had already been based in other regulations of the Polish law, first of all in the

[5] Jolanta Jabłońska-Bonca, *Wprowadzenie do prawa. Introduction to law,* 2nd ed., Warszawa: LexisNexis, 2008, p. 157.

Constitution of the Republic of Poland through the imposed on the public authorities duty of respecting and protecting human dignity, in the Civil Code through legal protection of human dignity and in the Labour Code itself due to the prohibition of discrimination in employment through sexual harassment, but these regulations refer to something else. They do not directly refer to a particular situation of an employee in a workplace, only generally protect some values.

The term 'mobbing', had functioned also in the general Polish language, in 2003 it was included in the *Uniwersalny słownik języka polskiego* (Universal Dictionary of Polish Language). According to the dictionary definition 'mobbing' belongs to the book lexis and means:

> ... applying various forms of psychological violence in the team of persons working together, violence that aims at isolating a person from the environment, ridiculing them and humiliating; office terror.[6]

It was not, however, a definition for a particular situation resulting in particular legal effects. The dictionary definition itself is not too precise, either. It does not specify a person, who can be a mobber, a person, who is a victim of mobbing and it doesn't specify who is responsible for mobbing.

Till the moment, when a situation of mobbing was legally regulated, with reference to the situation, which we nowadays refer to as *mobbing*, the following terms - synonyms - were used: *mental terror, pestering, mental harassment, moral molestation, bullying at a workplace*. These terms, however, reflect more of a mood and situation of a person mobbed rather than the essence of 'mobbing' as a phenomenon. They do not also specify direction of actions referred to as *mobbing*, neither the fact, who can be defined as a mobber. Introduction of proper legal regulations for mobbing has considerably changed the situation.

According to the legislator's decision, *mobbing* in the Polish law means:

---

[6] *Uniwersalny słownik języka polskiego* [Universal Dictionary of Polish Language], ed. by Stanisław Dubisz, Warszawa: Wydawnictwo Naukowe PWN, 2003, p. 691.

> ... any action or behaviour relating to an employee or directed against the employee consisting of persistent and long-lasting harassment intimidation of an employee resulting in his or her decreased evaluation of professional capabilities, as well as resulting in or aimed at humiliating or ridiculing an employee, isolating him or her or eliminating him or her from a work team. (Article 94.[3] § 2 Polish Labour Code)[7]

At the same time, according to the regulations of the Polish law "an employer shall prevent mobbing" (Article 94.[3]§ 1. Polish Labour Code).

Whereas

> ... an employee, who suffers from health disturbance as a result of mobbing may claim a relevant sum from the employer as cash compensation for the incurred harm. (Article 94.[3]§ 3. Polish Labour Code)

Also:

> ... an employee, who terminated the employment contract inconsequence of mobbing shall have the right to claim compensation from the employer in the amount of at least the minimum remuneration for work established pursuant to separate provisions ... (Art. 94.[3] § 5. Polish Labour Code)

Obviously mobbing in the workplace existed long before it was defined as such. However, only when action or behaviour of employer, boss or employee against some other employee was defined as in the legal definition above, the problem was noticed not only in the dimension of a particular phenomenon researched by scientists with reference to behaviour of particular members of a given community towards one of their members.

The term 'mobbing' started to be using in the middle of 20th century, only by the scientists, however, and with relation to described aggressive behaviour of wild animals toward one of their group. Thanks to a Swedish doctor and psychologist Heinz Leymann, the term started to function in the social sphere. Leymann used the term 'mobbing' to describe mental terror towards individual employees of

---

[7] Journal of Laws Dz.U. 1998 no. 21, item 94.

economic institutions.[8] According to this scientist the word mobbing comprises the whole system of psycho-social relations at the workplace, characterized by hostile attitude and harassing employees by their mates or superiors. According to Leymann mobbing results from a conflict, which over time intensifies due to the lack of counter action. In the final effect it becomes long-term action turned against one of the employees. In the public discourse between various European countries *mobbing* appeared already in the seventies of the last century, along such terms as: *moral harassment, victimation and psychological terror* or *bullying*. Different words for hostile behaviour are used in different countries, but in most European countries the term 'mobbing' is used.[9]

Appearance of the word *mobbing* in the Polish legal discourse, let undoubtedly to changes in the terminology of the language of law and legal language. Initially introduction to the language of law this word that sounded totally alien, etymologically stemming from the English *mob* (which has both meaning of a verb and noun) was not associated in Poland with the phenomenon it described, which was a problem. There was also a question of how reasonable it is to use an internationalism in a text of the Polish act of law since Polish dictionaries provide a Polish synonym for *mobbing*: *office terror*. Due to the fact that Polish is an inflective language, there was an even bigger issue of how to inflect this term through persons and how to form verbs from it. A request was thus directed at the Commission of the Legal Language at the Polish Language Council how shall these grammatical issues connected with the term 'mobbing' be solved.

Despite the fact that since 1997 an act on Polish language has been in force and it puts on public authorities the obligation to protect Polish language, a proposal to introduce the term 'mobbing' into the texts of the Polish act of law did not meet negative reaction on part of the Polish Language Council, which is an advisory and opinion body

---

[8] *The Mobbing Encyclopedia*, available at <http://www.leymann.se/English/ 11320>.

[9] Anna Larson, "The Conceptual History of 'Mobbing'," *Proceedings of Annual Conference ECER 2008: From Teaching to Learning?*, available at <http://www.eera.ecer.eu/publicationdatabase/conference/2008/contribution/the_conceptual_historyof_mobbing>.

of the Polish Academy of Sciences. The answer of the Polish Language Council to the question about the issues connected with inflection of the word 'mobbing' was very liberal. The Council made reference to the general rules binding in this case by Polish language, but it also decided that the custom (that is a language practice of Polish native speakers) is finally going to decide about, which grammatical form of the word *mobbing* will form.

A much more important consequence of introduction of the term 'mobbing' to the Polish legal discourse is the one taking place in the social dimension. Changes caused by the transformation of the political system in Poland both in the political and economic aspects, positioned Poland closer to the European Community zone with regard to the relations at a workplace as well, although it was more referring to the institutional issue, e.g. new forms of employment. At the same time relation employer-employee was redefined. Employment as such used to be no problem in Poland, it became a good sought for and work became a value.

As we know unemployment is conducive to abuse on part of an employer and peers at work. Position of an employee due to the work deficit, remains in asymmetry towards the employer's position. However, despite various forms of harassment, an employee had problems with taking any action. They chose staying silent instead, in fear of losing their job. Introducing the term 'mobbing' in the Polish Labour Code first of all, influenced change of social awareness in the issue. One may even say that situations that had previously been perceived as *personal problems in the workplace*, started to be perceived as actions posing threat to the position at work that is as a problem of social character. Mostly because the effects of actions defined as mobbing affect not only an employee, who usually is affected negatively in helth and almost always loses a job, but also the whole society. This dimension of social costs covered with relation to treatment of the victims, costs of social benefits for those, who became unemployed as a result of harassment in the workplace, had not been noticed before.

Therefore not only there were no actions taken against the results of mobbing, but prevention was not applied, too.

Mobbing is an example of internationalism, which has not only enriched a domestic pool of words making Polish legal discourse more communicative, but it also influenced change in attitudes and cultural changes in the Polish society.

2. Universalism or separatism

As much as in the development of national languages:

> ... two contrasting and complementing trends are intertwined: a tendency to differentiate, divide and separate languages and the tendency to approximate and amalgamate languages,[10]

thus on the one hand there is a striving for separatism, and on the other hand - for cultural universalism, in Polish legal discourse the second one - universalism - seems to be stronger. This is visible in the presence of internationalisms in the legal discourse, which speak in favour of the stronger position of the unification tendencies over the individualistic tendencies.

Universalism in the legal discourse, determined by political and social processes, referred to as internationalization or globalization, is show not only at the level of lexis of the Polish texts of the acts of law. Internationalisms in the legal discourse lead to the similarities in the linguistic depictions of the worlds - legal world, and as a result also the world of values protected by law.

In the specialized discourse, to which the legal discourse undoubtedly belongs, the process of internationalization of a language, in particular lexis is ahead of language purism. Enriching lexis of the legal discourse resulted and still results from practical reasons. It happens because of necessity to reach certain aim in communication. It leads, through the attempt to unify terminology and ways of expression, not only to communicating understood as exchange of information, but also to forming a certain community.

---

[10] Jolanta Maćkiewicz, „Wyrazy międzynarodowe a kształtowanie się europejskiej ligi słownikowej" [International words and creating of European vocabulary league], *Język a Kultura* 1992, vol. 7, p. 145.

APPENDIX

Legal Rules in the Name of Democracy and Democracy in the Name of Legal Rules: Parallel Deaths of Socrates and Julius Caesar

edited by Romina Amicolo
University of Naples "Federico II", Italy

Abstract: The complete picture of the deaths of Socrates and Julius Caesar allows to represent, in an exhaustive and problematic way, a concept of democracy and legal rules, traditional, but by now inadequate to the increasing social complexity, that, with the sentence of Socrates and the murder of Julius Caesar, executes its extreme attempt of self-defense and self-maintenance.

Key words: Democracy, legal rules, parallel convergences, justice, freedom, ethics, equality, politics, republic, tyranny

1. The death of Socrates: legal rules in the name of democracy

Socrates "quite calmy and with no sign of distaste"[1] "drained the cup in one breath,"[2] while most of his comrades, who, up till that time, "had been fairly successful in keeping back"[3] their tears, when they "saw he was drinking, that he had actually drunk it,"[4] they "could do so no longer"[5]: and also Phaedo's tears, in spite of

---

[1] Plato, *Phaedo*, 117 C 5.
[2] Ibidem, 117 C 6.
[3] Ibidem, 117 C 7.
[4] Ibidem, 117 C 8.
[5] Ibidem, 117 C 9.

The death of Socrates, Jacques-Luis David, 1787

The murder of Caesar, Vincenzo Camuccini, 1798

himself, "came pouring out, so that he covered his face and wept brokenheartedly – not for him,"[6] but for his "own calamity in losing

[6] Ibidem, 117 C 10.

such a friend."[7] And Crito had given up even before Phaedo, and "had gone out when he could not restrain his tears."[8] Apollodorus, who had never stopped crying even before, now broke out into such a storm of passionate weeping that he made everyone in the room break down, except Socrates himself, who, hearing the friends crying, invited them to have courage:

> Really, my splendid friends what a way to behave! ... I am told that one should make one's end in a tranquil frame of mind. Calm yourself and try to be brave.[9]

When, after he finished drinking, the body of Socrates became by now cold, Crito, seeing him, closed his mouth and eyes. This was, the end of the best man, without comparison "the wisest and most upright man,"[10] that, inviting to follow the virtue, didn't hesitate to refuse public positions and to abdicate the politics, as he had told in his Apology:

> You may be quite sure, Athenians, that if I had tried long ago to engage in politics, I should long ago have lost my life, without doing any good either to you or to myself. Please do not be offended if I tell you the truth. No man on earth who conscientiously opposes either you or any other organized democracy, and flatly prevents a great many wrongs and illegalities from taking place in the state to which he belongs, can possibly escape with his life. The true champion of justice, if he intends to survive even for a short time, must necessarily confine himself to private life and leave politics alone.[11]

2. The murder of Julius Caesar: democracy in the name of legal rules

Brutus, as some other conspirators, held the praetorship and therefore he had, before the murder of Caesar, to hear the cases, in one of which an obstinate contender, refusing his judgment, lost the control

[7] Ibidem, 117 C 11.
[8] Ibidem, 117 D 2.
[9] Ibidem, 117 D 6–9.
[10] Ibidem, 118 A 15.
[11] Plato, *Socrates' Defence (Apology)*, 31 E–32 A.

and began to shout against him, that he would appeal to Caesar. Brutus, then, without losing his composure, articulated a provocative answer: "Caesar doesn't prevent me neither he will prevent me from acting in accordance with legal rules."[12]

In front of the body, by now to the ground of Caesar, stabbed and dripping blood, Brutus, with the other assassins, apostrophizes the death of Caesar as the death of the tyranny: "Liberty! Freedom! Tyranny is dead!"[13] "Liberty, freedom and enfranchisement!"[14] "Ambition's debt is paid."[15]

When by now the play of the politics is next to its epilogue, Brutus, during a quarrel with Cassius, cries angered:

> Did not great Julius bleed in the name of legal rules? What villain touched his body, that did stab and not for legal rules[16]? What, shall one of us, that struck the foremost man of all this world but for supporting robbers, shall we now contaminate our fingers with base bribes, and sell the mighty space of our large honours for so much trash as may be grasped thus? I had rather be a dog and bay the moon that such a Roman.[17]

3. Parallel convergences between the deaths of Socrates and Julius Caesar

As legal rules and democracy proceed side by side, without ever touching themselves, but giving the observer, the impression of parallel convergences, that, in many cases, are more than simple optic illu-

---

[12] Plutarch, *Brutus*, 14, 7.

[13] William Shakespeare, *Julius Caesar*, III, i, 78.

[14] Ibidem, III, i, 81.

[15] Ibidem, III, i, 83.

[16] We changed the word "*justice*," used by Shakespeare, with the words "*legal rules*" because "*justice*," in this context, is meant as "the respect of legal rules" that is able to guarantee the political power of the republican aristocracy. The correctness of this interpretation is confirmed by the real-life event related by Plutarch in *Brutus* 14, 7: the administration of justice realized by the praetor Brutus is the application of legal rules that Caesar, with his power, democratic because based on the consense of people, wanted to stop.

[17] W. Shakespeare, *Julius Caesar*, IV, ii, 70–79.

sions, so, the deaths of Socrates and Julius Caesar, don't escape a game of identity and differences, that involves not only the illustrious and charismatic personalities of a philosopher and a political man and their worlds, the Greek and the Roman ones, but, above all, the dynamics both of the legal rules that don't hesitate to put their tools, the trial and the punishment of the death sentence, to the service of the democracy, and of the democracy, that, in the name of freedom and the legal rules' defence, doesn't admit the tyranny, but arrives to kill.

4. Legal rules in the name of democracy: Socrates and the crisis of the Athenian democracy

The Socratic dialogues both of Plato and Xenophon, show how legal rules defend democracy, that is in crisis, because of the separation of the Greek man from the community and the transformation that the conception of the democracy suffers because of the death of Socrates: it is the same democracy to die, as genially realized by Hannah Arendt, because of that conflict between the philosophy and the polis, that Socrates opens and Plato exasperates.

5. Socrates appears in front of the Court: the accusations

In the year 339 B.C., Socrates, a seventy year-old Athenian, climbing for the first time, in his by now long life, in the courthouse, has called to answer some accusers of impiety and corruption of the young people, according to the charge formulated by the accusatory Anytus and Meletus:

> Socrates is guilty of corrupting the minds of the young, and of believing in deities of his own invention instead of the gods recognized by the state.[18]

---

[18] Plato, *Socrates' Defence (Apology)*, 24 B 8–10; Xenophon, *Memorabilia*, I, 1.

The reading of the charge in the courtroom, in the presence of the judges and his slanderers, as required by the procedure, is only the last action of a persecution started a quarter of century before the trial, when, in 423 B.C., Aristophanes, in his play *The Clouds*, had represented Socrates as "a wise man who has theories about the heavens and has investigated everything below the earth, and can make the weaker argument defeat the stronger,"[19] uttering a great deal of nonsense and other foolishness, in his walks on air, in the clouds.

If these people, the disseminators of these rumors, are "the most dangerous accusers, because those who hear them suppose that anyone who inquires into such mutters must be an atheist,"[20] the true defendant, is not the man but his philosophy, responsible of having shaken from its torpor the Athenian democracy of the 5th century B.C. The polis was inactive and stunned by the appearance, so much that, just to keep on sleeping, in its numbness, without caring about itself, it sentenced to death the man who, not only had dared to wake up it, with his "maieutic art,"[21] but, also after having been silenced, with a law that forbade him to practice the art of the word, had kept on conversing in the city with the young people, the cobblers, the artisans, the blacksmiths, and those who wanted to stop and talk with him: how could Socrates have given up "the consequences that he drew from them, namely the correctness, the holiness and similar other things?"[22]

6. Socrates "head of Janus" in the crisis of the Athenian democracy

"The Socrates' urgent need to focus his research on the human things is indicative of the crisis"[23] of the Athenian democracy. With

[19] Plato, *Socrates' Defence (Apology)*, 18 B.

[20] Ibidem, 18 C.

[21] Xenophon, *Memorabilia*, II, 31-35.

[22] Ibidem, II, 37-38.

[23] Walter F. Otto, *Socrate e l'uomo greco*, Milano: Marinotti Edizioni, 2005, p. 30.

regard to it, Socrates is a "head of Janus,"[24] for his double character, both innovating, because he destroyed the preceding philosophy and the existing democracy, and, at the same time, "incredibly conservative, because he defended the legal rules and took a stand against the sophists and their sense of omnipotence and relativism."[25]

In his attempt to do honour to the legal rules and to save them from the unbelief and the contempt, Socrates destroys the ancient democracy and brought to the light that "the political sphere didn't obviously handle all the superior activities of the man,"[26] according to the Greek traditional concept of democracy as "a form of peculiar and freely chosen life,"[27] "not mere form of necessary action for the unification of men in a regular way,"[28] but "*bios politikos*"[29] or "kingdom of the human business,"[30] "autonomous way of life and authentically human."[31]

Socrates affirmed that he "suddenly had not to found something different, additionally to what it was already known, but he had to found a superior principle to replace the old democratic principles which governed the polis."[32]

The Socrates' interrogative "what is it?", reassumes the claim of a divine arrangement, rooted in a native nature, which is "the epochal novelty of Socrates,"[33] who resolves the crisis of the Greek man. According to Socrates' ethics, the justice, the beauty and the whole other human qualities have to be universally considered "immediately evident realities,"[34] as before the sophistical relativism. But in this way, Socrates opens the road to something of completely new, destructive

---

24 Ibidem, p. 25.

25 Ibidem.

26 Hannah Arendt, *Vita Activa. La condizione umana* (1958), Edizioni Bompiani, 2008, p. 14.

27 Ibidem, p. 11.

28 Ibidem.

29 Ibidem.

30 Ibidem.

31 Ibidem.

32 Ibidem, p. 14.

33 Ibidem.

34 Francis M. Conford, "Plato's Commonwealth," in: idem, *The Unwritten Philosophy and Other Essays*, Cambridge: Cambridge University Press, 1950, p. 54.

of the tradition and founder of our political thought, that, far from understanding and conceptualizing all the political experiences of the humanity of the West, comes from a specific historical constellation: the trial of Socrates[35] and the conflict between legal rules and democratic principles in the Athens of the 5th century B.C.

7. The democratic principles: action and discourse in the experience of the *polis* before Socrates

"The establishment of democracy in the 5th century meant for the man to receive, locked up in his private life, a second life, his *bios politikos*,"[36] characterized by the two only activities reputed necessary and constitutive of the political communities, "that is the action (praxis) and the discourse (lexis),"[37] considered, in the pre-Socratic thought, complementary and superior to all the others, because only from them "originates the dominion of the human business."[38]

According to the native conception of the Greek world, before the Socratic philosophy, "not only the political action, which was unconnected with the sphere of the violence, realizes itself in the discourse, but - and it was the decisive factor - the right word at the right moment, apart from its meaning, was the action."[39]

The experience of the Athenian democracy is the history of the progressive separation between the action and the discourse, which, progressively becoming more important than the action, „was a means of persuasion rather than a specifically human way of answering, beating and reacting to everything happened or was made in the polis."[40]

In the primitive Greek community of the archaic epoch, where the individual recognized the same values which were acknowledged by the community, legal rules, were above everything else. Justice, in the

35 H. Arendt, *Vita Activa. La condizione umana*, op. cit., pp. 10–11.

36 Ibidem, p. 20.

37 Ibidem.

38 Ibidem.

39 Ibidem.

40 Ibidem.

meaning of application of legal rules, was the tendency to act in his own entourage, so that everyone received what belonged to him, and didn't pass the limits of the own entourage, in the exercise of a virtue that was the "universal good."[41] Life brought a lasting imprint, divine, and every action assumed so a universal value, "since it corresponded to the uses of the tradition,"[42] in the total absence of doubts on the value of the life, that survived to the man because it was conform to the divine order and involved in respecting it. This principle of the Athenian democracy was consecrated in the poets' songs, which were carrier of glory and immortality.

More difficult became to define the virtue when the ancient chivalrous ideal, universally recognized in Greece, collapsed and it was delineated, as testified by the Homeric story of the quarrel for the weapons of Achilles, a more and more marked "inclination for the differentiation of the values, since it was possible to speak of the different virtues of the men. As the new social class became aware of his own value, less and less it adapted itself to the ideal of virtue imposed by the old social class."[43] The discovery that the lives of the men were different and that in the most different professions it was possible to follow a particular αρετή (vitue) marked not only the crisis of the divine order, until then unanimously shared, but the con-sequent sinking of the differentiation of the life into the uncertainty of a man who felt to be mutable and exposed to the influence of different things, without the firm belief in the affinity of the man with the God, because of the feral sophistical philosophy. The new men identified their natural condition with "the situation in which the strong men gave free outlet for their strength of passions and gave themselves up to pleasure."[44]

In opposition to the Sofists, Socrates marked the turning point from the classical-archaic thought to the post-classical Hellenic one. He didnt't shake the ingenue instinctive safety with fruitless reasonings, as if the Greeks, before him, gave cheerfully themselves up to

[41] Bruno Snell, *La cultura greca e le origini del pensiero europeo*, Turin: Ed. Einaudi, 1963, p. 191.

[42] Ibidem.

[43] Ibidem, p. 192.

[44] Ibidem, p. 202.

the spontaneity of the instinct, but, when the human soul had already been consumed, overcome by the uncertainty, Socrates rebuilt the ethics. He didin't introduce himself "with the tone of the teacher who knows and recommends," but exercised the maieutic art with the goal of teaching the virtue and helping "to point out the knowledge that everyone had to draw from himself."[45]

8. The worse evil for Socrates: his renunciation of philosophy and legal rules

Socrates, before the judges who condemn him, is heedless of death, because "you are mistaken, my friend, if you think that a man who is worth anything ought to spend his time weighing up the prospects of life and death. He has only one thing to consider in performing any action - that is, whether he is acting rightly or wrongly, like a good man or a bad one."[46] Socrates' attitude in front of the Court in Athens is the same which he assumed in the battles of Potidaea and Anmphipolis and Delium: "where a man has once taken up his stand, either because it seems best to him or in obedience to his orders, there he is bound to remain and face the danger, taking no account of death or anything else before dishonor."[47] As in the battles Socrates, risking the death, remained at his post like anyone else and faced death, because the officers whom the city of Athens chose to command him assigned him his position, so, equally, he doesn't desert his post in front of the court that sentences him to death, because the God appointed him to the duty of leading the philosophical life, examining himself and the others, also when, as now, he is in fear of death or of any other danger.[48]

The search of the virtue and the disclosure of ignorance is extended by Socrates to everyone that he meets, young or old, foreigner or fellow citizens, but especially to fellow citizens, inasmuch as they are closer to him in kinship and above all because this was what his God

[45] Ibidem.

[46] Plato, *Socrates' defense (Apology)*, 28 B 5–10.

[47] Ibidem, 28 D.

[48] Ibidem, 28 E.

commands, and it is his belief that no greater good has ever befallen in the city of Athens that his service to his God.[49]

Socrates describes his philosophy, whose objects are the man, the citizen of Athens and the same *polis*, whose attainment is the good of the city, that is not a transcendent entity, but the invitation "to make their first and chief concern not for your bodies not for their possessions, but for the highest welfare of their souls, proclaiming as he goes, Wealth does not bring goodness, but goodness brings wealth and every other blessing, both to the individual and to the state."[50]

Socrates defends his philosophy, clarifying the terms, the formalities and the contents of his search, that is a preaching, and, as the God commands, a mission, an invitation to the exercise of the virtue and not cause of corruption of the Athenian youth.

The training in the exercise of virtue is the foundation of the Socrates' philosophy: it's necessary if you want that in the democracy both legal rules would be respected and, consequently, justice could reign. Socrates will remember the importance of virtue, at the end of his Apology, where he asks to take care of his children after his death:

> When my sons grow up, gentlemen, if you think that they are putting money or anything else before goodness, take your revenge by plaguing them as I plagued you; and if they fancy themselves for no reason, you must scold them just as I scolded you, for neglecting the important things and thinking that there are good for something when they are good for nothing. If you do this, I shall have had justice at your hands, both myself and my children.[51]

9. The Socrates' death as the end of the Athenian democracy

"I assure you that if I am what I claim to be, and you put me to death, you will harm yourselves more than me."[52] With the affirma-

[49] Ibidem, 30 A.
[50] Ibidem, 30 B.
[51] Ibidem, 41 E.
[52] Ibidem, 30 C.

tion that his death sentence will cause a damage to the Athenians, who will act "against the gift of the God," Socrates begins the part of his defense that mostly will succeed tiresome to the judges and will irremediably mark his death sentence:

> If you will kill me, you will not easily find another like me, that God has appointed to this city, as though it were a large thoroughbred horse which because of its great size is inclined to be lazy and needs the stimulation of some stinging fly. It seems to me that God has attached me to this city to perform the office of such a fly, and all day long I never cease to settle here, there and everywhere, rousing, persuading, reproving every one of you.[53]

The action of Socrates has woken up the democracy "from its drowsing and, once it will finish the philosopher off with a single slap, it will go on sleeping till the end of its days, unless the god, in his care for the city sends someone to take the place"[54] of Socrates, who sacrificed his existence: he "neglected his own affairs and endured the humiliation of allowing his family to be neglected for all these years, while he busied himself all the time on his citizens' behalf, going like a father or an elder brother to see each one of them privately, and urging them to set their thoughts on goodness"[55] and convincing them to practice the virtue and to respect legal rules in the name of the Athenian democracy. The invitation of Socrates to take care of his own soul is an element of breakup, not only toward the traditional conception of the virtue in the *polis,* but also in comparison to the relationship between legal rules and democracy. Socrates has not held public offices because he knew well that Athenian democracy was the kingdom of the injustice, as breach of legal rules; he has stirred in the private sphere, approaching his citizens to one to one and inviting them to follow, not the street of the public honors but that of the individual improvement, through the knowledge and the care of themselves. Socrates "goes around giving advice ... and busying himself in people's private affaire, and yet never ventures public-

[53] Ibidem, 30 E.

[54] Ibidem, 31 A.

[55] Ibidem, 31 B.

ly to address people as a whole and advise on matters of state"[56] because he is "subject to a divine or supernatural experience, which Meletus saw fit to travesty in his indictment."[57] This spirit debared him from entering public life, since the democracy is incompatible with the respect of legal rules:

> You may be quite sure, gentlemen, that if I had tried long ago to engage in politics, I should long ago have lost my life, without doing any good either to you or to myself.[58]
>
> Do you suppose that I should have lived as long as I have if I had moved in the sphere of public life, and conducting myself in that sphere like an honorable man, had always upheld the cause of right, and conscientiously set this end above all other things? Not by a very long way, gentlemen; neither would any other man.[59]

The philosophy, as call to the reflection and the knowledge, which uses the discourse to show that none knows, enters in the city and distroys the democracy, because the search of the justice and the good is an exercise not of the *polis*, as collectivity, but of the man, as human being, even if without the quality of citizen. Socrates, to obey to his daimonion, disobeys the city and it is his internal voice that forbids him to practice political activity, because the road of the "knowledge," as search of the virtue and improvement of themselves, is not public, but private anymore.

The Athenians send Socrates to death and believe that through it they will be delivered from submitting their conduct to criticism, but Socrates says that the result will be just the opposite:

> ... they will have more critics, whom up till now I have restrained without your knowing it, and being younger they will be harsher to you and will cause you more annoyance. If you expect to stop denunciation of your wrong way of life by putting people to death, there is something amiss with your reasoning. This way of escape is neither possible nor

---

[56] Ibidem, 31 D.

[57] Ibidem.

[58] Ibidem, 31 E.

[59] Ibidem, 33 E.

> creditable. The best and easiest way is not to stop the mouths of others, but to make yourselves as good man as you can. This is my last message to you who voted for my condemnation.[60]

According to the concept of democracy of all the "Greek philosophers, even if contrary to the life of the Athenian democracy, everything, in the political life and the democratic experience, was decided with the words,"[61] while the violence was used to oblige the others, instead of persuading them, in the life out of the Athenian democracy, in the pre-politics relationships, in the sphere of the private domestic organization, where everything is justified by the necessity. In the democracy everyone becomes "free from the inequality connected with every type of dominion" and moves himself "in a sphere where it was not allowed neither to comand neither to be comanded."[62]

Equality was the true essence of the democracy, as synonymous of liberty, whose field of exercise was marked by the boundaries of the polis. It's underlined by the "Aristotelian definition of the man as «a living being able of speaking» (*zoon logon ekhon*)"[63]: "whoever was out of the *polis*, slave or barbarian, was *aneu logou*, deprived, naturally, not of the faculty of speaking, but of a way of life where only the discourse had sense and the fundamental activity of all the citizens was the discourse."[64] The few "equals" (*homoioi*) men live in the city among own peers, in a public sphere happily permeated by a competitive spirit, where everyone constantely had to distinguish himself from the others, as the best citizen (*aien aristeuein*), who respects not only the legal rules, but also the values of the community.

Conditions of survival of the Athenian democracy, "the most individualistic and least conformist of the ancient known political bodies, were not only „the reduced number of citizens – as a big number of people develops an almost irresistible inclination toward the des-

---

[60] Ibidem, 39 D.

[61] H. Arendt, *Vita activa*, op. cit., p. 23.

[62] Ibidem, p. 24.

[63] Ibidem, p. 21.

[64] Ibidem.

potism, both of a person and of the majority,"[65] but also "the distance between the private and the public life which the ancient people had to daily overcome if they wanted to transcend the circle of the domestic life and to ascend to the sphere of the democracy"[66] as the city was founded on the exclusion of the violence and the strenght from the politics.

As soon as the social complexity grows and "a new middle-class society comes to be in conflict with the ancient aristocratic order,"[67] the tendency to the differentiation of the values, because of the missed recognition of the dominant class' unitary ideal, does not only determine the laxity of morals, but also "the hostility"[68] of the democracy, whose survival is based on the respect of the traditional virtues, against the philosopher, who discusses with the other citizens, his peers, about the virtues which are now different and plural. "Such enmity became clear and evident with the trial and the death sentence of Socrates,"[69] "an episode which shakes the trust of Plato in the use of the persuasion to drive the men."[70] The use of the capital punishment to hush up the philosopher, who for all his life persuaded his citizens to follow the virtue and respect the legal rules, was "the end of the Greek democracy, as the space of the word, where the violence is not admitted."[71]

10. Legal rules talk to Socrates

Crito, a Socrates' friend, who visits him in the prison before his death, talks him into escaping from the jail and again the legal rules become the theme of the Socratic discourse. Socrates disapproves of Crito's opinion, which is unfair his behavior of accepting the death instead of escaping. According to Socrates the democracy is founded

---

[65] Ibidem, p. 32.

[66] Ibidem.

[67] B. Snell, *La cultura greca e le origini del pensiero europeo*, op. cit., p. 192.

[68] Hannah Arendt, *Between Past and Future*, Milano: Garzanti, 1991, p. 150.

[69] Ibidem.

[70] Ibidem.

[71] Ibidem.

not upon the authority and the coercion, practiced by the city's institutions, but upon the respect of the legal rules: the man, who is driven by the reason and the identity between "to know" and "to do" the good, pursues the justice and finds it through the respect and application of legal rules.

The Athenian legal rules themselves explain why the Socrates' escape from the prison is unfair:

> If any of you chooses to go to one of our colonies, supposing that he should not be satisfied with us and the state, or to emigrate to any other country, not one of us laws hinders prevents him from going away wherever he likes, without any loss of property. On the other hand, if any of you stands his ground when he can see how we administer justice and the rest of our public organization, we hold that by so doing he has in fact undertaken to do anything that we tell him. And we maintain that anyone who disobeys is guilty of doing wrong on three separate counts: first because we are his parents, and secondly because we are his guardians, and thirdly because, after promising obedience, he is neither obeying us nor persuading us to change our decision if we are at fault in any way. And although all our orders are in form of propols, not of savage commands, and we give him the choice of either persuading us or doing what we say, he is actually doing neither.[72]

Socrates refuses to run away because his escape would destroy the legal rues and the democracy. The final judgment, because of its non-observance, would lose strength, becoming insecure and would be finally destroyed. If also the city committed injustice against him, because it didn't pronounce a correct sentence, nothing is possible to reproach the laws, which have allowed him to be born, bring up and educated. Such was the relationship between the citizen Socrates and his *polis* that if the legal rules try to put him to death in the belief that it is right to do so, he, on his part, doesn't have the same right to destroy his country and its laws in return:

> ... both in war and in the law courts and everywhere else you must do whatever your city and your country command, or else persuade them in

---

[72] Plato, *Crito*, 51 E–52 A.

> accordance with universal justice, but violence is a sin even against your parents, and it is a far greater sin against your country.[73]

The violence, the strength and the fraudulent action, are excluded from the *polis* and the Socrates' escape is a break of the agreement with the legal rules, so much serious as you keep in mind that there were very few people in Athens who have entered into this agreement with them as explicitely as he had. The legal rules had substantial evidence that he was satisfied with them because he had never left the city to attend a festival or for any other purpose, except on some military expedition:

> You have been content with us and with our city. You have definitely chosen us, and undertaken to observe us in all your activities as a citizen, and as the crowning proof that you are satisfied with our city, you have begotten children in it. Furthermore, even at the time of your trial you could have proposed the penalty of banishment, if you had chosen to do so – that is, you could have done then with the sanction of the state what you are now trying do without it. But whereas at that time you made a noble show of indifference if you had to die, and in fact preferred death, as you said, to banishment, now you show no respect for your earlier professions, and no regards for us, the laws, whom you are trying to destroy. You are behaving like the lowest type of menial, try to run away in spite of the contracts and undertakings by which you agreed to live as a member of our state. Now first answer this question. Are we or are we not speaking the truth when we say that you have undertaken, in deed if not in word, to live your life as a citizen in obedience to us?[74]

The Legal Rules of Athens leaves the citizen free to operate his choices and don't impose o take his own decision against his will or under constraint. After that the decision has been assumed, and the citizen is entered into agreement with the city, he must live his life in obedience to the legal rules. The democracy is the space of the accord, where the citizen can persuade the legal rules, but, when the sentence has been pronounced, justice demands that the citizen respects it, in strength of the initial agreement with the city.

---

[73] Ibidem, 51 C.

[74] Ibidem, 52 C–D.

The Socratic image of the justice is divided into two meanings, according to the moment of the political choice or of the juridical decision: when Socrates acts in the city, speaks in its roads with whoever wants to converse with him and defends himself in the courthouse, he listens to his internal voice, takes position against the opinion of the others and persuades his citizens to follow the virtue; but when the political choice has been assumed and juridical decision is formed, legal rules personify the justice and there is place only for the obedience.

11. Democracy in the name of legal rules: Julius Caesar and the democratic nugde

Equally rich of implications is the connection between legal rules and democracy in the reconstruction of Julius Caesar's murder, through the reading of sources as Plutarch and Suetonius, that allows to go over the historical event of the charismatic leader's death, to show the attempt, only temporarily successful, to stop the political project, successively realized by the "Caesar's child," who institutionalized the *regnum* and realized a project of pacification and social justice, which involved not only Rome and the italic peninsula but the whole known world.

The analysis of the William Shakespeare's play devoted to Julius Caesar is an element of modernity set in the antiquity, which, with the use of the Roman History, gives a suitable and potentially neutral representation of the clash between the absolutist-monarchic model and that republican one in the modern State. Once more legal rules and democracy meet in a knot, which, with the unification of past and present, helps us in the preparation of our future.

12. Caesar between the republic and the tyranny

Caesar, walking in the cram, hears a voice that calls him, acuter than the others, and invites him to beware the Ides of March: he is a diviner; seen him, reacts and exclaims: "He is to dreamer. Let us leave him. Pass."[75] The connection between this scene and the immediately precedent one, where the new master of Rome, believes in the symbolic nature of the world, and is submitted to it, because he aspires to the political recognition and constitutional consecration of his power, shows the image of a Julius Caesar as point of break and, at the same time, of convergence between two political models, the republic (*Res Publica*) and the tyranny (*Regnum*).

The sudden passage from the preceding superstition to the incredulous arrogance of the actual exchange, both markes the Caesar's affiliation to the republican political world, which quickly turns at the end, but continuous to despise the superstition, as the metaphysical base of the power, reflects also the Shakespeare's concept of the Caesar's politics, which was a novelty.

Caesar, always took care of protecting that good traditional relationship with the urban populace and its clams, which however from the origin had been the foundation of his political fortunes, and at the same time, overcame the old and traditional democratic party, in the attempt to give a result and a new solution to the conflict, by now pathologically unstable, between optimates and urban popular mass. This was the novelty of the Caesarian dictatorship "that had induced Plutarch (or his source) to imagine the scene of the aching confession of Caesar at the time of his first turbulent consolate"[76] (59 A.D.):

> ... the optimates were opposed him in the senate and he, who for a long time looked for a pretext, started to protest and to shout that against desire, rather against his will, Caesar had to throw himself in the arms of the popular mass, who was of necessity favored by him because of the violence and the insensibility of the Senate; and in fact he went out in front of the people.[77]

Cicero, "at the end of the Second Philippic, one of his harder discourses,"[78] outlines the Julius Caesar's profile, and, even if he accuses him to have introduced, "in a free people, the habit to the enslave-

[75] W. Shakespeare, *Julius Caesar*, I, ii, 24.

[76] Luciano Canfora, *Giulio Cesare Il dittatore democratico*, Rome: Ed. Laterza, p. 385.

[77] Plutarch, *Caesar*, 14, 3.

[78] L. Canfora, *Giulio Cesare*, op. cit., p. 384.

ment, with the terror and the resignation," to have seduced the people as the big part of his adversaries, and to have transformed "clemency, generally recognized him, in a *clementiae species*,"[79] a mask, because of the "*regnum*,"[80] "the true passion of his whole anxious existence, precociously broken,"[81] keeps silent around "the accusation, fluently turned to the juvenile years of Caesar," "that he launched or imposed or only tried also to impose the traditional «revolutionary» programme of assault to the wealth."[82]

"After Caesar became in fact «consul without colleague,» but with the benevolence of the Senate, openly performed footsteps conformable to a democratic politics", as the "distributions of countryside of Campania among 20,000 citizens with at least three children," but he took into consideration "exclusively the public property" and "inserted, in the agrarian legislation, clauses of guarantee for the owners": the optimates, "killing him, didn't perceive to have eliminated the more far-seeing exponent of their class."[83]

13. Honors for Caesar: the scene of the Lupercalia

The fear of the republicans is that "people choose Caesar for their king"[84] and the danger is perceived as imminent, on the scene where Cassius, who would prefer „not be as live to be in awe of such a thing as I myself,"[85] flares up the mind of Brutus, who "had rather be a villager than to repute himself a son of Rome under these hard conditions as this time is like to lay upon us,"[86] inflamed, in his decision to take part to the conspiracy, from the sound of fanfares and cries of acclamation for Caesar, which are heard from far and are incorrectly interpreted as the cry of the crowd, who is preparing to crown him.

[79] Ibidem.
[80] Ibidem, p. 385.
[81] Ibidem.
[82] Ibidem.
[83] Ibidem.
[84] W. Shakespeare, *Julius Caesar*, I, ii, 79.
[85] Ibidem, I, ii, 94–96.
[86] Ibidem, I, ii, 172–174.

From the following story of Casca to Brutus, it will result to be exactly the opposite: Caesar, when the crown is offered him by Anthony, during the cerimony of the Lupercalia, has refused it with the back of the hand and the people, happy of that refusal, felt a-shouting, while to every offer, happened for well three times, Caesar refused "every time gentler than other."[87] The scene of the Lupercalia,[88] which is present in the sources, is the drama of the refusal of Caesar, that estranges from himself the crown, feeling that people don't want to crown him, and nevertheless he passionately desires it so much that, when "he perceived the common herd was glad he refused the crown, he plucked me ope his doublet and offered them his throat to cut."[89] Shakespeare, when imagines Caesar that, before fainting, suffers emotional raptus, combines the historical episode of the missed crowning of the Lupercalia, with the attitude to offer in sacrifice his throat, as the first one told by Plutarch, both in the *Life of Caesar*, and in the *Life of Anthony*, and expressive of the sacrificial paradigm of the leader, who, refusing the kingdom, desired it so much as he arrived for it at the immolation of himself:

> The Senate had decreed him exceptional honors, and he was casually set on the rostrums when consuls and magistrates and the whole Senate drew near him: he didn't get up, but as if he treated with private citizens he affirmed that they would have had to decrease and not already to increase these honors. This not only irritated the Senate, but also the people, convinced that in the Senate the whole city had been offended. The people, who were possible to go away, went away very dejected, so much that Caesar perceived it and immediately returned home, and, after that he removed the mantle from the neck, he said that he was ready

---

[87] Ibidem, I, ii, 228–229.

[88] Celebrated in Rome on February 15, 44 B.C., it was a Roman winter cerimony: old men and young people, who were naked, greasy, surrounded, took part in a procession. They mocked everyone they met and beat them with strips of goat's skin. That year the procession was driven by Anthony, who, without success, looked for crowning Caesar, sat on the rostrums, on a gold throne, and wound in a mantle of purple. The amplest story of this episode is "drawn by the *Life of August* edited by Nicolaus Damascene, the devoted biographer of the «child» of Caesar". L. Canfora, *Giulio Cesare*, op. cit., pp. 312–313.

[89] W. Shakespeare, *Julius Caesar*, I, ii, 261–264.

> to leave to be struck by whoever wanted it. Later however he alleged to his justification the illness: he said that, when he is standing to speak in front of a crowd, his faculties are immediately shaken and misled, and he suffers dizziness and loses consciousness.[90]

The sour and dramatic wisecrack of Caesar who, irritated for the scene of his crowning, and also for the failure, raised him stood up, discovered his neck, and said that "he offered it to whom wanted to cut his throat,"[91] "can only mean that Caesar reported in this way, publicly, the danger of initiatives of that kind and accused them, who tried to openly force his hand in monarchic sense, that they wanted his death."[92]

Julius Caesar, "in the last times (*tempore extremo*),"[93] beginning from the autumn of 45 B.C., inaugurated his politics of opening toward the aristocracy and allowed "finally, not only that all those people, that until then he had not forgiven, returned in Italy and accessed the magistracies, but that the statues of Pompey and Lucius Silla, who people had upset, were raised again."[94] His politics aroused the reaction of his adversary Cicero, "the first who seems to have suspected and feared the calm of the Caesar's political activity which was as the sea. Cicero feared the power of his character, dissimulated by the hilarious and amiable tone and said that he saw a tyrannical understanding in all of his thoughts and political actions."[95] He ironically, commented "that, Caesar, erecting the statues of Pompey, had consolidated his own ones."[96]

As it's indicated from the "conspiracies and direct night-time reunions against his person," about which Caesar chose not to inquire, but he made only to know, with an edict, that he was aware of the political climate which was poisoned from a rooted distrust and a diffused suspect towards that man, who however, had folded up

[90] Plutarch, *Life of Caesar*, 60, 4–7.
[91] Plutarch, *Life of Antony*, 12, 6.
[92] Plutarch, *Life of Caesar*, 4, 8.
[93] Suetonius, *Caesar*, 75, 4.
[94] Ibidem.
[95] Plutarch, *Life of Caesar*, 4, 8.
[96] Ibidem, 57, 6.

the Romans, because of his fortune. The Romans accepted his break, because they believed that the monarchy was a relief to the evil of the civil wars, and elected him dictator to life, *dictator perpetuus*. This election, according to the common consent, had the same value as a tyranny, because the perpetuity in the time, transformed the republican institution in a monarchic one. Cicero proposed to the Senate the first honors, whose greatness was always in the limits of the human power."[97] But "the Senators put on him that honors - as the historian Florus writes[98] - as the infules are put on the sacrificial victim that is going to be killed,"[99] and in this climate also the failure attempt of Anthony to crown Caesar during the Lupercalia, "not less than other events, contributed to stimulate the conspirators to a quick action. It had given in fact, a more concrete test of what they suspected"[100]: the Caesar's "φιλοτιμία,"[101] his "aspiration to the kingdom, that was for the people the first cause of hating him, and instead for those people, who for a long time opposed him, the best pretext."[102]

Moreover it competes to delineate the political picture of the Caesar's death, also "the uncontrollable initiative of private soldiers and followers that "don't understand their leader anymore" and start to undergroundly act by themselves"[103] as Anthony, who is "among those that don't understand anymore how far Caesar wants to push himself after the life dictatorship, which, accumulated to the renewable consulate for ten years, is already a hugeness."[104] Anthony plots against him, as confirmed also by Plutarch, who reports that

[97] Caesar obtained the official title of dictator perpetuus, life dictator, in the February 44 B.C., before the cerimony of Lupercalia. Plutarch, *Life of Caesar*, 57, 1-3.

[98] He was *Florus*, who reinforces the judgment of Plutarch „about the provocative complicity of the future assassins in the authoritarian turn realized during the passage from the 45 B.C. to the 44 B.C." It was a thin fold of the psychology of the future conspirators, that was not unknown to Cicero when he wrote the Pro Marcello». L. Canfora, *Giulio Cesare*, op. cit., p. 304.

[99] Ibidem.

[100] Nicolaus Damascene, *Life of Augustus*, 20–21 (§§ 69–75), ed. by Barbara Scardigli e Paola Del Bianco, Siena, 1983, 40–43, in: L. Canfora, *Giulio Cesare*, op. cit., p. 313.

[101] Plutarch, *Life of Caesar*, 58, 4.

[102] Ibidem, 60, 1.

[103] L. Canfora, *Giulio Cesare*, op. cit., p. 313.

[104] Ibidem, pp. 313–314.

"an accusation of rebellion was turned against Anthony."[105] About Anthony's plot, Caesar answered that he din't have "fear of these men, fat and with well-kept hair,"[106] but also Cicero accused Anthony, in a footstep of the Second Philippic, that he has been, "with the comedy of the Lupercalia, the true motor of the Caesar's killing,"[107] "*ob metum proximi dictatoris*,"[108] "for «fear» of the dictator Caesar."[109]

> Despite the extreme uncertainty that reigns on that dark episode, those words would make to slant more for the provocative gesture of a man that had conceived a real *metus dictatoris* than not for the fruit of the monarchic exaltation of a private soldier that climbs over and anticipates the desires of his leader. Over everything – as the same Cicero observes – the dictatorship was already by now "a kind of monarchy."[110]

14. The Republican defence of Legal Rules: Caesar *abusus dominatione iure caesus*

In addition to the sources, also the Shakespearean play, paints Caesar "as a tyrant in action,"[111] in the scene where, Cassius, busy in the work of persuasion of Casca to join himself in the conspiracy, reduces the *dictator perpetuus* to his debatable human proportions, to his defects, describing him as a "poor man, that would not like to be a wolf, but that he sees the Romans are but sheep. He were no lion were not Romans hinds."[112] For the conspirators, the fear, express for mouth of Cassius, is that "Caesar has to get the start of the majestic world and bear the palm alone."[113] The purpose of his killing is to prevent that he has power, taking it away from the other Roman no-

[105] Plutarch, *Life of Caesar*, 62, 10.

[106] Ibidem, 62, 10.

[107] Cicero, *Second Philippic*, 84–87.

[108] Ibidem, 84–87.

[109] Ibidem, 91.

[110] L. Canfora, *Giulio Cesare*, op. cit., p. 315, that in the note n. 17 quotes the latin text of Cicero, *Philippic*, I, 3: *vim regiae potestatis obsederat*.

[111] W. Shakespeare, *Julius Caesar*, I, iii, 103.

[112] Ibidem, I, iii, 104–105.

[113] Ibidem, I, ii, 130–131.

bles. Different from the position of all these Republicans is the attitude of Brutus, who, as Casca says, "holds a very elevated position in the heart of people"[114] and interrogates himself, in his soliloquy, about the power, seen in his mechanism, dynamics and inevitable corruption: Caesar "would be crowned: how that might change his nature, there's the question."[115]

For Brutus, unlike for the other Republicans, and particularly Cassius, the murder of Caesar is not the murder of the man, but of the monarchy that he desires, of the power which is *absolute, absolutus* in Latin, because it's loosened by the ties of the legal rules. The monologue of Brutus, that opens the first scene of the third action, is not more contradictory or confused, but shiny and psychologically unbalanced, really because of its exquisitely ideological character, as it is deduced from the central opposition between *"no personal cause"*[116] and *"the general."*[117] The reason of the Brutus' solution of Caesar's death is not personal - "for my part I know no personal cause to spurn at him"[118] -, but political, the „general,"[119] which is individualized according to an urgent rationality, that not only doesn't leave space to the feelings, but reduces the reasoning to a syllogism: if the absolute power contaminates him and makes him tyrannical - major premise - and if Caesar, even if now not corrupt, wants to make himself king - minor premise -, then, the necessity of killing Caesar, "It must be by his death,"[120] expressed in opening of his soliloquy, but only apparently out of every logic and consequentiality, is the necessary and inevitable conclusion.

---

[114] W. Shakespeare, *Julius Caesar*, I, iii, 157. The ability that Shakespeare attributes to Brutus, to put together opponents of different political matrix, rather opposite, and to act from element of conjunction of the "two «souls» of the conspiracy," the Pompeian one, led by Brutus, and that Caesarian one, which was more and more hostile to the dictator (Decimus Brutus, Trebonius), is confirmed by the sources: the conspirators at the end, accept to pass to the action, solicited naturally by Cassius, but "only on condition that Brutus was to lead the action" (Plutarch, *Brutus*, 8, 2).

[115] W. Shakespeare, *Julius Caesar*, II, i, 13–14.

[116] Ibidem, II, i, 11.

[117] Ibidem, II, i, 13.

[118] Ibidem, II, i, 11.

[119] Ibidem, II, i, 13.

[120] Ibidem, II, i, 10.

The conviction that the absolute power becomes tyrannical, because its concentration in the hands of only one man, produces, as inevitable consequence, an abuse in its exercise, is expressed with the image of the bright day, whose effects are equivalent to the crowning's ones: as "it is the bright day that brings forth the adder, and that craves wary walking,"[121] so crowning Caesar, "then, we put a sting within him that at his will he may do danger with."[122] If the attribution of the title of *rex* (king) is the bright day that brings forth the adder, Caesar must be thought „as a serpent's egg, which hatched, would as his kind grow mischievous"[123]: the Caesar's murder is the killing of Caesar "in the shell,"[124] before that, crowned, he could grow mischievous. Recognized to Caesar the worth of balanced person, as Brutus has never "known when his affections swayed more than his reason,"[125] „augmented, would run to these and these extremities,"[126] from the moment that the tyranny, the contrary of democracy, separating "remorse from power,"[127] inevitably determines an "abuse of the greatness:"[128]

> But it's a common proof that lowliness is young ambition's ladder, whereto the climber-upward turns his face; but when he once attains the upmost round he then unto the ladder turns his back, looks in the clouds, scorning the base degrees by which he did ascend.[129]

Despite the purely rational and political reason, set at the base of his adhesion to the conspiracy, Brutus, since is part of it, is sleepless and gets excited, as in "a phantasma, or a hideous dream."[130] He feels himself as "a little kingdom,"[131] which is torn to bits by the inside

[121] Ibidem, II, i, 14–15.
[122] Ibidem, II, i, 15–16.
[123] Ibidem, II, i, 32–33.
[124] Ibidem, II, i, 34.
[125] Ibidem, II, i, 20.
[126] Ibidem, II, i, 31.
[127] Ibidem, II, i, 19.
[128] Ibidem, II, i, 18.
[129] Ibidem, II, i, 21–27.
[130] Ibidem, II, i, 65.
[131] Ibidem, II, i, 66.

conflicts, by "the nature of an insurrection,"[132] because of the awareness of the "monstrous visage"[133] of the conspiracy, that will never find a cavern dark enough to mask itself, but it can hide only "in smiles and affability."[134]

Brutus, that, in the name of the Logos, the Reason and the absolute control of the passions, would like to maintain the conspiracy "pure," as action for the defense of the republican legal rules, in presence of the proposal of an oath in the name of the reason and the republican ideology, unleashed his anger in a series of invectives against whoever is so weak that has to commit himself in a similar symbolic action, without the legitimation of *mores*, which have the function of legal rules, and therefore in contrast with the republican political model, which abhorred every ceremonial selfcongratulation.

> But do not stain the even virtue of our interprise nor th'insuppressive mettle of our spirits, to think that or our cause or our performance did need an oath, when every drop of blood that every Roman bears, and nobily bears, is guilty of a several bastardy if he do break the smallest particle of any promise that hath passed from him.[135]

Brutus excludes that the murder can also touch others, as particularly, Anthony: "our course will seem too bloody, Caius Cassius, to cut the head off and then hack the limbs, like wrath in death and envy afterwards for Antony is but a limb of Caesar"[136] and "he can do no more than Caesar's arm when Caesar's head is off."[137] Brutus tries to sublime the barbarity of the real murder, inviting the conspirators to be "sacrificers but not butchers,"[138] who aim to brake the body of Caesar "as a carcass fit for hounds,"[139] appearing to the eyes of the people not murderers, but "purgers,"[140] who raise themselves against his spirit,

---

132 Ibidem.

133 Ibidem, II, i, 81.

134 Ibidem, II, i, 82.

135 Ibidem, II, i, 132–140.

136 Ibidem, II, i, 163–166.

137 Ibidem, II, i, 183–184.

138 Ibidem, II, i, 167.

139 Ibidem, II, i, 175.

140 Ibidem, II, i, 182.

monarchist and absolutist, well knowing that "in the spirit of the men there is no blood. O that we then could come by Caesar's spirit, and not to dismember Caesar! But, alas, Caesar must bleed for it."[141]

The character of Brutus in the play of Shakespeare is contradictory. Brutus in fact, embodies the republican spirit, and desires to preserve the nature of political action of the Caesar's death, consumed in the name of the legal rules. For such reason Brutus excludes any oath, which throws back in such way, on the ritual paradigm of the monarchic symbolic model. Nevertheless he resorts contradictorily to the oath, because he wants to turn the monstrous murder into a rite, that kills the body, but only as action "necessary and not envious,"[142] with the purpose of purifying Caesar's spirit. The contradictoriness of this character finds perfect comparison in the sources. The resentful catalogue of the constitutional violations committed by Caesar, "almost identical, once more, in Suetonius, Plutarch and Appianus"[143] and "which show that he abused his power (*abusus dominatione*) and that therefore was killed according to Legal Rules (*iure caesus*),"[144] "cohabits with the conviction, expressed in other parts of the same works, that the Caesar's murder was a crime and that the assassins finally ran into the necessary punishment."[145]

„There is a compact tradition about the Caesar's actions and the behaviors that, in a certain sense, legitimated the attack against him, according to the expression of Suetonius. This tradition is summerized in a «list,» substantially stable of embezzlements, which were the constitutional innovations (all in monarchic sense) introduced by Caesar after Mundus"[146] and reassumed by Suetonius: (1) the concentration, in his own person of too many positions and external honors, "as the continuous consulate, the perpetual dictatorship, the prefecture of the customs, and also the *praenomen* of *Imperator* and the *cognomen* of *Pater Patriae*"; (2) the "recording of a series of discourtesies to the constitutional routine, as, for instance, the nomination no

---

141 Ibidem, II, i, 169–171.

142 Ibidem, II, i, 179.

143 L. Canfora, *Giulio Cesare*, op. cit., p. 304.

144 Suetonius, *Caesar*, 76, 1.

145 L. Canfora, *Giulio Cesare*, op. cit., p. 304.

146 Ibidem, p. 301.

less than eight urban prefectis or the systematic debasement of the consulate, which he ruled «in name only»;"[147] and, finally, (3) a series of provocative behaviors; "the greatest and implacable ill-will"[148] was the reception of the whole Senate, who had come to give him big honors, sat, without getting up. Such coincidence is explained only if we hypothesize the oneness of the source from which Suetonius, Plutarch and Appianushave drawn. He's "Asinius Pollion,"[149] contemporary of Julius Caesar, who is the author of the judgment that the dictator perpetuus was "killed according to legal rules."[150] "*Abusus dominatione iure caesus*" is in fact, an expression too sour to be habitually shared "in the entourage of Adrian,"[151] because Suetonius reports that, after the death of Julius Caesar, "August went to the Senate with the caress under the robe and the senators were searched before having access to the Curia"[152], while the conspirators "were killed with the same dagger with which they had violated the body of Caesar."[153] This expression means that the assassins had received the correct punishment and a security system has been adopted for Caesar's child. Asinius Pollion, in the history of the Roman Law, and Brutus, in the play of Shakespeare, are interpreters of the reasons of the republican aristocracy, "an elite, very well selected and able of tenacious self-defense and self-maintenance,"[154] who had arrived to kill Julius Caesar, the richest and illustrious exponent of the republican and conservative class. The Republicans' purpose was to prevente the institutionalization of Caesar's charismatic power. The violent end of Caesar was not only justified, but correct, according to legal rules, because it turns to pre-vent "a real tyranny (*dominatio*), which denied the liberty (*libertas*)"[155] of the optimates and its constitutional base, the autority (*auctoritas*) of the Senate.

[147] Suetonius, *Caesar*, 76, 1.
[148] Ibidem, 78, 2.
[149] L. Canfora, *Giulio Cesare*, op. cit., p. 306.
[150] Ibidem, p. 304.
[151] Ibidem.
[152] Suetonius, *Augustus*, 35, 2.
[153] Suetonius, *Caesar*, 89.
[154] L. Canfora, *Giulio Cesare*, op. cit., p. 309.
[155] Ibidem, p. 306.

15. The democratic dictator: the evolution of legal rules in the Caesar's life and Roman politics

According to Plutarch the basic connotation of Julius Caesar's character (ἤθος)[156] was the *φιλοτιμία*, as lust for power and glory. The "ambiguity"[157] of φιλοτιμία, literally "love of honour,"[158] but whose "sense oscillates between love of «ambition,» with a negative shade too, and pure ardour of glory,"[159] reveal as, in the case of the political man, glory and power sometimes coincide, but often enter in conflict, so that the love of power contaminates that of glory. It happens to Julius Caesar, who, pleaded on bended knee to revoke the bandishment against Publius Cimber, so to give him back his freedom, refuses:

> I could be well moved, if I were as you; If I could pray to move, prayers would move me. But I am constant as the northen star, of whose true-fixed and resting quality there is no fellow in the firmament.[160]

The function of the absolute leader, of the *rex* (king) is described according to the typical correspondence between political world and macrocosm. As in the skies the sun and the polar star distinguish themselves from the planets and all other stars for their unique and irreplaceable function, the first one, as giver of light and the second one, as synonymous of fixity, and therefore, of reference, so also among the men an unchangeable hierarchy is necessary. The leader has the function of representing, in the mutability of the time and the history, the immutability of a transcendent order:

> The skies are painted with unnumbered sparks, they are all fire, and every one doth shine, but there's but one in all doth hold his place. So in the world: 'tis furnished well with men, and men are flesh and blood, and

156 Antonio La Penna, "Cesare secondo Plutarco," in: Plutarch, *Vite parallele di Alessandro e Cesare*, Milano: Rizzoli, 1992, p. 234.

157 Ibidem, p. 284.

158 Ibidem.

159 Ibidem.

160 W. Shakespeare, *Julius Caesar*, III, i, 58–62.

apprehensive; yet in in the number I do know but one that unaissailable holds on his rank, unshaked of motion; and that I am he, let me a little show it, even in this that i was constant Cimber and constant do remain to keep him so[161].

The emphasis on the "not change of the leader, projection of the eternity in the world, of the motionless motor in the mutability, turned to ransom the transitoriness, the horizontal plan in the history,"[162] and identified with the republican ideology, is the peak of the life of Caesar, that is reconstructed by Plutarch as a route. The result of the life of Caesar, "systematically wanted from the very beginning,"[163] is the tyranny, that upsets "the traditional order of the state,"[164] through forms more and more clear and strong of domination (*dominatio*), from the dictatorship, to the life dictatorship, to the tyranny (*βασιλεία*),[165] through the crowning, final action of the struggle that he, "driven by the democratic love for people (δήμος)"[166] had conducted against the Senate. But, in Plutarch, the idea that the tyranny was the natural "evolution" of the ambition, vice of Caesar and core of his nature, since the adolescence and the beginning of the political career, coexists with the other, that the "need of monarchy"[167] was caused by the "moral crisis"[168] of the aristocratic Republic (*Res Publica*), corrupted, because of the shameless trading of the public positions, and destroyed by the anarchist and more and more frequent and uncontrollable demonstrations of violence.

The candidates for public positions put the benches in the street and shamelessly contaminated the masses, and hired people went down then to fight for who paid them not with the vote, but with arcs, swords and slingshots. The contenders often separated them after that they have contaminated the gallery with the blood and with the dead bodies and left

---

161 Ibidem, III, i, 63-73.

162 A. Serpieri, *Giulio Cesare*, Milan: Ed. Garzanti, note 85, 210.

163 A. La Penna, "Cesare secondo Plutarco," op. cit., p. 285.

164 Ibidem.

165 Ibidem.

166 Ibidem, p. 245.

167 Ibidem, p. 254.

168 Ibidem.

> the city in the anarchy as a ship without helmsman so much beaten here and there, that who had sense was happy if from such illogical condition and serious storm could derive them nothing worse than the tyrannical power. Many were also those people who said that the monarchy was necessary and accepted this remedy since a mild physician offered it (and they alluded to Pompey).[169]

"It really is owed to Plutarch a scene, we don't know how much truthful, that makes clear the meeting, in a dramatic moment, of these two conceptions,"[170] the monarchist and the republican ones: the dialogue between Pompey and Cratippus of Pergamus, where, the disappointment of Pompey, who would like to demand an explanation for his own political calamities to the "Providence,"[171] is contrasted to the realism of Cratippus, who individualizes the remedy, by now necessary, of the "serious roman political problems"[172] in the monarchy: "if Caesar had not established it, Pompey, finally, would have establish it."[173]

The voice of Plutarch, who, according to the "judgment of the Greeks,"[174] considered Rome "since a long time a monarchy"[175] and its government tyrannical already at the time of the "dictator"[176] Cinna (adversary, with Gaius Marius, of Cornelius Silla), echos, unexpectedly, in the Cicero's political reflection. Cicero, brave defender of the Republic political model, already "in the work *De Re Publica*, therefore even before the civil war,"[177] had thought that the "constitutional tool"[178] of the dictatorship, was able to resolve political problems and ungovernable situations, as the Greek tyranny, but with a nomination limited in the time. He had avoided the reactivity of the public to the only use of the term "dictator," with the skilled gimmick

[169] Plutarch, *Life of Caesar*, 28, 4–6.
[170] L. Canfora, *Giulio Cesare*, op. cit., p. 422.
[171] Ibidem.
[172] Ibidem, p. 423.
[173] Ibidem.
[174] Ibidem, p. 422.
[175] Ibidem.
[176] Plutarch, *Life of Caesar*, 1, 1.
[177] L. Canfora, *Giulio Cesare*, op. cit., p. 303.
[178] Ibidem.

of the Scipio Emilianus' dream, the „only man who could support the salvation of the city"[179] and could restore the State, if he had succeeded in escaping the cruel hands of his relatives.[180] Julius Caesar identified his absolute power, which was unknown for its enormousness, with the traditional constitutional figure of the dictatorship, because of its "native function of mediation and resolution of the foreign and domestic conflicts,"[181] but he deprived it of its previous temporal limitation (six months), which has been connected with its exceptional character. It was not a "capricious initiative against the general trend,"[182] but it was, at the same time, both his "salvation," as "the only political and constitutional tool"[183] which gave him the "freedom of action also against his advocates"[184] and his "political downfall," as the prevailing, if not the only, reason of that political crisis, which was due to its "endless (*sine die*) dilatation."[185]

The conspirators thought of resolving the political problem of his absolute power with his murder and it was also the opinion of Cicero, who branded the Caesar's murderers as "heart of lion, brain of children."[186] With these words, Cicero intended "to say that the slaughter of the Ides of March would have had to include Antony too"[187]: after Antony's death, the ancient republican legal rules, founded upon the Senate's auctoritas, could have recovered their power. In this way Cicero "shows to reduce the conflict by now endemic in the last century of the republic, to the responsibility of single ambitious personalities, whose deaths would put everything back in order."[188] To tell the truth, the new "political parties"[189] in the Roman politics, for the increasing social complexity, were so much consistent and socially re-

[179] Cicero, *De Re Publica*, VI, 14.

[180] Ibidem, VI, 14 "Dictator rem publicam constituas oportebit, si impias propinquorum manus effugeris."

[181] L. Canfora, *Giulio Cesare*, op. cit., p. 303.

[182] Ibidem.

[183] Ibidem, p. 316.

[184] Ibidem.

[185] Ibidem.

[186] Cicero, *Letter to Atticus* XVI, 21, 3.

[187] L. Canfora, *Giulio Cesare*, op. cit., p. 357.

[188] Ibidem.

[189] Ibidem.

markable, as they would not certain "vanish into thin air,"[190] and would not return to be politically non-existent, "only because of the disappearance of the «tyrant»."[191] The Roman politics had in fact a new protagonist, the people, defined, in the description of the missed crowning of the Lupercalia, that Shakespeare puts in mouth to the republican Casca, "a rabblement,"[192] who, hooting and clapping their chopped hands and throwing up their sweaty nightcaps, "uttered such a deal of stinking breath, because Caesar refused the crown, that it had almost choked Caesar, so for he swooned and fell down at it."[193] But the people were able to influence Caesar's behavior, so much that he gave up the so desired crowning only because "he perceived the common herd was glad he refused the crown."[194]

Caesar was aware of the existence of those new "more extended parties, who were interested in the social and political conflict, and he imagined to win them with his victory. Caesar thought that this popular party would not have been inactive if its leader would be brutally killed,"[195] and convinced himself that it was "at least unadvisable"[196] a conspiracy against him. For these reasons also Caesar decided "disconcertingly to dismiss the armed escort."[197] The political diagnosis of Caesar that the possible violent elimination of his person, would have meant the resumption in great style and greater virulence of the civil conflict was fruit not of determinism, but of previsional ability: "his physical survival was not a personal interest of himself, but a public interest of the Republic because if something terrible happened to him, Republic would be fallen in civil wars, which could have been heavier than the previous ones."[198] The same "theorization of the uselessness of the Caesar's death"[199] for a "rebirth of the free-

---

190 Ibidem, p. 358.

191 Ibidem.

192 W. Shakespeare, *Julius Caesar*, I, ii, 243.

193 Ibidem, I, ii, 245.

194 Ibidem, I, ii, 261-263.

195 L. Canfora, *Giulio Cesare*, op. cit., p. 357.

196 Ibidem, p. 358.

197 Ibidem, p. 357.

198 Ibidem.

199 Ibidem, p. 349.

dom"[200], that cannot be restored "in absence of an enough number of citizens able to appreciate it, to desire and protect it,"[201] is at the base of the answer to Brutus, who looks for the adhesion to the conspiracy against Caesar, of Favonius, the republican man, who was "entusiast of Cato"[202] and thought that "it was better an illegal monarchy that a civil war."[203] The dictatorship is felt as an evil that the Roman citizen, lover of his country and having republican feelings, preferred, because smaller than civil wars, which could have been back after the Caesar's murder.

When the body of the dictator fells lifeless to the ground, the spirit of Caesar still dominates the Roman politics. In the moment where the republican government would have stabilized and grown stronger, by the cry of Brutus "Liberty! Freedom! Tyranny is dead,"[204] the new Caesar, who is embodied by Anthony, changes the face of the history with his prayer to the people on the dead body of Caesar.

The conflict between the republican authority (*auctoritas*) and the tyrannical kingdom (*regnum*), that the Caesar's murderers intended to solve definitely, with the death of the tyrant, has still opened. The rite officiated by Brutus, who invites the Romans to stop themselves, to bathe their "hands in Caesar's blood up to the elbows,"[205] and to besmear their swords, as the washing from the bad blood of Caesar symbolizes the bleeding done for reclaiming the world, becomes, for mouth of Anthony, the shedding of the "nobler blood of this whole world,"[206] that continuous, also after his death, to enrich the swords of the conspirators.

Brutus asks to the people to be delighted by the regained freedom (*libertas*).

> Roman libertas was a legacy transmitted by the founders of Rome to the Roman people; their liberty was tied up to the beginning which their an-

---

[200] Ibidem.

[201] Ibidem.

[202] Plutarch, *Brutus*, 12, 3.

[203] Ibidem.

[204] W. Shakespeare, *Julius Caesar*, III, i, 78.

[205] Ibidem, III, i, 106.

[206] Ibidem, III, i, 156.

> cestors had established founding the city, whose business the descendants had to manage, whose consequences they had to bear, and whose foundations they had to increase. All these were the *res gestae* of the Roman Republic.[207]

The defense of freedom (*libertas*) for Brutus was the *res gestae*'s defense. The people didn't comply with the invitation of Brutus because Caesar "*mortus adhuc loquebatur*,"[208] "even dead, he still had the unbelievable authority which he had alive. This authority was based not on the violence, the astuteness or also the genius,"[209] as thought by Brutus, but on the use that he made of them, on the unbelievable improvement that he was able to carry out and on the ability to reconcile the brutish political power with legal rules. Caesar "defeated roman people in a commun adhesion to his own power and he justified his own equal authority for everybody as absolute for everybody, in the name of legal rules so much acceptable as made more flowing and efficient because of the administrative simplification according to the éliteses' desires. It was asserted the existence of natural legal rules, which were anterior and superior to the plurality of the civil and temporary rules. Simplified by the elimination of the positions, disciplined by the constant rules of the new government and by the exemplary repression of all the abuses, even if committed by influential people, these legal rules were finally peace-makers with justice which was, as Caesar well knew, necessary for the safety and continuity of conquests."[210] Caesar remained "victim of the traditional castes of the roman politics,"[211] but he continued, also after his death, to be "a star for the remote but well present people also in the multi-ethnic kaleidoscope of the capital of the Empire,"[212] as it was confirmed by the imposing "homage of the foreigners to the Caesar's coffin"[213]: "all the foreigners, associating themselves to that immense mourning, made

207 Hannah Arendt, *Between past and future Eight Exercises in Political Thought* (1968), Harmondworth: Penguin Books, 1987, p. 157.

208 J. Carcopino, *Giulio Cesare* (1935), Milano: Bompiani, 2006³, p. 541.

209 Ibidem.

210 Ibidem, p. 579.

211 L. Canfora, *Giulio Cesare*, op. cit., p. 376.

212 Ibidem.

213 Ibidem.

their lamentations around the fire, each according to their own customs. In particular way the Hebrews, who wanted to return to make him homage in the place of the funeral"[214] for many nights.

> The Roman Republic was, as known, an oligarchical Republic: everything of its political executives was recruited among the lines of a patrician-plebeian nobility who was recognizable as such, because its ancestors had covered the consulate, which was the maximum political and military position. It was an oligarchy which asked and piloted the popular vote to immortalize itself.[215]

It was not "rigidly closed to the contribution of other family groups, which, after the civil war, had come also from the italic ruling classes,"[216] but subordinates the access to the politics of the men of the new ruling classes, called *homines novi*, not only to the wealth of their rich families, which were able "to pay" their political entry, but also to the "connection to the great families that conduct the political game,"[217] so that they shared its ideal and accepted its record. It assumed the characters of a real co-optation to the Republic and its oligarchical ideology. The Common Good was identified by the Republican ideology with the Country and the Freedom, and, in name of their defense, it could have been prepared to sacrifice everything, as Brutus made.

The people was not involved with the politics, which was reserved to the oligarchical aristocracy, and the insensibility of the crowd to the key of the liberty and the struggle against the tyranny is underlined, during the discourse of Brutus, by the silence, which is suddenly broken by a "Live, Brutus! Live! Live!"[218], when Brutus promises that also for them there will be "a place in the Republic."[219] If it is the ambition of the people to win, the final applause of the plebeians, who proclaim that Brutus is the new Caesar – "Let him be

---

[214] Suetonius, *Caesar*, 84, 5.

[215] W. Shakespeare, *Julius Caesar*, III, ii, 43–46.

[216] L. Canfora, *Giulio Cesare*, op. cit., p. 37.

[217] Ibidem.

[218] W. Shakespeare, *Julius Caesar*, III, ii, 47.

[219] Ibidem, III, ii, 47.

Caesar"[220] – and it proposes to bring him with triumph – "Bring him with triumph unto his house."[221] "Give him a statue with his ancestors"[222] –, makes to fall as a castle of paper, to the wind of a thin irony, dissolver of every urgent logic, the rational construction of a republican, who, killed Caesar, to destroy his tyrannical spirit, but risks himself to be proclaimed king: "Caesar's best parties will be crowned in Brutus."[223]

With the death of Caesar, the republican ideology went down because of the democratic push whose Julius Caesar was interpreter: he had tryed to operate the transformation of the sovereignty which the increasing complexity in Rome seemed to require. And if Julius Caesar dies, without realizing his democratic political project, the monarchic ideology, whose he had been "the contradictory and passionate supporter," finds in Octavianus, "emblem of the Caesar's politics," his thinner and icy interpreter. Shakespeare reserves to Octavianus the last words of the Politics' play, endless as the History, which, between pretense and truth, simulation and dissimulation, returns, so, "circularly, to its beginning."[224]

---

220 Ibidem, III, ii, 49.

221 Ibidem, III, ii, 48.

222 Ibidem, III, ii, 49.

223 Ibidem, III, ii, 50–51.

224 A. Serpieri, note 177, 226.

DIA-LOGOS
Schriften zu Philosophie und Sozialwissenschaften
Studies in Philosophy and Social Sciences

Herausgegeben von
Edited by
Tadeusz Buksiński & Piotr W. Juchacz

"*Dia-Logos. Studies in Philosophy and Social Sciences* is a peer-reviewed book series publishing valuable monographs and edited volumes on various aspects of philosophy and social sciences. The series is intended to be an interdisciplinary forum of deliberation according to our firm belief that challenges of the contemporary world require common and multilevel research. The *Dia-Logos* series does not represent a single ideology or school of thought, but it is open to different trends and various styles of reflection, trying to understand better the contemporary world. We invite the submission of manuscripts of monographs and edited volumes from academic philosophers and social scientists."

Bd. / Vol. 1 Piotr W. Juchacz / Roman Kozłowski (Hrsg.): Freiheit und Verantwortung. Moral, Recht und Politik. 2002.

Bd. / Vol. 2 Norbert Leśniewski / Ewa Nowak-Juchacz (Hrsg.): Die Zeit Heideggers. 2002.

Bd. / Vol. 3 Marek Kwiek (ed.): The University, Globalization, Central Europe. 2003.

Bd. / Vol. 4 Ewa Czerwińska-Schupp (Hrsg.): Philosophie an der Schwelle des 21. Jahrhunderts. Geschichte der Philosophie, Philosophische Anthropologie, Ethik, Wissenschaftstheorie, Politische Philosophie. 2003.

Bd. / Vol. 5 Danuta Sobczyńska / Pawel Zeidler / Ewa Zielonacka-Lis (eds.): Chemistry in the Philosophical Melting Pot. 2004.

Bd. / Vol. 6 Marek Kwiek: Intellectuals, Power, and Knowledge. Studies in the Philosophy of Culture and Education. 2004.

Bd. / Vol. 7 Marek Kwiek: The University and the State. A Study into Global Transformations. 2006.

Bd. / Vol. 8 Andrzej Przylebski (Hrsg.): Das Erbe Gadamers. 2006.

Bd. / Vol. 9 Ewa Czerwińska-Schupp (ed.): Values and Norms in the Age of Globalization. 2007.

Bd. / Vol. 10 Tadeusz Buksiński (ed.): Democracy in Western and Post-Communist Countries. Twenty Years after the Fall of Communism. 2009.

Bd. / Vol. 11 Marek Zirk-Sadowski / Mariusz Golecki / Bartosz Wojciechowski (eds.): Multicentrism as an Emerging Paradigm in Legal Theory. 2009.

Bd. / Vol. 12 Bartosz Wojciechowski: Philosophical Approach to the Interculturality of Criminal Law. 2010.

Bd. / Vol. 13 Marek Nowak / Michał Nowosielski (eds.): (Post)transformational Migration. Inequalities, Welfare State, and Horizontal Mobility. 2011.

Bd. / Vol. 14 Tadeusz Buksiński (ed.): Religions in the Public Spheres. 2011.

Bd. / Vol. 15 Bartosz Wojciechowski / Piotr W. Juchacz / Karolina M. Cern (eds.): Legal Rules, Moral Norms and Democratic Principles. 2013.

www.peterlang.de

www.ingramcontent.com/pod-product-compliance
Ingram Content Group UK Ltd.
Pitfield, Milton Keynes, MK11 3LW, UK
UKHW020834290926
15470UKWH00004B/1333

9 783631 640081